Spanish as a Contact Language

An Ecological History

Israel Sanz-Sánchez

EDINBURGH
University Press

Edinburgh University Press is one of the leading university presses in the UK. We publish academic books and journals in our selected subject areas across the humanities and social sciences, combining cutting-edge scholarship with high editorial and production values to produce academic works of lasting importance. For more information visit our website: edinburghuniversitypress.com

© Israel Sanz-Sánchez, 2025

Edinburgh University Press Ltd
13 Infirmary Street
Edinburgh EH1 1LT

Typeset in 10/12 Times New Roman by
Cheshire Typesetting Ltd, Cuddington, Cheshire

A CIP record for this book is available from the British Library

ISBN 978-1-4744-2909-2 (hardback)
ISBN 978-1-4744-2910-8 (paperback)
ISBN 978-1-4744-2911-5 (webready PDF)
ISBN 978-1-4744-2912-2 (epub)

The right of Israel Sanz-Sánchez to be identified as the author of this work has been asserted in accordance with the Copyright, Designs and Patents Act 1988, and the Copyright and Related Rights Regulations 2003 (SI No. 2498).

Contents

Dedication	viii
List of Maps, Figures, and Tables	ix
Series Editors' Preface	xiii
Preface	xiv
Abbreviations	xvii

1. Spanish as Myth, Spanish as Contact — 1
- 1.1. Introduction: Centering the margins — 1
- 1.2. What is Spanish? The birth of a mythical creature — 3
- 1.3. The erasure of variation: Forgetfulness in the historical linguistics of Spanish — 7
- 1.4. Do languages exist? — 10
- 1.5. The centrality of language users — 13
- 1.6. The ecology of language — 16
- 1.7. Language as contact — 17
- 1.8. Hitting the wall: Testing the limits of traditional approaches to contact — 19
- 1.9. Approaching contact in Spanish ecologically: What this book is and what it is not — 24
- 1.10. Structure of this book — 28
- Discussion questions — 28

2. The Ubiquity of Contact: Toward an Ecological Approach to Language Change — 29
- 2.1. Introduction: Centering contact — 29
- 2.2. Where do our ideas about contact come from? Earlier articulations of contact processes — 30
- 2.3. The limitations of contact typologies: Dialect vs language contact — 37
- 2.4. Languages as populations — 42

2.5. Language change: Ecology rolls the dice 45
2.6. How contact works: An ecological reassessment of contact processes 50
2.7. Conclusion 54
Discussion questions 54

3. **Spanish Before Spain: Ancient, Roman Era, and Medieval Contacts** **56**
3.1. Introduction: Imagining Spanish 56
3.2. Solving contact enigmas in remote times 58
3.3. Indo-European: Fragmentation vs. contact 60
3.4. Contacts in Hispania: The Latinization of the Iberian Peninsula 63
3.5. Linguistic outcomes of the spread of Latin in Hispania 67
3.6. After Rome: Looking for the roots of Romance varieties 72
3.7. Later medieval contacts: Birthing Castilian 78
3.8. Reconciling sociolinguistic and linguistic evidence in medieval Castilian 81
3.9. Conclusion 86
Discussion questions 86

4. **Spanish Beyond Spain: Contact Ecologies in the Colonial Era** **88**
4.1. Introduction: Transplanting Spanish 88
4.2. Early colonial contacts in the Americas: Sociodemographic context 91
4.3. Early American colonial language ecologies 93
4.4. Some contact outcomes in the early colonial Americas 98
4.5. The later colonial period in the Spanish Americas: Sociodemographic context 102
4.6. Late colonial American language ecologies 106
4.7. Some contact outcomes in late colonial American ecologies 109
4.8. Colonial osmoses: Spanish influence on Indigenous repertoires 115
4.9. Colonial contacts in Asia and the Pacific: A sociodemographic and ecological sketch 118
4.10. East Asian and Pacific linguistic contact outcomes 121
4.11. Conclusion 125
Discussion questions 126

5. **Spanish in the Post-colonial World: New Nations, New Citizens, New Contacts** **127**
5.1. Introduction: Questioning Spanish 127
5.2. New borders in the Spanish Americas: Historical and ecological context 129
5.3. The linguistics of the new Latin American borderlands 132
5.4. The internal historical ecological dynamics of the new Latin American republics 135
5.5. The emergence of national varieties of Latin American Spanish 140
5.6. Immigrants, indentured workers, and slaves 143

5.7.	Linguistic outcomes: Native and exogenous pools in contact	149
5.8.	New contacts in the old metropolis: The language ecology of post-colonial Spain	152
5.9.	The linguistics of early post-colonial Spain	157
5.10.	Conclusion	161
	Discussion questions	161

6. Recent Contacts: New Language Ecologies in a Transnational World — 163

6.1.	Introduction: Glocalizing Spanish	163
6.2.	Intranational Hispanic ecologies: Contacts within national borders	166
6.3.	Outcomes of contact in non-migration-based intranational ecologies	171
6.4.	Outcomes of contact in intranational ecologies based on internal migration	176
6.5.	The sociodemographics of transnational Hispanic ecologies	179
6.6.	Transnational environmental complexities across and beyond borders	182
6.7.	Migration-based transnational contact outcomes	186
6.8.	The linguistics of transnational contacts along borders	192
6.9.	Twenty-first-century post-colonial continuities in the Maghreb	195
6.10.	Beyond borders: Contacts in the digital world	198
6.11.	Conclusion	200
	Discussion questions	201

7. Toward New Ecological Narratives in Language Histories — 203

7.1.	What have we learned?	203
7.2.	What is language change? Put yourself in the speakers' shoes!	205
7.3.	Who can change language? Everybody!	207
7.4.	Final words: On not throwing the baby out with the bathwater	209
	Discussion questions	212

References — 213
Index of Languages and Families — 245
Index of Subjects — 248

A mis abuelos (Andrea y Víctor, Celestina y Ángel),
que tanto trabajaron por nosotros.

Maps, Figures, and Tables

Maps

1.1.	Proposed dialectal continua in Europe	11
2.1.	Some proposed cuts along the Asturian dialect continuum and their associated isoglosses	39
3.1.	Reconstructed linguistic areas in pre-Roman Iberia and locations named in this chapter	64
3.2.	Distribution of four spoken Latin reflexes for 'tomorrow' in present-day Romance	69
3.3.	Chronological progression of the *Reconquista*	79
3.4.	Menéndez Pidal's Castilian dialectal wedge	82
4.1.	Select Spanish foundations (towns, garrisons, missions) across the northern colonial borderland and foundation year	104
4.2.	The Spanish colonial Philippines and the western Pacific area	119

Figures

1.1.	Mesoamerican parents disciplining their children with chili smoke, Codex Mendoza (1540s, central Mexico)	2
1.2.	The *Glosas Emilianenses* manuscript	4
1.3.	Spain's official *Route of the Spanish Language* website	6
1.4.	Starlings creating an ephemeral murmuration in Scotland	15
1.5.	Palenquero on a wall in the streets of San Basilio de Palenque	21
2.1.	A tentative tree of linguistic descent in Romance	31
2.2.	A wave-based representation of the spread of geographical innovations	32
2.3.	A representation of a social network	34
2.4.	A tentative visualization of the individual ecology of cognition	44
2.5.	Percentage of noun phrases showing gender agreement across three groups of Spanish-speaking children	47
2.6.	Factors influencing the application of Muysken's bilingual optimization strategies	52

3.1.	First lines of Nebrija's *Gramática de la lengua castellana* (1492)	57
3.2.	Stages of Indo-European fragmentation with some contact	62
3.3.	Iberian (Paleohispanic)-Latin bilingual and biscriptal inscriptions from Tarraco	65
3.4.	The Bronze of Ascoli	67
3.5.	Horseshoe arches in (1) Santa Eulalia de Bóveda (Lugo, fourth-fifth centuries), (2) San Juan de Baños (Palencia, seventh century) and (3) Jerez de la Frontera mosque (Cádiz, eleventh-twelfth centuries)	73
3.6.	Visigothic slate slab	77
4.1.	Mexico-Tenochtitlan and Cuzco in *Civitates Orbis Terrarum, vol. 1* (ff. 58v–59r), 1572	89
4.2.	Mexico City Cathedral and other colonial-era buildings atop the foundation of the Mexica *huey teocalli* ('main temple', Sp. 'templo mayor')	94
4.3.	Felipillo interpreting between the Spaniards and the Inca	97
4.4.	Distribution of *seseo* in a corpus of documents from the Gulf of Mexico	101
4.5.	*De mestizo y d[e] india, coyote* ('from a *mestizo* father and an Indigenous mother, a *coyote*'). Miguel Cabrera, Mexico, 1763	106
4.6.	Lima's *plaza mayor* in the late 1600s (anonymous painting)	107
4.7.	Present-day participants in a Güegüense performance in Nicaragua	114
4.8.	Indigenous Mariana Islanders supplying food to the crew aboard a Spanish ship, Boxer Codex, late sixteenth century	120
4.9.	Young Filipino and *mestizo* women reading pro-independence newspaper *La Independencia,* ca. 1898	122
5.1.	Early-independence Bogotá in the 1820s–1830s in Alcide D'Orbigny's *La relation du voyage dans l'Amérique méridionale pendant les années 1826 à 1833*	128
5.2.	Population of Lima, 1820–1961	137
5.3.	Population of Mexico City, 1824–1950	137
5.4.	The *Ferrocarril Central Mexicano* at a stop in rural Mexico in the late 1800s	139
5.5.	Miners (*salitreros*) in a sodium nitrate mine in northern Chile, ca. 1900	142
5.6.	Black and white population in Cuba, 1792–1899	145
5.7.	Buenos Aires conventillo in 1905	147
5.8.	Chinese indentured workers in a rural settlement in Cienfuegos province, Cuba, ca. 1884, from Edwin Atkins *Sixty Years in Cuba* (1926)	148
5.9.	Afrodescendant sugar cane cutters in rural Cuba, late 1800s, from Robert Porter's *Industrial Cuba* (1899)	148
5.10.	Population of Madrid, 1842–1950	153
5.11.	Population of Barcelona, 1842–1950	153
5.12.	Population of Mondoñedo, 1842–1950	154
5.13.	A *corrala* in the Madrid neighborhood of Puente de Vallecas, early 1900s	156

Maps, Figures, and Tables xi

6.1.	A trilingual (Chinese, Spanish, English) store sign in Madrid	164
6.2.	Neighborhood on the outskirts of Ecatepec, Mexico	168
6.3.	The rural foothills of Cerro Imbabura in Ecuador	170
6.4.	Spanish and Guarani in a Paraguayan governmental campaign about a pregnancy subsidy	174
6.5.	Vehicles crossing from Mexico into the United States at the Tijuana-San Ysidro checkpoint	181
6.6.	Levels of self-reported conversational Spanish proficiency across three generations of US Latinxs	183
6.7.	Mural with Latinx, Chicanx, and Mexican Catholic and Indigenous references in Barrio Logan, San Diego, California	185
6.8.	A Bolivian confraternity parading in the streets of Arica, Chile, in 2012	187
6.9.	Currency exchangers on the Guatemalan side of the border with Honduras	193
6.10.	A bilingual Arabic-Spanish dental clinic sign in a Sahrawi refugee camp in Tindouf, Algeria	197
7.1.	Waves, sea foam, grains of sand, seaweed … or a beach?	204
7.2.	The funnel view in language histories	208

Tables

2.1.	Relationship between select contact effects and specific sociolinguistic environments	36
2.2.	Pronoun rates for NYC Spanish speakers from two regions and two generations	41
3.1.	A few Indo-European cognates	60
3.2.	Definite articles in Leonese, northern Castilian and Aragonese vs post-Burgos Castilian	83
3.3.	Pre- and post-Toledo singular possessive adjectives	83
3.4.	Pre- and post-Seville 1sg possessive adjectives	83
3.5.	Asturian third-person clitic system	84
3.6.	Maximally reduced (semantically based) Castilian third-person clitic system	84
3.7.	Case-based (Andalusian) third-person clitic system	85
4.1.	Taxpayers and total Indigenous population in colonial Peru	91
4.2.	Slave arrivals in the Spanish American colonies, 1525–1820	92
4.3.	Population of select colonial Spanish American cities at two points in time	103
4.4.	Presence of *yeísmo* merger in spelling in selected writers from colonial New Mexico	110
4.5.	Select analogical processes in traditional varieties of Latin American Spanish	112
4.6.	Stages of incorporation of Spanish elements in colonial Nahuatl texts and sample associated features	116
4.7.	Subject personal pronouns in three Philippine Spanish-based creole varieties	123

5.1.	Percentage of population age 10 and older unable to speak English in four US Southwest regions, 1890 and 1900	131
5.2.	Foreign immigration to Argentina, by nationality, 1857–1940	144
5.3.	Estimated percentage of speakers of Basque by province, 1866–8	157
6.1.	Population for select dates in Bogotá, Lima, Madrid, and Mexico City, in thousands	167
6.2.	Emigrants and immigrants, absolute balance (in thousands), and relative balance for select countries in 2020	180
6.3.	Relative frequency of variants for the expression of futurity in Barranquilla and NYC Colombian Spanish	190

Series Editors' Preface

We are delighted to present this new volume in the Edinburgh University Press *Historical Linguistics* series of advanced textbooks on language change and comparative linguistics. Each individual volume provides in-depth coverage of a key subfield within historical linguistics. As a whole, the series provides a comprehensive introduction to this broad and increasingly complex field.

The present volume exemplifies the kind of content, tone and format we aim for in the series, and the volumes that are coming down the pike do as well. The series is aimed at advanced undergraduates in linguistics and students in language departments, as well as beginning postgraduates who are looking for an entry point. Volumes in the series are serious and scholarly university textbooks, theoretically informed and substantive in content. Every volume contains pedagogical features such as recommendations for further reading, but the tone of the volumes is discursive, explanatory and critically engaged, rather than 'activity-based'.

Authors interested in writing for the series should contact us.

Joseph Salmons (jsalmons@wisc.edu) and
David Willis (david.willis@ling-phil.ox.ac.uk).

Preface

For many people today, the word 'ecology' (and related forms, like 'ecosystem,' 'eco-friendly,' etc.) have become familiar concepts. Their use is often connected to our growing awareness about the causes and consequences of climate change. As I write these lines in late 2023, we close yet another year of unprecedented weather extremes: freak cold snaps, record heat waves and droughts alternating with bursts of excessive rain and flooding have been recorded all over our planet. Ocean temperatures are continuing to rise at an unprecedented pace. We are also witnessing the pressures that these rapid environmental changes are exerting on all forms of life on Earth, humans included. As many natural species are expanding or restricting their ecological range in response to these changes, human populations are also seeking refuge in regions where life conditions may remain more sustainable in the future.

This book is not about these environmental changes, but it does apply an environmental lens to language change. The basic premise of this book is that languages are not totally unlike natural species: languages too are made up of populations of interacting individual organisms (speakers and their linguistic repertoires) that adapt to the characteristics of their environment. In the case of natural organisms, the environment comprises their climate, topography, and sources of nutrition; in the case of speakers, the ecological embedding includes demographic and social triggers, as well as the physical architecture of the human body and brain. And just like the changing environment of a natural species determines the genetic makeup of its organisms, the speakers' ecological environment determines their linguistic makeup.

At first sight, this might seem a rather uncontroversial premise. And yet, much of what has been written about the history of individual languages is based on the proposition that a language is not a population of organisms, but a type of organism. In this traditional view, prevalent in Western linguistics, we are used to hearing about the so-called 'birth' of a language, how speakers transmitted it through generations, or how it 'died' when speakers ceased to use it. Just like an organism's appearance changes with age, so do languages (in this organic approach) experience changes throughout their lives but retain their genetic essence. For a long time, the history of Spanish has been narrated precisely from this perspective: we have often been told that this linguistic (genetically Indo-European) organism was the offspring of spoken Latin, spread out of Europe to three continents during the colonial era, and has by now grown into an internationally diverse but essentially unitary entity, best epitomized in the standard language.

As historically accurate as parts of this narrative are, its underlying organic premise is questionable in several respects: it assumes that speakers are 'carriers' of a language or 'vehicles' of linguistic processes, rather than agents of language change; it takes for granted that human communicative resources can be packaged into discrete languages; and, in identifying the essence of these organic entities, it privileges some sets of linguistic resources (and, tacitly, their users) while rendering other resources (and their users) invisible. This is certainly not a new argument: over a century ago, German linguist Hugo Schuchardt already articulated a version of this critique. More recently, language scholars like Suresh Canagarajah, William Croft, Ofelia García, Michel DeGraff, Ricardo Otheguy, Mary Louise Pratt and, most notably, Salikoko Mufwene have also shared articulations of language that are compatible with or fully emphasize the ecological, contact-based nature of language use and change.

This book is the first one to revisit the traditional narrative of the emergence and development of Spanish in explicit ecological terms. This is what I propose: instead of (again) approaching this history as a chain of transmission of a historical essence, let's think about it as a range of contexts (that is, ecologies) where speakers have actively created, reinterpreted, and reshaped a broad spectrum of communicative resources, some of which we have happened to label as 'Spanish.' In other words, let's center individual speakers as the true agents of language use, and contact among them as a universal process in all forms of language change. To do so, we must join ecologically inspired linguists and scrutinize deep-seated notions about language (and people!): the difference between 'language' and 'dialect', 'monolingualism' and 'bilingualism', 'native' vs. 'non-native speaker', and even the very idea of a 'language' as a unit of linguistic variation.

In this book, I apply this protocol to a panoramic selection of sociohistorical contexts where populations of speakers in contact have produced their own versions of Spanish. I piggyback on the available demographic, sociocultural and linguistic information, and especially on contact-conscious studies of language variation and change in Spanish. In choosing which ecologies to focus on, my goal has been to offer a balance between some that have been studied fairly thoroughly (and for which we may consequently have more data) and others that have figured less prominently in historical accounts of Spanish, but which may shed light on processes of contact and change besides those apparent in the more commonly quoted contexts. I have written this book with a broad audience in mind (from advanced college students with at least some background in linguistics to specialists in the field), giving just the necessary amount of linguistic theory to understand the book's ecological thread line but explaining important concepts as needed, and not assuming much shared sociohistorical knowledge. Every chapter is followed by a few questions that are intended as steppingstones to further discussion and connections. Overall, my goal is to encourage readers to engage critically with their received knowledge about the history of Spanish and its speakers, and to pose their own questions.

Before starting, I must acknowledge several people who have made this project possible. I am thankful to several colleagues in the field (Suzanne Aalberse, Jerry Craddock, José del Valle, Borja Díaz, María José Estarán, Mark Lauersdorf, Sonia Kania, Irene Moyna, Sergio Romero, Naomi Shin, Ignacio Simón, Fernando Tejedo, Don Tuten, Isabel Velázquez), who over the years have shared helpful insights or materials. I am also grateful to Mahmoud Amer, Noelson Chery, and Naoko Rotunno, who answered language-specific queries about Arabic, Krèyol, and Japanese, as well as to Aída Cajaravile, Elena González, Luisa Martín, Jasmín Soto and Raquel Oviedo (from EquiLing Madrid) and Armin Schwegler for granting me permission to use their photographs. I owe a great debt of gratitude to Laura Quinn, Sam Johnson, Joannah Duncan, and the rest of the editorial team at EUP, as well as to the *Edinburgh Historical Linguistics* series editors, Joe Salmons and David Willis, for their extended patience with this project, their assistance and their feedback (especially Joe, who took the time to read several drafts of the book and provided many detailed and insightful comments). I am also thankful to an anonymous reviewer, who shared invaluable comments on the whole manuscript, and to Jenna Dowds for her detailed copyediting of the manuscript (needless to say, I alone am responsible for all remaining errors and inaccuracies). Lastly, I extend special thanks to friends (María José Cabrera, Marcos Campillo, Marga Herrero, Eirini Panagiotidou, Stacey Schlau, Laura Verrekia, Esther Voces) and family (my parents María Teresa Sánchez and Jesús Sanz, my sister Penélope Sanz, and most especially my partner Allen Rozelle) who have indefatigably cheered me on during this process and encouraged me to bring this book to completion.

Abbreviations

1	first person	IND	indicative
2	second person	INF	infinitive
3	third person	MASC	masculine
ACC	accusative	NOM	nominative
ADJ	adjunct	PART	participle
AGNT	agent	PERF	perfect
AUX	auxiliary	PL	plural
CONJ	conjunction	POSS	possessive
DEF	definite	PRES	present
EMPH	emphatic	PRET	preterite
FEM	feminine	PROG	progressive
FOC	focus particle	PST	past
FUT	future	REFL	reflexive
GER	gerund	SG	singular
HAB	habitual	SUBJ	subjunctive
HON	honorific	TOP	topic marker
IMP	imperfect	UNINF	uninflected verbal form

1

Spanish as Myth, Spanish as Contact

Mucho se engaña por cierto, quien en la cosa mas instable, y flaca, busca perpetuidad, y firmeça.
(Bernardo de Aldrete 1674 [1606]: 41v, *Del origen y principio de la lengua castellana o romance que oi se usa en España.*)

1.1. Introduction: Centering the margins

In 1574, an African slave by the name of Antón Yaruniga brought a case before the Mexican branch of the Inquisition against his wife Juana Ramírez, a *mestiza* of Indigenous and African descent. He accused her of eloping from their home in the silver mining town of Taxco to marry another slave. Juana had moved far away and even changed her name to María to avoid being located, but she was eventually found and forced to stand trial. Such bigamy proceedings were common in the Spanish colonies, at a time of social fluidity when a new home and a new marriage offered opportunities to escape a situation of dissatisfaction or abuse, or simply to better one's lot.

The records for this legal case afford us many glimpses into Antón and Juana's everyday life, painting a fascinating tapestry of multilingual and multicultural interactions. For starters, Antón is introduced as a *bozal*, that is, a slave born in Africa, probably along the coast of present-day Senegal, Sierra Leone or Guinea, where many slaves in the European colonies were abducted from in the 1500s (§4.2). Therefore, he must have grown up speaking one or several western Niger-Congo languages and possibly others. At the trial, however, he did not require an interpreter, which shows that he must have spent several years in the Spanish colonies. As for Juana, her background likely included some familiarity with the slaves' languages, as well as with Spanish and Nahuatl: her mother Francisca was a Nahuatl-speaking *india* who had raised her daughter and two other sisters, conceived from unions with African-born slaves. Such diverse personal ethnolinguistic histories were far from unusual in colonial Mexico in the late 1500s.

Everyday life in the streets of a mining boomtown like Taxco required skills and resources to negotiate a culturally, ethnically, and linguistically kaleidoscopic environment. Notably, these resources were not only linguistic: in a revealing anecdote in these proceedings, Juana complained that abusive Antón had forced her to breathe chili smoke, a traditional form of punishment for children among the pre-Columbian cultures of central Mexico that her husband must have picked up after arriving in the Americas (see Figure 1.1 for a contemporary representation). In these documents, beyond the legalese of the professional Inquisition scribes, we discover a dynamic web of demographic, cultural, and linguistic exchanges where Taxco residents engaged in the reproduction, rejection, or reinterpretation of the communicative resources available to them. The result was characterized by continuity, but also by innovation. More details about Juana's and Antón's case are provided in Schwaller (2016: 124–30).

All around the planet, in environments like multilingual, multiethnic, multicultural Taxco, millions of speakers of varied backgrounds have continued to engage in similar processes, recombining communicative resources of global provenance and developing their own versions of them. Centuries later, some of these repertoires have come to be known as 'Spanish.' Juana and Antón did live in a world where people talked about 'language' and 'languages': but neither were these systems of belief uniform, nor did everybody's linguistic behavior necessarily abide by these beliefs. Instead, these speakers must have done what all other humans have done since language emerged as a technology for communication, being more 'concerned with whether or not they are understood and with what they gain from communicating in particular ways on specific occasions than with what or how they contribute to the emergence of their communal norms' (Mufwene and Vigouroux 2017: 81). And yet, much of what has been written about the history of Spanish tacitly assumes that human communication is biased toward the reproduction of these norms. In these narratives, the linguistic behavior of bilinguals or multilinguals has often been approached tacitly as an exception to the otherwise assumed normal behavior of monolinguals. This way of writing language histories silences the experiences of individuals who, like Juana and Antón, produced new modes of communication

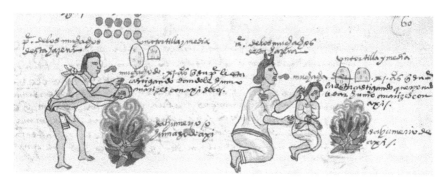

FIGURE 1.1. Mesoamerican parents disciplining their children with chili smoke, Codex Mendoza (1540s, central Mexico) (Bodleian Library 2023, f. 60r, © Bodleian Libraries, University of Oxford, license: https://creativecommons.org/licenses/by-nc/4.0/deed.en)

born out of necessity and opportunity, rather than loyalty to anybody's previous linguistic traditions.

In this book, I question this received narrative. What would the history of Spanish look like if we do not think of it as a set of language elements transmitted from generation to generation for centuries? In other words, what would this history look like if we do not think of Spanish as *a language*? To answer this question, I propose that Spanish (the same as any other language) can be thought of alternatively as a cultural myth, constructed to impose uniformity over a heterogeneous constellation of language features resulting from contacts among individuals whose primary goal has always been to communicate in linguistically and socially effective ways. Amid these contacts, assessments about what constitutes 'Spanish' have changed over time and have come to include many elements that were not always thought of as being a part of the language.

To understand this approach, we first need to revisit some deep-seated notions, starting with the very idea of Spanish as a historical entity – that is, Spanish as a language.

1.2. What is Spanish? The birth of a mythical creature

In 1926, Spanish philologist Ramón Menéndez Pidal published *Orígenes del español: Estado lingüístico de la Península Ibérica hasta el siglo XI* ('The Origins of Spanish: The Linguistic Situation in the Iberian Peninsula up to the Eleventh Century') (1950). This was a key milestone in a sturdy historical tradition that sees Spanish as a linguistic entity originating in an early medieval Romance dialect spoken in the north of the Iberian Peninsula. Elements of this tradition can be traced in much earlier works, such as Antonio de Nebrija's *Gramática de la lengua castellana* (1492) (Biblioteca Digital Hispánica 2023a), Juan de Valdés's *Diálogo de la lengua* (1535) (Biblioteca Digital Hispánica 2023b), Bernardo de Aldrete's *Del origen y principio de la lengua castellana* (1674, first published in 1606) and Gregori Maians i Siscar's *Orígenes de la lengua española* (1737), some of whom Menéndez Pidal explicitly acknowledged in the prologue to *Orígenes* (we will come back to Nebrija in Chapter 3). Menéndez Pidal's goal was philological: he used archival texts from northern Castile, dated between the ninth and the eleventh centuries (for instance, the *Glosas Emilianenses*, a series of Romance and Basque annotations to a Latin text, often deemed the earliest example of written Castilian, see Figure 1.2), to document the birth of Spanish as a written language, and thus, as a historical object (1950: vii).

By pinpointing the emergence of Spanish in these texts, Menéndez Pidal was doing more than just dating the first written records in the language. He was also laying the foundation for a form of thinking and writing about Spanish as a historical living entity that naturalized the link between the forms found in tenth- and eleventh-century northern Castile with those used by several hundred million speakers in the early twenty-first century (Del Valle 2013a). That these early medieval annotations were only (at best) remotely intelligible to Spanish speakers of his age was irrelevant for Menéndez Pidal's main point. To him, these parchment pages gave witness to the first stages of development of the Castilian/

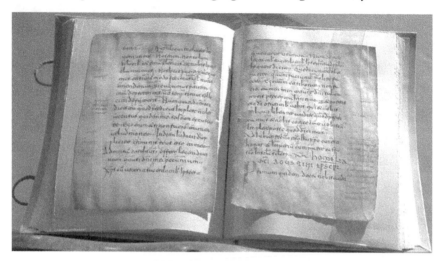

FIGURE 1.2. The *Glosas Emilianenses* manuscript (Víctor Gómez via Flickr, license: https://creativecommons.org/licenses/by-nc-nd/2.0/deed.en)

Spanish 'embryo'[1] as it started to grow by leaps and bounds, still feeding from its mother (Latin) but ready to being life as an independent entity (1950: 528–9). Just like an embryo looks different from the adult individual but shares the exact same genetic blueprint, so is Menéndez Pidal inviting us to see these early medieval documents as representing an earlier life stage in the development of this linguistic organism that we now call 'Spanish.'

In all fairness, the 'language as organism' metaphor was not Menéndez Pidal's invention. It had already been predicated by nineteenth-century comparative linguists as they researched the origins, expansion, and diversification of the Indo-European language family (§2.2 and §3.3; see also Jakobs and Hüning 2022). But Menéndez Pidal elevated this historical-organic conception of Spanish to the status of intellectual dogma. An example is *Historia de la lengua española* by Rafael Lapesa, one of Menéndez Pidal's students. This was an immensely popular textbook with nine editions since its original publication in 1942 and with multiple reprints of its last 1981 edition, spanning until 2005. In this book, prefaced by Menéndez Pidal himself, Lapesa relies fully on his professor's metaphors to depict Spanish as a growing, evolving body, led by an intrinsic drive to become a homogeneous, international, and culturally elevated instrument of communication. Lapesa paints a vivid portrait of a daring linguistic entity with a mind of its own that is ahead of other less self-assured Iberian Romance varieties: it soon eliminates variation by choosing more stable, assumedly more advanced forms (1981: 175–8); it absorbs the less lively, more underdeveloped dialects of Muslim Spain to the south (180). As it shakes off phonological, morphological, and syntactic hesitations (197–204), it walks toward its regularization ('camina hacia su regularización', 247) and spreads across the ocean. In Lapesa's eyes,

---

1 Throughout this book, all non-English quotes are translated into English, unless otherwise noted.

by the end of the twentieth century, Spanish had reached its destiny as 'the expressive instrument of a community that envelops two worlds, Spain and Latin America, including men ["hombres"] of all races' (442), expressed in its ideal form as a homogeneous language of literature and culture ('lengua culta', 444–5). Here, the Castilian embryo adumbrated by Menéndez Pidal has finally grown into a fully-fledged international and refined creature that, nevertheless, has preserved its original essential genetic traits.

As quirky as the images in this storyline might seem to us, Menéndez Pidal's and Lapesa's underlying conception of Spanish as a living organism with a traceable genealogy was fully embraced by subsequent generations of linguists (and speakers). Together, they contributed to solidify what is by now a well-established narrative about the history of Spanish. This tradition is apparent in the very titles of many of the works that, in the wake of Menéndez Pidal's *Orígenes*, have sought to trace the history of this linguistic object: Spaulding's *How Spanish Grew* (1943), Lloyd's *From Latin to Spanish* (1987), Penny's *A History of the Spanish Language* (2002), Pharies's *A Brief History of the Spanish Language* (2015), among others. The titles of works for a non-specialized audience often reveal a similar approach: Alatorre's *1001 años de la lengua española* (1979), Nadeau and Barlow's *The Story of Spanish* (2013), Moreno Fernández's *La maravillosa historia del español* (2015a), and Pons Rodríguez's *Una lengua muy larga* (2016), to name a few. This literature has undoubtedly shed light on many aspects in the history of Spanish and has given generations of students tools with which to interpret the vast amount of data furnished by historical corpora, dialectal studies, and other sources. At the same time, however, many of these contributions have embraced (to various degrees of explicitness) the same understanding of Spanish as an entity with origins, growth, expansion, and direct linear evolution toward its full development as a standardized international language (Del Valle 2016).

This narrative has permeated how we still think and talk about the history of Spanish today. It continues to be reproduced, with various degrees of explicitness, in research articles and textbooks. It is upheld by institutions of higher learning and language planning, and commonly heard outside academia – for instance, as a lure used by Spain's official tourism board to attract visitors to the 'birthplace' of the language in several locations of north-central Spain, as shown in Figure 1.3. This attitude is certainly not exclusive to Spanish: it is typical of a *monoglossic* positivistic form of thinking about language characterized by a split between speakers and the forms they use that is common in Western thinking (Canagarajah 2014: 19–24). From this perspective, languages are assumed to exist as historical realities, and users are seen as carriers (that is, speakers of x), rather than as agents. Observed changes in a language must be reconcilable with their organic essence: just like organisms come to life and grow, experiencing changes in shape, size, and metabolic functions while preserving individual genotypical characteristics, so should a language be described in its historical trajectory, from beginning to present, as a changing but essentially unitary entity (for a critique of the organic metaphor, see Gal and Irvine 1995: 968; Mufwene 2008: 12–6 and §2.4).

6   *Spanish as a Contact Language: An Ecological History*

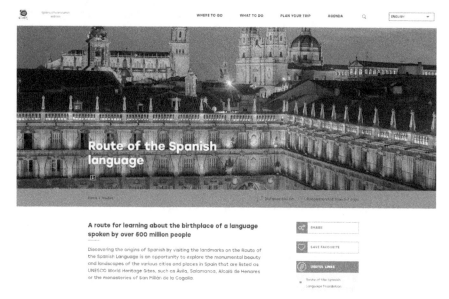

FIGURE 1.3. Spain's official *Route of the Spanish Language* website (source: https://www.spain.info/en/route/route-of-spanish-language/)

But this narrative is not just a framework to talk about the history of Spanish. It is, ultimately, the reflection of an understanding of Spanish as an object that can (and should!) be defined, observed, analyzed, and regimented. These goals become apparent in prescriptive presentations of the language. For instance, the *Nueva gramática de la lengua española* (Real Academia Española and Asociación de Academias de la Lengua Española 2009), a normative text published by ASALE, a collection of language standardizing bodies under the aegis of Spain's Real Academia Española, specifies in its preface that its goal is 'to describe in detail the many structures shared by the majority of Spanish speakers' (xlii). The preface acknowledges diversity but makes clear that there are 'value judgments that reflect the implicit consensus about *a system shared by millions of speakers*', while 'calling the speakers' attention about the language they use, which belongs to them and *which they must take care of*' (xliii, my emphasis).

Even some dialectal descriptions are still partially reflective of the same approach, presenting Spanish as endowed with essential characteristics accrued throughout its historical development and shared by an international community of speakers. For instance, Moreno Fernández and Otero (2008) and Moreno Fernández (2015b) have proposed the following six salient essential denominators of Spanish: high relative homogeneity, with low risk for fragmentation; official status in many countries around the world; main language in a geographically cohesive linguistic area; demographic growth; high index of communication (understood as its preferential use as a language of communication by bi/multilingual speakers in many areas); and, again, first-order language of culture (literature, media, bureaucracy, etc.). These prescriptive and dialectal articulations of what Spanish is today share in at least some of the ingredients in Menéndez Pidal's and Lapesa's storyline: the current stability and dialectal cohesion of the language, expressed most transparently in the literary standard, is exactly what we would expect as the logical consequence in the history a self-aware creature with a thirst for standardization and geopolitical spread.

Einar Haugen's (1966) already noted that this *discourse of homogeneity* is typical in the construction of standard languages: only a tiny subset of the variation attested in the community is acknowledged, and only some forms are accepted as part of the standard. But the arbitrariness behind the criterion governing this selection is rarely made explicit. We are invited to accept the rationale governing it, as well as the authority of the subjects who establish it, as a matter of fact. Now, as the chapters in this book will show, it would certainly be unfair to brand all historical grammar or historical dialectological literature in Spanish as a mere rendition of Menéndez Pidal's or Lapesa's ideas – my argument here is that some of the assumptions about what languages are and how they change that have spurred research on the history of Spanish since the nineteenth century may have helped us see some things (but not others) and may have led us to write certain versions of what happened (but not others). If that is the case, what (and who) have we left out, and what might happen if we try to write a different kind of narrative?

1.3. The erasure of variation: Forgetfulness in the historical linguistics of Spanish

Dialectologists and sociolinguists have long stressed that language heterogeneity is a central aspect of language use (Weinreich et al. 1968), and Spanish is no exception. Faced with this evidence, the historiography of Spanish has often responded by either explaining it away as unrepresentative of the essential characteristics of the language or (more commonly) by interpreting it as a surface manifestation of some form of underlying homogeneity.

Historical grammars, focusing on so-called 'internal' developments (§2.5), have often exemplified this attitude. In Spanish, Menéndez Pidal (who else?) articulated the prototype for this genre in his *Manual elemental de gramática histórica española* (first published in 1904), another best-seller with multiple editions throughout the twentieth century. In this textbook, he explicitly circumscribed his object of study to the changes connecting spoken Latin to the current literary standard (1958 [1904]: 30). As dialectal surveys and archival research in the early twentieth century began to offer incontrovertible proof of pervasive geographical variation, subsequent historical grammars had to somehow reconcile this evidence with the strong tradition revolving around the description of the literary language. Thus, in the opening to his *Gramática histórica española*, and carefully trying to not step on Menéndez Pidal's revered toes, an almost apologetic García de Diego justified his inclusion of dialectal variants because 'Castilian is a cluster of dialects' ('complejo dialectal'), even if they ultimately fed into the emergence of the historical standard language (1961: 18–9). Along a similar vein, in *The Evolution of Spanish: An Introductory Historical Grammar* (the first such work for an English-speaking audience), Lathrop candidly admitted that, since his goal was to describe standard Spanish, 'it would be inappropriate to complicate and confuse issues by discussing dialectal developments' (1980: x).

Fortunately, more recent historical grammar textbooks are usually explicit in their acknowledgment of sociolinguistic variation: unlike what used to be the case decades ago, current scholarship in Spanish does not sweep social and dialectal variation under the rug. But even so, today's historical grammars are still mostly concerned with tracking the linguistic genealogy of the standard language (Núñez Méndez 2012; Pharies 2015; Ranson and Quesada 2018): the phonological correspondences, morphological evolution, syntactic rearrangements, and processes of lexical diversification that these texts tell us about are by and large those leading to normative Spanish. Dialectal variants are acknowledged, but typically only when they are well represented in prominent regional norms (for instance, variation in forms of address, as in non-deferential *tú* vs. *vos* 'you-2SG').

In a way, this focus is understandable: historical grammar textbooks cannot logically aspire to explain all attested forms of variation, so those that comprise the pan-Hispanic standard language would seem at first sight like a good target. But the end result, perhaps unintendedly, is often not too far from that of prescriptive works. For instance, the compilers of ASALE's prescriptive grammar reassure readers that acknowledging dialectal variants 'does not endanger the unity of the Spanish language, but instead helps to strengthen it' (2009: xlii) – implicitly confirming, ironically, that the homogeneity of this linguistic object should after all not be taken for granted (by the way, this anxiety about the unity of Spanish is not new; see §3.1, §5.1 and §6.10 for other historical examples). In short, it is clear that recent historical work on Spanish does not ignore sociolinguistic variation, often recognizing that variation is at the root of language change. At the same time, by espousing the same bias in favor of the explanation of the standard language, these historical grammars and prescriptive texts have contributed to reify this purportedly homogeneous entity as an ideal representation of the whole language and its assumed historical essences.

This insistence on narrating the history of Spanish as the evolution of a bundle of forms endowed with a clear-cut, easy-to-follow genealogy of descent evidences various degrees of *erasure* (Gal and Irvine 1995) and *invisibilization* (Havinga and Langer 2015) of linguistic heterogeneity that are typical of discourses on standard languages. Del Valle interprets this erasure as a form of mandatory forgetfulness that protects the canonical narrative from the articulation of alternatives (Del Valle 2016: 19). From this perspective, the history of Spanish becomes *a history of that which is worth being remembered*. In contexts where the operation of normative discourses is paramount (such as academic publishing, institutions of higher education, public discourse on Spanish), this form of forgetfulness is still often prescribed. As a result, both historical and prescriptive discourses often emerge as faces of the same coin, each a crutch to the other, collaborating in the reproduction of the same cultural myth of homogeneity via the erasure of difference and heterogeneity.

This operation of historical amnesia becomes harder to sustain when diachronic narratives dare to contend with the stubborn reality of heterogeneity emerging from dialectal or archival data. This problem is paramount in Penny (2000), to date one of the few approaches to the history of Spanish that have attempted to reconcile variability and heterogeneity with a genealogical narrative of the language. Armed with the tools of late twentieth-century dialectology and sociolinguistics, Penny questioned many of the assumptions inherent to the standard narrative of descent and homogeneity. But even Penny, who explicitly framed sociolinguistic and historical data as inconsistent with strict linguistic boundaries, set out to study the history of Spanish as one of descent and regularity, embracing the axiom of its core Latin ancestry. Sociolinguistics, as he interpreted it, allows us to study 'the seamlessness of language variation: the fact that language presents itself to us in the form of orderly but undivided heterogeneity' (ix). Sociohistorical linguistic data might be messy, but under this messiness (we're told) lies the essential orderly makeup of the language, which researchers will find as long as they are willing to look hard enough.

To date, the clearest form of questioning of this discourse of homogeneity or orderly variability in Spanish comes from the literature on contact in bi/multilingual or bi/multidialectal settings. By providing evidence of deviations from the patterns typical of monolingual or dialectally homogeneous areas and their incorporation in Spanish varieties, dialect and language contact literature has implicitly (but unmistakably) questioned the myth of Spanish as a historical linguistic essence (Chappell and Drinka 2021; Dworkin et al. 2024; Klee and Lynch 2009; Núñez Méndez 2019; Ortiz López et al. 2020). It is true that even contact-focused literature sometimes still takes for granted models that approach multilingualism as an individual's or a community's ability to use more than two named and otherwise different languages (for instance, Thomason and Kaufman 1988; Van Coetsem 2000; Weinreich 1953; §2.2). It follows, then, that contact situations are historically and sociolinguistically restricted: some situations qualify as 'contact settings', and others do not. This approach is captured in the by-now commonplace collocation *Spanish in contact with...* (or 'el español en contacto con...'), which is featured in the title of multiple studies, monographs, chapters, and edited collections published over the past two decades (e.g. Blas Arroyo 2011; Escobar 2011; Klee and Lynch 2009; Núñez Méndez 2019; Poch Olivé 2016; Sanz-Sánchez 2014; Sayahi 2011). It may be argued that relying implicitly on a conceptual divide between contact and non-contact situations leaves the monolingual myth of Spanish as a historical linguistic entity largely unexamined. And yet, contact-focuses studies remind us that we cannot simply continue to tell the history of Spanish as a narrative of unadulterated descent. Contact literature in Spanish (and other languages) opens exciting avenues for novel approaches to the historical relationship between speakers and their communicative resources in these linguistically diverse environments.

For decades now, post-structuralist critiques of Western linguistics as a field have approached language varieties as ideological constructs, used in the naturalization of ethnic or national ideologies (Gal and Irvine 1995; Pratt 1987; see also §1.4 for more recent critiques). These criticisms have in turn fed a search for alternatives in the linguistics of Spanish (e.g. Del Valle 2013a, 2016; Lynch 2018, 2020; Mar-Molinero 2008, 2020; Otheguy et al. 2015, 2022; Villa and Del Valle 2015) that consciously veer away from the structuralist, monoglossic, positivist discourses on Spanish and its history. Instead, they call for a reassessment of Spanish as a socio-political mirage, and for its forms and meanings not as given but emerging in communication among speakers whose behavior may or may not match definitions of native or monolingual proficiency. In these articulations, hybridity and heterogeneity are consubstantial with language use, rather than marginal. To date, however, these calls have had little effect on the linguistic historiography of Spanish, and the imprint of structuralist paradigms on narratives of language change continues to be strong.

To understand this reluctance to question the received dogma of Spanish as a historical essence, we need to explore the very core of this narrative: the existence of languages and the role that speakers play in language change, a point to which we now turn.

1.4. Do languages exist?

Even though the historiography of Spanish (and other languages) commonly relies on the 'discrete language' construct, this idea has proven problematic for language change theory. The blurriness of the distinction between *languages* and *dialects*, acknowledged to be based on political or cultural factors (Chambers and Trudgill 1998: 3–12; Erker 2017; Otheguy et al. 2015; Penny 2000: 15–6; Thomason 2001: 2), is often mentioned as an example of the limitations of this construct (this distinction will be critiqued in more depth in §2.3). But the ontological status of named language varieties as units of linguistic variation and change is much less commonly scrutinized.

In a classical formulation of this problem, Kloss (1967) proposed that languages can be identified as distinct entities on the basis of two perspectives, either *Ausbau* (lit. 'expansion, development'), which applies to varieties developed as standard languages; and *Abstand* (lit. 'distance, separation'), which expresses differences based on linguistic distance. For instance, across the traditional Romance dialects of northern Iberia, the standardized *Ausbau* varieties ('Portuguese', 'Galician', 'Spanish', 'Catalan') are linguistically discrete, but *Abstand* differences across regional and social dialects are much more gradual. As a matter of fact, dialectal variation across northern Iberian Romance varieties is usually described as a gradual *dialect continuum* within the western Romance area (see Map 1.1). Within this spectrum, political and cultural differences have given rise to sociocultural definitions of linguistic difference ('Portuguese', 'Spanish', 'Catalan', etc.), but historical dialectal variation in the region is a bad match for these purported discrete distinctions (see Penny 2000: 80–107). We'll return to the issue of dialect continua in §2.3.

To circumvent these sociopolitical or ideological difficulties in the definition of these named linguistic units, *mutual intelligibility* is commonly invoked as an alternative criterion. For instance, a widely used introductory textbook for historical linguistics laconically defines a language as 'any distinct linguistic entity (variety) which is mutually unintelligible with other such entities' (Campbell 2004: 186) and moves on from there. But mutual intelligibility can only go so far as a universal criterion to locate language boundaries. For one, historically related varieties share many *cognate* forms that are phonologically (and often semantically) similar because of a shared origin: compare, for instance, the Romance reflexes for 'tooth: Port. and It. *dente*, Sp. *diente*, Cat., Fr. and Occit. *dent,* Rom. *dinte*, all of which still share the same meaning and a similar pronunciation to what is reconstructed for Lat. *dent(em)*. Romance

MAP 1.1. Proposed dialectal continua in Europe (Kanguole, via Wikimedia Commons, license: https://creativecommons.org/licenses/by-sa/2.5/deed.en)

languages in particular have been estimated to share high percentages of cognate lexicon and numerous orthographic similarities, which allow for partial mutual cross-linguistic intelligibility at the spoken and written level (Heeringa et al. 2013). Furthermore, besides formal similarities, intelligibility is also mediated by several non-linguistic factors, including individual speakers' previous exposure to the other language and cultural attitudes (Gooskens and Van Heuven 2020). As a result, the same as geographical or social boundaries, mutual intelligibility is anything but a reliable criterion if we want to draw linguistic borderlines.

Criticism to the premise that language variation and use can be described on the basis of discrete languages has come from various fronts, including *individual-cognitive* approaches (where language is seen as knowledge represented in the speakers' brains), and *socio-pragmatic* literature (where language is seen as cultural practice actuated in communication). Isac and Reiss (2013) exemplify the individual-cognitive approach, describing languages as sets of computational rules represented in the mind of individual speakers. They rely on the generativist tradition (as articulated in, for instance, Chomsky 1986) in labeling these individual mental representations as *i-languages,* and they reject the idea of homogenous communal languages as linguistic entities. Using English as an example, they point out that

> [t]here is no entity in the world that we can characterize as 'English'. There is just a (large) bunch of people with fairly similar mental grammars that they can use to communicate in a way that is typically more efficient than between what we call Japanese and English speakers, because the so-called English mental grammars are more similar to each other. (2013: 16–7)

In this line of thinking, communal language abstractions (*e-languages*) are constructed based on these perceived commonalities among each user's mental grammar.

Socio-pragmatic approaches, informed by post-structuralist theory, have also been critical of the discrete language myth, although for other reasons. Socio-pragmatic criticism has to do with how this myth directs linguistic inquiry away from what speakers *do* in favor of a reductionist vision of what they supposedly *know*. In turn, this approach privileges monolingual language behavior as the ideal object of linguistic theorization. Makoni and Pennycook stress that '[l]anguages do not exist as real entities in the world and neither do they emerge from or represent real environments; they are, by contrast, the inventions of social, cultural, and political movements' (2006: 2). Unlike structuralist approaches, which viewed individuals as speakers of 'a' language, socio-pragmatic approaches think of them as users of *repertoires* (Gumperz 1980; Matras 2020) of communicative elements that take on local meanings in specific contexts of use. In this view, norms emerge dynamically in local negotiation among groups of individuals. Examples include *communities of practice* where speakers come together for a shared goal, like school cliques, work teams, or denominational confraternities (Eckert 2000, Mendoza-Denton and Gordon 2011) or *social networks* of frequently communicating individuals (Milroy and Milroy 1985, 1992; §2.2 and §2.6). Speakers in these kinds of contexts play an active role in the negotiation of their repertoires, which may come to include elements of varied provenance: language varieties (dialects, stylistic registers, etc.) are thus combinations of 'mobile resources' (Blommaert 2010: 6–7) that we can activate and combine for multiple (and always changing) communicative purposes.

This approach has political implications. For socio-pragmatically inspired authors, self-contained, community-based definitions of languages reflect ethnocentric colonial views on linguistic hybridity or non-standard communicative practices. Canagarajah (2014) locates the emergence of this ethnic concept of language in European nineteenth-century nationalism, exported via political and academic colonialism to other parts of the world. In this ethnocentric approach, languages exist in mutually exclusive geographical and social spaces with clear boundaries (for instance, 'Spanish is spoken in Spain', 'French people speak French', 'Koreans don't speak Chinese', etc.), and homogeneity and/or monolingualism are assumed as the norm across ethnic groups or geographical areas (Jakobs and Hüning 2022).

Instead of this Western paradigm based on the assumption of uniformity and clean-cut descent, some authors have proposed a new *translingual* paradigm to better capture the dynamic, hybrid nature of all uses of language (Canagarajah 2014; see also García and Li 2014 and Otheguy et al. 2015, 2019, 2022 for a similar articulation). In this paradigm, the differentiation and labeling of languages is an ideological act of demarcating certain codes in relation to specific identities and interests. However, in actual communication, users draw from all resources available to them, regardless of whether they are believed to belong to the same or different languages. A speaker's competence does not fall into separate spheres of experience or knowledge for each language. Language is not separate from other non-linguistic, semiotic resources but is multimodal (including oral, written, and visual modes). A present-day texting chain, which may combine lexical material, onomatopoeias, emojis, voicemails, photographs, memes, and other signifying elements (often in the same turn) epitomizes the multimodality of language use.

Although both the individual-cognitive and socio-pragmatic views differ in their motivation and goals, they share their understanding of communal languages as cultural constructs rather than real linguistic entities. If we accept this basic position, the obvious next question is what this all means for linguistic historiography. How can we write the history of *a* language if languages do not exist? Or, as Warren put it, 'how can one tell the history of language when there is no "language beyond language"?' (2003: 28).

1.5. The centrality of language users

In this book, I will explore this question in relation to Spanish by advocating for an alternative way of thinking about its history. My starting point will not be the assumed linguistic genealogy of Spanish, but *the role of individual speakers in specific ecologies of communication* as the source of all continuities and all change.

To say that whatever a language is, it must exist because individual humans use it may seem a tautology. But the precise role of individual speakers in theories of language change has been controversial. We know languages change, but how do individuals contribute to these changes? In some sociolinguistic approaches, individual speakers are theoretically meaningful only insofar as their actions contribute to the emergence of communal norms: '[l]inguistic analysis cannot recognize individual grammars or phonologies. Individual rules or constraints would have no interpretation and contribute nothing to acts of communication. In this sense, the individual does not exist as a linguistic object' (Labov 2001: 34; see Eckert 2019 for a recent articulation of a similar perspective). Other sociolinguistic approaches, however, have engaged much more actively with the role of individual speakers as originators and transmitters of change: '[we need] a route for constructing a two-level sociolinguistic theory, linking small-scale structures such as networks, in which individuals are embedded and act purposively in their daily lives, with larger scale and more abstract social structures' (Milroy and Milroy 1992: 16); 'we need to go to the individual to understand the behavior that leads to the adoption or rejection of potential changes' (Kerswill and Williams 2000a: 65). Recent approaches to the spread of innovations across communities of speakers have also focused on individuals as transmitters of change (Baxter and Croft 2016; Blythe and Croft 2021; Hall-Lew et al. 2021).

Socio-pragmatic post-structuralist interpretations have foregrounded real-life communicative practices among individuals as the medium whereby language norms emerge and change. This approach centers individuals' *cognition*, understood both as a dynamic mental and social competence, as the site of language use and change:

> Meaning-making requires the work of creative and active social agents to employ the disparate and conflictual elements of a language or cognitive system … Cognition is embedded. Thinking occurs not separated from the environment but in engagement with it … [C]ognition is extended: it doesn't occur within the mind alone. The environment and others help us think (Canagarajah 2014: 32; see also García and Wei 2014 and Otheguy et al. 2015).

Note that, in this approach, language is not a system (of sounds, grammatical rules or words), but a *practice*: it does not reside in one individual, nor in the whole community, but in the act of individual-to-individual communication. As they engage in this collective 'meaning-making' (as Canagarajah puts it), individuals as socially situated cognitive agents participate with their mental affordances as well as their social knowledge of context, including any local discourses on what counts as 'a language', and their ability and motivation to adhere to or to modify these norms (Hill and Hill 1986; Makihara 2013; Matras 2020).

Newer articulations have embraced this understanding of language to examine the relationship between language acquisition and language change. One such line of inquiry follows Hopper's (1987) views on grammar as emerging from discourse, that is, communicative practices as primary and structure as derived (Backus 2021; Bybee 2010; Ortega et al. 2016). With this *usage-based* view as their starting point, researchers have proposed the notion of language as a *complex adaptive system* (CAS) (Ellis and Larsen-Freeman 2009; Kretzschmar 2015; Larsen-Freeman 2007). In this view, the interaction among individual units, elements or agents gives rise to generalities and differences at the level of the population. CASs are *emergent*: one cannot predict these population-level effects by looking at any one given interaction among agents, but in the general patterns resulting from these interactions. Examples include weather systems, traffic patterns, or swarms of animals, like flocks of birds (Figure 1.4). From a CAS perspective, language is a system of dynamic usage with the following characteristics: multiple speakers interact with each other adaptively, where past interactions inform current and future interactions; competing factors (from perceptual mechanics to social motivations) shape every user's behavior; and language patterns (that is, structure) emerge from the users' experience, cognitive processes, and social networks of communication (Ellis and Larsen-Freeman 2009).

In this view, individuals are not subject to any central control. Instead, as they communicate with each other, they reinforce some behaviors and others

FIGURE 1.4. Starlings creating an ephemeral murmuration in Scotland
(© Walter Baxter, geography.org.uk/photo/4302954, license:
https://creativecommons.org/licenses/by-sa/2.0/deed.en)

become less frequent (Nölle et al. 2020). Collective patterns emerge from these interactions, but these patterns are never completely stable, and the very dynamics of communication may introduce changes at any point. These stages of seeming stability are akin to sociolinguistic norms, or even so-called languages and dialects (for instance, *punctuated equilibrium*, Nevalainen et al. 2020; see also *sedimentation* in Canagarajah 2014: 28–9). An important corollary in many CAS-informed and post-structuralist approaches is that users never completely 'learn' a language (there is no fully baked language to learn) but continuously recreate and modify it in context and together with other non-linguistic elements of communication throughout their lifespan. Acquisition, therefore, is not the learning of structure, but the life-long development of features, meanings, etc. through usage, so usage and acquisition are inextricably connected: '[i]t is not that you learn something and then you use it; neither is it that you use something and then you learn it. Instead, it is in the using that you learn – they are inseparable' (Larsen-Freeman 2007: 783). In a similar vein, linguists from various subareas have begun to explore the ways in which individual speakers can contribute to (or resist) communal trends of change throughout their lives (Baxter and Croft 2016; Sankoff 2018).

In CAS-influenced and post-structuralist approaches, *context* takes on a critical role: context is not just limited to what has traditionally been called 'external' factors of language use and change (demography, sociocultural conditions, language ideologies, etc.). It also includes the interaction among the various components of language and their transformation as individuals communicate, or in other words, 'the intersubjective space between interlocutors' (Larsen-Freeman

2007: 783). By stressing the continuity between the speakers' cognitive representations of communication and their contextually situated interactions with other language users, CAS approaches emphasize the interdependence between so-called mental and social/pragmatic aspects in language (§1.4). They also provide for possibilities to situate the emergence of communal norms at various levels of articulation, from the individual to the local network, the dialect, the language, or even the global (see languages as populations, §2.4).

1.6. The ecology of language

The critical role played by context is central to approaches that view language change as the by-product of individuals' responses to their *language ecology*, comprising both the conditions of language use and the relationships among linguistic elements in the speakers' cognition. Haugen (1971) was the first to explicitly analogize language context to a biological ecology, understanding the language variety (for instance, Tegucigalpa Spanish, Australian English, or Nenets) as the unit of ecological adaptation to the speakers' social lives. This perspective subsumed the then growing fields of sociolinguistics and language contact, but also the sociology of language (as in the study of language attitudes, policies, maintenance, and loss). A more recent area stemming from Haugen's work is *ecolinguistics* (Fill and Penz 2018), which sees language and biological diversity as mutually correlated, with language as a mediator of the relationship between humans and their natural environment.

Other ecological approaches have taken a closer look at the role of speaker-to-speaker communication in shaping population-wide patterns of historical stability and change. This line of thinking commonly relies on a biological-evolutionary framework (Clements 2018; Croft 2000, 2008, 2021), whereby language change is the result of the accumulation of innovative choices (*differential replication*) across populations of interacting subjects. Mufwene's work on the *ecology of language* (2001, 2008, 2018; Mufwene and Vigouroux 2017) has offered the most explicit articulation of this approach. Here, languages are no longer analogized to organisms, but to *populations* of organisms of the parasitic type, where speaker idiolects are the organism, and the speakers' minds are the hosts (do keep in mind this is just an analogy: these authors are *not* saying that language is a parasite! As we will see in §2.4, this analogy has both advantages and limitations). The ecology of language comprises the environmental conditions in which individuals access language and use it to communicate, all the way from cognitive and articulatory constraints to large-scale social structures. Individual repertoires emerge as their users select from the aggregate of features (*feature pools*) that they have access to in their personal ecologies. For instance, for a bilingual English/Spanish speaker, this may include constructions from standard and non-standard versions of either language, code-switching patterns between both, and even elements from other languages encountered throughout life.

In true CAS and evolutionary fashion, this approach predicts that individuals in similar environments will behave similarly in linguistic terms, but total uniformity is never reached: '[i]ndividual speakers/signers have singular life, hence interactional, trajectories; and these have shaped their personalities and social identities in different (though often similar) ways' (Mufwene and Vigouroux 2017: 81). If population patterns emerge from individual selections determined by the environment, it follows that theories of language evolution, including change and stability, will benefit from attending to how universal cognitive dispositions mediate these selections in specific social contexts. As in other recent approaches (for instance, CAS, post-structuralist, sociolinguistic) 'acquisition' in ecological terms takes a broad meaning: it is not the successful reproduction of some hypothesized adult or native target, but the constant formulation of communicative repertoires in interaction with those of other users throughout the speaker's lifespan (Leather and Van Dam 2003: 13–4). In this process, individuals' cognitive resources play a critical role: the architecture of the human brain, its developmental characteristics throughout the lifespan, its computing possibilities and limitations (production, perception) and human memory all interface with the individual's context to provide a platform for socially situated language use (see *cognition* in §2.4).

1.7. Language as contact

Central to ecological approaches is the fact that 'every setting of language use and human interaction is a contact setting' (Mufwene and Vigouroux 2017: 76). This is hardly a new idea: for decades now, approaches to dialectology, social variation, and language contact have underscored that, insofar as every form of language use is ultimately the consequence of exposure to the language of others, language change is always a matter of contact: '[i]n some sense, all languages are contact languages, [since l]anguage is the ultimate, uniquely human tool used to establish and to maintain contact between people' (Bakker and Matras 2013: 1; and Chapter 2). But old habits die hard, and narratives of language change often continue to conceptualize contact in terms of contact among linguistic entities, whether 'dialects' or 'languages.' From this perspective, contact is an exception to the more usual or basic contexts of change, identified with assumed language-internal tendencies in monolingual communities. As discussed above (§1.2 and §1.3), this has been the case in much of the historiographical tradition on Spanish.

Many scholars are now open to acknowledging the role of contact processes in the history of many languages in a more encompassing perspective: '[i]n many cases, the contact history of a language is underexplored in linguistic scholarship', but this reassessment is often 'largely a question of us metaphorically polishing the spectacles through which we look at the language in question, and of jettisoning a priori assumptions that are not as watertight as we might once have believed' (Grant 2021: 7). In thinking about the history of Spanish from this perspective, I align myself with Hundt and Schreier, who in their volume on English as a contact language have decried the fact that 'historical linguistics have long concentrated on language-internal processes and treated language contact as marginal' (2013: 17). In full ecological spirit, we can take their argument one step further: it is not only that 'contact-induced language change plays a significant role in English and elsewhere' (17), but contact *is* language, and *all language change is contact-induced* (Bakker and Matras 2013: 3; Matras 2020). The centrality of contact in language change poses yet another challenge to the assumption that languages may be thought of as self-contained entities with clear geographical or social borderlines (§1.4, §2.3). If we accept the view of *language as contact* as a potential starting point for new narratives of change in named language varieties like Spanish, we must question the usual take on language history as a chain of inheritance. Instead, we can envision change as a dynamic, context-dependent process, where hybridity is the norm rather than the exception. I develop several important implications of this ecological contact-based approach to the writing of language histories in Chapter 2.

In this book, I am inspired by Mary Louise Pratt's almost four-decades-old call to walk away from the traditional *linguistics of community* based on the ideological mirage of homogeneous languages shared by homogeneous groups, and to instead envisage a *linguistics of contact*, where historically situated acts of communication and negotiation of language take the center stage:

> Imagine ... a linguistics that decentered community, that placed at its cent[er] the operation of language *across* lines of social differentiation, a linguistics that focused on modes and zones of contact between dominant and dominated groups, between persons of different and multiple identities, speakers of different languages, that focused on how such speakers constitute each other relationally and in difference, how they enact differences in language. Let us call this enterprise a *linguistics of contact*, a term linked to [the] notion of contact as a component of speech events (Pratt 1987: 60, author's emphasis).

Pratt's classical call still sits well with the more recent socio-pragmatic views on language reviewed above, including newer sociolinguistic and translingual approaches, usage-based studies, language as CAS, and the ecology of language, all of which stress the *heteroglossic* nature of language as practice and process (Bakhtin 1981; note that recent approaches to the concept of 'community' also take difference and heterogeneity as central to how human beings come to construct shared spaces). To articulate a different narrative of the history of Spanish, I 'take the idea of linguistic repertoire as the foundation of social life ... and acknowledge that difference and variability are basic constitutive elements of communicative processes' (Woolard 2007: 142). Therefore, this narrative must be concerned with how contact among users has given rise to the linguistic repertoires named 'Spanish' throughout history 'without assuming the coherence of language systems and with attention to hybrid rather than normative processes' (Warren 2003: 97).

The challenges in this endeavor are both conceptual and methodological. Conceptually, the idea of a *history* or a *narrative* assumes some connection among the narrated events, predicated on the ultimate ontological status of that which is narrated (a history of *what*?). By way of illustration, the Oxford English Dictionary defines *history* (as a count noun, in the sense in which this word is used in the title of linguistic historiographies) as '[a] written narrative constituting a continuous chronological record of important or public events ... or of a particular trend, institution, or person's life', where 'each movement, action, or chain of events is dealt with as a whole and pursued to its natural termination or to a convenient stopping place' (2023). This definition fits like a glove in the traditional historiography of Spanish, where today's international standardized and systematically variable language (or even the organism-person, as conceived of by Menéndez Pidal, Lapesa, and others; §1.2) is the institution or entity whose history is to be narrated. But the match is less than perfect if we question the existential status of this object. Methodologically, the issue becomes how to apply much of the available theory on language learning, variation, and contact, which has traditionally relied tacitly on the existence of self-sufficient linguistic entities (as observed for Spanish by Erker 2017; Otheguy et al. 2015, 2022), to the study of language change and the telling of individual language histories.

In the next section, I exemplify these challenges with two situations of contact involving forms of Spanish: Palenquero (northern Colombia) and Nahuatl (central/ northeastern Mexico).

1.8. Hitting the wall: Testing the limits of traditional approaches to contact

Palenquero (also known as Palenkero or *lengua*) is a creole language spoken alongside Spanish in San Basilio de Palenque, a town south of Cartagena in northern Colombia (Lipski 2020a; Schwegler 2011; §4.6). The study of Palenquero and other *creole languages* (for instance, Hawaiian Pidgin, Haitian Kreyòl, Cape Verdean Creole, or Tok Pisin) has historically been a battleground for theories on language contact and change. These languages exhibit marked grammatical differences with respect to their *lexifiers* (the languages that creoles derive their basic lexicon from, as in French for Haitian Kreyòl, Portuguese for Cape Verdean Creole, or Spanish for Palenquero). These differences have often led to an interpretation of creoles as a typologically specific category of languages created via the interruption of the assumed normal intergenerational transmission (Bickerton 1981; McWhorter 2000, 2015; Thomason 2001; Thomason and Kaufman 1998). For others, creoles can be explained as the result of universal L2 acquisition processes (Plag 2008; Sessarego 2020). Ecologically informed approaches (Aboh 2015; DeGraff 2009; Mufwene 2001, 2008, 2010) oppose any compartmentalization of creoles into a separate linguistic category. They emphasize instead the linguistic continuities between creoles and the various codes in contact in creolizing environments, as well as the evidence for the application of universal acquisition strategies in the selection of specific structures.

The possibility that creoles and non-creoles may not be the result of qualitatively different processes of language transmission is controversial. For instance, McWhorter (2015) invokes several structural differences between Palenquero, on the one hand, and both Spanish and Kikongo (one of the languages spoken by the African slaves among whom Palenquero emerged), on the other. For instance, Palenquero lacks gender and number marking, subject-verb agreement, and differential object marking (as in Sp. *veo tu casa* 'I see your house' vs. *veo a tu madre* 'I see your mother'), all of which are present in Spanish and Kikongo. In light of these differences, McWhorter argues strongly for a qualitative distinction between creoles and non-creoles, both in terms of their structure and in terms of their history: 'there is a stark enough difference between creoles and their source languages to motivate our conceiving of their genesis as a discrete process' (2015: 51).

The linguistic differences that McWhorter underscores are real. What is not made clear in his analysis, however, is exactly how this assumed qualitative difference is to be conceptualized, since every linguistic or social criterion used to distinguish creoles or creole genesis (such as how pervasive specific grammatical structures are, how isolated the early creole speakers were from native users of the lexifier, or the initial relative proportions of native vs. non-native speakers) is necessarily a matter of degree. The existence of codes that share some of the structural and sociohistorical profiles of so-called full-fledged creoles (for instance, *creoloids, semi-creoles,* and other similar typologies, Mesthrie 2008) also questions these qualitative typological categories in linguistic and sociohistorical terms. From an ecological point of view, the question is whether the speakers among whom Palenquero emerged applied learning and communication strategies that were (as McWhorter puts it) qualitatively different from those applied in other social settings. Since these speakers must have relied on the same cognitive mechanisms, communicative motivations, and possibilities for symbolic indexation of features as speakers in other situations, the answer would seem to be negative.

Even if we are open to the idea that creole languages like Palenquero are not a typologically separate category of languages and did not emerge via qualitatively distinct processes, it is a fact that speakers (of Palenquero, or Spanish, or both) do conceive of Palenquero as somehow separate from Spanish. As it turns out, there is a well-established discourse in the community that Palenquero is, for all practical purposes, a *different* language from Spanish – supported not just by the morphosyntactic differences between canonical Spanish and Palenquero, but also by the low level of intelligibility of Palenquero by monolingual Spanish speakers (Schwegler 2011). Critically, however, the way in which bilingual or multilingual users conceptualize language boundaries is not always consistent with pre-existing definitions of the 'languages' in contact. Much on the contrary, speakers' ideas on linguistic boundaries constitute yet another site of conflict between conventional discourses on language differences and actual linguistic repertoires.

Specifically in the case of Palenquero, Lipski (2015, 2020a) has tested its speakers' psycholinguistic awareness of boundaries between Spanish and Palenquero experimentally. In these studies, participants were asked to identify utterances as either Palenquero, Spanish, or 'mixed.' Despite well-established discourses among linguists and speakers alike on the existence of two separate languages (reflected, among other contexts, in public uses of Palenquero as a symbol of the town's identity, see Figure 1.5), the speakers' actual everyday performance questions this separation: 'A major confounding factor is the high degree of lexical overlap, including a very high proportion of cognate items whose phonological realization varies little or not at all between the two languages. Perhaps most [crucial] for determining the boundaries between Spanish and [Palenquero] is the fact that there are no monolingual [Palenquero] speakers whose grammar can be compared with monolingual Spanish speakers' (Lipski 2015: 156).

Revealingly, Lipski's experiments show that older speakers tend to be more likely than younger speakers to label mixed utterances (i.e. simultaneously

FIGURE 1.5. Palenquero on a wall in the streets of San Basilio de Palenque (courtesy of Armin Schwegler)

containing elements grammatically considered either 'Spanish' or 'Palenquero') as only Palenquero, a demonstration that different generations have internalized different definitions of the language. Additional porousness can be seen in elements that operate as Palenquero 'flaggers', leading speakers to identify the whole utterance that they occur in as Palenquero, regardless of the presence of other elements in the sentence that are canonically ascribed to Spanish (Schwegler 2011: 448). For instance, speakers commonly associate mixed utterances including Spanish verbal person-number agreement (for instance, verbal endings like -*mos* for 1PL) to the 'mixed' category. By contrast, whenever these same Spanish grammatical or lexical features occur in proximity to Palenquero constructions indicating verbal tense, mood, or aspect (TMA particles), speakers tend to label the whole utterance as Palenquero. Examples (1a-c) illustrate some of these particles: note TMA particles *ta* (present progressive), *asé* (habitual) and *asé-ba* (past habitual) in combination with Spanish lexicon (*kumé* 'eat', see st. Sp. *comer*; *maí totao* 'roasted corn', see st. Sp. *maíz tostado*)[2] (examples adapted from Schwegler 2011: 452):

(1a) Yo   ta   kumé   maí   totao
     I   PRES.PROG   eat   corn   roasted
     'I am eating/eat roasted corn'.

---

2   In the remainder of the book, 'st. Sp.' stands for standard (or otherwise canonical) Spanish.

(1b) Yo asé kumé maí totao
    I   HAB eat corn roasted
    'I usually eat roasted corn'.

(1c) Yo asé kumé-ba maí totao
    I   HAB eat-IMP corn roasted
    'I usually ate roasted corn'.

According to Lipski, the ecological history of the community has led to a situation where grammatical performance does not match perceptions of language boundaries, making it impossible to identify two separate feature pools. Lipski still defends the existence of specific 'Spanish' and 'Palenquero' morphosyntactic settings in reference to specific grammatical features, but he stresses that these settings do not map onto speakers' (or linguists') external definitions of two separate languages. Similar experiments and conclusions in a trilingual contact situation in Ecuador involving Spanish, Kichwa and Media Lengua are provided in Lipski (2020b) (see also §6.4).

Granted, Palenquero has derived much of its lexicon from Spanish. But analogous confounding factors can also be found in situations of contact among lexically very distant languages. For instance, in an overview of 'heavily Hispanicized Nahuatl' varieties in a situation of long-term bilingualism with more recent language shift to Spanish, Flores Farfán (2008) lists a plethora of innovative forms uncharacteristic of older forms of Nahuatl. One such case concerns the substitution of the traditional plural verbal morpheme of Nahuatl –*h* [ʔ~h], shown in (2), by –*n* [n], shown in (3), partially modeled on the 3PL morpheme in Spanish, as shown in (4):

(2) Traditional Nahuatl:
    nemi-ʔ
    live-PL

(3) Hispanicized Nahuatl:
    nemi-n
    live-PL

(4) Spanish:
    vive-n
    live-PL

    'They live'.

According to Flores Farfán, the emergence of Nahuatl plural verbal –*n* in these modern varieties (as in 3) is not simply a copy of the Spanish morpheme. It can be traced back to colonial Nahuatl, where some non-verbal plural suffixes included nasal elements (plural absolutive suffix *-tin*, plural possessive suffix *-huān*). Flores Farfán attributes the construction in (3) to a bilingual *convergence* strategy (Aalberse et al 2019: 155–8; Klee and Lynch 2009: 20–2; Silva-Corvalán 1994; see §2.5 and §2.6 for a discussion of convergence) yielding cognitively economical options. For these speakers, -*n* now also has the value of a verbal morpheme, a consequence of simultaneous environmental triggers in the bilinguals' mind (such as the availability of -*n* as a plural verbal morpheme in Spanish and its similarity with Nahuatl plural endings). As was the case in Palenquero, speakers regard some of these 'new Nahuatl' forms as deviations from assumed traditional monolingual models, but this criterion is far from reliable: at times, structures that are attested historically in Nahuatl are mistakenly identified by speakers as originating in Spanish (15–6; see also §6.3). By contrast, other features not historically present in Nahuatl (such as verbal -*n*) fly under the purist radar and are not censored.

Historical contact situations like Palenquero and Nahuatl confirm that speakers' constructions of named languages are sociohistorically contextual and do not always map clearly onto straightforward linguistic boundaries or lines of descent. All we can hold on to in these situations is the role of various forms of speaker-to-speaker contact in the emergence of communal repertoires. This is not to say that discourses on linguistic difference cannot play an ecological role: ideas about language and languages often mold speakers' awareness and motivate them to favor specific forms, sometimes in tangible ways – recall the emergence of linguistically more-or-less discrete languages in areas where, historically, dialectal variation was gradual (see discussion of *Ausbau* and *Abstand* differences in §1.4). These linguistic differences have in recent times been reinforced by a host of factors (education systems, media, national borders, discourses on ethnolinguistic identity), but the same can be said for more historically remote periods. For instance, between the fifteenth and sixteenth centuries, as Castile gained the geopolitical upper hand in the Iberian Peninsula, bilingualism with Spanish became widespread among Portuguese social élites. Spanish-based structural adaptations gained currency in this social milieu, as in occasional uses of differential object marking (with *a*), uncharacteristic of Portuguese: 'a funda de David derrubou *ao* gigante' 'David's slingshot knocked the giant down' (Haffner 2009: 229). In addition, literary and lexicographic sources in Portugal around this period show hundreds of Castilian adjectives, including *alcançável* 'reachable' (< Sp. *alcanzable*), *madrugador* 'early-riser', *sangrento* 'bloody' (< Sp. *sangriento*) (Venâncio 2014: 3). While some of these innovations (e.g. differential object marking) never gained much social traction and fell out of use as Portugal regained its independence in 1640, many others became *entrenched* (§2.4) in Portuguese repertoires, especially at the lexical level. Throughout this book we will see many such cases showcasing the very real role that language ideologies can play to motivate speakers to select specific options.

At this point, readers familiar with research on bi/multilingual acquisition may wonder whether this ecological approach clicks with what we know about how language is represented in the human brain. Echoing this question, MacSwan (2017) has argued that any psycholinguistic evidence in support of discrete mental representations for each language in bilinguals would undermine the translingual thesis that named languages are socio-political constructs (§1.4). Whether bi/multilingual speakers possess separate mental representations for each language is certainly an old question. Answers range from separate representations (Meisel 2018) to a unitary, shared representation from which bi/multilinguals select features according to sociolinguistic factors (Matras 2020; Otheguy et al. 2015, 2019). Intermediate proposals accept the existence of separate components but with frequent cross-activation (Kroll and Ma 2018).

As important as this question undoubtedly is from a psycholinguistic perspective, the answer does not constrain how human beings actually *use* language to communicate, which as shown in the cases of Palenquero and Nahuatl, often involves combining and even fusing material from so-called 'separate' languages. Unless it can be proven that, all other things being equal, language users exhibit a cognitive bias in favor of staying within the borders of these posited separate mental representations, the answer to this question should not constrain narratives of language change. Instead, the opposite seems to apply. Out of the many physical, mental, or social environmental triggers that can be shown to have motivated language users historically, an innate cognitive bias to reproduce other users' internal representations of language is certainly not one. As a matter of fact, psycholinguistically rooted language contact models have stressed the operation of bilingual language processing principles that involve the application of structural or semantic patterns of one language to the lexicon of the other language (see *imposition* in Van Coetsem 2000; also Winford 2005, 2020) or the creation of options that blend formal or semantic characteristics from both languages (see *rely on two languages* strategy, Aalberse et al. 2019; Muysken 2013). Similarly, as will be shown repeatedly throughout this book, the overwhelming evidence for structural convergence in contact settings strongly suggests that speakers follow ecological motivations rather than externally defined lines of linguistic descent. As we will see in more detail in Chapter 2, speaker repertoires are always *hybrid* (§2.5). In short, an ecological approach to contact does not imply commitment to any given psycholinguistic model of bi/multilingualism – although, undoubtedly, models that do not rely on compartmentalized language-specific mental representations are likely better suited to explain the evidence for hybridization and cross-linguistic influence in language change.

If we accept this ecological proposal as a starting point, what would a contact-based history of Spanish look like? I start to address this question in the next section.

1.9. Approaching contact in Spanish ecologically: What this book is and what it is not

As we start walking toward this goal to centralize the role of speaker-to-speaker contact in the history of the repertoires known as 'Spanish', I rely on an evolutionary-ecological approach to language as an emergent system (§1.5). I am therefore influenced most directly by applications of evolutionary and/or ecological theory to specific situations of language change (including Aboh 2015; Aboh and Vigouroux 2021; Clements 2009; Efrat-Kowalski 2021; Mufwene 2014; Negrão and Viotti 2014; Otheguy et al. 2022; Winford 2017, 2020), and more generally by approaches to contact that recognize the multicausational triggers on language users (Adamou 2013; Matras 2020; Otheguy and Zentella 2012). I also wholeheartedly embrace the spirit and techniques of recent approaches in *historical sociolinguistics* (Auer et al. 2015), which have prioritized writings by speakers of non-standard varieties (immigrants, non-native speakers, rural or working classes, etc.). This focus calls for the incorporation of linguistic experiences other than those of the socioeconomically privileged literate speakers of European descent typically favored in the historiographical tradition. This can be done, for instance, by incorporating the texts produced by *semiliterate* speakers: individuals without formal education and limited access to written norms, whose texts are in principle less constrained by the models typical of high registers and may reflect patterns of variation rejected by standard or formal language norms. When this evidence is available, it allows us to explore patterns of variation among speakers and populations not typically acknowledged in the historiography of standard languages (see also *language history from below*, Elspass 2007).

An ecological take on language history is necessarily *deconstructive*: it analyzes processes of linguistic selection of elements traditionally labeled *x* (Spanish, German, Burmese) from an evolutionary, selective perspective, but with no commitment to the (re)production of the type of orderly linguistic genealogy preconized by Menéndez Pidal, Lapesa, and others after them (§1.2). Thus framed, one can still speak of 'a history of Spanish', but only while engaging with and scrutinizing the metalinguistic discourses that have historically operated to impose homogeneity onto heterogeneous idiolects and collective repertoires (Del Valle 2013a: 14–8). What counts as 'Spanish' in each ecology is necessarily contingent to each time and place. Consequently, a 'history of Spanish' becomes a 'history of communication and language learning in the ecologies that have been classified as sites for the use of Spanish.' In addition, this focus on contact can also take us in directions usually disregarded in traditional language historiographies. For instance, we can examine how speakers have incorporated 'Spanish' features into other ecologies (in other words, how contact with 'Spanish' shaped non-Spanish repertoires).

An important point to stress before proceeding is that this ecological approach should not be understood as the 'good' kind of historical linguistics, with historical grammar or other avenues that have not focused on contact processes as the 'bad' (or the 'traditional', 'obsolete', or 'inefficient') kind. Let's not forget that the formal continuities and discontinuities described in the accumulated research on the history of Spanish are outcomes of diachronic processes for which abundant evidence is available. When we read about the regular changes that transformed the sound system or the verbal paradigms of spoken Latin, or the syntactic rearrangements that resulted in the present-day word order of Spanish (all of which are common topics in the historiography of the language), we are dealing with *real* changes. As far as we can tell, many Latin consonants did palatalize before front vowels (for instance, see Lat. /t/ and /k/ *ratiōne(m)* 'reason', *caelu(m)* 'sky' > Sp. /s/ or /θ/ in *razón*, *cielo*), some Latin neuter nouns that survived into Spanish became masculine (Lat. *templum, vīnum* 'temple, wine' > Sp. *templo, vino*) and others feminine (*lignum, pirum,* 'timber, pear' > Sp. *leña, pera*, apparently via Latin plurals *ligna, pira*), subject-verb-object became the default word order in Romance, and so forth. In other words, historical grammar and other approaches that focus on the formal evolution of standard Spanish are not wrong. It follows that a solid knowledge of these correspondences, built collectively by generations of scholars, continues to be a key part of the picture of change in Spanish that students and researchers in this area should become proficient in. But these formal aspects are only one of the dimensions of the history of a 'language', in whatever way we define this construct. And if this dimension is all we focus on, we will miss an important part of why and how languages change, and most importantly, who changes them. The idea here is that, if we agree that language change is carried out by individuals as they come into contact with each other, then we have much to gain by approaching the history of Spanish as an exploration of the contexts in which these contacts have taken place, and of the speakers' role as the ultimate agents of all forms of language evolution. And we can use this knowledge to supplement and enrich (rather than to replace) other viewpoints. I return to this argument toward the end of the book (§7.4).

The general approach in this book is uncommon in the linguistic historiography of Spanish, but in some ways it is still probably more conventional than I would want it to be. For instance, although linguistic features are not ecologically isolated from other meaning-making resources (§1.5), I do focus on the elements that have been privileged by accounts of contact in historical linguistics (phonological, morphological, syntactic, and lexical features), rather than other meaning-making elements. This is admittedly a narrower approach than one might expect from an ecological approach to language history. At the same time, by focusing on these kinds of resources, we can reassess previous narratives of language change in Spanish, which have focused precisely on these linguistic features. Also, the historical chapters of the book (Chapters 3–6) are organized chronologically, but this sequence should not be interpreted in genealogical terms: in this narrative, the speakers in, say, sixteenth-century Taxco (like Juana and Antón in §1.1), nineteenth-century Manila or twenty-first-century Miami are not imagined to be the linguistic heirs of those in tenth-century Castile. Instead, we will be treating these speakers as socially embedded agents that have always built their own repertoires from (their respective linguistic) scratch.

Also, the ecologies featured in the book are but a very small selection of all the sociohistorical contexts where we could potentially explore the role of contact. I acknowledge that, in my selection of historical ecologies to cover, there is a bias for situations and data that have been privileged in previous analyses, especially from the Iberian Peninsula and certain dialects of Latin American Spanish. There is a risk that this overrepresentation may perpetuate some of the underlying assumptions about the centrality of certain speakers to the definition of Spanish. I have tried to deactivate this bias, at least partially, by incorporating discussions of settings that are rarely included in histories of Spanish (for instance, contact within Indo-European in Chapter 3; in colonial Philippines in Chapter 4; in nineteenth-century rural Cuba or northern Chile in Chapter 5; or in Latin American Indigenous communities, the Maghreb or online communication in Chapter 6; to name a few). Overall, I advocate for a more critical, inclusive form of writing about the history of Spanish that incorporates a variety of sociolinguistic experiences and not just those that can be seen as reflections of the trends of change in the standard language.

In other ways, however, this book is unlike most other previous approaches to the history of Spanish. Most notably, I do not seek to approach contact ecologies to produce sociolinguistically informed answers to historical grammar questions (of the kind 'who shifted the second-to-last syllable stress of Latin *cantābāmus* to third-to-last syllable, as in Spanish *cantábamos*, and for which purpose?' or 'why did speakers eliminate the future subjunctive forms like *estuviere* and *trajere* from spoken Early Modern Spanish?'). Many excellent historical grammar textbooks (such as Penny 2002; Pharies 2015; Ranson and Quesada 2018) and countless individual studies have already proposed answers to some of these questions, and they should very much remain the go-to resource for these types of grammar- or structured-focused queries, as I argued earlier. Instead, I focus on how socially situated interactions among communicating individuals have given rise to vastly different population-level combinations historically, going beyond the usual presentation of the 'external history' of Spanish (on 'internal' vs. 'external' factors of change, see §2.5). For instance, when discussing the southward spread of Castilian features in medieval Iberia, the transplantation of Spanish to the early American colonies or the emergence of post-colonial national varieties, I am less concerned with the description of geopolitical events (invasions, foundations, revolutions) than previous approaches. My historical focus is on how these large-scale historical events set the stage for the local conditions of communication where speakers of varied ethnolinguistic backgrounds were motivated to select specific features as they interacted with each other.

Before moving forward, a note on terminology is warranted. If socio-political definitions of discrete languages are unreliable, it seems that we should heed calls (García and Wei 2014; Makoni and Pennycook 2006; Namboodiripad and Henner 2022) to do away with labels that take such definitions for granted. These include *language* (and *language contact*), *dialect* (and *dialect contact*), *bilingualism*, *multilingualism, monolingualism, language proficiency* or *competence,* and even the dichotomy between *native* vs. *non-native speaker*. In this book, I do reframe some of these notions in explicit ecological terms (for instance, *languages* as *populations*; §2.4). But thinking, writing, and reading are also ecological processes. Neither I as the author of this book (a 6'2"-tall Spain-born, middle-aged, college-educated male living in the United States who self-identifies as an L1 Spanish, L2 English and L3 Greek speaker and who cannot drink coffee after 4:00 pm) nor my audience (who I assume also has multiple backgrounds and positionalities) can completely distance ourselves from our accumulated knowledge and experiences, and these are ideologically shaped. Remember, too, that socio-political language constructions are socio-politically real: they mediate and often shape our linguistic experience and behavior in tangible ways (§1.4). I concur with Otheguy et al. that, although these categories 'have nothing to do with individuals when seen from their own internal linguistic perspective', they are nevertheless 'appropriate and legitimate in discussions of social identity and sociolinguistic behavior because they are defined socially' (2015: 293) and can still be used as long as they are contextualized and critiqued. As you read on, I encourage you to think about the tensions and contradictions inherent to these labels when we use them as designators for realities that, by nature, transcend the very linguistic constructions that such labels designate.

1.10. Structure of this book

This book is structured as follows. Chapter 2 offers a panoramic view of historical approaches to contact in linguistics as the background to many of our current prevalent notions on contact (such as the divide between 'language' and 'dialect' contact as fields of inquiry). It also elaborates on several important aspects of the contact-based ecological approach adopted in this book. In the remainder of the book, I apply this approach to reassess the evolution of Spanish in a number of sociohistorical contexts. In Chapter 3, I re-examine the clean, canonical Indo-European > Latin > Romance line of inheritance as a succession of linguistic recombination events. In Chapter 4, I focus on the emergence of multiple contact settings resulting from the transoceanic colonial expansion of Spain between the sixteenth and the early nineteenth centuries. In Chapter 5, I revisit the ecological consequences of the end of colonialism, including the effects of the emergence of new national identities and mass immigration and urbanization in the nineteenth and twentieth centuries. In Chapter 6, I study a variety of additional recent contact environments since the mid-twentieth century, including intranational migratory and non-migratory contexts, transnational ecologies, and other settings of language negotiation and learning (for instance, digitally mediated communication). Chapter 7 summarizes and concludes this book by suggesting avenues for future ecological approaches to language contact and change in Spanish.

Discussion questions

1. Origin narratives are not exclusive to Spanish. What other similar narratives about the 'birth' of other languages are you familiar with? Which specific locations, texts, or historical events or personalities do they highlight to make sense of the subsequent history of the language?

2. Using one of the more recent textbooks on the history of Spanish (Núñez Méndez 2012; Pharies 2015; Resnick and Hammond 2011; Ranson and Quesada 2018), select a description of a change (e.g. a phonological evolution or the development of a verbal paradigm). What factors are mentioned and what additional questions could we ask to supplement this account?

3. The discourse of homogeneity has shaped the way in which many linguists (me included!) have learned to conceptualize language change (§1.2). In many language communities, non-linguists actuate this same discourse by appealing to correctness ('"Jack and me" is not correct') or authority ('that's not in the dictionary'), or even by denying the evidence around them ('"haiga" is not a word!'). But speakers can also push back – e.g. by engaging in multilingual practices or by insisting on using stigmatized forms. If we wanted to incorporate these practices to a history of Spanish, where would we start looking for this kind of evidence?

2

The Ubiquity of Contact: Toward an Ecological Approach to Language Change

2.1. Introduction: Centering contact

In Chapter 1, I revisited the prevalent discourse on Spanish as a centuries-old organism endowed with a linguistic essence. I argued that this vision is rooted in an understanding of languages as historical objects that is common in Western thinking as a key component of discourses on ethnicity or nationality, naturalizing the connection between group identity and language use. These discourses conceal the emergence of named language varieties as cultural constructions. Drawing from evolutionary and ecological interpretations of language change (Aboh and Vigouroux 2021; Croft 2000, 2008; Efrat-Kowalski 2021; Mufwene 2001, 2008, 2018; Mufwene and Vigouroux 2017) as well as from approaches that see language use as a process of recombination of features by individuals (Matras 2020; Otheguy et al. 2022; Winford 2017, 2020), I advocated for an alternative view of the history of Spanish rooted in the role of speaker-to-speaker *contact* in linguistically heterogeneous environments. To summarize, languages (Spanish included) emerge in populations of individuals interacting within their respective ecologies, with communicative and social efficiency as their goals.

In this chapter, I further develop several important aspects of this contact-based ecological frame and its implications for the study of language change. I start by offering a summary of the history of contact as a factor in the explanation of language change in linguistics (§2.2). I then critique some of the conceptual categories in which several of these explanations are rooted, especially typologies of contact (such as 'dialect' vs. 'language' contact) (§2.3). I join socio-pragmatically and ecologically inspired authors in arguing that these conceptual partitions are ultimately a by-product of the tendency to conceive of language as an *object* of study rather than as a dynamic *process* (as advanced in §1.5 and §1.7). Then, I unpack two important ingredients of the contact-based ecological approach: languages as populations (§2.4) and the components of the ecology of language (§2.5). I conclude (§2.6) by providing an ecological reassessment of some previously proposed contact mechanisms as a step toward the ecological narrative of the history of Spanish developed throughout the remainder of the book.

This chapter does not seek to offer a comprehensive review of the literature on contact, but simply a reassessment of some prominent processes for the purposes of this book – readers are encouraged to consult the literature reviewed in this chapter for further discussion and examples of contact processes.

2.2. Where do our ideas about contact come from? Earlier articulations of contact processes

As advanced in Chapter 1 (§1.2 and §1.3), since the nineteenth century, Western linguists have been concerned with the properties of human languages and the mechanisms whereby these properties are subject to historical instability (Jakobs and Hüning 2022). But even though the historical effects of contact are everywhere, linguists have struggled to define it and to devise methodological protocols to study it.

In the late 1800s, the Neogrammarians sought to get to the roots of the processes of change unearthed by early nineteenth-century comparative linguistics in the study of the Indo-European language family (§3.3). For them, contact had a largely marginal role in language change. This marginalization is apparent in Osthoff and Brugmann's 1878 'Neogrammarian manifesto' (in reality, the introduction to the first volume of *Morphologische Untersuchungen auf dem Gebiete der indogermanischen Sprachen*). Here, they argued that sound changes are regular and exceptionless. Diachronic irregularities must be due either to the effects of analogy or to unrepresentative or otherwise inaccurate data. Although they admit that linguistic innovations proceed from individual to individual as they gain currency in the speech community (1878: iv), their treatment of historical processes makes it clear that they viewed the inter-generational transmission of language systems as the default diachronic mechanism. Later Neogrammarian-influenced authors acknowledged at least some of the effects of contact, if only as a conduit for the spread of changes exhibiting the expected regular patterns (for instance, Paul 1920 [1880]) – foreshadowing some of the ideas developed more recently in social network approaches to language change (Auer 2015: 186–7; §2.6).

The Neogrammarians' generally lukewarm stance toward contact as a factor in language change was not universally shared. One of their most prominent skeptics was Schuchardt, who criticized the Neogrammarians' emphasis on regularity and fragmentation, as captured in their use of the tree metaphor (*Stammbaum*) as originally articulated by, for instance, Schleicher (1853) as a valid representation of diachronic connections among related languages (see Figure 2.1 for a recent interpretation of descent and fragmentation within Romance according to the tree model).

Instead, Schuchardt saw the gradual expansion of innovations via speaker-to-speaker contact (*Mischung*) as the basic mechanism of change: language change is a constant ebb-and-flow of difference and similarity that never results in discrete language communities. Contact, therefore, is not an exception, but

The Ubiquity of Contact in Language Change 31

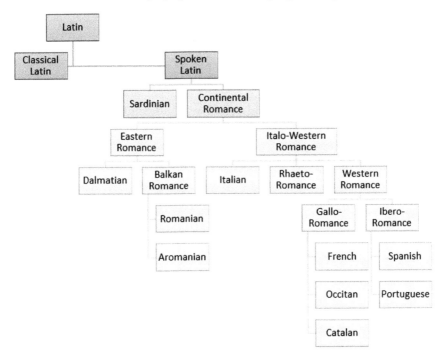

FIGURE 2.1. A tentative tree of linguistic descent in Romance
(source: author)

'permeates every form of language development' (1917: 522). Similar views on the gradualness of the geographical spread of linguistic innovations can be seen in Schmidt's (1872) articulation of the wave model (*Wellentheorie*) as an alternative to the tree model: in this conceptualization, changes spread outwards from innovating/focal areas via speaker contact, and the language of a given community is the historical summation of innovations spreading from various origins and in various directions (see Figure 2.2). Ascoli's (1881) theory of substrate (*sostrato*) as a factor in dialectal development emphasized the historical effects of bilingualism, and thus provided another critical early contribution to the contact conversation. By emphasizing the central role of various kinds of contact in the emergence of specific varieties, these researchers anticipated many of the themes in more recent approaches to language variation and change (§2.6).

The advent of structuralism in the early twentieth century did little to further the cause of contact as a primary factor in language change. Saussure's articulation of languages as self-sufficient abstract systems downplayed the role of variation ('all of [the speakers of a language] will reproduce – *doubtless not exactly*, but approximately– the same signs linked to the same concepts', 1986 [1916]: 13, my emphasis). In his view, languages are 'never complete in any single individual, but [exist] perfectly only in the collectivity' (13). Saussure understood that language or dialect contact could introduce changes into a community's language, but he followed the Neogrammarians in considering them marginal

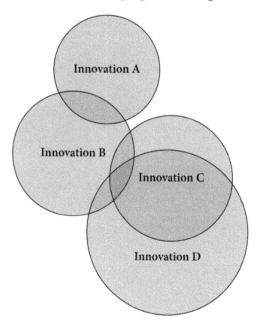

FIGURE 2.2. A wave-based representation of the spread of geographical innovations (Whimemsz~commonswiki, via Wikimedia Commons, license: https://creativecommons.org/licenses/by-sa/2.5/deed.en)

factors. For instance, substratum effects are typical of 'circumstances which occur only rarely' (150); and while some communities might be linguistically diverse, 'geographical diversity ... *in its ideal form* [occurs when] different areas correspond to different languages' (265, my emphasis). Some innovations may spread socially in a gradual manner as advocated for by Schmidt and Schuchardt, but the result is always a new stable system: contact and instability are therefore only historical anomalies (205–8).

While Saussure's articulation of language as an abstract system was immensely influential, a growing number of researchers in the early 1900s started to think of the sociolinguistics of contact as important to the relationship between individual speakers and language change. A primary representative of this emergent approach was Haugen (1950). Informed by his own personal experience as a bilingual heritage speaker of Norwegian, he proposed a typology of contact effects, understood primarily as changes at the structural and lexical level. For Haugen, contact can always be essentially defined as *borrowing*, that is, a form of incorporation of elements into a recipient matrix system, which constrains what can and cannot be borrowed: '[e]xcept in *abnormal cases* speakers have not been shown to draw freely from two languages' (1950: 211, my emphasis). In some ways, Haugen still followed in the steps of the structuralist tradition: while speakers are the agents of contact, it is ultimately language systems that come into contact and are influenced by it. Even so, his work laid the ground for the study of language contact as a function of the environment of communication, as noted (§1.6).

Another instrumental landmark in the study of contact was Weinreich (1953), who emphasized the role of bilingual individuals as linguistic agents and not simply as exceptions to the assumedly normal behavior of monolinguals. In his view, factors that play a role in contact at the individual and social level include the speakers' level of proficiency, the age of onset of bilingualism, and the existence of ideologies about the prestige or usefulness of each language (71–115). Weinreich advanced some of the central topics in more recent contact literature, including the relative likelihood of contact effects in specific areas of lexicon and grammar (63–8), contact as a source of new languages (104–6), and the relationship between community-wide language shift and grammatical change (106–10).

Not that everybody was listening. Starting in the 1950s, generativism revived elements of Saussurean structuralism by defining human languages as abstract, internally organized systems manifested in the linguistic knowledge of ideal speakers (*i-languages*, see Chomsky 1986; §1.4). In principle, this approach left little room to consider the effects of contact on language variation and change. But recent generativist-inspired applications have paid much closer attention to contact processes than earlier proposals, especially in the form of approaches to bilingual language acquisition (Rothman and Slabakova 2018) and the study of the acquisition of variation (such as the *multiple grammars* framework, Roeper 2016). Generative acquisition frameworks have in turn been applied to the explanation of specific historical changes (Lightfoot 2006; Meisel et al. 2013). Underlying many of these proposals is the idea that language change happens when individual learners derive an innovative grammar from variable input – i.e., input from other speakers that offers evidence for more than one underlying analysis, essentially the outcome of contact among language users.

The advent of variationist sociolinguistics following Weinreich et al.'s (1968) proposal to treat the linguistic and social constraints of variation as central to an understanding of language breathed new life into the study of contact. Among other key questions issues, Weinreich et al. articulated the *actuation* question, which they considered 'the very heart' (102) of any explanation of change. The actuation of a change involves the mechanisms determining when and where a specific change takes place, and these critically imply the spread of an innovation through the social space via interaction among speakers, as others adopt the new element and imbue it with some kind of social meaning (186–7).

Variationists, however, have disagreed on how much attention one should pay to the behavior of individual speakers. Early variationist studies were focused on the variable grammar of the speech community as the object of study of linguistics, and as such were often skeptical about the possibility that paying attention to the behavior of individuals may be informative of the progression of a change (§1.5). But starting with applications of *social network* theory to the spread of innovations (Laitinen et al. 2020; Milroy and Milroy 1985, 1992; see Barajas 2022; Martín Butragueño 2016 and Villena-Ponsoda 2005 for examples from Spanish-speaking areas; §6.4), sociolinguistic approaches to language change have been much more concerned with how speaker-to-speaker contact may lead to the spread of linguistic changes. In a social network approach, the likelihood that a given innovation may be introduced and spread across a group of speakers is a direct function of the patterns of communication among them. A schematic representation of the social links among the members of a network is shown in Figure 2.3. Note the relative position of individuals in this network: outsiders (represented with a star) initially introduce innovations from other networks, but they spread in the network once they are adopted by more central members. In addition, connections among members sometimes occur in only one type of social context (dotted line), but other members communicate in a variety of settings (solid lines). Stronger, more diverse links favor the spread of changes (see §2.6 for further discussion of this model):

Other influential sociolinguistic models (for instance, Labov 2007, Sankoff 2018, Tagliamonte and D'Arcy 2009) incorporate the role of age-based acquisition behavior in the study of the spread of innovations. In these accounts, the sociodemographic structure of the community determines who will be active in the spread of an innovation: younger learners will usually closely approximate the grammar of the community, older children, adolescents and even young adults may advance changes in progress, and older speakers may introduce new, less systematic options from other communities or, if native to the community, will typically continue using the variety they settled in as young adults (Sankoff 2018). In general, sociolinguistic approaches share a basic conception of language change as a collective cultural process: individual speakers innovate, but these innovations only lead to language change if they are imbued with social meaning and adopted by other speakers. This is a very different take on change from generative (or otherwise innatist) models, where change is instantiated in individual speakers' systems as they use input from other speakers to generate a new grammar (on the role of individuals in these different perspectives, see Hall-Lew et al. 2021). Different as these proposals are, they all unavoidably lead us back to communication among individuals as the gateway to understanding how linguistic elements are transmitted or modified over time.

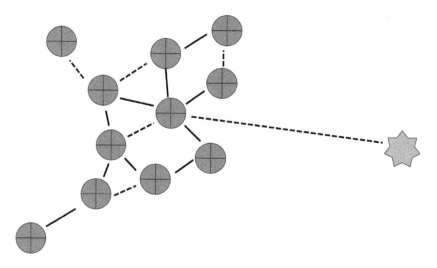

FIGURE 2.3. A representation of a social network (source: author)

By now, the study of contact processes and their outcomes has become central to the analysis of language variation and change. Broadly speaking, contact studies have developed into two strands: *language contact* (among others, Aalberse et al. 2019; Aboh 2015; Adamou 2021; Grant 2021; Matras 2020; Montrul 2022; Muysken 2013; Polinsky 2018; Sessarego 2021; Silva-Corvalán 1994; Thomason and Kaufman 1988; Van Coetsem 2000) and *dialect contact* (Auer and Hinskens 2005; Britain 2016; Chambers and Trudgill 1998; Fernández Ordóñez 2012a; Kerswill and Williams 2000a; Siegel 2010; Trudgill 1986, 2004) (see §2.3 on the premise that language and dialect contact may be two separate processes). In these studies, attention is paid to the characteristics of the structures in contact, the social embedding of contact, and the role of speakers as language learners. Interest in these factors is apparent, for instance, in a very strong tradition in contact studies that seeks to correlate specific sociolinguistic contexts of language use with their linguistic effects.

In a classical formulation of this relationship (Thomason and Kaufman 1988), *borrowing* (of lexicon but also of structural units) can be seen in situations of long-term bilingualism; by contrast, the mapping of structural or semantic patterns from one language or another (*interference*) is said to occur primarily in situations of language shift. In cognitive-focused proposals, by contrast, the goal is to explain the outcome of contact as a result of psycholinguistic processes involved in language representation and learning applied by individual speakers (Winford 2005, 2020). Van Coetsem (2000) was an influential contribution in this direction: in his model, relative dominance in one language predicts the direction of influence. According to this principle, changes may be classified into two main processes. In *borrowing*, an element from the source language is integrated into the speaker's dominant language (the recipient language). Conversely, in *imposition*, competence in the recipient language is lower than in the source language: as a result, elements of the source language (typically grammatical or semantic patterns) provide a blueprint to produce the recipient (here, non-dominant) language. These are individual psycholinguistic processes but can be understood to operate collectively in populations where speakers share a similar language dominance profile. More recent cognitively rooted models (De Bot and Bülow 2021; Matras 2020) rely on an even more flexible understanding of cross-linguistic effects: speakers are not 'borrowing', 'imposing' or 'transferring' elements from one linguistic system to another but making choices from shared linguistic repertoires (§1.4) in ways sensitive to social expectations about communicative appropriateness (for instance, 'speak A' or 'speak B'). Cognitively based models question a strict distinction between contact among named language varieties (as traditionally assumed in language or dialect contact studies) and the sociolinguistics of so-called monolingual communities.

A tentative non-exhaustive summary of the relationship between some contact effects and specific forms of sociolinguistic embedding is provided in Table 2.1. Here, the goal is to explain how necessary a given sociolinguistic environment is for each contact effect. The contact effects in the table are *lexical borrowing* (the use of one lexical item from one language in another, as in *fútbol* in Spanish < Eng. *football*); *full relexification* (when the lexicon of a language is replaced with lexicon from another source, but structural/grammatical elements

TABLE 2.1. Relationship between select contact effects and specific sociolinguistic environments (adapted from Grant 2021: 31)

Contact process	Social mechanism			
	Social bilingualism	Language shift	Adult-to-child transmission	Transmission among adults
Lexical borrowing	Sometimes	Rarely	Rarely	Rarely
Full relexification	Always	Usually	Never	Usually
Simplification	Always	Sometimes	Sometimes	Always
Complexification	Usually	Usually	Never	Usually
Koinéization	Always	Sometimes	Never	Always
Creolization	Sometimes	Rarely	Always	Sometimes to always

are maintained, as in Ecuadorian Media Lengua, which combines Spanish vocabulary and Kichwa morphology; §6.4); *simplification* (when a certain grammatical category is lost, as happens with the distinction between indicative and subjunctive in many heritage Spanish speakers in the United States; §6.7); *complexification* (when new grammatical categories are introduced, as in the use of past perfect as a marker of evidentiality in forms of Andean Spanish; §6.3); *koinéization* (the emergence of a new language variety via contact among two or more intelligible varieties, as proposed for medieval and colonial Spanish; §3.8 and §4.4); and *creolization* (the emergence of a new language via pervasive contact with significant grammatical restructuring, as in the case of Palenquero; §1.8).

While the table invites us to think of some contact effects as more likely in certain sociolinguistic environments, counterevidence may be invoked. For instance, contrary to what the table suggests, koinéization has often been described as requiring the action of child learners in order to result in a new variety (Kerswill and Williams 2000a; Sanz-Sánchez 2013; Trudgill 2004; Tuten 2003, 2024): adults initiate the process, but do not carry it to completion (see §4.4 for examples from colonial Latin American Spanish). Similarly, the relationship between language shift and lexical borrowing is equivocal: in the history of Spanish, many situations of shift have left lexical borrowings as their only obvious historical trace (for instance, shift to Latin in Roman Iberia, or to Spanish among many Latin American Indigenous communities, see §3.5 and §4.4 for examples, respectively). Regardless of how predictive some of these proposed correlations may be, current research on language contact leaves little room to doubt that a full understanding of the dynamics of language variation and change must incorporate the role of socially situated communication and learning among speakers as a mechanism for both the emergence of innovations and their spread across the social space.

The pendulum has clearly swung a long way from the days of the Neogrammarians and the earliest structuralists when the role of contact in language change was deemed as marginal. But echoes from yesteryear linger, and some of the ways in which we still think of contact are symptomatic of our reluctance to see language as anything other than an organic entity that is somehow separate from its speakers. A primary example is the distinction between 'language' and 'dialect' (and, therefore, 'language contact' and 'dialect contact' typologies), which still guides much of the overarching thinking about language change in many linguistic traditions, including the historiography of Spanish. In the next section, I reflect on how this truncation hinders our ability to fully understand the dynamics of change in many contexts.

2.3. The limitations of contact typologies: Dialect vs language contact

A very common way to approach contact has been to establish contact typologies: languages have sometimes been classified as 'non-contact' vs. 'contact' languages, and the latter labelled according to various structural or sociolinguistic criteria as 'pidgins', 'creoles', 'semi-creoles', 'creoloids', 'mixed languages' or 'koinés', to name but a few typologies (see Mesthrie 2008, and the debate about whether creoles constitute a separate category of languages, §1.8). From the perspective of the process giving rise to new varieties, arguably an influential classification is the distinction between *language contact* and *dialect contact*. This separation has a long history in the study of the history and sociolinguistics of European languages, which have been deeply shaped by the comparative tradition emerging from the study of the Indo-European language family (§3.3). In this tradition, linguistic differentiation from the proto-language is conceived as a process of dialectal fragmentation (e.g. Spanish, French or Romanian as dialects of spoken Latin; English, Swedish or Gothic as dialects of proto-Germanic, and so forth).

This distinction is particularly relevant to this book, because it relies on assumedly straightforward linguistic boundaries that allow us to classify some forms of variation as internal (that is, dialectal) rather than external (cross-language) differences. The history of Spanish has focused primarily on the former, with other contact situations and their outcomes analyzed as the result of the influence of 'other' languages on the lexicon or grammar of Spanish, and somehow external to the evolution of the language. A traditional example is the analysis of some processes of contact as *strata* (recall Ascoli's stratum theory, §2.2), where language contact is conceptualized as layers of influence on the grammar of a language: one can consequently speak of a Basque 'substratum' or a Germanic 'superstratum' on early Iberian Romance (§3.2). A more recent example concerns the influence of English or Spanish in the United States, which is said to have given rise to lexical and grammatical options that are uncharacteristic of other varieties and are presented as prime examples of a language contact environment (Escobar and Potowski 2015; Otheguy and Zentella 2012).

However, insofar as the difference between a 'language' and a 'dialect' is commonly acknowledged to rely on ideological factors (§1.4), this distinction between language contact and dialect contact would seem to be less than discrete: 'the difference ... is more one of degree than of kind' (Hickey 2010: 4). In many settings of language contact, researchers also observe the simultaneous effects of contact among varieties of the same language (e.g. dialect contact in US Spanish, Escobar and Potowski 2015: 157–84; see this section below and §6.7).

The common practice in contact studies, however, has been to assume that these are indeed two separate processes, with different mechanics and different outcomes: '[t]here are certain language contact phenomena we can expect to find if there has been language contact ... whereas we cannot necessarily expect the same phenomena if there was dialect contact' (Jahr 1999: 131). In Spanish, studies of the historical effects of contact can also largely be seen to have fallen on either side of the dialect contact (Fernández Ordóñez 2012a; Martín Butragueño 2020; Penny 2000; Tuten 2003) or the language contact (Clements 2009; Klee and Lynch 2009; Lipski 2022) divide. Recent overviews of the history of Spanish (Cano 2005; Dworkin et al. 2024; and, for Spanish in the Americas, Eckkrammer 2021) by and large also embrace this distinction, as they discuss (for instance) the dialectal effects of fragmentation processes in early Iberian Romance, dialectal koinéization in medieval Castilian Spanish, the effects of language contact in the transatlantic expansion of Spanish during the colonial period or its use alongside other officially acknowledged languages in various areas of Spain.

Because the limits of language varieties beyond the repertoires of individual speakers are elusive (Erker 2017, and §1.5), linguists have been hard pressed to establish criteria to tell cross-dialectal from cross-linguistic differences. To justify this division, *structural factors* are commonly invoked. For instance, Kerswill and Williams (2000b) proposed an adaptation of Poplack's *equivalence constraint* in code-switching (1980) whereby in dialect contact 'items can be mixed apparently at will and with minimal loss of intelligibility' (2000b: 82) without necessarily having to abide by the grammar of an underlying language matrix, as is assumed to occur in language contact. Other times the difference is presented in terms of *intelligibility*, understood as a binary: 'dialect contact [occurs] between speakers of mutually intelligible ... varieties. The linguistic relationship between the varieties in contact inevitably determines the outcome of the contact, and in this respect dialect contact differs importantly from language contact' (Wilson 2010: 117); 'it is still generally the case that first and second dialects ... are more similar to each other than first and second languages, and therefore more mutually intelligible' (Siegel 2010: 2).

One problem with these definitions is that they often rely on measures along relative scales. Therefore, any determination about where the cut along these scales should be made is necessarily arbitrary. As examined in §1.4, none of these criteria will do to explain why contact among structurally similar varieties exhibiting partial mutual intelligibility is sometimes approached as language contact (for instance, Spanish and Catalan, Blas Arroyo 2011) and sometimes as dialect contact (e.g. dialects of Italian). In these cases, the ultimate factor seems to be the existence of recognized language standards (recall the difference between *Ausbau* and *Abstand* differences), largely a sociocultural and not a linguistic criterion. Another problem with these definitions is that they assume internal homogeneity in the community, with all speakers in a variety displaying the same relative degree of structural difference and intelligibility vis-à-vis those of the other variety.

But structural differences are usually socially and geographically gradual rather than abrupt: as we saw in Chapter 1, this gradualness is apparent in *dialect continua*, where the distribution of the linguistic boundaries of specific features do not overlap and fail to exhibit clear geographical or social breaks, as in the traditional northern Iberian Romance dialects (Chambers and Trudgill 1998: 3–12; Penny 2000: 80–107). In these situations, partitions along the continuum are feasible only if we focus on the distribution of selected features (*isoglosses*), or if we consider the *Ausbau* (i.e., standardized) languages in the area. By way of illustration, consider the spectrum of geographical variation in the Asturian region ranging from traditional 'Galician' dialects in the west to 'Cantabrian' (*montañés*) in the east, represented in Map 2.1. This is an area where standardized codes today include Galician, Spanish and Asturian (the latter as a more socially contested standard variety). As for intelligibility, as advanced, it is mediated by subjective factors and by each speaker's previous linguistic experience (Gooskens and Van Heuven 2020; Heeringa et al. 2013). These limitations are particularly clear at a diachronic level, where varieties are commonly seen morphing into new ones without clear chronological or structural breaks (Thomason 2001: 2). For instance, in the history of the Romance languages, the break between 'Latin' and 'Romance' has been identified with the emergence of Romance-specific orthographies (largely a sociocultural event) rather than with any specific historical break in the linguistic evolution of the spoken languages (Wright 2016).

If differences between 'dialects' and 'languages' are not qualitative or typological, it would seem desirable to apply a unified theoretical framework to both dialect contact and language contact: '[t]here seems to be no need to assume fundamental structural differences between dialects and languages that would make a comparison between dialect contact and language contact impossible when investigating structural changes or stability' (Kühl and Braunmüller 2014: 14). However, the usual practice has been to approach these as different processes exhibiting different mechanisms. For instance, as seen (§2.2), language contact is often conceptualized in terms of the borrowing of elements from language B by users of language A, or the transfer of structural elements onto system B by users of system A via L2 language acquisition (Muysken 2013; Thomason and

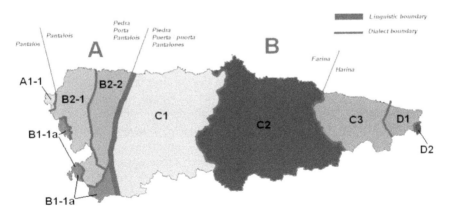

MAP 2.1. Some proposed cuts along the Asturian dialect continuum and their associated isoglosses (Susana Freixeiro via Wikimedia Commons, public domain)

Kaufman 1988; Van Coetsem 2000; see §2.6 for an ecological discussion of these processes). For dialect contact, speaker-to-speaker *accommodation* has been proposed as the most prominent mechanism, prompting speakers to approximate each other's dialectal repertoire, eventually leading to the emergence of new dialects (Auer and Hinskens 2005; Chambers and Trudgill 1998).

Despite these proposed differences, there are many indications that language contact and dialect contact have more in common than meets the eye, especially if approached as the result of processes of individual acquisition (Hendriks 2024). For instance, both dialect and language learners are sensitive to *age effects*, with native proficiency commonly described as possible only if acquisition is initiated during (and sustained throughout) childhood (Montrul 2022; Tagliamonte and Molfenter 2007). Attainment has also been seen to be affected by personal *motivation* in both forms of learning (Dörnyei et al. 2015; Rys 2007). In both language and dialect acquisition, speakers respond to the *frequency* of elements in their input: the more frequent an element is, the more likely it is for learners to acquire it (Diessel 2007; Nycz 2013). Frequency, in turn, is often seen as contributing to *salience*, understood as the likelihood that a certain feature will be noticed, which has also been claimed to operate in both dialect and language learning. For instance, dialects in contact may exhibit 'superficial similarities' that are hard to acquire because they are difficult to notice (Siegel 2010: 141–5), as when two phonemes differ in their allophonic detail or present two cognate forms with different semantic distributions. But similar constraints have been invoked for language acquisition too, and explicit awareness about characteristics of the input has been hypothesized to be key to the overall process (Ellis 2005). Finally, acquisition in both situations may lead to forms of *convergence* (§1.8 and §2.6), whereby aspects of the grammars in contact become more similar (see *structural convergence* in language contact, Adamou 2021; Babel and Pfänder 2014; Silva-Corvalán 1994; and *mixed/fudged dialects* in dialect contact, Chambers and Trudgill 1998; and Wiemer 2021 for an overview of various convergence processes). In both language contact and dialect contact, therefore, we have evidence that individual speakers apply similar learning principles: differences in the outcomes may have to do with the grammatical distance among the options that learners are presented with, the age in which they access various features, and the sociocultural pressures for speakers to select specific options, rather than with the application of fundamentally different processes.

The limitations of this distinction are made clear in sociolinguistic situations where both 'language' and 'dialect' contact can be seen to co-occur in the same population. For instance, in their study of subject expression in New York City Spanish, Otheguy and Zentella (2012) found that language contact between English and Spanish interfaces with dialectal convergence among speakers of various Latin American Spanish-speaking origins (namely, Caribbeans comprising speakers of Dominican, Cuban, and Puerto Rican descent, and 'Mainlanders' including individuals of Ecuadorian, Mexican, and Colombian origin). The result is a new community grammar. In it, the rate of overt subject pronouns (such as *yo, tú, ella, nosotros* 'I, you-SG, she, we-MASC') is higher among NYC Spanish speakers than in any of the contributing Spanish dialects. Table 2.2 shows the pronoun rates for two dialectal groups across two generational cohorts of NYC

TABLE 2.2. Pronoun rates for NYC Spanish speakers from two regions and two generations (adapted from Otheguy and Zentella 2012: 108)

	Latin American-raised			NYC-raised		
	N	Pro	SD	N	Pro	SD
Caribbean	19	*36*	8	13	*44*	11
Mainland	20	*24*	9	13	*33*	8
p		$p < .01$			$p < .01$	

Spanish speakers: Latin American-raised speakers, and NYC-raised speakers. As can be seen in the table, pronoun rates (Pro) are higher in the latter than in the former in both dialectal groups.

The authors attribute this increase in the rate of pronouns among NYC-raised speakers to the combined effects of dialectal accommodation and bilingualism on their individual systems. Their analysis did uncover what seem to be somewhat separate effects for bilingual Spanish-English proficiency (general to the whole community) and dialect contact (with Mainlanders accommodating to Caribbeans more than the other way around). Significantly enough, though, both forms of contact conspire to yield a common effect on the grammar of subject expression in this variety of Spanish (see §6.7 for an additional similar example).

Such cases are far from exceptional. A look at the history of Spanish reveals multiple situations of contact that are difficult to interpret either linguistically or sociolinguistically exclusively in terms of either dialect or language contact (to name but a few, contact between L1 and L2 varieties of Castilian in medieval Spain, §3.8; between Spanish and Portuguese along the border between Brazil and Uruguay, §5.3; or between coastal varieties of Peruvian Spanish and Quechua-influenced Spanish in Lima, §6.3 and §6.4). In these situations, speakers have been presented with a wide range of options, some stemming from the interpretation of linguistically similar features in native learning, others due to non-native learning, and others (as in the case of the pronoun rates in NYC Spanish) owing to the action of learning across so-called dialectal and language boundaries. In these contexts, therefore, the question is not whether speakers' selections can be attributed to 'dialect contact' or 'language contact', but whether the available options presented learners with acquisitional, structural, or sociolinguistic (dis)advantages, regardless of how twenty-first-century linguists happen to classify them (Erker 2017; Otheguy et al. 2022). Just like other categories with a long history in Western research on language structure and language change (§1.8), the distinction between *language contact* and *dialect contact* (and, for that matter, between *language* and *dialect*) fails to capture the actual dynamics of contact environments, and the ways in which speakers contribute to the emergence of new repertoires. By contrast, ecologically inspired typologies (e.g. Clements 2018; Croft 2021) focus on how specific social circumstances tend to lead to certain linguistic outcomes, emphasizing the spectrum nature of contact repertoires.

Throughout this book, my argument will be that these kinds of messy contact contexts where speakers of various backgrounds have shaped patterns of language transmission and change are the rule rather than the exception. How can we approach contact in these complex settings if we question these categories? A population-based approach to contact as an ecological process offers some promising avenues to tackle this complexity.

2.4. Languages as populations

At this point, we are ready to entertain some of the practical implications of the contact-based ecological framework to the study of language change. To summarize the argument presented in Chapter 1 (§1.6 and §1.7), this framework is informed by approaches to language as a *complex adaptive system* (Bybee 2010; Ellis and Larsen-Freeman 2009; Kretzschmar 2015; Larsen-Freeman 2007), where patterns emerge as the result of communication among interconnected agents. In this respect, language change is like other forms of *evolution* in non-linguistic adaptive systems, including 'biological evolution ... and other phenomena of evolutionary change such as cultural evolution' (Croft 2008: 220). Evolutionary processes in language involve not only structural changes (such as the changes in lexicon, grammar or pragmatic patterns that have typically been the object of historical linguistics), but also changes in the social embedding of language users. Speakers develop repertoires throughout their lifespan in contact with other speakers (Baxter and Croft 2016; Matras 2020) by selecting features according to a host of ecological triggers (Mufwene 2001, 2008; Aboh and Vigouroux 2021). As such, an ecological approach to language and language change subsumes both internal (articulatory, cognitive) and external (social, ideological) factors, as discussed below (§2.5).

The similarities between languages and biological species, introduced in Chapter 1 (§1.6), exemplify the parallelisms between language and other systems shaped by evolutionary processes. Both languages and biological species are based on *replication*, where an agent copies an element (a gene, or a linguistic element or pattern), and the resulting copy either preserves most of the original features of the replicated element or introduces an innovation. Another similarity is that the replication process is sensitive to the *environment* in which it takes place. A third characteristic shared across biological species and languages is that they are organized as *populations*: groups of individuals that come to share structural characteristics as they interact. In the case of a biological species, these structural similarities are expressed in the organism's genome. In the case of a language, they consist of shared linguistic features, expressed in idiolects constructed via selection and recombination of options from the *feature pools* that speakers have access to: 'just like one needs more than one organism to speak of a species, a language is an extrapolation from idiolects which are governed by similar and pragmatic principles or that may be traced back to the same ancestor' (Mufwene 2001: 149; see also Mufwene 2018; Mufwene and Vigouroux 2017).

How can this biological analogy help us understand the dynamics of contact in language history? Let's take the southward expansion of medieval Christian kingdoms into Muslim territories in the Iberian Peninsula (tenth to fifteenth centuries), one of the periods treated as foundational in the historiography of Spanish, as an example. Traditional narratives have underscored this general geopolitical event and the associated resettlement of northern speakers in southern regions as key catalysts in the development of Iberian Romances as separate languages (e.g. Lapesa 1981; Lleal 1990; Menéndez Pidal 1950; Penny 2002; §3.7). Sociolinguistically, however, things must have been more complex, as the incoming settlers interacted with the existing population of the Muslim territories. In the cities taken by the new Christian rulers (Toledo, Cordoba, Seville, Granada), a diverse population soon lived side by side: settlers arriving from the north speaking mutually intelligible Romance varieties or Basque; French and Italian merchants; local residents speaking forms of Hispanic Arabic and, in some cases, Mozarabic varieties or even Berber. As speakers were presented with feature pools containing elements of varied provenance, they must have been motivated to replicate and recombine some of them in ways that were sometimes coincident with those of other speakers, sometimes different. For instance, while most of the consonantal system typical of early Castilian was replicated with few changes, diphthongs such as /wa, wo, we/ and /ja, je/ replaced the mid open vowels /ɔ/ and /ɛ/, respectively. Similarly, the clitic system (pronouns *lo/la/le* and their associated forms) was subject to various social and dialectal interpretations during this period. In all these replications, socially situated processes of contact and learning were key (Fernández Ordóñez 2012a; Tuten 2003, 2024; Sanz-Sánchez and Tejedo-Herrero 2021). As the repertoires resulting from these recombinations took shape in socially diverse populations, they must have often not been clearly classifiable in terms of dialects (or even separate languages within the Romance continuum); but they were eventually classified as named varieties as new geopolitical and ethnic boundaries were established (see §3.7 and §3.8 for a more detailed ecological interpretation of this period).

If a language population is a collection of interacting idiolects, where does the agency of speakers fit in? Recall (§1.6) that authors like Mufwene have analogized speakers to the hosts of a biological species of the parasitic or viral kind. Both need a carrier organism to perpetuate themselves (a host in the case of a parasite or a virus, and a speaker's mind in the case of language); their fate is determined by the ecological patterns of interaction among the carriers or by coexistence with other parasitic systems (other viruses, or in the case of languages, other adaptive systems in the mind of the user, such as culture, gender and power ideologies); and both the genotype of a virus and the profile of an individual's idiolect can shift over the carrier's lifetime (Mufwene 2008: 19), for instance via age-related increase or decrease of sociolinguistic frequencies (Sankoff 2018), language attrition (Montrul 2022; Polinsky 2018; §2.5) or simply exposure to new dialects/languages. Note that this analogy is not perfect: for instance, a virus starts its life with a full biological genotype, whereas an idiolect is constructed throughout its speaker's life. Also, while the genes of a parasite can be transmitted from host to host, idiolects are not transmitted whole, but constructed piecemeal via acquisition (Mufwene 2008: 26–7; see also Otheguy et al. 2022).

This analogy does underscore some of the shared aspects between a biological species and a language, but I will argue that the relationship between speakers in a population and their idiolects can be conceptualized in an even more integrated way, precisely along the lines of *cognition* as presented in Chapter 1 (§1.5).

From this perspective, language use and language change can still be seen as determined by the ecology of the population of idiolects, but speakers are not merely idiolect carriers. Instead, it is in the ecology of communicating individuals (of collective 'meaning-making', in Canagarajah's words, 2014: 32) that linguistic resources take shape and meaning as a shared practice. Cognition includes language elements as pieces of experience, and is shaped by the ecological characteristics contributed by speakers at the cognitive (processing and memory); physiological (neurological, articulatory) and social levels, all of which are part of the communication act in and of themselves. Figure 2.4 tentatively represents several key ecological elements that feed into a speakers' cognition. I return to this point below when describing the ecology of language change (§2.5).

This approach to languages as populations of idiolects and speakers integrated in cognition differs from structuralist approaches to language, where a species is a *type*, 'defined by a set of properties, that is not located in space or time but in an abstract domain of biological traits' (Croft 2000: 12; see also §1.4). By contrast, in an evolutionary population-based approach, a species is a 'sociotemporal [reality], not an eternal essence', consisting of a 'population of organisms ... circumscribed by the region in time and space collectively occupied by the individual members of the species' (Croft 2000: 12). Since populations emerge via contact, frequent communication among individuals sharing similar individual ecologies will lead to the focusing or sedimentation of communal norms (for instance, via diffusion across social networks, dialectal focusing in new dialect formation, or creolization in situations of pervasive language contact) in and across individuals. The idea that frequency of use leads to the cognitive *entrenchment* of specific features in an individual's repertoire, with shared patterns of entrenchment across a population resulting in the types of linguistic differences that we call 'languages' or 'dialects', also sits well with usage-based accounts, where changes are the result of accumulated interactions by and among

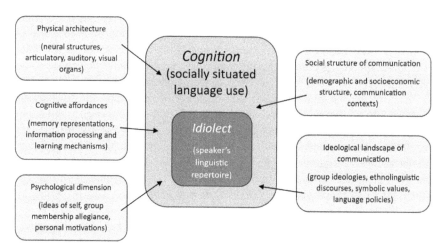

FIGURE 2.4. A tentative visualization of the individual ecology of cognition (source: author)

individual speakers (Backus 2021: 113). Similarly, linguistic differences among the members of the population will occur whenever their ecology of communication is disrupted (through migrations, the drawing of national borders, changes in socioeconomic structure or the emergence of ethnolinguistic differences). From a population-based perspective, borderlines between language varieties are simply an outcome of their speakers' ecology of communication.

Note that there is no contradiction between defending a *language as population* approach and rejecting the 'linguistics of community', as we advocated for in agreement with Pratt in Chapter 1 (§1.7). From an ecological point of view, a population is not a culturally or ethnically defined community (an identity-based group, a social class, a nation, and so forth), but a set of idiolects, embedded in their speakers' cognition as they engage in the collective negotiation of linguistic resources. Ethnolinguistic identities may certainly operate in language change, but only when they become accepted by a population of speakers and they shape their communication patterns accordingly. Whether such ideologies are at work in a particular ecology and whether they have led to the emergence of a language variety is often unclear. We can see a good example of this unclarity in the current conversation about whether Spanish in the United States can be regarded as varieties of the same 'macrodialect' or simply as a geographical aggregate of separate speech communities (or, in other words, *United States Spanish* vs. *Spanish in the United States* 'español *de* los Estados Unidos' vs. 'español *en* los Estados Unidos') (Escobar and Potowski 2015: 300–4).

2.5. Language change: Ecology rolls the dice

If languages emerge from interactions among the members of a population (and their idiolects) via cognition, it follows that the factors that determine these interactions should also shape the course of language stability and change. As advanced in Chapter 1 (§1.6), these factors constitute the *ecology of language*. This approach shifts the focus of language change explanations from formal or systemic aspects of change to the ecological conditions that determine where, when, and how languages change. In language change, 'ecology rolls the dice' (Mufwene 2001: 145).

To understand the key role of ecology in language change, it helps if we think of idiolects as being conformed via the *selection* of features among the various linguistic options available to speakers in a population, in a process analogous to the *competition* of genes in viral species (Mufwene 2001: 147). Recall that speakers select from among the competing variants in their feature pool, consisting of every linguistic element that they can access within their personal communication ecologies (Mufwene 2008: 17). When presented with more than one variant, speakers may select one or several, in which case sociolinguistic variation will ensue (151). In (1a-g) we see several choices made by speakers across ecologies in the history of Spanish, and the functions assigned to some of these choices:

(1a) Stylistic or contextual stratification: *asigún* (stigmatized) / *según* (non-stigmatized/standard) 'according to' and other similar couplets like *asina* / *así* 'this way'; *naiden* / *nadie* 'nobody'; *haiga* / *haya* 'there is/are-3SG.PRES.SUBJ' in rural Michoacán (Mexico) (Santa Ana and Parodi 1998; §6.2).

(1b) Dialect contact: in word-final /n/, velar [ŋ] vs. alveolar [n] in Spanish in Houston, with a tendency among Salvadorans to accommodate (§2.3) to [n] to avoid the negative perception of [ŋ] as an index of ruralness and non-Mexicanness (Hernández 2009; §6.7).

(1c) Borrowing of elements from other languages (for instance, loanwords): *alcachofa* 'artichoke', *almíbar* 'syrup', *marfil* 'ivory', *tarea* 'task' from Hispanic or Classical Arabic, amid Islamic cultural and material influence in medieval Spain (Giménez-Eguíbar 2024; §3.7).

(1d) Combination of options from more than one language in a paradigm: *tu* and *bos* as the 2SG address subject pronoun (from Spanish), together with *kamí* (exclusive) and *kitá* (inclusive) as 1PL, or *kamó* as 2PL subject pronouns (from Cebuano) in Philippine Spanish-based creole Zamboagueño (Lipski 2012; §4.10).

(1e) Structural or semantic mapping from one language (*imposition*, Van Coetsem 2000 and §2.2; also 'rely on L1' strategy, Muysken 2013 and §2.6): stylistic alternation between standard Sp. syllable-final and non-standard Nahuatl-style second-to-last syllable stress (*corrál – córral* 'livestock pen'; *razón - rázon* 'reason') in bilingual communities in central Mexico (Hill and Hill 1986: 221–2; §6.3).

(1f) Simplification of existing options (for instance, elimination of contrasts, selection of more analytic structures): preference for prepositional phrases over case marking with inflectional endings, and SVO vs. SOV syntax in late spoken Latin (Bentz and Christiansen 2015; §3.5).

(1g) Innovative reinterpretation of elements in the source repertoires via L2 acquisition strategies: prepositional phrases used as subject pronouns (*pa mi*, see Sp. *yo* 'I'), lack of subject-verb agreement (*pa mi no sabe*, see Sp. *(yo) no sé*), lack of gender agreement in nominal phrases (*gente suleto*, see Sp. *gente insurrecta*) in the Spanish of Chinese indentured workers in nineteenth-century Cuba (Clements 2009: 102–23; §5.7).

These selections can proceed horizontally, regardless of speakers' age, and vertically, via acquisition by younger speakers from adults or older peers (Mufwene 2010). Critically, when making these selections, speakers weigh out the advantage of each form (Musyken 2013) in their individual ecology: presented with the same or similar options, what may be cognitively and socially advantageous in a context of strong sociocultural pressure to assimilate to a language other than Spanish or to avoid certain forms may not be the same whenever sociolinguistic stratification favors the combined use of forms with different social values (Matras 2020: 65–106).

Let's consider an example. Research on *heritage speakers* of Spanish in the United States has identified grammatical patterns that depart from the monolingual varieties that have historically fed into these heritage populations. We can see these differences in the semantic constraints that govern the choice between preterite or imperfect tense, indicative or subjunctive mood, or gender agreement in noun phrases, and in the frequency of use of specific features (Escobar and Potowski 2015: 81–112; Silva-Corvalán 1994; §6.7). These kinds of differences are commonly invoked as evidence of either *attrition* or *incomplete acquisition* in the systems of heritage speakers (Montrul 2013: 207–38,

2022; Montrul and Silva-Corvalán 2019; Polinsky 2018; see also §6.7). In other words, heritage speakers are seen by these authors as not fully acquiring something that monolingual speakers have acquired fully. This differential acquisition path is usually attributed to a decrease in heritage language dominance after early childhood as bilingual speakers come into increasing contact with the majority language outside the home. Less dominance in the heritage language causes bilingual speakers to lose some of the structural constraints typical of monolingual speakers acquired in their early years (attrition), or to not develop these constraints in the first place (incomplete acquisition). Other approaches emphasize instead the parallelisms between monolingual and heritage grammars, with both types of speakers exhibiting the same acquisition order and linguistic constraints of use, even if overall frequencies are different (Requena 2022; Shin et al. 2023). In these approaches, heritage speakers have not failed to acquire something, but they have simply acquired it differently. Figure 2.5 illustrates this difference in a picture naming activity to study the acquisition of gender agreement in noun phrases (as in *el zorro blanco* 'the-MASC white-MASC fox', *la oveja blanca* 'the-FEM white-FEM sheep') among monolingual children from central Mexico and among bilingual Spanish/English-speaking children in Chicago, ages six to eleven (Montrul and Potowski 2007). Here, MON stands for the monolingual children, SEQ for sequential bilinguals that were exposed to English after age four, and SIM for simultaneous bilingual children exposed to both languages since birth. As can be seen, both bilingual groups exhibited lower rates of gender agreement than their monolingual peers, especially in the feminine.

To explain these differential selections in each group of speakers, the literature has proposed a complex mix of environmental factors like the amount of input available to each speaker, their sociocultural motivation to use the minority

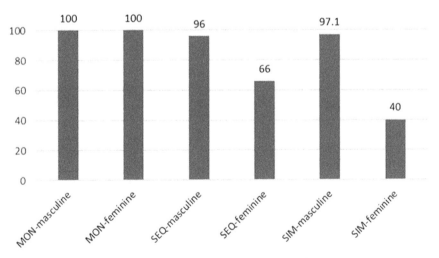

FIGURE 2.5. Percentage of noun phrases showing gender agreement across three groups of Spanish-speaking children (figure by author; data from Montrul and Potowski 2007: 315)

language, or the age of exposure to the majority language. Ultimately, these differences explain why, although the *forms* in Spanish that monolingual and heritage speakers have been exposed to are the same (that is, phrases with gender agreement), their *selections* are different: both monolinguals and bilinguals rely on the same mechanisms to develop their repertoires, but these mechanisms produce different results across different acquisition settings, feature pools, and language use experiences (Adamou 2021; Higby et al. 2023).

Another important take-away from the literature on monolingual and bilingual speakers is that language users always create their idiolects from scratch: historically, the local ecology will determine whether speakers in a population will select the same features present in other speakers' idiolects, or different features. An accumulation of the same selections across members of a population leads to linguistic stability (*stasis,* Croft 2000: 24; see *entrenchment* in §2.4). By contrast, linguistic diversification at the level of the community (*speciation,* Mufwene 2001: 3) occurs when speakers in a population converge on selections that depart from those of other speakers (151). Since no two speakers share the exact same ecology, the selection process is always prone to innovations. Following this reasoning, Mufwene rejects the idea of *transmission* (Labov 2007) to refer to the process where speakers select and copy features from other speakers, and instead proposes *restructuring* (2008: 18). At the risk of seeming overly persnickety, I prefer to refer to this process as *recombination* (Mufwene 2008: 118–20) to highlight the fact that, from an evolutionary perspective, 'structure' never exists as a complete product, but rather emerges over time from language use by the individuals in a population (see Hopper 1987, Bybee 2010, and §1.5). Note that, in this process, speakers may select features regardless of whether they correspond to the same or different named 'languages' or 'varieties', and use them variably, which Mufwene (2008: 121–4) terms *hybridism* (see also *introgression* in Croft 2000: 180): there is no built-in loyalty on the part of the speakers to replicate elements of specific named languages or varieties (of, say, Latin, Spanish or Kinyarwanda). If they happen to, this is simply an outcome of their ecology of language use and not part of the evolutionary nature of language change as a process.

From this perspective, an ecological approach stands in contrast to proposals that see every form of language variation as necessarily symbolic of some form of identity ('language change is linked to variation, variation to difference, and difference to identity, [so] it's impossible to consider any of the structural changes ... without reference to identity', Mendoza-Denton and Gordon 2011: 562–3; Eckert 2019). By contrast, in the present approach, some forms of variation may be recruited for social indexical purposes (see *enregisterment,* Johnstone 2016), but others may not. The fact that a form has acquired social meaning may make it more salient to speakers in a given population, and this sociolinguistic saliency may encourage them to either reject or favor the form.

For instance, Erker (2017) reflects on how speakers of Spanish in the United States accommodate to each other in different contexts. An example is syllable-final /s/, which varies across the Spanish-speaking world between full [s] and lenited articulations, including [h] or full elision. He contrasts data showing that Miami-born speakers produce higher rates of full /s/ than Cuban-born speakers, with data from New York City, where speakers accommodate to a new interdialectal mean somewhere in the middle of the various contributing dialects (rather than sharing a community-wide trend, as in Miami). In his analysis, the production of /s/ has different social values in Miami than in New York City, which (the author hypothesizes) explains the different selections by speakers in each location. Revealingly, however, social indexing is not necessary for language change: together with socially salient variables, Erker discusses other features (for instance, overt subject pronouns, §2.3) that seem to not be socially indexed but which are also subject to change in US Spanish. In this case, cognitive biases in favor of convergent structures in bilingual repertoires (and not social identity) are invoked as the reason for change in these areas of grammar (see Fernández-Mallat 2018 for a similar argument about the Spanish of Bolivian immigrants in northern Chile; and Michnowicz et al. 2023 about contact features in North Carolina Spanish).

Understanding language change as an ecological process can help us reconceptualize the traditional dichotomy between 'internal' (formal) vs. 'external' (social) causes of change, and between 'internal' and 'external' language histories commonly seen in language historiographies, including in Spanish (for instance, Penny 2002: 2; Pharies 2015: xi; Resnick and Hammond 2011: 292). Insofar as an individual's cognition is both mental and social (§2.4), there is no clear-cut separation between what is 'internal' and 'external' to an individual's idiolect, and a strict distinction between 'internal' and 'external' motives for language change is untenable (Mufwene 2008: 31). Events in the life of populations (including language expansion, language speciation, language shift, language death) can be studied in their ethnographic, anthropological, or sociological dimensions, but they are ultimately ecologically driven outcomes of the linguistic feature selection patterns of individuals in the population.

Lastly, the role of the ecology of communication is theoretically *deterministic*, as ecological factors precipitate feature selection (in a 'cascading' fashion, see DeGraff 2009: 946–8; Mufwene 2018: 75–6). In practice, however, an ecological approach cannot predict language change. This is because multiple ecological triggers with different weights operate simultaneously on the individual speakers of a population (Nölle et al. 2020). Since ecologies are complex, language change is always due to *multiple causation* (Adamou 2013; Thomasson and Kaufman 1988: 59–61). This approach is helpful to understand the multilayered nature of language change in several ways. For instance, an ecological approach can shed light on why relatively homogeneous language communities may over time give rise to very divergent varieties following the fragmentation of the original population of speakers, as when Latin evolved into the current Romance varieties, Spanish included (Lipski 2022; Smith 2020). It can also be useful to explain how the same feature may spread in more than one community without diffusion due to environmental similarities in the forms that speakers accessed and filtered through universal learning processes (*vernacular universals*, Chambers 2004), as in the case of the striking morphological parallelisms among mutually isolated rural varieties of Spanish (Sanz-Sánchez 2011; §4.7). Finally, an ecological explanation can go also go further than structural explanations to account for the actuation (§2.2) of a given innovation across different ecologies, as when the same phonemic merger can be seen to spread at different times via different social routes in specific Spanish varieties (see *yeísmo,* the merger of /ʎ/ and /j/, Sanz-Sánchez 2013; §4.7, §5.5 and §5.9).

In the next section, I apply this ecological lens to briefly revisit several mechanisms of contact that have figured prominently in the study of language change and which are particularly relevant to the ecological approach in this book. This reassessment, in turn, will provide us with a fresh pair of eyes with which to approach the historical sociolinguistic processes that we will see at work in the history of Spanish in the chapters that follow.

2.6. How contact works: An ecological reassessment of contact processes

As noted, language change contexts have tended to be classified into contact and non-contact situations, and into different types of contact settings (§2.3). From an evolutionary perspective, however, individual speakers are foreign to these typologies. With this axiom in mind, an ecological approach dovetails with many previous approaches to contact and change, with the understanding that these theories address prominent aspects of how individual speakers learn and negotiate language in their respective historical contexts, rather than essentially discrete processes.

Sociolinguistic approaches to the spread of innovations across the social space are particularly relevant to an ecological understanding of contact. Sociolinguists focusing on stratified, monolingual language communities of the kind typical in many Western, industrialized nations have explored the effect of social structure, gender, age, and other social variables in the social progression of change. For instance, many studies have identified the role of specific age cohorts in the promotion of new vernacular norms or conservative linguistic behavior (Labov 2007; Sankoff 2018; Tagliamonte and D'Arcy 2009; §2.2). Research on *social networks* (Laitinen et al. 2020; Milroy and Milroy 1992), as also advanced above (§2.2), has focused on the correlation between the structure of the communication networks in a population and the spread of innovations. Once an innovation has entered a network, it will spread faster across networks where members tend to have more multiplex ties (that is, when the same individuals communicate in various social contexts) than those where members have fewer multiplex ties. These network-wide effects are predicated on the action of individual speakers, whose ties to other speakers and their position within the broader network predict their sociolinguistic behavior. In this sense, the classical distinction between *innovators* and *early adopters* (Milroy and Milroy 1985: 367) is useful to understand the difference between the initial actuation of an innovation and its spread: innovators are marginal members that generate a change, while early adopters aid in its spread by virtue of their more central place in the network (recall Figure 2.3). Over time, what started as innovations in a small population of idiolects may, via contact among speakers within the network, become incorporated into idiolects at a much larger (social or geographical) scale (see the distinction between *microstructure* and *macrostructure* in Croft 2000: 190–3): social networks can therefore be conceptualized as intermediate-level populations between the speaker and larger populations. Several studies of the spread of innovations in specific Spanish-speaking ecologies have made use of this approach (Barajas 2022; Martín Butragueño 2016; San Juan and Almeida 2005; Villena-Ponsoda 2005).

Most social network approaches see language change deterministically as a function of network structure and not of collective psychological factors, such as identity (but not everyone agrees: recall that identity is central in the work on communities of practice, which are also essentially a kind of social network, §1.4). From this perspective, situations of pervasive demographic contact (for instance, via colonial settlement, displacement, or mass migration), are particularly interesting because they often result in a thorough rearrangement of social networks and the renegotiation of any social or symbolic values previously attached to specific features. As such, they allow us to test hypotheses on the relative role of deterministic vs. psychological factors in the ecology of language change (Trudgill 2008; §2.6). Settings of *new dialect formation* or koinéization (Britain 2016; Kerswill and Williams 2000a; Trudgill 1986, 2004) illustrate the interplay between both kinds of factors. In the initial stage of contact, most speakers participate in loose networks where they have access to very diverse features, and as a result their personal feature pools are very *diffuse*: there is a lot of variability, and the social meaning of specific features is not established yet. As speakers accommodate to each other (§2.3), communication patterns across the population stabilize and local networks with varying degrees of strength emerge. Younger learners in the population further solidify variability into a more systematic norm (Labov 2007). This process is conducive to the *focusing* of specific linguistic variants in the community, but also to their reinterpretation as social or stylistic markers (Croft 2000: 177–8; see also *reallocation* in Trudgill 1994, 2004; Font-Santiago et al. 2022).

Several situations of contact in the history of Spanish and their linguistic effects have been studied through this lens, including medieval Spanish (Fernández Ordóñez 2012a; Tuten 2003), the emergence of new varieties of colonial Spanish (Fontanella de Weinberg 1992; Granda 1994; Sanz-Sánchez 2013, 2019), the settlement of northern Chile in the late 1800s (Avilés 2016), and dialect contact among varieties of Spanish in US cities, which includes the negotiation of features originating in various dialects of Spanish as well as contact with English (e.g. Los Angeles, Parodi 2011; New York City, Otheguy and Zentella 2012; North Carolina, Michnowicz et al. 2023).

In addition to considering the role of network structure and the relative role of linguistic and social factors in the emergence of new varieties, an ecological view of language change can also feed from acquisitionally informed perspectives. Some ecologically informed authors have warned against assuming that individual psycholinguistic processes involved in language acquisition hold the key to explaining the outcomes of contact processes at the population level (Mufwene 2010). Other authors have advocated for a holistic approach, where individual acquisition processes are one of the factors involved in the selection of features at the population level (Winford 2020).

An ambitious proposal along these lines relies on individual *bilingual acquisition strategies* (Aalberse 2024; Aalberse et al. 2019; Muysken 2013) to account for a range of effects along the language contact spectrum. These include both on-the-spot conversational strategies (code-switching) and population-wide outcomes (like creolization and mixed language emergence). The idea here is that, in every act of communication, speakers strategically rank each of the language features they have access to according to the psycholinguistic and social requirements of their setting. These decisions can be subsumed under four main rubrics: (1) rely on your L1 (for instance, by inserting morphemes or lexicon from one's L1 when speaking the L2, or by mapping a structural pattern from one's L1 onto the L2); (2) rely on your L2 (for instance, by borrowing elements from the L2); (3) rely on both your L1 and your L2 (as when bilingual speakers favor convergent structures that are available in both languages); and (4) rely on universal principles (UP) of language processing (narrate events in chronological order, use reduplication and iteration for emphasis, etc.). Specific linguistic and sociolinguistic factors increase or decrease the likelihood of application of each strategy, as shown in Figure 2.6.

As an example, Quechua speakers have historically incorporated Spanish morphemes. At first sight, this is a straightforward case of borrowing (§2.2), but upon closer examination, this general process subsumes various bilingual strategies. For instance, following the 'rely on your L1' strategy, some of these borrowed morphemes have taken on the semantic properties of affixes already existing in Quechua (as in Inga Quechua in Colombia, where agentive morpheme -*k* has been replaced by semantically similar Spanish -*dor*, which has also developed a meaning as a past habitual marker, just like the Quechua affix it replaced). In Ecuadorian Kichwa, Spanish plural markers (-*s, -es*) have been generalized and replaced the original Quechua markers, illustrating the 'rely on your L2' strategy. Lastly, properties of both the L1 and the L2 are sometimes combined, as when

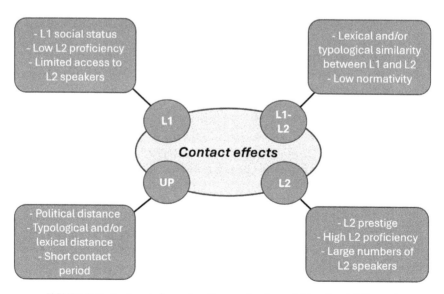

FIGURE 2.6. Factors influencing the application of Muysken's bilingual optimization strategies (figure by author, based on Muysken 2013: 726)

Spanish diminutives *-ito/-cito* are incorporated in Bolivian Quechua as *-itu/-situ*, exhibiting Quechua phonology but Spanish semantics (Muysken 2013: 719–20). An advantage of approaching contact processes from this perspective is that we can go beyond earlier models that relied on broad dichotomies (for instance, *borrowing* vs. *transfer* in Thomason and Kauffman 1988, *borrowing* vs. *imposition* in Van Coetsem 2000; §2.2). Instead, we can paint a more nuanced picture of the various reasons why individual speakers may choose to apply specific feature selection strategies, and the social circumstances favoring these selections at a population level. It also allows us to understand *structural convergence* (Wiemer 2021) as a manifestation of the speakers' ability to access the structural or grammatical settings of two 'languages' simultaneously, and to rely on both to select among specific variants or to create new ones.

Another way in which paying attention to individual learning processes may inform our understanding of language change from a population perspective is by considering the role of *cognitive acquisition biases* (Backus 2021; De Bot and Bülow 2021). These may be relevant insofar as some forms may be more learnable, which in turn increases their chances of being selected (Chambers 2004). For instance, Clements (2009: 1–27) discusses the role of *bootstrapping* in both L1 acquisition by children and L2 acquisition by adults as a general process whereby structures emerge progressively from previously acquired elements. In this process, learners show a preference for forms that are easier to process perceptually, semantically, or syntactically (even when they are not the most frequent options in the input). For instance, present-tense copulas in most Spanish and Portuguese-based creoles as well as L2 Spanish in naturalistic contexts tend to be consonant-initial (such as *son, sã* 'to be') rather than vowel-initial, even though the latter are by far much more frequent in L1 forms of both Portuguese and Spanish (for instance, vowel-initial *eres* 'to be-2SG.PRE.IND' and *es* 'to be-3SG.PRE.IND' account for almost 80% of all forms of the present indicative copula in present-day Spanish corpora). This preference is connected to the enhanced acoustic perception of CV combinations (Clements 2009: 22–3). All other things being equal (which, by the way, they often are not!), easier-to-learn forms will have a diachronic advantage. Understanding feature selection as responding to acquisitional biases among the various triggers that speakers respond to can help explain many of the observed effects of contact as well as cross-linguistic typological distributions (Clements 2009: 19; Mufwene 2008: 128–31).

From an evolutionary-ecological point of view, this range of observed contact effects is not problematic – recall that age-related cognitive and social factors in the individual are also part of the ecology of each speaker's cognition (Mufwene 2008: 83; §2.4) and speakers may interact both horizontally and vertically. The question, therefore, is not whether specific groups of speakers (age cohorts, social classes, communities of practice, etc.; §1.4) are the agents of language change. Instead, the focus is on which types of changes are more likely to occur in a population at a specific time given the local ecological triggers, and which role various kinds of learners may have in promoting or inhibiting the social spread of a particular innovation.

2.7. Conclusion

This chapter has elaborated on several important aspects of the ecological framework of contact. To summarize, this approach necessarily transcends many of the taxonomies of contact that have been proposed in the past, by centering speaker-to-speaker communication as the source of all forms of change. It does not negate the validity nor the usefulness of most theories and methodologies that have been developed to interpret the dynamics of contact situations. But it does require that we take a step back and proceed to re-engage with these proposals from the only locus where contact can be proven to be active: not whole age categories, social groups, regions, nations, or linguistic essences, but the cognition of individual language users in communication with each other. From this perspective, thinking and writing about language history ceases to be a matter of describing a series of changes that are sometimes due to contact, sometimes not.

So, what does this all mean for our understanding of the history of Spanish? In the remainder of this book, I will revisit some of the ecologies that have traditionally been covered in genealogical narratives of the history of Spanish, interpreting the available social and linguistic record through the contact-based evolutionary approach articulated so far. My goal is to propose a different type of narrative, one that does not deny the applicability of other frameworks, but which gives contact processes (rather than transmission or inheritance) the upper hand. In doing so, I abide by the principles of language use and change introduced in Chapter 1 and developed in this chapter. The picture emerging from this narrative will ultimately reaffirm the socio-political nature of named language varieties (like 'Spanish'). It will also demonstrate the central role of communication and learning via contact among speakers in specific sociohistorical settings as the universal driving force for language change.

In the next chapters, I will stick to the principle that 'ecology rolls the dice' (§2.5) to revisit a range of sociohistorical settings, by following three steps: I will first survey the available demographic and sociolinguistic information for each setting, I will then offer a reconstruction of the environmental embedding of language learning for speakers in each context, and lastly, I will present the linguistic outcomes of contact-led recombination in each ecology.

Discussion questions

1. Most linguists today are comfortable researching and describing contact situations, but as we have seen (§2.2), this has not always been the case in Western linguistics. Why not? Which assumptions about human cultures and human behavior are reproduced by models that assume lack of contact as the sociolinguistic default?

2. Much of our knowledge of how languages change is based on research in industrialized Western societies. Here, sociolinguists have often attributed the progression of change to older children and adolescents, as they adjust their early acquired home systems to their local dialectal norm. Are these acquisition conditions generalizable to other cultural or chronological

contexts? What may we be missing if we assume Western societies are representative of how individuals contribute to language change?

3. Go to the *World Atlas of Language Structures Online* (https://wals.info/). Under 'features', select one or two that you are familiar with and examine their overall distribution (both in quantitative terms, as in 'which options are more/less frequent cross-linguistically', as well as in their geographical patterning across the planet). What factors might determine these distributions? Cognitive? Acquisitional? Patterns of demographic movement or contact in specific regions?

3

Spanish Before Spain: Ancient, Roman Era, and Medieval Contacts

3.1. Introduction: Imagining Spanish

If an *annus mirabilis* award competition in the historiography of European languages was ever held, 1492 and Spanish would likely be among the strongest contenders. Any language planner with a knack for manifest destiny myths could have hardly imagined a more felicitous combination of events. For one, the power couple formed by queen Isabella of Castile and King Ferdinand of Aragon, masters of over three fourths of the Iberian Peninsula, succeeded in taking over the Nasrid Emirate of Granada, ending almost eight hundred years of Muslim rule north of the straits of Gibraltar and setting the stage for the forced conversion of Muslims and Jews. A few months later, a Castilian-sponsored expedition led by Cristopher Columbus landed on the coast of the Bahamas, kickstarting the European colonial era in the Western Hemisphere. And just weeks before the Christian rulers in the Castilian-Aragonese dynastic union expanded their geopolitical control beyond the Iberian Peninsula and the Canary Islands, humanist Elio Antonio de Nebrija published the first grammar of a vernacular European language, the *Gramática de la lengua castellana*, which he personally dedicated to Isabella, 'born queen and ruler ["reina i señora natural"] of Spain, the islands, and our ocean' (Biblioteca Digital Hispánica 2023a: 5; see Figure 3.1).

In the prologue to his grammar, Nebrija justified the publication of this innovative text (a vernacular Romance grammar) in explicit geopolitical terms: 'language has always been a companion to power ["siempre la lengua fue compañera del imperio"]; and the former follows the latter so closely, that they begin, grow, and flourish alongside each other, and when they fall, they fall together' (Biblioteca Digital Hispánica 2023a: 5). Clearly, Nebrija did not just want to provide a description of the rules of the language. He also wanted to contribute to a higher end: strengthening the place of Castile as the core of the emerging Spanish state and ensuring that its language would be ready to operate as the new nation's symbolic instrument. Nebrija's conception of Castilian is in many ways a direct antecedent of the more recent discourses on Spanish that we surveyed in Chapter 1: like many others after him (§1.2), he spoke of Castilian as if it were a person, born as the offspring of Latin, a child during the times of the early kings

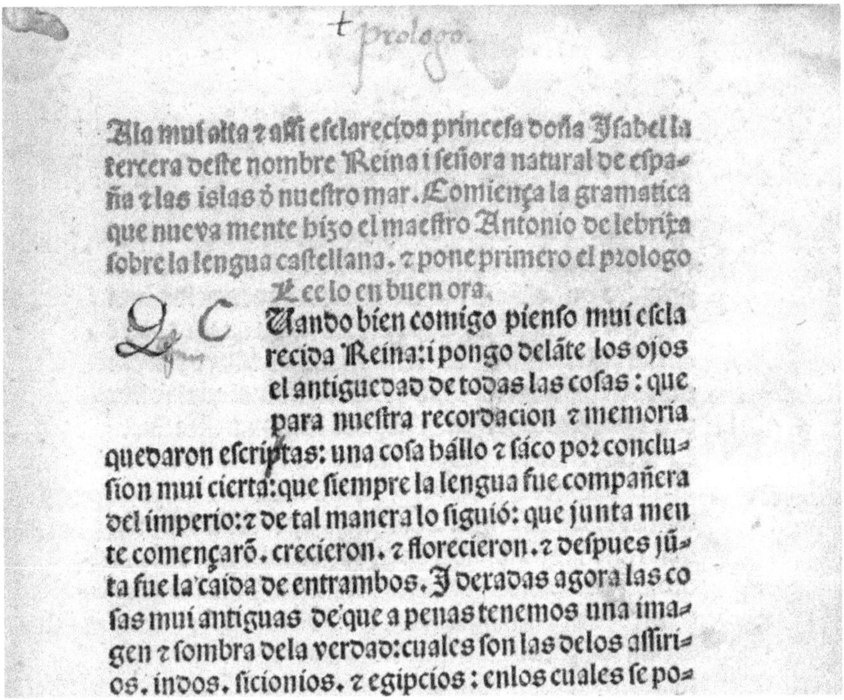

A la mui alta z assi esclarecida princesa doña Isabel la
tercera deste nombre Reina i señora natural de españa z las islas d nuestro mar. Comiença la gramatica
que nueva mente hizo el maestro Antonio de lebrixa
sobre la lengua castellana. z pone primero el prologo.
Lee lo en buen ora.
Quando bien comigo pienso mui escla
recida Reina: i pongo delãte los ojos
el antiguedad de todas las cosas: que
para nuestra recordacion z memoria
quedaron escriptas: una cosa hallo z saco por conclusion mui cierta: que siempre la lengua fue compañera
del imperio: z de tal manera lo siguió: que junta men
te començarõ. crecieron. z florecieron. z despues jũ-
ta fue la caida de entrambos. I dexadas agora las co
sas mui antiguas de que a penas tenemos una imagen z sombra dela verdad: cuales son las delos assiri-
os. indos. sicionios. z egipcios: enlos cuales se po-

FIGURE 3.1. First lines of Nebrija's *Gramática de la lengua castellana* (1492) (Biblioteca Digital Hispánica 2023a, © Biblioteca Nacional de España, license: https://creativecommons.org/licenses/by-nc/4.0/deed.en)

of Castile and growing into adulthood in this golden age of political supremacy and territorial expansion. His grammar was the confirmation that this linguistic child had come of age.

But Nebrija was also aware that this process was anything but irreversible: just like other empires and their languages had lost their influence, this could happen to Spain unless Castilian as its leading language was codified and fixed: 'so that whatever is written in it from now on may remain in one fixed form and may endure for the rest of times' (Biblioteca Digital Hispánica 2023a: 7). Nebrija was explicit, therefore, that the object that he was describing was a linguistic and an ideological construction: many forms of speaking existed in Castile at this time, but not all of them would do for the purpose of his grammar. As for other languages in the Peninsula, their role in this process of national unification was out of the question.

What Nebrija did not say is that this direct line of descent of Castilian as the reincarnation of Latin was also a cultural mirage. This narrative may have fit the mood at a time when Castile was consolidating itself as the core of a new (and expansionist) political unit, a kind of modern Rome where linguistic development and political power went hand in hand. Ideologically, a homogenizing narrative that emphasizes descent and conceals diversity and discontinuity can be particularly useful at a time when a nation-state is being built. But the history of standard languages like Spanish is as much a history of commonalities as it is a history of differences, mediated by a complex web of contacts. For instance, as Trudgill has pointed out, '[a]ll the major standard language varieties in Europe today are relatively high contact koinés and creoloids ... resulting from dialect contact' (2011: 238). Likewise, Penny (2000) has explored the role of selection processes in the creation of standard Spanish. The background of the collection of forms that Nebrija packaged in his grammar was a lot more complicated than he may have realized or wanted to admit – and nothing ruins the mood of nation building and linguistic standardization like historical complexity.

The vision of Castilian articulated by Nebrija in his *Gramática* has been invoked often in the historiographical tradition of Spanish to naturalize an apparently seamless transition from 'Castilian' as a medieval Latin-derived variety to 'Spanish' as the modern language of a new national unit (§1.2 and §1.3). In this chapter, I will use Nebrija's prologue as the steppingstone for an ecological questioning of this historical narrative of direct transmission of essential characteristics. I will focus on how interactions among speakers of diverse provenance in their historical communities resulted in the pool of features that Nebrija selected from for his version of standard Castilian in 1492, starting with the same prehistoric construct chosen by most histories of Spanish: Proto-Indo-European (PIE). The chapter will highlight several historical ecologies during this time span for which the available sociohistorical and linguistic record provides evidence of the role of contact: the diversification of Indo-European (§3.3), the spread of Latin in Hispania (§3.4 and §3.5), the Visigothic period (§3.6), and medieval Spain (§3.8 and §3.9). But before diving into these remote settings, we first need to be clear about what we can and cannot expect from the available evidence.

3.2. Solving contact enigmas in remote times

The study of the consequences of contact leading up to the standard languages of the early modern period is not new. The literature on topics like the Indo-European expansion, the spread of Latin in the Roman Empire or the emergence of medieval Romance varieties is rife with references to contact. Many of these approaches share the perspective that there is some type of linguistic matrix providing a thread of continuity between the early Indo-Europeans and the speakers of modern Romance varieties like Spanish. According to the tenets of the *comparative method* (Campbell 2004: 122–83, and §3.3), this matrix is said to be apparent in several areas of language that are assumed to be diachronically more stable than others, and therefore more easily passed on from an original language to its derived dialects. These include basic vocabulary (including numerals, core family relations, and at least some biological and technological concepts), some grammatical material (personal pronouns, verbal endings) and basic typological characteristics (grammatical gender marking, inflectional morphology, basic word order, etc.).

Having established that the intergenerational transmission of these elements reflects this shared diachronic matrix, reflections on the role of contact in the remote history of individual languages typically focus on how external influences have operated on this inherited component. These influences have been commonly conceptualized as linguistic layers of non-native acquisition or *strata* (recall Ascoli's work in §2.2), including *substrates* (via shift to an L2), *superstrates* (via borrowing of non-native elements by L1 speakers) or *adstrates* (as in situations of long-term bilingualism). In the case of Spanish, the languages of pre-Roman Iberia are often seen as a substrate to Latin; Gothic, medieval Latin, and other European languages like Italian and French as superstrates; and other Iberian languages like Portuguese or Catalan as adstrates (Echenique Elizondo 2003). These accounts conjure up images of generations of speakers whose default behavior is to pass their linguistic legacy on to the next generation with as little change as possible, except when one of the abovementioned contact scenarios apply.

But as Smith (2020) has recently argued in relation to the study of contact in the history of Romance languages, the strata-based approach is only useful if the social conditions that would yield such one-dimensional contact effects can be shown to have been in place. Under closer scrutiny, the acquisitional and demographic mechanisms involved in chronologically remote contact settings are often more complex. By way of illustration, in the history of Spanish, Basque has been claimed to be either a substrate to early Castilian or an adstrate or both (Echenique Elizondo 2003). The verdict depends on whether Castilian is posited as having developed out of Basque speakers shifting to forms of north-central Iberian Romance, or from a situation of long-term bilingualism along a geographical linguistic boundary – but in reality, both scenarios may have alternated with each other historically. Smith's critique of the stratum approach is ultimately a reflection of the complexity in the sociolinguistic history of individuals and their populations, which are never linguistically homogeneous groups in contact with each other.

At first sight, reconstructing these ecological conditions and their linguistic outcomes in historically remote societies might seem like a daunting task. The written record for most of these environments is scant or non-existent, especially since we are largely dealing with pre-literate societies. Additional remains shedding light on the demographics, socioeconomics or culture of these communities are typically missing, highly fragmentary, or even of contested validity (see, for instance, the controversy about the authenticity and the linguistics of the *fibula of Praeneste*, the first putative text in Latin, dated seventh century BC, Mancini 2021). Similarly, archaeological and genetic data, when available, is difficult to interpret in linguistic terms (after all, we cannot ask a skeleton which language they spoke...). Nevertheless, the more we examine whatever scraps of evidence have been preserved to reconstruct the historical sociolinguistics of the speakers living in the roughly 5,000 years between PIE and medieval Spanish, the clearer the central function that various forms of contact must have had in the linguistic life of their populations becomes. In the following sections, I survey some representative work on several of these historical populations, underscoring the key role that contact processes played in all of them.

3.3. Indo-European: Fragmentation vs. contact

The development of Western linguistics since the nineteenth century (§2.2) owes much to the study of the formal and lexical correspondences among a group of languages that, at the onset of the European colonial area in the fifteenth century, stretched from Iceland to the Bay of Bengal, and which came to be known as the Indo-European family. A selection of these *cognates* (that is, historically related forms, §1.4) can be seen in Table 3.1 (non-cognate forms are italicized).

TABLE 3.1. A few Indo-European cognates (adapted from Mallory and Adams 2006: 2, 5)

English	Latin	Greek	Spanish	Czech	Sanskrit
mother	maːter	meːteːr	madre	matka	maːtar
brother	fraːter	phreːteːr	*hermano*	otec	bhraːtar
one	uːnus	en	uno	jeden	ekam
two	duo	duo	dos	dva	dve

The systematic study of these correspondences as a gateway to the historical relationships of descent from the *proto-language* (a posited common linguistic source) became the core of the comparative method (Campbell 2004: 122–83), and this approach was eventually applied to postulate other language groupings. In the Indo-European case, the archival record for some of these languages, reaching as far back as the second half of the second millennium BC (Mycenean Greek and Vedic Sanskrit), also helped comparativists get closer to the form of this posited proto-language. Since then, additional archival evidence, as well as archeological findings and, more recently, genetic studies have also been enlisted. This body of data has allowed researchers to sketch a clearer image of the history of Indo-European languages than of any other language family. But, unsurprisingly, it has also complexified old questions about the spread of these languages and generated new ones. One of these questions concerns the original homeland of Indo-European speakers, a conversation that is closely linked to the dating of the Indo-European linguistic expansion (Anthony and Ringe 2015; Chang et al. 2015; Renfrew 1987). Indo-Europeanists also debate the internal grouping of the family, an area where researchers must address whether the observed cognates are due to shared inheritance or to spread among subgroups (Garrett 2006). All these questions are ultimately about the sociolinguistics of the populations where these varieties emerged (Drinka 2020, 2022).

In relation to the homeland question, many authors support some version of the *steppe hypothesis* (also known as 'Kurgan hypothesis'), according to which PIE was spoken somewhere in the Pontic-Caspian plains, roughly the area between the Dnieper and Volga rivers, around 4500–4000 BC (Anthony and Ringe 2015; Chang et al. 2015; Drinka 2022). Other proposals have situated the Indo-European homeland further south (in Anatolia or Armenia), and have linked the linguistic fragmentation of the family to the spread of farming into Europe and the Middle East as early as 7500–7000 BC via small-scale contact rather than large-scale migrations (Renfrew 1987). Recent intermediate proposals identify an original homeland south of the Caucasus, with early branching into the Pontic-Caspian area (Heggarty et al. 2023).

Regardless of the location of this homeland, contact with other nearby communities appears to have contributed to the basic lexicon and grammar of PIE even before fragmentation. For instance, proponents of the steppe hypothesis have called attention to PIE cognates with Uralic and Kartvelian words, suggesting an original location between (and in contact with) these language groups north of the Caucasus (Anthony and Ringe 2015). Examples include PIE *wodr 'water' and Proto-Uralic *wete 'water', and PIE *sm̥h₂l-/ *smeh₂l- 'apple' and Proto-Kartvelian *msxal- 'pear'. Similarly, proposed Semitic loanwords have been invoked to defend a homeland or at least early contact south of the Caucasus (Mallory and Adams 2006). These include PIE *tauros < Proto-Semitic *tawr- 'bull, ox' and PIE *woinom < Proto-Semitic *wayn 'wine'. The overall picture emerging from these reconstructions is one of interethnic communication and cultural exchanges as part of the sociolinguistic environment of early PIE speakers.

The sociolinguistic embedding of contact in PIE is particularly critical in connection to the internal classification of the Indo-European family. In the traditional *fragmentation* model (§2.2), groups of speakers split off from the main community, giving rise to new languages via isolation and internal innovation. Upon closer examination, however, specific branches exhibit shared linguistic characteristics, bearing on the question of whether they constitute shared innovations or they are due to waves of diffusion (§2.2) among geographically contiguous IE groups, and even local contact with non-IE communities. Even branch-specific elements may be due to a more complex sociolinguistic contact history than meets the eye. For instance, Garrett (2006) has suggested that the traditional fragmentation model as applied to portions of the IE family may be a mirage propelled by an ideologically fueled search for the origins of ethnic groups in nineteenth-century comparative linguistics. Instead, a closer look at linguistic evidence suggests that at least some of these branch-specific features may be due to the sedimentation of local contact phenomena that originally diffused across a continuum of related dialects. If they look like separate branches to us today is primarily due to the loss of intermediate dialects across this dialect continuum. Figure 3.2 shows an adapted version of the fragmentation model (assuming a steppe origin) incorporating some of these contact effects, such as among Celtic, Germanic, and Italic (branch 3b on the map).

The evidence for both transmission of inherited elements within IE communities and contact among speakers of IE and non-IE varieties has motivated Drinka to advocate for a vision of PIE as a dynamic 'proto-conglomerate' (2013: 402). This would be made up of various layers of contact, rather than the 'traditional, idealized image of PIE as a compact entity existing at one point in space and time' (402) and then fragmenting into discrete branches.

This vision is directly relevant to the history of the Italic branch and to the emergence of Italic languages, including Latin. Connections among Italic, Germanic, and Celtic languages appear to have been particularly common (as suggested in Figure 3.2). Some of these connections may stem from internal

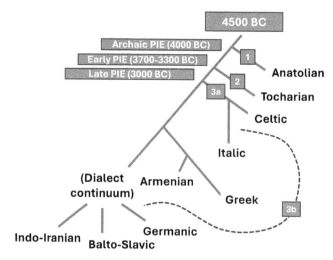

FIGURE 3.2. Stages of Indo-European fragmentation with some contact (figure by author, adapted from Anthony and Ringe 2015: 209)

diffusion among these groups and others to language contact (for instance, accentual patterns calqued on a Proto-Finno-Ugric model, Salmons 1992). However, to make matters more complex, these three branches do not always share the same similarities. Examples (1–3) illustrate a selection of these features (from Drinka 2020):

(1) Shared by Italic and Celtic:
Assimilation of *p...ku̯ > ku̯...ku̯
PIE *penku̯e 'five' > Latin *quinque* 'five', Old Irish *cóic* 'five'
(2) Shared by Italic and Germanic:
Formation of a collective number word in *-no-
PIE *du̯is-no 'twice' > Latin *bīnī* 'two', Old English *getwinne* 'twins'
(3) Shared by Italic, Germanic, and Celtic:
Word for 'chin' from PIE *men- 'to protrude' > *mn̥to- > Lat. *mentum* 'chin', Welsh *mant* 'jaw, mouth', Gothic *munþs* 'mouth'

These complex contact effects are again a bad match for a strict fragmentation-based model, and instead evoke a scenario of contiguous communities in contact, with features diffusing as populations and cultural innovations traversed north-central Europe in prehistoric times.

Contact among speakers of IE dialects, and between these and speakers of non-IE languages appears to have been particularly intense in the Italic Peninsula. In the vicinity of the historical cradle of Latin in the Lazio region of central Italy, other recorded IE varieties included Faliscan, Umbrian and South Picene, to the north, as well as Oscan to the south. Etruscan, a non-IE language, was spoken just to the north. Phonological, lexical, and structural similarities among these languages are numerous, inviting questions about the sociolinguistic mechanisms that may have resulted in these similarities (whether inter-dialectal diffusion, transmission from a proto-Italic ancestor, or transfer via long-term

Spanish Before Spain 63

bilingualism) (Drinka 2020: 309–13). The concept of a 'Central Italic koiné', where these groups shared cultural and linguistic innovations that progressively sedimented into local varieties, has been proposed to conceptualize this sociolinguistic environment (Clackson and Horrock 2007: 37–76). What is clear is that, since the very beginning of Rome's expansion around the Mediterranean, its language already bore the marks of multiple ancestral rounds of contact.

3.4. Contacts in Hispania: The Latinization of the Iberian Peninsula

The spread of Latin in the Iberian Peninsula was a sociolinguistically complex process that advanced at different rates in each region (Beltrán Llorís 2005; Díaz Ariño et al. 2019; Luján 2024). Contact with Latin speakers via trade and diplomatic missions preceded the arrival of Roman troops in 218 BC as Rome tried to counteract Carthage's growing influence over the Western Mediterranean. Occupation of the whole peninsula was not complete until two centuries later. Enhanced motivation for the local populations to adopt and eventually shift to Latin obtained as Rome consolidated its political, legal, and cultural presence (*romanización*) and promoted the settlement of soldiers, merchants, and officials from various parts of Italy. This process was anything but a *tabula rasa* transplantation of Latin. Instead, the new settlers from Italy interacted with a remarkably diverse pre-conquest sociolinguistic landscape that we can partially reconstruct from a variety of sources, including comments by Greek and Roman historians, as well as epigraphic evidence (in funerary inscriptions, numismatic materials, and ceramics). These epigraphic remains showcase a variety of spelling systems: Latin, Greek and Punic alphabets, and several local systems combining syllabic and alphabetic elements collectively known as 'Paleohispanic' writing (Díaz Ariño et al. 2019; Lorrio and Sanmartí 2019; see this section below for an example).

The evidence suggests three major linguistic groups in pre-Roman Iberia: Celtic (IE), Iberian and Basque (both non-IE). The Celtic area spread over the center and north of the Iberian Peninsula. Iberian texts are found along the Mediterranean coast and the lower Ebro River valley. Along the eastern fringe of the central Iberian plateau, we find groups referred to as Celtiberians, linguistically Celtic but exhibiting idiosyncratic cultural and material characteristics. Basque (the only pre-Roman language not to be displaced by Latin) was spoken along the western Pyrenees area and in present-day southwestern France. In addition to these three major linguistic groups, the local linguistic landscape included Tartessian (also known as Turdetanian), a seemingly non-IE language in the southwestern area; Lusitanian, an IE language sharing elements with Celtic; and both Greek (IE) and Punic (Semitic), used in the Greek and Phoenician colonies along the Mediterranean and southern coasts, respectively (Lorrio and Sanmartí 2019). Map 3.1 outlines the distribution of these main pre-Roman linguistic areas, as well as several locations (in italics) in pre-Roman and Roman Iberia named in this chapter.

Questions linger concerning the linguistics of these groups, especially Iberians and Tartessians, whose texts have been transliterated but not deciphered.

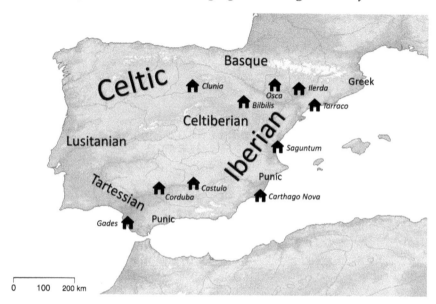

MAP 3.1. Reconstructed linguistic areas in pre-Roman Iberia and locations named in this chapter (map data by author, base map by Diotime, via Wikimedia Commons, license: https://creativecommons.org/licenses/by-sa/3.0/deed.en)

The relationship between Iberian and Basque, which were in contact long before the Roman invasion, is also debated. Observed lexical and structural similarities between Basque and forms in Iberian texts have been interpreted either as proof of a common original ancestor, or more commonly as the function of mutual borrowing and areal diffusion due to long-term contact (Orduña 2019).

By comparison to the pre-Roman period, the sociolinguistic record of the transplantation of Latin to the Iberian Peninsula is somewhat less murky. The outcome of this process is universally described as one of shift to Latin. Linguistic assimilation appears to have been quicker in the areas that were conquered first (the Mediterranean area, the lower Ebro valley, and the south). These areas received significant numbers of settlers from Italy, speaking Latin and possibly other closely related Italic varieties. They were also the areas where local populations were granted official recognition as Roman municipalities the earliest, and where Roman citizenship was more prevalent. For these areas, large-scale shift to Latin appears to have been complete as early as the end of the first century BC. Further inland, the process seems to have been slower and more sociolinguistically spotty, with indications that local languages continued to be spoken well into the first century AD. For instance, Tacitus writes about a Celtiberian farmer who murdered a Roman official in AD 25; when interrogated, he answered in Celtiberian (*sermōne patrio* 'native speech/language') (Adams 2003: 289). Some communities may have continued to use languages other than Latin even later, but besides a few anthroponyms and except for Basque, the historical record offers no clear evidence of them past the second century AD (Beltrán Lloris 2005).

The demographics of this period offer additional clues as to how these populations interacted. Recent tallies of the population of Roman Hispania in the beginning of the Christian era hover around 4 million. The south and the Mediterranean coast appear to have been more urbanized and more densely populated than other regions. Most of the population (as much as 75%) was rural, but higher densities were found alongside rivers and the trade routes that communicated cities, mining areas and commercial harbors (Sinner and Carreras 2019). Importantly, many of the urban centers founded during this period were co-located with or adjacent to earlier Hispanic settlements, such as Carthago Nova, Clunia, Corduba, Gades, or Tarraco (Sinner and Carreras 2019: 312; see Map 3.1). If so, it is reasonable to expect that these hybrid settlements would have provided opportunities for Iberian and non-Iberian populations to interact.

As Latin repertoires spread, bi/multilingualism appears to have been common, particularly in the cities along the Mediterranean coast and the Guadalquivir valley, where epigraphic remains give proof of hybrid linguistic practices. For instance, cities like Saguntum (present-day Sagunto) minted coins with bilingual legends in Latin and Iberian. Bilingual inscriptions, including also occasional Greek and Punic elements, can also be found in cities like Tarraco (Tarragona) and Castulo (near Linares). Figure 3.3 shows two such bilingual/biscriptal inscriptions, where the non-Latin part is Iberian in Paleohispanic script.

FIGURE 3.3. Iberian (Paleohispanic)-Latin bilingual and biscriptal inscriptions from Tarraco (Díaz Ariño et al. 2019: 408, courtesy of authors)

Further inland, the Latin-script Celtiberian inscriptions from the Peñalba de Villastar sanctuary (in present-day Teruel) include several Latin loanwords and even a line from Virgil's *Aeneid* (Díaz Ariño et al. 2019: 411), providing a tantalizing testimony of some of the contexts in which local populations were exposed to Latin. The overall picture emerging from this epigraphic record is that of a multilingual cultural environment where Indigenous populations became increasingly exposed not just to Latin but also to Roman cultural institutions, literacy, and literature.

The overall pattern in the spread of Latin proficiencies appears to have been gravitational (from the larger towns into the rural areas) and geographical (from east and south to west and north; Beltrán Lloris 2005: 91–8), but this pattern must have interacted with a broad array of individual contexts and motivations for language learning. For some, contact must have started early in life, as in the case of children born to mixed unions between Roman soldiers and Hispanic women. For instance, in 171 BC, the citizens of the Punic city of Carteia (in the vicinity of present-day Gibraltar) petitioned the Roman Senate to be conferred the status of landowners (*colōni*) since, as the children of Italian soldiers and Punic women, they could not enjoy the full benefits of Roman citizenship. For other young learners, exposure to Latin seems to have occurred in more public settings: for instance, an academy was founded in Osca, present-day Huesca, in the first century BC to teach Latin and Greek to the children of the local Iberian élites (Díaz Ariño 2019: 402, 405–6).

Contacts outside the family or one's immediate ethnic group across the lifespan also played a role, especially whenever proficiency in Latin offered economic or cultural advantages. As many speakers' commercial and cultural networks became connected to other areas in the Peninsula and across the empire, interaction in Latin must have been progressively favored. New institutions also created conditions favorable for language learning. For instance, the Roman military comprised a plurilingual force where acquisition of Latin provided a necessary means of interethnic communication. Slavery was another instrumental institution: slaves were often Indigenous captives of military campaigns, and their integration into Latin-speaking households further disrupted the traditional ecologies of pre-Roman Hispania (Adams 2003: 760–3). The attainment of Roman citizenship, granted to at least a half a million individuals in the Iberian Peninsula (Beltrán Lloris 2005: 95), must also have motivated many to acquire elements of Latin given its use in the process to obtain citizenship (Adams 2003: 560–2).

The extant evidence also affords us glimpses into the symbolic dimension of this process. A well-known witness is the Bronze of Ascoli, a tablet dated 89 BC honoring the *turma salluitana*, an Iberian military unit, reproduced in Figure 3.4. The tablet lists the cities of provenance of the members of the *turma* in the Ebro River valley. All names are presented following the formula *x y f(ilius)* 'x son of y'. For most son-father pairs on the tablet, both names are Iberian. Interestingly, a few of the sons carry Iberian names with Latinate endings (*Sosimulus, Elandus*), and for the three name entries from Ilerda, the fathers' names are Iberian but the sons' are Latin (e.g. *Q. OTACILIVS SUISETARTEN F* 'Q[uintus?] Otacilius, son of Suisetarten'). This generational difference suggests a shift in ethnolinguistic

FIGURE 3.4. The Bronze of Ascoli (Papix via Wikimedia Commons, license: https://www.gnu.org/licenses/fdl-1.3.html)

allegiance in these families (Adams 2003: 281). Indications of similar changes can be seen elsewhere: for instance, a tomb in Torreparedones (central Andalusia), dated first century BC to first century AD, contains the remains of several generations of the same family. The oldest names are Iberian. By contrast, the more recent names combine Iberian and Latin elements, and follow Latin onomastic formulae (Díaz Ariño et al. 2019: 402).

Latin poet Martial, born in the Celtiberian town of Bilbilis, provides an eloquent example of the correlation between large-scale linguistic assimilation and shifts in ethnolinguistic allegiance. In one of his poems, dated AD 88–9, he introduces several indigenous toponyms of Roman Hispania with these words: 'Let us, born from Celts and Iberians, be unashamed to recall in grateful verse the harsher [place] names of our country' (quoted in Díaz Ariño et al. 2019: 415–6). This literary vindication confirms that, as of the late first century AD, many already looked down on local non-Latin linguistic elements and the identities they symbolized as unsophisticated and undesirable.

3.5. Linguistic outcomes of the spread of Latin in Hispania

In this environment of cultural and linguistic assimilation, individual speakers were motivated to create innovative repertoires incorporating elements of the various pools to which they had access. While indigenous languages were still used, incorporation of Latin elements must have occurred: epigraphic materials sometimes seem to offer evidence of semantic or structural calques from Latin (for instance, in the lower inscription in Figure 3.3, the expression *aretake/ areteki*, commonly found in Iberian epigraphy, is possibly a calque from Latin *heic est situs* 'is placed here', Díaz Ariño et al. 2019: 408). Similarly, inscriptions in pre-Roman languages incorporate morphological or otherwise structural elements borrowed or modelled after Latin. For instance, some Celtiberian inscriptions combine indigenous anthroponyms with Latin genitive endings and the 'x son of y' formula calqued from Latin but using the Celtic word *gente/kenti* 'son' (Adams 2003: 282). The general picture emerging from these (very fragmentary) records is that, before large-scale shift to Latin, speakers of pre-Roman languages adapted their local linguistic resources to express the new cultural frames brought in by the Roman masters (as in the case of family relations).

Because of the overall power balance shift in favor of Roman culture, the long-term result of contact during this period largely implied recombination (§2.5) toward forms of Latin. The sociolinguistic context of Roman Hispania has been of interest to historical accounts of Spanish inasmuch as some elements distinguishing Spanish from other Romance varieties may be traced back to contact processes during the Roman period. Did the local conditions of contact favor local selections that differed from those in other repertoires across the Roman dominion? And can some of the selections preserved diachronically in Spanish be attributed to the L2 learning of Latin Indigenous speakers?

In relation to the first question, several authors (Clements 2009: 28–36; Penny 2002: 8–14) have described the local variety of Latin as archaic and conservative. In this view, the fact that Hispania was among the first territories outside Italy to be settled by the Romans, combined with its remoteness, caused local users of Latin to either preserve terms that fell out of fashion elsewhere (see *founder effect,* Mufwene 2001) or to not adopt innovations that diffused elsewhere across the empire. According to this thesis, the social networks of speakers in Roman Hispania were largely oriented inwards, with little contact with other Roman provinces.

Adams (2007) has assessed this hypothesis by combing through a vast diachronic body of written Latin covering the whole Roman and early medieval periods. The results are mixed: some items do seem to have largely disappeared from Latin after the period when the Iberian Peninsula was settled (e.g. *cūius/a/um* 'whose' in its use as a possessive adjective, see Sp. *cuyo/a*, with reflexes also in Port. *cujo/a* but nowhere else except Sardinian). Likewise, some items used only in Spanish or shared exclusively with nearby varieties do seem to have been privative of regional spoken Latin, for instance *thius* 'uncle' (see Sp., Port. *tío*, It. *zio*, Sard. *tiu-ziu*, compare to Fr. *oncle* or Rom. *unchio* < Lat. *āvunculus*) or *māneāna* 'tomorrow' (see Sp. *mañana* and Port. *amanhã* vs. Cat. *demá*, Fr. *demain*, It. *domani*, Sard. *cras*, Rom. *mâine*), suggesting local innovations (see Map 3.2). But other forms commonly cited as evidence of a local trend toward archaism or conservatism can be found elsewhere. For instance, reflexes of *vacīuus* (Sp. *vacío* 'empty') appear in regional dialects of French and Italian. Forms derived from *fābulor* 'to chat' (Sp. *hablar*) are present in Provençal, several Italian dialects and Sardinian. Based on this evidence, Adams concludes that there is some evidence for local dialectal uses, but '[i]t cannot ... be demonstrated that there is a significant element of archaic Latin reflected in Ibero-Romance' (2007: 399), or that speakers of Hispanic Latin remained completely isolated from innovations originating in other areas of the Roman world.

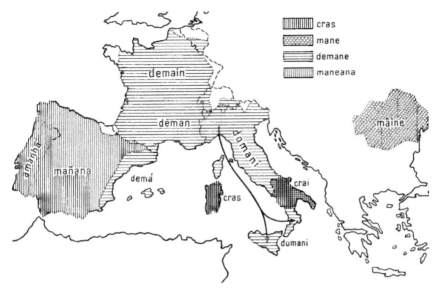

MAP 3.2. Distribution of four spoken Latin reflexes for 'tomorrow' in present-day Romance (Rohlfs 1954, map 14; public domain)

The influence of processes of non-native learning on the emergence of local Latin pools is even more controversial. As noted (§3.4), the sociohistorical evidence strongly suggests that local varieties of Latin evolved in a context where many speakers had pervasive access to or produced L2 features. An early strand of literature located contact effects from Italic languages like Oscan and Umbrian in the Latin spoken by the first Roman settlers of Hispania (Lapesa 1981: 90–6), but the linguistic evidence for this theory is rather flimsy (Adams 2007: 403–21). In a more commonly quoted scenario, speakers of pre-Roman Hispanic languages shifting to Latin introduced elements into the emerging local vernaculars that eventually came to define the emerging Romance varieties of the Iberian Peninsula (Clements 2009: 28–35; Echenique Elizondo 2003; Lapesa 1981: 35–48; Luján 2024), a thesis fully in line with the *stratum* tradition (§3.2). The following (4a–e) are among the features that these sources have attributed to transfer from indigenous languages, mostly Celtic (for Basque influence, §3.8):

(4a) Lexical items lacking a Latin etymology, including *barro* 'mud', *cama* 'bed', *cerveza* 'beer', *morcilla* 'blood sausage', *losa* 'slate/stone plank', *páramo* 'high plain' and *perro* 'dog'

(4b) Typologically unusual phonological elements among Romance languages, such as the contrast between two rhotics: /ɾ/ and /r/ (as in *foro* 'forum' vs. *forro* 'wrap')

(4c) Lenition of intervocalic plosives (*prātu(m)* > *prado* 'field') and palatalization of [kt, ks] > [tʃ, ʃ] (Lat. *nocte(m)* > Sp. *no[tʃ]e* 'night'; Lat. *laxāre* > med. Sp. *le[ʃ]ar* 'to loosen')

(4d) Plural of masculine nouns in *-o* > *-os*, instead of *-i* (from Latin 2nd declension)

(4e) Denominal adjectival suffixes like *-arro/-orro* (*machorro* 'macho man'), and *-iego* (*andariego* 'wandering')

Besides the fact that our knowledge of the linguistics of pre-Roman languages is rather faulty, one of the problems in gauging these substrate claims is that the Roman-era documentary archive of bilingual performance is virtually non-existent. The few textual witnesses of Latin produced by bilinguals in Hispania are very fragmentary and far less linguistically extensive than some of those found in other parts of the empire like Egypt or Gaul (Adams 2003). Except for a few of the lexical items noted in (4a) that happen to be attested in Roman-era texts and that do seem to be loanwords (see discussion of *lausia* > *losa* and *paramus* > *páramo* in Adams 2007: 423–6), most of these features are not recorded before the medieval period. Others, like (4d), have been explained as analogical options not requiring the action of L2 speakers (Penny 2002: 118–9).

And yet, what we know about the ecology of Roman Hispania (§3.4) makes it reasonable to hypothesize that language learners contributed innovative forms to their local pools. For instance, several authors have pointed out the overall geographical overlap between some Romance phenomena, most notably plosive lenition (feature 4c), and the recorded range of Celtic languages in western Europe (Clements 2009: 31–2; Martinet 1952). Local learners may have also boosted the frequency of forms already present in the contact pool that provided articulatory or processing advantages. For instance, lenition may be attributed to universal articulatory tendencies affecting intervocalic consonants rather than to non-native phonological interference (Smith 2020: 429–30).

In reality, both explanations (traditionally considered as examples of 'external' and 'internal' factors; §2.5) are not mutually exclusive. Specifically in connection to phonological features, we know that Latin in Hispania exhibited a distinctive local pronunciation: classical observers characterize speakers from Roman Spain as having strong, unsophisticated accents. For instance, emperor Hadrian, born in southern Spain, was described as *agrestius prōnuntians* 'pronouncing in a rough way' at the time of his arrival in Rome (Adams 2007: 231–3). It is legitimate to expect that mass assimilation to Latin resulted in innovative accentual and articulatory patterns among the local Hispanic population, as happened in other regions of the empire where undesirable accents are explicitly presented as a function of L2 learning (most notably Greeks, Adams 2003: 432–7). As luck would have it, epigraphic evidence from a bilingual pottery corpus found at the La Graufesenque site in southern France (first century AD) shows that Celtic-Latin bilinguals produced forms that deviated phonologically from those typical of non-bilinguals (for instance, the Greek loanword in Latin *paropsides* 'desert dishes' appears as *paraxidi*, suggesting a Celtic articulation of [ps] as velar [x], see Adams 2003: 438–9). As predicted by acquisitionally informed models of language contact (§2.6), in a context where individuals were exposed to many forms of speaking, phonological options offering acquisitional advantages and demographically frequent as non-native approximations would have been primary targets for selection.

The acquisitional advantages that some options in this variable input may have offered various kinds of speaker-learners may also account for the spread of grammatical features. Recall that, in situations of pervasive contact, options that are easier to process cognitively may have a built-in advantage (Aalberse et al. 2019; Clements 2009; §2.6). This kind of effect does not require transfer from an existing structure in the local population's original feature pool and is therefore not what linguists usually have in mind when speaking of substrates. The evolution of word order during the Latin period constitutes an intriguing area to explore the contribution of these learner strategies to diachronic change.

The historical corpus of Latin shows a clear move from variable but default SOV (subject-object-verb) orders toward more frequent SVO constructions throughout the Roman period (Bauer 2009), anticipating the syntax of Romance languages. Compare SOV in (5), where the object is before the verb, with SVO in (6):

(5) Virgil's *Aeneid*, Book 3 (first century BC):
Fāta   viam   invenient
fate-NOM.PL way-ACC.SG   find-3PL.FUT.IND
'The fates will find (their) way'.

(6) *Itinerārium Aetheriae*, Part 1 (fourth century AD)
Nam invēni   ibī   aliquam   amīcissimam   mihi
So find-1SG.PRET   there some-ACC.SG   dear friend-ACC.SG of mine
'And I found there a very dear friend of mine'.

Bentz and Christiansen (2015) have suggested that the generalization of SVO in late spoken Latin was the result of L2 learner strategies. In this proposal, the grammar of pre-classical Latin, which included rich inflectional marking in the form of case endings and flexible (but default) SOV order, was acquisitionally challenging at two levels: it involved the learning of a large amount of morphological material (case endings), and it required two-way cognitively high-cost operations to ensure morphological agreement and syntactic role assignment between the verb and other sentence constituents (nominative morphology for the subject, accusative morphology for the object, and so forth). The authors point out that the simplification of nominal inflection is historically parallel to the generalization of SVO orders and submit that this parallelism can be explained as a function of L2 processing strategies. In their view, SVO was cognitively advantageous for non-native speakers because it eliminated the need to back-project the syntactic role from the verb onto the object, allowing all sentence constituents to be processed left-to-right and rendering much of the original inflectional marking unnecessary. In this scenario, the large numbers of non-native speakers in many regions of the Roman domain tipped the frequency scale in favor of SVO diachronically.

While this explanation is a good fit for the available sociohistorical record on the expansion of Latin, additional factors were likely at play, including the phonological and morphological variability of the input. Case marking, already variable in the earliest texts in Latin, appears to have become increasingly unstable as time went by. This instability included the accusative (*-am* in v*iam*, *aliquam amīcissimam* in 5 and 6) – a critical case to mark subject vs. object distinctions in Latin, which speakers progressively extended into the functions of the nominative (Adams 2013: 201–56). Vowel contrasts, another cornerstone of the inflectional system, were also a primary area of variation in spoken Latin (Adams 2013: 37–70; Clackson 2016). Increased variability due to non-native learning can be expected to have contributed to an even more diffuse (§2.6) pool for the acquisition of case distinctions in the Roman provinces. For the speakers in these provincial populations, linguistic models based on the norms of the educated élites eventually became inaccessible or irrelevant. Instead, the selection of structurally transparent, cognitively simpler options can be interpreted as a diachronic effect of acquisition in sociolinguistically diverse environments (see *multiple causation*, §2.5), as will be seen repeatedly throughout this book.

3.6. After Rome: Looking for the roots of Romance varieties

The breakdown of the Western Roman Empire is usually seen as a watershed event in the external history of Europe, but it was actually a centuries-long process with much earlier social, economic, and cultural roots. By the time child emperor Romulus Augustulus was deposed by the new Germanic leader of Italy in AD 476, the Iberian Peninsula had been under the military control of Germanic (Suebi, Vandals) and Iranian (Alani) groups for decades. In the fifth century, another Germanic tribe, the Visigoths, entered the Peninsula from eastern Europe and subdued the previous chiefdoms. After seizing the areas held by the Byzantines in the south, the Visigoths came to rule most of the Iberian Peninsula by the early seventh century. This rule came to a sudden end in 711, when Muslim troops (mostly Berbers under Arab leadership) crossed the straits of Gibraltar, advancing to the foothills of the Pyrenees in just a few years. The newcomers either failed or did not care to control the regions north of the Cantabrian mountains, where a series of Christian kingdoms emerged and eventually challenged Islamic control of the areas to the south starting in the ninth and tenth centuries.

The events in this (very summarized) history of early medieval Iberia are familiar ingredients in the historiography of the Spanish language. The underlying assumption is that these geopolitical shifts operated as sociolinguistic milestones because they brought about social and cultural changes leading to the emergence (or, in the traditional historical metaphor, the 'birth') of the language (§1.2). This assumption is ultimately anchored in the teleological approach shared by early modern language discourses and some of the more recent work in the historical linguistics of Spanish. Recall that Nebrija already framed the manifest destiny of Castile and its language as the core of the new Spanish nation against the backdrop of the fall of the Roman Empire and the rise of the Christian kingdoms (§3.1). As discussed in Chapter 1, these same external events continue to make frequent cameos in historical accounts of Spanish as key steps in its growth as a linguistic entity. And yet, as momentous as all these military campaigns and border fluctuations may seem in a *language from above* (Elspass 2007) perspective, they are only ecologically significant insofar as they can be shown to have altered the conditions of communication and learning for speakers in the late Roman and early medieval Iberian Peninsula.

Several of these political shifts evidently triggered social and cultural changes with far-reaching ramifications for language use. For instance, the Muslim invasion has been said to have had 'enormous linguistic consequences' (Penny 2002: 16). Not only did it usher in a new ruling class and a new religion, but also settlers from northern Africa and, more critically, a new sociopolitical hierarchy symbolized by various forms of Arabic. Crucially, the same as the Romans, Muslim rulers were never able to get a firm grip on the northern fringe of the Peninsula, including the Basque area. What seems to have resulted in this area was an environment where speakers of late Hispanic Latin (or early Romance, whichever denomination one prefers) continued to use or be in close contact with Basque, a fact that may have shaped their repertoires in significant ways (§3.8).

While some forms of language change can be linked to these geopolitical transformations, the historical record also gives evidence of sociocultural continuity between the Roman and the early medieval periods. For instance, archaeological evidence between the fifth and the tenth century exhibits remarkable material similarities in aspects like the structure of dwellings, food storage facilities, burial site arrangement, domestic objects, or construction techniques. The centuries-long use of the horseshoe arch in late Roman, Visigothic, and medieval (both Muslim and Christian) architecture (see Figure 3.5) provides a visually striking example. These cultural continuities suggest that many aspects of everyday life in the Iberian Peninsula remained relatively unchanged throughout this period (Vigil Escalera-Guirado and Quirós Castillo 2012). The goal, therefore, is to paint a picture of language evolution centered around the experience of the speakers rather than historical blocks of time based on political or military events.

FIGURE 3.5. Horseshoe arches in (1) Santa Eulalia de Bóveda (Lugo, fourth-fifth centuries), (2) San Juan de Baños (Palencia, seventh century) and (3) Jerez de la Frontera mosque (Cádiz, eleventh-twelfth centuries) (authors: (1) Potoma15, (2) Nelida a.c. and (3) Diego Delso; via Wikimedia Commons, licenses: (1) https://creativecommons.org/licenses/by/2.0/deed.en, (2) https://creativecommons.org/licenses/by-sa/3.0/deed.en, (3) https://creativecommons.org/licenses/by-sa/4.0/deed.en)

From a historical sociolinguistic perspective, this is a challenging endeavor. The demographic evidence and the archival record of everyday spoken language is spotty, and until the development of Romance-specific spelling traditions starting in the ninth-tenth centuries (Wright 2016), virtually all the earlier western Roman dominion continued to be pegged to the spelling of Latin. As a result, the available materials are often frustratingly opaque from a sociolinguistic perspective. These obstacles have shaped narratives of language change in ways that are perhaps more reflective of our ability to interpret the extant evidence than of the actual conditions of language variation and change during this period.

We can take the Visigothic period as an example. The roughly three centuries between the arrival of the Visigoths and the Muslim invasion have typically been either dismissed as a sort of vernacular language research black hole or acknowledged only as a harbinger of more linguistically consequential events. For instance, Lapesa (1981: 117–22) speaks of a 'primitive' Romance variety in the earliest ('incipient') stages of evolution, isolated from other Romance regions but already showing signs of unity. In this view, the everyday language of the Visigothic kingdom was a 'pre-Castilian Romance' (122). More recently, Ranson and Quesada have echoed the same perception: the Visigothic period was important 'for non-linguistic reasons', most notably the social detachment of the Iberian Peninsula from the rest of the Roman domain as well as the isolation of the Cantabrian region where Castilian eventually developed (2018: 51–2). Even Penny, who calls attention to sociolinguistic conditions leading to dialectal diversification in this period, characterizes it as a kind of archival 'dark ages' and describes the Visigothic kings' choice of Toledo as their capital as the one significant external event of this period because of the symbolic role that this city was to play during the southward expansion of Christian kingdoms (2002: 16; §3.7). In this prevalent line of thinking, the Visigothic years matter primarily as a linguistic prequel to the medieval era's unquestioned main act: the emergence of Castilian.

Contact-focused approaches to this period are concerned fundamentally with the introduction of Gothic elements to local repertoires, which is universally described as almost negligible (Dworkin 2012; Kremer 2005; Penny 2002: 14–6). It can be identified only in a few lexical incorporations (such as *banda* 'group of soldiers', *espía* 'spy', *estaca* 'stake', *ganso* 'goose', *rico* 'rich', *ropa* 'clothing', *sacar* 'to take out'). These differ from other Germanic loans in Iberian Romance attested in Latin texts or other Romance varieties, which therefore appear to stem from earlier contacts with Germanic-speaking peoples during the Roman period (as in *guerra* 'war' or *yelmo* 'helmet') (see Kremer 2005: 139 on the challenges involved in identifying the precise Germanic source of many of these items). Besides these loanwords, Visigothic influence is invoked to explain a few morphological features of limited historical productivity (e.g. nominal *-engo* 'descending from, pertaining to' from a hypothetical Germanic source *-ing/-ink*, as in Sp. *abolengo* 'ancestry', lit. 'pertaining to one's grandparents', *realengo* 'pertaining to the king') and a number of anthroponyms, some of which became popular in medieval Spain (for instance, *Álvaro*, *Elvira*, *Gonzalo*, *Rodrigo*). The paucity of Germanic (or specifically Visigothic) elements in Iberian Romance is in principle what we would expect from a situation where the newcomers were a minority, and the motivation for most of the population to incorporate elements indexical of this heritage was largely limited to elements that symbolized an association with the new ruling class, like *-engo* or the anthroponyms. As such, this Germanic-Visigothic component has been classified as a form of *superstrate*, that is, a layer of contact from a culturally or politically prominent minority without widespread bilingualism (Echenique Elizondo 2003: 618; §3.2).

While these elements were probably among the options negotiated by speakers of Visigothic Hispania, their retention in Spanish does not provide a real-time snapshot of the ecology of contact that they emerged from. Instead, it is the result of subsequent sociolinguistic negotiation. Consider the words for 'glove': medieval Spanish used to have a noun *lúa*, another likely Gothic loan (Kremer 2005: 139), seemingly a cognate of English *glove*, and still in current use in Portuguese as *luva*. In Spanish, the form was replaced by *guante* (another Germanic loan) and seems to have become obsolete by the sixteenth century: its most recent use in the CORDE historical corpus is from 1512 (Real Academia Española 2023). Its listing as a result of contact with Gothic is thus but a historical anecdote among other relics from Visigothic Hispania. But whether *lúa* and other elements of putative Gothic origin are still in use today says little about the sociolinguistics of the Iberian Peninsula during this period, and more about much later patterns of lexical selection (in other words, this is a genealogical issue; §1.2). Ecologically, the question is not whether the speakers of the Visigothic period contributed to the emergence of a Romance variety that they could not have possibly anticipated. Instead, we want to better understand which communication patterns developed during this period, and to which degree these contexts and their linguistic outcomes can be surmised from the extant evidence.

Information is scant, but we can reconstruct at least some of these environmental aspects. Demographic studies agree that, despite gaining the political and military upper hand in the fifth century, ethnic Visigoths were but a slim share of the population of post-Roman Hispania, probably just about 100-200,000 individuals over a total population of 6 to 10 million (Ripoll López 1989). Upon arrival, they settled in the north-central region of the Iberian Peninsula, between the Tagus and the Douro rivers, although other areas show evidence of later Visigothic settlement, especially in the northwest. These settlements appear to have brought about few changes to the overall demographic landscape of the Iberian Peninsula, which continued to be based on a handful of small urban centers amidst a mostly rural population (Vigil Escalera-Guirado and Quirós Castillo 2012). Initially an ethnically separate group, the Visigoths progressively merged with the local post-Roman Hispanic population: they officially renounced Arianism (a form of Christianity that rejected the divinity of Jesus), adopted Roman Catholicism, and came to be governed by the same legal code as the non-ethnically Visigothic majority by the mid-sixth century. Linguistically, by the time they entered the Iberian Peninsula in the early fifth century, Visigoths seem to have already been in contact with Latin and had either partially or completely shifted to it (Kremer 2005: 136–7).

Studying the sociolinguistics of contact during the Visigothic period is methodologically challenging. What has been preserved (church documents, royal proclamations, laws) is mostly in ecclesiastical or legal Latin and seems to be removed from more colloquial language (Barrett 2024). The one significant exception involves a corpus of more down-to-earth texts engraved on slate slabs from central Spain, mostly the current provinces of Cáceres, Salamanca and Ávila, dated between the second half of the sixth and the first half of the seventh centuries (Velázquez 2024; Velázquez Soriano 2004). Many such texts deal with prosaic transactions among local rural residents (land sales, promissory notes, donations, and even a few letters) and appear to be the work of *semiliterate* writers (§1.9) and therefore closer to the everyday sociolinguistics of most speakers than learned texts. Once deemed too paleographically obscure for linguistic analysis (Lapesa 1981: 118), these slabs have been recently reassessed as offering evidence of at least some features of the spoken language. An example is shown in Figure 3.6.

Consider the fragments in (7), from a letter where a landowner delivers harvesting orders to a subordinate (from the slab in Figure 3.6), and (8), part of a declaration of rights to a property.

(7) Late sixth century-early seventh century:

[Domno] Paulo Faustinus salute tuam / … em et rogo te domne ut comodo consu/[etum] facere est p(er) te ipsut oliba illa quollige, / [cur]a ut ipsos mancipios in iuramento / [coger]e debeas ut tibi fraudem non fa[cian]t illas cupas collige calas / [d]e cortices et sigilla de tuo anulo et uide / [ill]as tegolas cas astritas sunt de fibola quo/[modo] ego ipsas demisi.

'Faustinus to [master] Paul: I greet your [dignity] and ask you, sir, to pick the olives by yourself as is usually done. Remember to compel the slaves not to commit fraud against you under oath. Gather the cups, the strips of bark, and seal them with your ring. And make sure that the tiles, which have been fastened with a clamp, are left as I left them'.

(text from Velázquez Soriano 2004: 362–3; my translation)

(8) First half of the seventh century:

'Ego Vnigild(us) de locum Langa / Tomanca, dum uenisse ad loc[um] tu litigare ad domo Froilani, ego aduxsi teste ipse Froila, fraude ad do/mo Desideri, dum istare in dom(o) Desideri / fu(i)t ueniens Froila et dix(it) mici: 'leua, leuita, / et uadam(us) ad domo Busani et Fasteni'. / Sucisit fuim(us) ad domo Busani'.

'I, Unigildus, from the place called Langa Tomanca, when I had come to the place … to litigate at Froila's house, I brought Froila himself as a witness, because of the fraud at Desiderus's house. While I was in Desiderius's house, there came along Froila and he said to me: 'Get up, raise, and let us go to Busanus's and Fastenus's house'. So it transpired, we went to Busanus's house'.

(text from Velázquez Soriano 2004: 223; translation adapted from Adams 2013: 371)

For Barrett (2024), the deviations from earlier linguistic norms found in these texts are primarily in spelling, which he interprets as demonstrating the overall continuity of the written Latin norms of the late Roman period. But one can

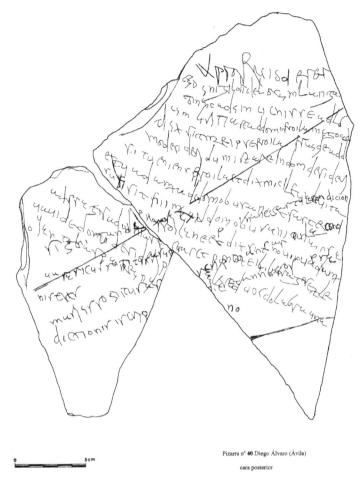

FIGURE 3.6. Visigothic slate slab (Velázquez Soriano 2004: 222, courtesy of author)

also find more innovative features here. On the one hand, some of these spelling deviations are likely linguistically motivated (the form *domne* in (7) points at a loss of the intertonic vowel in Latin *dom_i_ne*; and in (8), the initial vowel in *istare* suggests a prothetic vowel of the kind we see in Sp. *_e_star*). On the other, these texts contain several grammatical features of interest. For instance, in (7) many demonstratives appear to be used as something close to articles (*ipsos mancipios* 'those/the slaves', *illas cupas* 'those/the cups', *illas tegolas* 'those/the tiles'), pointing at the emergence of a new grammatical category in the local variety that had not been a part of the Latin feature pool: Romance definite articles (in Sp. *el, la, los, las*) are quite clearly derived from Latin historical demonstratives (Penny 2002: 145–6). In (8), the high proportion of prepositions (*ad domo* 'to the house', *de domo* 'from the house', *in domo* 'in the house', *de locum* 'from the place') stands in contrast even with late Latin texts, where some of these combinations were still expressed with inflectional morphology (Adams 2013:

257–320; 482–527). Both texts contain innovative uses of inflectional endings: for instance, in (7) the old accusative plural feminine ending *-as* is used in subject function (*c<u>as</u> astrit<u>as</u> sunt* 'which have been fastened'), which would have called for nominative *-ae* in normative Latin (§3.5), while in (8) the word *domo* appears with an invariable form (compare the form *ad domo* used in the text with normative *ad domum*). While we are not aware of the ethnic identity of the authors or the individuals mentioned in these texts, we do find several Germanic anthroponyms in (8) (*Vnigildus, Froila,* and possibly *Busani*), mixed with Latin ones (*Desideri*).

Sociolinguistically, it would be wrong to consider this corpus as simply an expression of rustic language in opposition to high-register texts (Velázquez 2024): many of these slabs contain religious or legal formulae (Velázquez Soriano 2004: 542), demonstrating that at least some of these speaker/writers in rural Visigothic central Spain were familiar with elements of learned culture. But other texts do exhibit features that continue or even enhance trends of sociolinguistic variation already attested in late Latin (§3.5), such as frequent departures from normative Latin case morphology or a preference for prepositional rather than inflectional marking. The high frequency of such features in these unlearned texts appears to be reflective of their generalization across the social space (Adams 2013: 371–5, 509–10). More importantly, these choices provide a linguistic parallel to the forms of social and cultural continuity observed between the late Roman and Visigothic sociolinguistic landscapes discussed above. For instance, whenever the texts stray away from legalistic formulae, the syntax is predominantly SVO (as in 8, 'ego (S) aduxsi (V) teste ipse Froila (O)'; Velázquez Soriano 2004: 542–4), confirming the preference for this arrangement as the unmarked word order following the centuries of contact that had fed into the local vernaculars. These texts also contain at least some elements of clear Germanic origin (such as anthroponyms), demonstrating their adoption during this period well beyond the ethnic Visigothic population.

Texts such as these might prove unfulfilling to those looking to use them to trace the emergence of specifically 'Castilian' (or, for that matter, 'Spanish' features). But they do contain many valuable indications of at least some forms of social and dialectal variation specific to the language of the Visigothic period. From a historical ecological perspective, they are a powerful reminder that we may study the sociolinguistics of this period in its own right.

3.7. Later medieval contacts: Birthing Castilian

The roughly 500-year period between the earliest extant texts classified as Romance in the Iberian Peninsula, usually dated in the second half of the tenth century (and first studied extensively by Menéndez Pidal in *Orígenes*; §1.2), and the beginning of the Spanish colonial enterprise in the Americas in the late fifth century saw several remarkable geopolitical shifts. Many were connected to the *Reconquista*, the southward military expansion of the northern Christian polities traditionally considered the political and cultural successors of the Visigothic kingdom. These included initially Asturias-Leon and Navarre, and a series of small Aragonese and Catalan counties along the Pyrenees that eventually merged as the Crown of Aragon. Two additional units split from Asturias-Leon on its western and eastern flanks, respectively: Portugal and Castile. Following the definitive union of Leon and Castile in 1230, only Portugal, Aragon and Castile continued the annexation of Muslim territories, with Castile taking the lion's share of these territorial gains. Portuguese and Aragonese expansion ended in the thirteenth century, whereas Castile continued its territorial growth until the seizing of the kingdom of Granada in 1492, just a few months before Nebrija published his *Gramática* (§3.1). While maps of this process (see Map 3.3 – note that the national borders shown in this map are present-day ones) usually suggest a steady progression in this southward expansion, in reality periods of sweeping Christian territorial gains alternated with others when the border between Muslim and Christian land did not move or even retreated.

This period has been featured much more prominently in histories of the Spanish language than earlier centuries. From an interpretive point of view, this enhanced focus is understandable: the archival record is simply much richer and more representative. As a result, we generally have a comparatively much better grasp of what was going on sociolinguistically in, say, thirteenth-century Castile than in the Visigothic capital of Toledo in the sixth century. This more abundant corpus reveals complex patterns of sociolinguistic diversity that resist being reduced to modern dialect or language categories, and which were associated to (but not coterminous with) the political division between Christian and Muslim areas.

For instance, after the emergence of Romance-specific spelling traditions in the eleventh century, the Christian polities have been described as *diglossic* societies where (besides Basque) varieties of spoken Romance were used for

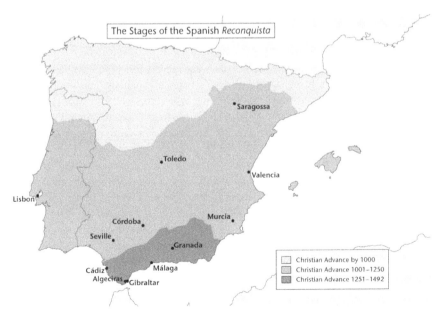

MAP 3.3. Chronological progression of the *Reconquista* (© PBS Learning Media 2015)

everyday communication, and Latin was initially still the preferred language in most forms of writing (Wright 2016). In the Muslim territories (*Al-Andalus*), the local linguistic ecology included, at minimum, Classical Arabic as a learned and ritual language, spoken Arabic, Berber as used by settlers from northern Africa, and the Romance varieties that continued evolving from those of the Visigothic period, referred to as *Mozarabic* or *romanandalusí* (Beale-Rivaya 2011; Minervini 2024) and best exemplified in the refrains to bilingual Arabic-Mozarabic poetic compositions (*jarchas* or *kharjahs*; Galmés de Fuentes 1994). In both Christian and Muslim territories, these environments were dynamic. In the Muslim territories, romanandalusí appears to have been largely abandoned in favor of spoken Arabic by the twelfth century (Beale-Rivaya 2011). In the Christian-controlled areas, Romance varieties progressively started being used in some forms of writing at the expense of Latin, blurring the earlier diglossic opposition; for instance, Castilian started being used in learned written registers since the reigns of Fernando III and Alfonso X in the thirteenth century (López Izquierdo 2024).

In both areas, social networks brought speakers in contact with yet additional pools. For instance, Jewish communities in both Christian and Muslim territories used Hebrew as a liturgical language; and French merchants setting up shop along the pilgrimage route connecting the Pyrenees with the shrine of Saint James in Galicia (*Camino de Santiago*) imported their Gallo-Romance features. Significantly, the border between Christian and Muslim territories was porous in times of both war and peace. In the learned centers of both areas, scribes translated Arabic, Hebrew, and Greek texts into Latin and Romance, and vice versa. Some of the linguistic consequences of these medieval multilingual ecologies are undeniable: the best-known case concerns the incorporation of hundreds of Arabic lexical items into the Romance pools of both areas (Giménez-Eguíbar 2024; §2.5), many of which can be located already in medieval texts and are still in use in Spanish, Portuguese, and Catalan.

The comparative robustness of the archival record for this period is not the only reason for its prominent position in histories of Spanish. The Reconquista has generally been understood as the time when Iberian Romance varieties accrued their defining characteristics, both linguistically and dialectally (Lapesa 1981: 163–253; Lleal 1990). But language historians have also presented this era as foundational in the history of Spanish for reasons that are every bit as political and cultural as they are linguistic: the southward advance of the Christian kingdoms, the geopolitical hegemony of Castile and the development of written registers in Castilian are all seen as critical to the emergence of Spanish as a national language (Penny 2002: 16–20). In turn, this process has often been naturalized as the manifestation of a form of sociocultural distinctiveness that made Castilian a symbol of competitiveness and overall sociocultural allure in medieval Spain: 'Castile, politically rebellious and ambitious, legally revolutionary, epically heroic, was the most innovative region linguistically' (Lapesa 1981: 165); '[f]rom the beginning, Castilian had a different personality than the other surrounding varieties' (Moreno Fernández 2015a: 32). This is a clear recasting of Menéndez Pidal's ideas on the essential expansive nature of Castilian ('nota diferencial castellana'), expressed in the innovative nature of its features as symbolic of Castilian identity (1950: 513; §1.2). Even less ideologically explicit approaches to language change in medieval Spain often present Castilian as an idiosyncratic variety that stood out linguistically among other, more conservative dialects (Lleal 1990: 167; Penny 2002: 18).

Historical grammars of Spanish have often tacitly shared in the consensus that this is a critical period in the development of the language. Even several recent textbooks (Núñez Méndez 2012; Pharies 2015; Ranson and Quesada 2018; Resnick and Hammond 2011) pay much more attention to the presentation of the phonological and grammatical processes taking place in medieval Spain than to those recorded for any other sociolinguistic context in the 500 years that followed (although some recent sociolinguistically informed panoramic contributions, like Eckkrammer 2021 and Dworkin et al. 2024, have adopted a more balanced view). Many of these historical grammar accounts are ultimately consistent with the language-as-organism lens, where the political and cultural history of Castile in the medieval period holds the key to understanding the organism's birth and development into adulthood, just like a person's youth is usually seen as a foundational time in their life (§1.2). Again, we are presented with a genealogical approach to language history: an ecological perspective can help us gain a more sociolinguistically accurate perspective.

3.8. Reconciling sociolinguistic and linguistic evidence in medieval Castilian

In much of the literature on medieval Castilian, the demographic resettlement of northern Christian populations into previously Muslim-held territory is assigned a primary sociolinguistic role. Menéndez Pidal articulated an influential image of this process of geographical expansion in *Orígenes del español* (1950; §1.2). He sketched the idea of a dialect spreading like an oil leak south and sideways from its original source in the Cantabrian region in a wedge-like (*cuña*) pattern, cornering other varieties (Galician, Portuguese, Astur-Leonese, Aragonese, Catalan) into the fringes of the Peninsula, and absorbing whatever was left of the Romance dialects of Muslim Iberia, as shown in Map 3.4. This narrative did allow some room for contact effects. For instance, the early Castilian dialect is said to owe some of its most distinctive traits to bilingual learning in Basque and Romance (among others, the five-vowel phonological system and the articulation of word-initial Latin /f-/ as [h]: Lat. *filiu(m)* > medieval Sp. [ˈhiʒo]). It also involved the selection of features from the northern Iberian continuum pool (§1.4 and §2.3), including the dipthongs /we, je/ from late Latin /ɔ, ɛ/, as in *puerta* 'door', *piedra* 'stone' vs. other dipthongized and monophthongal alternatives. In Menéndez Pidal's view, these features were selected precisely because of their association with the up-and-coming Castilian identity (§3.7). Sociolinguistic contact in this scenario was ultimately subordinate to the assumed cultural advantages offered by Castilian forms.

While echoes of this vision can still be felt in the historical discourse on medieval Spain, the reality is likely to have been more complex. Over the last two decades, sociolinguistically informed approaches to medieval Castilian have poked holes into the wedge narrative by articulating a more nuanced vision of the relationship between territorial expansion and language change

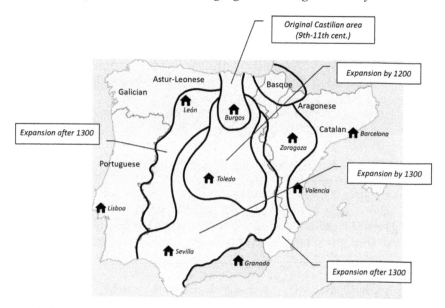

MAP 3.4. Menéndez Pidal's Castilian dialectal wedge (map data by author after Lapesa 1981: 184–5; base map by Gundan, via Wikimedia Commons, license: https://creativecommons.org/licenses/by-sa/4.0/deed.en)

in medieval Iberia (Fernández Ordóñez 2012a; Penny 2000, 2006). In these approaches, local patterns of settlement and contact were key triggers to the recorded linguistic results, rather than a casualty of the political expansion of Castile. For instance, Fernández Ordóñez (2012b, 2015) has pointed out that medieval archival data and twentieth-century dialectal surveys of the Iberian Peninsula reveal patterns of geographical diffusion along north-south or east-west axes that are a bad fit for the wedge model as the most prominent sociolinguistic explanation for the emergence of Castilian and for internal dialectal variation across Castilian varieties.

A remarkable contribution to this line of inquiry was Tuten (2003), who applied the koinéization via dialect contact model (§2.6) to the development of medieval Castilian (see also Tuten 2024). In this proposal, speakers of varied provenance applied the same general age-dependent language learning processes observed in other dialect contact situations: adult learners accommodated (§2.3) toward frequent forms that allowed them to reduce communicative distance in a context of dialect mixture, whereas children found some forms acquisitionally advantageous on the grounds of frequency or structural simplicity. The result, Tuten argues, was a series of stages of dialectal leveling corresponding to three phases of demographic resettlement: the Burgos phase (ninth-tenth centuries), the Toledo phase (eleventh-twelfth centuries), and the Seville phase (thirteenth century). In this model, the evolution of medieval Castilian pools should not be attributed to the prestige or putative vitality of Castilian features. Instead, it was the behavior of individual speakers as language users and learners in an environment of demographic mixture that determined the outcome of contact.

By way of illustration, consider the data in Tables 3.2, 3.3 and 3.4, which present some of the reconstructed dialectal input and the corresponding attested results at each of these stages.

TABLE 3.2. Definite articles in Leonese, northern Castilian and Aragonese vs post-Burgos Castilian (Tuten 2003: 117)

	Leonese	Northern Castilian	Aragonese	Castilian (post-Burgos)
MASC.SG	ele, elo, el, le, l, lo, llo	el, elo	lo, o, elo, el, ero, ro	el
FEM. SG	ela, lla	la, ela, l'	la, a, ela, era, ra	la, el
MASC.PL	elos, llos	los	los, os, elos, eros, ros	los
FEM.PL	elas, llas	las	las, as, elas, eras, ras	las

TABLE 3.3. Pre- and post-Toledo singular possessive adjectives (Tuten 2003: 204–12)

	Pre-Toledo		Post-Toledo	
	Masculine referent	Feminine referent	Masculine referent	Feminine referent
1SG	mio	mía, mi	mio	mi
2SG	to, tuo	túa, túe, tu	tu	
3SG	so, suo	súa, súe, su	su	

TABLE 3.4. Pre- and post-Seville 1SG possessive adjectives (Tuten 2003: 238–42)

Pre-Seville		Post-Seville
Masculine referent	Feminine referent	Masculine + feminine referent
mio	mi	mi

This data reveals various forms of systemic simplification via the reduction or elimination of allomorphy. Table 3.2 shows how Burgos-phase speakers settled the very diffuse range of articles they received from dialectal areas like Leon, Aragon, and northern Castile in favor of a much more restricted paradigm, with only one form for each gender-number pairing (except in the feminine singular). In Table 3.3, the marked allomorphy in the singular possessive adjectives typical of the documents from the decades immediately before the resettlement of Toledo has been reduced to two forms in the 1SG, and only one for 2SG and 3SG. Lastly, Table 3.4 illustrates the elimination of the rule that distributed the two remaining 1SG possessive adjective allomorphs (*mio* and *mi*), yielding *mi* as the only form in the Seville phase. In all cases, the data evokes the action of speakers that created simpler systems (that is, with fewer morphological distinctions) out of the many possibilities they encountered in their respective ecologies, achieving both communicative and cognitive efficiency (§1.5 and §2.5).

This application of the dialect contact framework to medieval Castilian goes far beyond more traditional accounts to explain the observed sociolinguistic effects of demographic resettlement. However, attention to even more local environmental factors might help us make sense of portions of the linguistic record not fully explainable on the basis of a single sociolinguistic trigger. An example is the emergence of 3rd-person clitic systems, an area of pervasive variation in Spanish historically (§5.9 and §6.4 for later examples). Dialects across the northern Iberian continuum have generally preserved morphological markers for semantic distinctions active in Latin (number, case, and gender) but have also added new distinctions based on the antecedent (such as mass/count in Asturian, human/non-human in the Basque area). These options contrast with the systems used to the south across Castile, which do not display these innovations and which exhibit leveling across case distinctions. The simplest Castilian version marks only semantic differences, with no morphological case marking. To illustrate these differences, Table 3.5 presents one of the northern systems, and Table 3.6 presents the Castilian system in its most reduced form:

TABLE 3.5. Asturian third-person clitic system (Fernández Ordóñez 2012a: 83)

	COUNT				MASS	NEUTER
	SINGULAR		PLURAL			
	Masculine	Feminine	Masc.	Femin.	Masc/fem	
ACCUSATIVE	lu	la	los	las	lo	lo
DATIVE	y		yos		y	y

TABLE 3.6. Maximally reduced (semantically based) Castilian third-person clitic system (Penny 2000: 92)

	COUNT			MASS
SINGULAR		PLURAL		
Masculine	Feminine	Masculine	Feminine	
le	la	les~los	las	lo

Tuten (2003: 173–203) interpreted these reductions as yet another manifestation of the koinéization process in the Toledo stage. Fernández Ordóñez (2012a) relied on social network theory (§2.6) to attribute these differences between the Castilian and the northern systems to language learning patterns in different social environments: in areas with tight social networks (as in the north), speakers may produce innovations that involve systemic complexification, whereas in areas with loose social networks (as in the demographic rearrangement accompanying the resettlement of Castile), they are more likely to prefer simpler options. How quickly this dialectal leveling progressed is also the object of debate: Sánchez-Prieto Borja and Vázquez Balonga (2018) have located counterexamples to the reduced Castilian system in medieval Toledo, which they attribute to a slower process of dialectal focusing than Tuten (2003) envisioned.

Surprisingly, however, the system that developed in Andalusia after the thirteenth century (Tuten's third dialect contact phase around Seville) restored the case distinction that eroded away in the Toledo phase – an unexpected outcome if one assumes that dialect contact situations should result in simplification. This system is featured in Table 3.7.

TABLE 3.7. Case-based (Andalusian) third-person clitic system (based on Penny 2000: 91)

	SINGULAR		PLURAL	
	Masculine	Feminine	Masculine	Feminine
ACCUSATIVE	lo	la	los	las
DATIVE		le		les

Both Tuten (2003: 242–5) and Fernández Ordóñez (2012a: 99) explain this outcome as a function of the local demographic mix in the south, which appears to have included high proportions of settlers from areas (Galicia, Asturias, León, Cuenca) where the case distinction was stable.

In a complementary account, Sanz-Sánchez and Tejedo-Herrero (2021) have called attention to the additional action of L1 speakers of non-Romance varieties, such as the varieties of Arabic not immediately displaced following the Castilian take-over. In their account, acquisition biases among adult non-native learners (of the kind overviewed in §2.6) played a critical role in the selection of the case-based clitic system. They find support for this hypothesis in the literature on the L2 acquisition of *module interfaces* (Sorace and Serratrice 2009), which argues that, all other things being equal, adult learners have an easier time acquiring elements that do not involve a grammatical interface than elements that do. They submit that the learning of the central Castilian clitic system, where syntactic case must be disambiguated semantically instead of being transparently represented in the input, posed an acquisitional challenge. This difficulty was compounded by the diffuseness of the input in an ethnolinguistically diverse environment. In these circumstances, individual learners reacted by selecting an option (the case-based clitic system) that posed advantages in demographic, structural and acquisitional terms.

Sociolinguistically and acquisitionally informed studies of medieval Spain remind us that our understanding of the dynamics of language change has much to gain from incorporating the cognitive principles and the communication routines that various kinds of individual learners (not just the linguistic majorities!) bring to the ecological table.

3.9. Conclusion

1492 may have felt like a consequential year to Nebrija and other fellow Castilians. Judging from the resounding military successes of Castilian troops, their kingdom's expansionist zeal, and the increasing prestige of Castilian among other languages of the Iberian Peninsula, one can hardly blame them. These signs of success, however, were but the result of an intricate historical web of geopolitical shifts, cultural exchanges and sociolinguistic rearrangements unfolding over the course of thousands of years. The various features that Nebrija codified in his *Gramática* as the embodiment of the new Spanish nation were only a few among the many linguistic outcomes of these historical interactions.

In this chapter, we revisited several of the ecologies usually included in genealogical accounts of the history of Spanish, dating back to Proto-Indo-European, passing through pre-Roman Hispania and Latin, the Visigothic kingdom, the Muslim period, and the Christian Reconquista. Rather than reproducing the traditional discourse that sees all these historical moments as connected by a thread of ancestral linguistic inheritance, the aim of the chapter has been to stress the inherent sociolinguistic diversity of each of these contexts. To do so, the chapter has foregrounded the processes of learning and negotiation via which speakers in these historically remote environments communicated with each other and contributed to their respective collective repertoires via a myriad of successive acts of recombination.

As the newly minted political unit called Spain initiated its colonial enterprise in the decades following 1492, bringing Europeans in contact with new communities and their languages, the assumed linguistic essence that Nebrija had in mind became even more questionable, and its cultural mythical nature even clearer.

Discussion questions

1. In §3.3, we explored how Indo-European languages can be seen to fit into specific sub-groups ('Germanic', 'Celtic', 'Italic', etc.), but we also quoted evidence for more convoluted patterns of contact among sub-groups or with non-Indo-European languages. Focusing on the role of *fragmentation* vs. *contact* will yield very different versions of the history of these languages. What other kinds of narrative (for instance, on ethnicity or nationality) could possibly be supported by each of these versions of history?

2. List the historical artifacts in the chapter giving evidence of bi/multilingual practices or forms of contact (e.g., multilingual inscriptions from the Roman era, Germanic anthroponyms on Visigothic slabs, Arabic-Mozarabic bilingual poetry, etc.). Are these bi/multilingual representations specific to their time periods, or do they share commonalities with present-day practices (for instance, are Mozarabic bilingual poems reminiscent of Spanish-English code-switching practices in today's reggaeton?)?

3. Historical models can help us make sense of historical data, but, inevitably, they also come with limitations. Consult Fernández Ordóñez (2012b and 2015), and the maps from the *Atlas Lingüístico de la Península Ibérica* (Navarro Tomás 1962; if your library does not own a copy, you may access some of the maps at http://www.alpi.csic.es/). Are any of the linguistic features charted or mapped in these sources a good fit for Menéndez Pidal's wedge idea (§3.8) of the spread of Castilian? Are any of them a bad fit? What might be the reasons why some linguistic features do (or do not) overlap with Menéndez Pidal's wedge?

4

Spanish Beyond Spain: Contact Ecologies in the Colonial Era

4.1. Introduction: Transplanting Spanish

In the years straddling the fifteenth and sixteenth centuries, populations all over the planet faced each other. Europeans had to face (or remember) the human beings that lived across the Atlantic, in Africa and in Asia; Indigenous populations in the Americas faced the presence of light-skinned people determined to exploit the natural and human resources of their land; sub-Saharan Africans faced an economic system that relied on their bodies and their blood to function; and Asian civilizations faced the arrival of traders and soldiers that saw them as producers of luxury articles and crops for far-away markets. Soon, a swarm of European ships crisscrossed the ocean transporting products, pathogens, slaves, and ideas, and life as these populations had known it was changed forever.

As Europeans attempted to grasp these new geographies, they turned to cartographers for help. In the beginning, many details were blurry: was there a quick passage connecting Florida and Japan? Was California an island? As new expeditions brought more clarity into this landscape of uncertainty, the cartographers' job became easier and their maps more accurate. Europeans also struggled to make sense of the people who inhabited these distant territories. The first Spanish expeditions brought back disturbing reports of grotesque, depraved creatures: one-eyed, one-legged, dog-faced humanoids; giants and Amazons; cannibals, sodomites, devil-worshippers. As time went by, tales about monstrous creatures became tales about monstrous people, and ideas about European cultural and moral superiority engendered new racial categories, legal systems, and ways of talking and writing about the colonial world that projected Western ideas of normalcy onto non-Westerners (Schwaller 2018).

One of the best-known products of this project of geographical and human cartography is *Civitates Orbis Terrarum*, a six-volume urban atlas published between 1572 and 1617 by German topographer Georg Braun and several collaborating engravers (Library of Congress 2023). It combined descriptions in Latin with colorful engravings displaying birds'-eye cityscapes and maps of over 500 cities from the known world. In these engravings, we also see a selection of characters donning outfits characteristic of each region, busy with everyday tasks: carrying wood, harvesting, fishing, dancing, chatting. We know that many of these details were intended as realistic portrayals because, in his introduction, Braun (somewhat naïvely) reassured his audience that the Turks would not be able to use these drawings to attack Europe's cities since, as Muslims, they would not dare to read a book that displayed human figures.

Perhaps unsurprisingly, most of the cities in *Civitates* are European. For the Americas, only two cities are selected: Mexico-Tenochtitlan and Cuzco, the old capitals of the Mexica and Inca empires respectively. The visual aspects of their presentations, based on previous accounts by European observers and shown in Figure 4.1, are intriguing. To be fair, a few details have a semblance of truth: Mexico, arranged around a central plaza, sits in the middle of a lake; Cuzco is at the foot of a fortress (likely the citadel of Saqsaywaman). Other details are harder to buy: there are towers with Gothic-style spires, defense walls are lined with medieval-looking battlements. We also cannot avoid noticing the people: Mexicas and Incas still inhabit these spaces, but unlike what was the case in the portrayals of Old World cities, they are not the real contemporary descendants of the pre-Columbian inhabitants. Mexica soldiers and aristocracy walk around wearing capes and feathers; and Inca soldiers sport Greco-Roman-looking outfits as they escort their ruler. What we see here is an approximation not to what sixteenth-century Mexico or Cuzco really looked like, but to the way Europeans must have imagined them: spaces of alterity, simultaneously historical and new, exotic and familiar, non-European and European, real and imagined at the same time. A construction designed to make sense to its audience.

Four hundred years later, we keep imagining the colonial world in ways that click with what we already know (by 'we', I am thinking specifically of Western audiences, but I'm aware that not every reader necessarily falls under

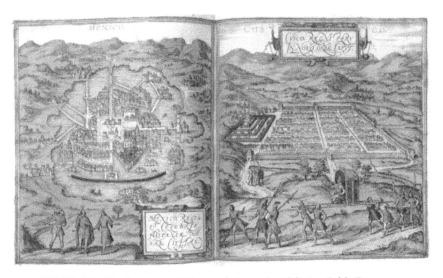

FIGURE 4.1. Mexico-Tenochtitlan and Cuzco in *Civitates Orbis Terrarum*, *Vol. 1* (ff. 58v–59r), 1572 (Library of Congress 2023, Geography and Map Division; public domain)

this umbrella). The spread of Spanish to the Western Hemisphere, for instance, has been presented as the colonial continuation of the familiar historical sequence that brought Castilian to political and linguistic supremacy in Spain (§1.2, §3.1), transplanting a growing language together with a growing culture: 'the men of Castile brought to America a reality that was shaped by their language' (Alvar 2000: 19). Once in the colonies, as the story goes, demographic and cultural contact changed Spanish, but its essence remained intact: '[i]n America and in Asia, across the immensity of the immeasurable territories, people from all regions of Spain came together, and their offspring and contact with the Indigenous peoples of each region and with the slaves brought from Africa gave life to the Spanish of the Americas' (Moreno Fernández 2015a: 87). While the historical details are complex, we are invited to think of this process as part of a larger chain of genealogical transmission where generations of speakers passed this centuries-long gift on to new speakers, modifying it, adapting it, supplementing it, but never altering its core character (Del Valle 2016).

And yet, as we survey the conditions in which speakers communicated and learned from each other across this vast colonial dominion, we are confronted with a heterogeneous landscape of experiences and voices that challenges this narrative of continuity and inheritance. What 'Spanish' became in the Americas meant very different things for different people, depending on whose perspective we take: the colonial officers in Lima, Santo Domingo, or Mexico-Tenochtitlan? The child growing up in a multilingual household, born to an Indigenous Quechua-speaking mother and a *mestizo* father? The West African slave sold to a new master in the harbors of the Caribbean? The Chinese trader setting up shop in Manila, selling goods to Spanish merchants and employing Tagalog workers? The question, therefore, is whether 'we' can conceive of these colonial language ecologies in new ways that do not take for granted the same vantage point as previous narratives… or whether, just like European map consumers of the sixteenth century, we are destined to keep looking at these historical experiences through the eyes of the linguistic myths that we have already become comfortable with.

Let's see what we can do. In this chapter, I survey several contact Spanish ecologies in the Americas and Asia between the 1500s and the 1800s. The chapter is structured as follows: I first (§4.2 and §4.3) focus on how several environmental conditions were instrumental in the emergence of new repertoires during roughly the first half of the Spanish American colonial period (until 1650), such as widespread non-native learning, new colonial social hierarchies, and contexts of interethnic communication. Some of the linguistic outcomes of these conditions are surveyed in §4.4. I then (§4.5 and §4.6) move on to the period after 1650, examining several factors that progressively altered these environments: the growth of colonial cities, economic diversification, and the role of the colonial borderlands as areas for linguistic negotiation. Some prominent linguistic effects of these changes are presented in §4.7. In §4.8, I focus on how Indigenous speakers negotiated the incorporation of elements of Spanish in their repertoires. To end the chapter, I survey some of the main sociolinguistic components of contact in the Spanish colonies in the western Pacific (§4.9), as well as their linguistic outcomes (§4.10). As elsewhere in the book, the goal is not to offer a comprehensive catalog of contact situations (for instance, contacts during the colonial era in northern Africa or Europe are not examined here), but to capture several salient trends in the sociolinguistic dynamics of this period and to provide a few illustrative examples.

4.2. Early colonial contacts in the Americas: Sociodemographic context

Early Spanish settlement in the Americas proceeded in roughly three stages: an early stage (1502–19) in the Caribbean; mainland expansion (1519–49), mostly in central Mexico and Peru, but also Paraguay, the River Plate and central Chile; and further expansion (after 1550) into northern Argentina, New Mexico, and Central America. Since the beginning, Spanish settlement targeted areas of high Indigenous population density and with potential for agricultural and mining activity, two preconditions for a colonial exploitative economy (Lockhart and Schwartz 1983: 86–92). Harbors on the Gulf of Mexico, the Caribbean, and the Pacific operated as transportation and commercial links between the American colonies and the Iberian Peninsula (and eventually southeast Asia, §4.9).

Coexistence and mutual adaptation among the ethnic groups in the early colonies were mediated, first and foremost, by their relative numerical proportions. Throughout the colonial period, Spain-born settlers were a small minority of the population. Many (but not all) came from southern Castile and Andalusia (Boyd-Bowman 1976). They were soon outnumbered by local-born *españoles* (individuals of Spanish descent perceived as ethnically European). Since the very beginning, this population of European origin interacted with a much larger Indigenous population. The importation of European pathogens to the Western Hemisphere and the environmental changes brought about by the system of economic exploitation instituted by the Spaniards led to catastrophic demographic losses among the Indigenous population in many areas (although estimates vary: for instance, for central Mexico, these losses have been calculated at anywhere between 35% and 90% of the pre-contact population, Ragsdale et al. 2019: 502). As an example, Table 4.1 presents a summary of the tax-paying and general population classified as Indigenous (*indios*) in colonial tallies for the territory corresponding to present-day Peru. As can be seen, a period of heavy losses was followed by relative stabilization starting in the mid-1600s, and partial recovery in the eighteenth century.

TABLE 4.1. Taxpayers and total Indigenous population in colonial Peru (Contreras Carranza 2020: 17)

Year	Taxpayers	Total Indigenous population
1561	269,336	1,164,434
1570	260,544	1,290,680
1573	241,046	n/a
1591	225,558	n/a
1620	136,235	671,505
1754	94,243	401,111
1793	141,248	619,190

As European pathogens and forced economic activities decimated the Indigenous population in many areas, African slaves were abducted and imported as substitute labor. Estimates typically put the number of slaves brought directly to Spanish America at between 1.3 and 1.5 million for the whole Atlantic trade period (1500–1867). Slaves also arrived via other European colonies like Brazil, Jamaica, and the Dutch Antilles (Borucki et al. 2015). The period before 1650 saw the largest numbers of arrivals in colonies like Mexico and Peru, but in some areas (Río de la Plata, Venezuela) slave arrivals resurged in the eighteenth century (Borucki et al. 2015: 437). Table 4.2 summarizes recorded African slave arrivals in the Spanish colonies for the period 1525–1820.

TABLE 4.2. Slave arrivals in the Spanish American colonies, 1525–1820 (Borucki et al. 2015: 440)

Period	Arrivals
1525–80	84,900
1581–1640	444,900
1641–1700	61,700
1701–60	56,800
1761–1820	298,900

Europeans occupied the highest position in the social hierarchy of the colonies, but multiple pieces of evidence confirm that demographic admixture became a part of everyday life from an early date. Contemporary European observers often decried the consequences. For instance, in a letter from 1552, friar Nicolas de Witte warned King Charles I about what he saw as the moral dangers of pervasive racial mixture in Mexico:

> [w]hat should one think of this land that engenders and populates itself with a mixture of a people so evil. It is clear that this land is full of mestizos, who are born with a very bad disposition; it is full of [black men and women] from whom are born the slaves; it is full of blacks that marry Indian women, who from are born the mulattos, it is full of mestizos that marry Indian women from whom are born a diverse breed without number (Schwaller 2016: 116).

Sociohistorical data confirm that De Witte's hyperbolic language was not completely unjustified, at least as far as the demographic aspect goes. For instance, between 1493 and 1600, only about 18% of Spaniards authorized to settle in the colonies were women (Boyd-Bowman 1976: 596–601), and data on European arrivals for the early seventeenth century continue to show a numerical bias toward men (Jacobs 1995: 218). Once in the colonies, many did not stick to ethnolinguistic lines: for instance, parochial data show that almost half of the marriages for the 1576–81 period in some parishes in Mexico-Tenochtitlan were classified as interethnic marriages (Schwaller 2016: 157).

The frequency and nature of such interethnic contacts were shaped by the economic and cultural goals of the colonizers. Economic life in this early colonial period became organized around activities distributed regionally: agriculture predominated in the central, more densely populated areas, while mining predominated in the Peruvian highlands and northern Mexico (for instance, the mines of Potosí, Taxco and Zacatecas). Cattle herding developed in more marginal regions (Río de la Plata, Central America). Manufacturing took place in small enterprises or *obrajes*, which produced a variety of items (like ceramics or fabrics). Much of the workforce necessary for these economic operations was supplied via mechanisms of forced labor. Indigenous workers were assigned to the Spanish landowners via allotment systems (*encomiendas* lit. 'assignments', *repartimientos* lit. 'distributions') (Lockhart and Schwartz 1983: 92–7, 118–9, 128–9). African and sometimes even southeastern Asian slaves (Seijas 2018; §4.9) provided an additional critical source of workforce. Other demographic changes stemmed from the Catholic Church's plans to spread Christianity in the new territories: in some areas, Catholic missions and *reducciones* (lit. 'concentrations') brought Indigenous populations into contact with Spanish speakers, disrupting pre-contact Indigenous demographic, social, and economic networks.

In addition to economic and cultural institutions, the Spaniards imported forms of social organization reflecting European models. An example was *hidalguía*, a medieval form of nobility based on ancestry with no admixture of non-Catholic blood, which in the colonies was re-interpreted as 'clean' European descent. In practice, however, ethnic admixture gave rise to new forms of social organization. According to Sánchez Méndez (2003: 146–7), a three-part hierarchical social structure soon obtained in the colonies: a small economically and culturally prominent class of prominent Spaniards and *criollos* (white colonists of European stock); a slightly larger middle group, including more humble Iberian settlers and their descendants, as well as most civil servants and the lower clergy; and a large lower class, which included the vast majority of the population, both Indigenous or *mestizo* (individuals of Indigenous and European stock). African slaves theoretically constituted a separate group.

This hierarchical structure, however, reflects an Iberian-centered understanding of colonial society. In Indigenous communities of the early colonial period, barring the demographic impact of contact, social structure was only partially affected by the arrival of the Spaniards. Many of the pre-Columbian social institutions survived either side-by-side or overlapping with new Spanish-inspired systems (for instance, the Mesoamerican *āltepētl* became Indigenous municipalities, Lockhart 1992). African slaves also developed new social institutions in many areas, including fraternities (*cofradías*) and, wherever they were able to escape their slave owners, maroon settlements (§4.3). As we will see in the next section, such contact ecologies beyond the direct reach of Europeans were to have profound consequences in how speakers negotiated the new social landscape, and their solutions shaped new linguistic repertoires from the very first days of the colonial period.

4.3. Early American colonial language ecologies

In the colonial masters' eyes, life in the colonies was to be organized into two parallel social orders with different institutions and legal systems separating the European and Indigenous populations: the *república de españoles* and the *república de indios* (Levaggi 2001). In cities like Mexico-Tenochtitlan, the Spanish borough was laid right on top of the foundations of the razed Mexica buildings, providing a striking visual representation of the new hierarchical order and the ideal ethnic separation that this order was predicated on (Figure 4.2). In practice, however, life in the colonies often challenged these ethnic and cultural boundaries. Everyday contacts abounded: whether in the coastal entrepôts of the Caribbean and the Pacific, the silver mines of Taxco and Potosí, the rural encomiendas of central Mexico, or the countless interethnic households, individuals of diverse ethnolinguistic background created new hybrid spaces of communication (Juana and Antón's story in §1.1 is a vivid example; see also Brain 2010; Schwaller 2012, 2016). Literature on the evolution of Spanish in the colonial period, however, has not always fully acknowledged these spaces and their linguistic consequences.

For instance, according to some versions of the sociolinguistics of this early colonial period, interactions between Spaniards and other ethnolinguistic groups were minimal (Escobar 2001: 82–7; Hidalgo 2016: 62–3; Lipski 2014: 47). Lipski summarizes the ecological embedding of language use at this time as 'the Spanish liv[ing] in walled cities or fortified coastal enclaves', in a sort of exometropolitan 'space station' (2014: 9). In similar terms, Hidalgo has argued for the existence of urban clusters of Europeans whose linguistic behavior accommodated to each other but was hardly modified by non-Europeans (Hidalgo 2016: 63). Sometimes we do see evidence of social separation among ethnic groups limiting the motivation for interethnic language learning. For instance, in cities like Lima and Cuzco, Indigenous people and Europeans inhabited different neighborhoods, separated by physical barriers, and interethnic marriage rates were low (Escobar 2001: 83–4). As a result, in these settings, only a few cultural brokers (clergy, scribes, interpreters, members of the Indigenous upper classes) developed bilingual repertoires.

FIGURE 4.2. Mexico City Cathedral and other colonial-era buildings atop the foundation of the Mexica *huey teocalli* ('main temple', Sp. *templo mayor*)
(source: author)

While this scenario of ethnic isolation did occur in some of these early settlements or within specific networks, what we tend to see across these colonies is a much more complex patchwork of contact routines that challenged pre-conquest ethnolinguistic practices. A good example are the Catholic missions or remote Hispanic outposts, where the sheer demographic weight of the Indigenous population motivated the Iberian population to develop bilingual proficiency (Escobar 2011: 324–5; González Ollé 1996). In some cases, ecological disruption resulted in the quick elimination of large parts of the pre-contact pools. Nowhere was this elimination clearer than in the Caribbean area (Cuba, Puerto Rico, Hispaniola). Here, the combination of new land exploitation systems introduced by the Spaniards and the ravaging results of contact with European pathogens led to the demise of the Arawak and Taíno as identifiable ethnolinguistic communities in only a few decades – as a result, most of the linguistic makeup of these groups is unknown (Aikhenvald 2012: 1–67). But even amid demographic decimation, elements of Indigenous culture and language were assimilated in new networks that developed beyond the confines of the early Spanish settlements (Raynor 2024; §4.7). Intermingling among individuals of European, African, and Indigenous descent gave rise to a hybrid population, as evidenced by studies of the genetics of the Caribbean (Moreno-Estrada et al. 2013), confirming a significant Indigenous component in present-day populations.

In some cases, environmental conditions granted most of the population access to the colonizers' repertoires alongside the pre-contact pools. Paraguay is a case in point. After the early settlement of Spaniards in the 1530s, extreme isolation and economic underdevelopment minimized social stratification: *españoles* continued to be at the top of the social scale, but *mestizos* played a more prominent role here than in other colonial areas. In this environment, opportunities for bidirectional learning abounded, starting in bilingual households where Guarani women bore children to Spanish men (Lipksi 1994: 304). As a result, both Guarani and Spanish continued to coexist during and after the colonial period (Granda 1994: 271; §6.3).

In addition to speakers of European and Indigenous descent, African slaves also played a key role in these early contacts. The slaves were linguistically heterogeneous and spoke a host of mostly Niger-Congo languages. Some may have gained familiarity with Iberian features via contact with Portuguese slave traders before arriving in the Americas (McWhorter 2000; Schwegler 1999). Once in the colonies, slaves from the same area constituted mutual aid societies (*cofradías*), allowing for some degree of ethnolinguistic continuity (Lipski 2005: 96–7). Forced resettlement motivated many slaves to learn elements from other pools in their environment, whether European (Spanish, Portuguese), African or Indigenous (201–3). For instance, highly stereotypical literary representations of *bozal* (non-native) speech by Africans, termed *habla de negros* (lit. 'blacks' speech'), give witness of at least some of the effects of these ecologies of learning as early as fifteenth-century Spain (Lipski 2005: 129–96; §4.4 and §4.7). *Palenques* (maroon communities) set up by *cimarrones* (escaped African slaves and Indigenous individuals) were another emergent ecology of contact in the Caribbean area. The resulting linguistic pools must have initially incorporated elements of varied provenance and shaped by language learning in this diverse environment (Raynor 2024 provides an example from Antioquia, Colombia, §4.7), even if over time demographic and social pressures favored Iberian features.

While many slaves lived among non-Africans (Sessarego 2017), sometimes local conditions created various forms of isolation between Africans and the early colonial Hispanic society. Besides the *palenques*, remote areas where high proportions of Africans were employed in plantation settings provide an example: here, many slaves would have had little motivation for frequent communication with Europeans, often communicating more frequently with their Indigenous neighbors, as in the Chota valley of Ecuador or the Yungas region of Bolivia (Lipski 2007; Sessarego 2021; see also §4.6). Such conditions of limited access to L1 Spanish models by Afrodescendants have led authors to posit the possibility that temporary pidgins or even creoles of the type found in other colonial settings may have emerged during this period (for instance, Schwegler 1999). Other authors reject this possibility on ecological grounds. For instance, McWhorter (2000, 2015) has traced the emergence of Atlantic creoles to the slave posts on the Western African coast and attributes the lack of Spanish-lexified creoles in the Americas to the fact that Spain owned no such establishments. Consequently, the slaves' first approximation to Spanish would have been on American soil, with enough input to acquire a non-creole form of Spanish. Sessarego (2017) points to legal reasons: in many areas, Africans were allowed to become much more integrated in Hispanic societies than was the case in other European colonies, and integration afforded learners the chance to approximate L1 Spanish models.

All these degrees and contexts of contact provided the optimal environmental conditions for various forms of learning across ethnolinguistic lines during the speakers' lifespan. For many, access to innovative feature pools started from birth, with many children growing up in ethnolinguistically diverse households and neighborhoods (Brain 2010), as in the case of Paraguay just mentioned. Contact also came from sources other than parentage: for instance, in sixteenth-century Mexico, African slaves tended to work as nannies and child nurses more often than European or Indigenous women (Hidalgo 2016: 104). For others, learning and use irrespective of traditional linguistic borderlines continued into adulthood. For instance, bilingual Indians and Spaniards served as interpreters (*lenguas*) in judicial proceedings and other transactions (Parodi 2001; Rivarola 2001; Schwaller 2012). An early example is shown in Figure 4.3, a rendition of the exchange between Spanish conquistador Francisco Pizarro and Inca emperor Atahualpa in Cajamarca (Peru) in 1532, mediated by Felipillo, an Indigenous interpreter (displayed to the right of the Spaniards, wearing European clothing). Other contexts included academic institutions that fostered language learning, such as ecclesiastical schools and universities (Hidalgo 2001: 64–7; see this section below); labor environments that brought together Indigenous workers, African slaves, and Spanish-speaking or bilingual supervisors in agricultural holdings, mines and manufacturing *obrajes* (§4.2) (Lockhart and Schwartz 1983; Lockhart 1992); markets or monasteries (Sierra Silva 2018); and ethnolinguistically mixed marriages, like Juana and Antón (§1.1).

As the position of Castilian Spanish as the language of the nation-state became consolidated in Spain (§3.1), norms of educated or literary use among

Spanish Beyond Spain 97

FIGURE 4.3. Felipillo interpreting between the Spaniards and the Inca (Guamán Poma de Ayala's *El primer nueva corónica y buen gobierno*, ca. 1615) (source: Wikimedia; public domain)

the colonial élites must have continued to follow metropolitan models. It was for the benefit of this small group at the cusp of the colonial hierarchy that the first schools and academic institutions were founded, geared exclusively at the education of the children of the élites and of the few Indigenous families that associated with them. These included the first universities in the Western Hemisphere (Santo Domingo in 1538, Lima and Mexico in 1551). Revealingly, some of these institutions were tailored to the colonial context. For instance, the Santa Cruz de Tlatelolco school was founded in 1536 on the outskirts of Mexico-Tenochtitlan to educate a new generation of Indigenous priests trilingual in Latin, Spanish, and Nahuatl. More informal, unsystematic forms of literacy (including basic penmanship and the reading of religious texts) were taught by rural schools, private teachers, and missionaries (Gonzalbo Aizpuru 2001), but much of the population appears to have been beyond their reach.

Beyond these European-influenced contexts, the enforcement of straightforward sociolinguistic norms must have been the exception rather than the rule during this early colonial period. Nevertheless, the question has been raised as to whether a new local dialectal norm could have emerged among the early settlers. Approaches that rely on a scenario where ethnic Spaniards interacted minimally with non-native learners have proposed that dialectal accommodation and L1 learning among the new generations of *españoles* led to the emergence of a new local variety via koinéization (§2.6) within a few generations (Fontanella de Weinberg 1992; Granda 1994; Parodi 2001; but see Rivarola 2001). More recently, however, this scenario has been called into question: relevant facts include the evidence for pervasive contact across ethnolinguistic lines outside the urban élites and the linguistic patterns attested in the archival record (Sanz-Sánchez 2013, 2019; Sanz-Sánchez and Moyna 2023; §4.4, and §7.2). This scenario is reminiscent of other incipient colonial European settlements, where norms among the settling strand (especially those at the cusp of the colonial society) are still oriented toward the metropolis and contact features have still not coalesced into sociolinguistically recognized, stable repertoires (Schneider 2007: 33–40). Over time, as we will see (§4.7), new features stemming from the local conditions of contact spread demographically and became symbolic of colonial identities.

4.4. Some contact outcomes in the early colonial Americas

Many approaches to early colonial Spanish have assumed that interethnic contacts left few long-term traces in the resulting Spanish pools. For instance, Sánchez Méndez rejects the possibility that bilingual contact codes with recognizable L2 features (*español de los indígenas*) may have shaped the local varieties of Spanish in the long run:

> This Indigenous Spanish could not have gone beyond the social group that created it, and [it] disappeared in the colonial period and during the nineteenth century, absorbed by the more polished and socially unmarked speech of the cities. If there was any influence on the [language spoken by] the [European] settlers, it must have occurred much later, because the colony was a context of social and racial segregation. In this context, although an ethnically marked, stable interlanguage did emerge, its social connotations prevented it from exerting any influence on the language of the colonial society (2003: 217).

This scenario is invoked to explain why many current monolingual varieties of Latin American Spanish appear to have retained few to no obvious structural influences from Indigenous languages (Lope Blanch 2000: 61–79; Moreno de Alba 1988: 49–87), contrary to what we would expect in situations of language shift: recall that language contact literature has identified such shift situations as optimal sites for speakers to generate innovative patterns (for instance, via the transfer or imposition of L1 grammar on the L2, or other bilingual acquisition strategies, as discussed in §2.6). In this view, the conditions of ethnolinguistic isolation often assumed for many early colonial societies (§4.2), coupled with the stigma associated with L2-influenced varieties in the colonial symbolic landscape, meant that these contact features stood no chance for selection once Indigenous populations shifted to Spanish (§4.6 and §5.5).

In this scenario, the diachronic effects of contact across ethnic barriers are only traceable in the lexicon, which is seen as a feasible form of selection in the absence of widespread social bilingualism (Lope Blanch 2000: 192–5; Moreno de Alba 1988: 56–65; Sánchez Méndez 2003: 391–201; see also §2.2).

Current Latin American Spanish lexicon does indeed feature many loanwords already in use in early colonial times, revealing both the adaptation of local vocabulary but also its spread well beyond the area of contact. Geographical diffusion of lexicon is apparent in the case of Taíno and Caribbean Arawak words originally incorporated in the Caribbean, but found today throughout Spanish-speaking Latin America (and also other languages via Spanish): *canoa* 'canoe', *barbacoa* 'grill' (see Eng. *barbeque*), *maíz* 'corn', and *(e)naguas* 'skirt', among others. Other loanwords remained closer to their original areas. Examples include lexicon from Nahuatl, such as *guajolote* 'turkey', *jacal* 'hut', *petate* 'rush mat', and *zacate* 'grass', common in Mexico and parts of Central America; or loanwords from Quechua, like *mate* 'plant for infused drink', *palta* 'avocado', *pampa* 'plain, grassland', and *quirquincho* 'armadillo', used in many South American varieties. Other loanwords tend to be even more regionally marked. Examples include loans from Mayan languages (*op* 'corn tortilla', *xux* 'wasp'), Chibchan languages (*chicha* 'fermented drink'), Aymara (*calancha/o* 'naked'), Mapudungun (*chope* 'stick to toil the soil', *malón* 'unexpected attack'), and Tupi-Guarani (*gaucho* 'cattle herder, horseman', *ñandutí* 'form of Paraguayan laced fabric decoration', *yacaré* 'alligator'), many of which never made it far from their respective contact areas (Martín Butragueño and Torres Sánchez 2022).

While preservation of lexical items in current Spanish varieties is one possible route to access the linguistic effects of contact in the early colonial period, attention to various kinds of archival data can be expected to yield a more complete picture (see §3.2 and §7.3 for a similar argument about other historical ecologies). Unfortunately, for many of these early colonial American ecologies, the archival record is minimal, non-existent, or of dubious representativeness. This is particularly the case for communities of non-European descent: for instance, the literary representations of Afrodescendants' speech in *habla de negros* by *bozal* African slaves (§4.3) are often clearly stereotypical and comedic (§4.7). In such cases, one may enlist additional sources (both historical and recent) to peek into these conditions of contact and some of their linguistic effects.

Loanwords from African languages are an example (Lipski 1994: 124–5). In her study of the Afrohispanic Costa Chica variety (Oaxaca, southern Mexico), Rosas Mayén identifies several items of African origin: *bembo* 'idiot, stupid' < Yoruba *bemba/bembon* 'thick-lipped person', *cuatete* 'catfish' < Kikongo *ŋkwá-* 'riverbank', or *cuco* 'small mosquito' < Bantu languages *kwkw/koko* 'small fly', Yoruba *kòkòrò* 'fly, worm' (2007: 155–83). In principle, it may seem unclear whether such lexical adaptations took place already in the early colonial period. However, remember that importation of African slaves dropped sharply in most Spanish colonies after 1650 (§4.2). Therefore, it is legitimate to think that at least some of these recently recorded items can be traced back to early colonial contact pools. I return to contact ecologies in Afrohispanic populations when discussing the late colonial period (§4.6 and §4.7).

In other cases, the written archival record is sturdier, and can be used to track historical contact effects that go beyond lexical borrowing. Structural innovations are apparent in the writings by bilingual speakers. For instance, Escobar (2001: 87–9) and Cerrón Palomino (2003: 137–61) cite as typical of sixteenth-century bilingual Quechua-Spanish writers the following elements: alternation between high vowels [i, u] and mid-vowels [e, o] (*cabildo~cabeldo* 'town council'); devoicing of voiced stops (*cabras~capras* 'goats'); non-canonical gender and number agreement in nominal phrases (*emagen bueno,* see st. Sp. *imagen buena* 'good image', *estes obra,* see st. Sp. *esta obra* 'this work'), use of a redundant clitic with intransitive movement verbs and with copulative verbs (*anduvimos merándolo las eclesias* 'we were looking at the churches', see st. Sp. *anduvimos mirando las iglesias*; *para que lo seays pentor* 'so that you will be a painter', see st. Sp. *para que seais pintor*).

An example of this type of competence can be seen in the writings by sculptor Francisco Tito Yupanqui (Titu Yupangui), a Quechua-dominant speaker from sixteenth-century Copacabana (Bolivia) (Cerrón Palomino 2003: 135–70). Consider (1), a fragment from a letter where Yupanqui narrates how he and his brother were taken by a local priest to learn the trade of wood carving:

(1) ... y nos fuemos andando, y me lo llevó in la casa di on maestro que lo llamavan Dego di Ortez, y me lo dixaron para que lo aprendira de aprindés, dispoés di quando lo sabíbamos on poco di algo di intalladura me lo fui a ondi istava con el mi hirmano don Alonso Viracocha Inca, y dispoés disto lo dixo que lo es oficio fácil, y que yo lo entiendo, que lo impesaría on hechora del Vergen ... (adapted from Cerrón Palomino 2003: 162).

'And we went by foot, and he brought me to the house of a master that they called Diego de Ortiz, and they left me [there] so that I would learn [the trade of carving] as an apprentice, later when we knew a little bit of wood carving I went with my brother don Alonso Viracocha Inca to where he was, and after this I (he?) said that it is an easy trade, and that I understand it, that I should start it [by working on] a statue of the Virgin'.

Here we see many characteristics typical of the Quechua-dominant Spanish written production of this period, including spellings suggesting non-canonical (i.e. non-L1) vowels and diphthongs (*di*, st. Sp. *de* 'of'; *dispoés*, st. Sp. *después* 'after'; *istava*, st. Sp. *estaba* 'was-3SG.IMP') or redundant *lo* clitics (*quando lo sabíbamos on poco de intalladura* 'when we knew a little bit of wood carving', st. Sp. *cuando sabíamos un poco de entalladura*). The presence of many of these features in present-day Andean pools (§6.3 and §6.4) shows that these early colonial contact ecologies are historical precursors of more recent patterns of selection.

The evidence for multiethnic, high-contact environments within just a few years of Spanish presence in the Americas can also be used to re-examine well-seated notions about communication within European-centered social networks. The hypothesis of an early colonial *koiné* (§4.3) emerging from accommodation and dialectal leveling among ethnic Spaniards is a suitable target for revision. In the most mainstream version of this account (Granda 1994; Fontanella de Weinberg 1992; Hidalgo 2016; Parodi 2001), several core elements of Latin American Spanish can be traced back to this levelled variety, which is assumed to have been assembled by L1 Spanish speakers via structural simplification and leveling. These features include the elimination of the 2PL paradigm of *vosotras/os* ('you-PL'; see §4.7 for other colonial interpretations of 2PL forms, and §4.10 for this form in Philippine creoles) and most notably *seseo*, the merger of several medieval sibilants (namely, dentoalveolars /s̪, z̪/, apicoalveolars /s̺, z̺/ and alveopalatals /ʃ, ʒ/) into /s/. This simplified sibilant system seems to have spread fairly quickly: most documents authored by scribes born in the colonies exhibit spelling evidence of this merger (e.g. *vezino* as *vesino/vessino* 'neighbor' or *casa* as *caza/caça* 'house') since the late 1500s, as shown in data from a diachronic corpus of documents from the Gulf of Mexico area, displayed in Figure 4.4.

The fact that these selections appear to have favored southern Castilian and Andalusian features is commonly explained as a logical function of the demographic predominance of speakers from these areas in the early settling contingent (§4.2). Dialectal counterevidence in the form of variation across Latin American Spanish dialects, such as the realizations of syllable-final /s/ (see §6.4 and §6.8 for recent examples), is interpreted as the product of later exposure by speakers of this leveled variety to competing metropolitan norms (for instance, Andalusian Spanish favoring aspiration or elision of coda /s/, and Castilian Spanish favoring retention; Boyd-Bowman 1988; Fontanella de Weinberg 1992). In short, this dialectal leveling scenario credits L1 speakers of Spanish as agents in the creation of the first colonial vernaculars, providing the basis for the posited general Spanish American koiné variety largely unaffected by contact with other languages, as seen earlier in this section.

While some of the social networks among the early colonial Spanish population (especially among the urban élites) seem to have shielded them from pervasive contact with non-Europeans, (§4.3), the evidence for widespread interethnic contacts and mutual learning among humbler ranks of the colonial society questions the sociolinguistic scenario of separation that the koiné hypothesis rests on. Remember too (§2.6) that simplification processes play a critical role

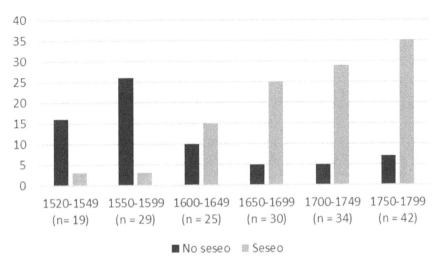

FIGURE 4.4. Distribution of *seseo* in a corpus of documents from the Gulf of Mexico (Sanz-Sánchez and Moyna 2023: 20, based on Melis and Rivero Franyutti 2008)

in bootstrapping in language acquisition (Clements 2009: 1–28; Winford 2005). These sociolinguistic and acquisitional clues make it legitimate to wonder whether speakers of Iberian stock were the only (or most influential) agents of phonological or morphological restructuring. Sanz-Sánchez (2019) has revisited this question in relation to *seseo* by studying the distribution of spellings for the historical sibilant sounds that merged into /s/ in a corpus of sixteenth-century letters written by Spain-born Spanish settlers. In this corpus, speakers from southern Spain exhibit much lower levels of sibilant simplification than what proponents of the colonial koiné commonly assume. Combined with other forms of evidence (metalinguistic comments, sibilants in Spanish loans in Indigenous languages, cross-linguistic phonological distributions), the data questions the assumption of a dialectal norm emerging exclusively from the action of L1 speakers. To account for the attested patterns of linguistic selection in these early colonial Spanish pools, the author proposes an alternative scenario that incorporates a broader range of ecological triggers, including the action of non-native learners and children growing up in a diffuse sociolinguistic environment. The hypothesis for the key role of child language acquisition in the actuation of new dialectal norms in the early colonial period has been developed more fully in Sanz-Sánchez and Tejedo-Herrero (2021) and especially Sanz-Sánchez and Moyna (2023). I return to this analysis in Chapter 7 (§7.2) to discuss several important implications of this ecological approach to contact in the early Spanish colonies.

Early colonial contacts affected not only the repertoires of speakers perceived as speaking a form of Spanish but also had tangible consequences in traditional Indigenous pools. These consequences will be surveyed explicitly in §4.8 below.

4.5. The later colonial period in the Spanish Americas: Sociodemographic context

Choosing 1650 as a mid-point between the 'early' and 'late' Spanish American colonial period may seem arbitrary, and in many ways it is. Many political, economic, and cultural systems can be seen to evolve gradually across this chronological divide. But the mid-seventeenth century was also a time when several important demographic and social developments were set in motion, and an exploration of their linguistic effects is justified from an ecological perspective.

Some of these changes are related to geopolitical shifts: as Spain's military supremacy in Europe faded, it found itself on the defense in the Americas too, losing several strategic stopovers (e.g. Jamaica in 1655 to Britain, and Haiti in 1670 to France). In turn, Spain's weakened grip over its transatlantic routes took a heavy toll on trade revenues, prompting colonial authorities to expand into marginal areas. Also, by the mid-seventeenth century, the two forms of use of Indigenous workforce typical of the earlier period (the *encomienda* and the *repartimiento*; §4.2) were largely replaced by rural estates (*haciendas*) where a mostly Indigenous and mestizo workforce was employed on a wage basis. These changes were motivated by the stark demographic losses among Indigenous communities of the first 100–150 years of Spanish colonial presence in the Americas, which caused increased competition for laborers, and a growing demand for a more diversified range of products for colonial and metropolitan markets. The new forms of production pushed some Indigenous populations into closer contact with Spanish speakers, a move which was to have important linguistic consequences (Lockhart and Schwartz 1983: 134–41).

In the central settlement areas of Mexico and Peru, the second half of the 1600s also marked the transition from a period of demographic and economic stagnation to one of stabilization and sometimes even moderate growth. Demographic gains came mostly from the Indigenous and the ethnically hybrid populations. By contrast, arrivals from Spain declined throughout the 1600s (Escandón 2014: 23–4) as did African slave arrivals in many areas (§4.2). Although rural areas continued to be home to most of the population (Sánchez Méndez 2003: 142–9), many cities rose in importance (Puebla, Guatemala, Bogotá, Cuzco, Quito, and Santiago; see Lockhart and Schwartz 1983: 125–6). Still, as in earlier decades, Mexico-Tenochtitlan and Lima continued to be the largest urban centers in the Spanish American colonies. Table 4.3 summarizes population estimates for some of these towns:

TABLE 4.3. Population of select colonial Spanish American cities at two points in time (Kinsbruner 2005: 30)

Lima	
1599	14,200
1755	54,000
Mexico-Tenochtitlan	
1591	50,000
1790	113,000
Santiago	
1657	1,600
1790	40,000
Buenos Aires	
1609	1,000
1778	24,200

Local economic factors sometimes resulted in exceptions to demographic growth. In a remarkable example, the depletion of silver ores caused the population of the Andean mining center of Potosí, which had stood at a staggering 140,000 residents in the mid-sixteenth century, to decline to just about 30,000 by the early 1700s (Kinsbruner 2005: 29). Also, some of the backwater areas of the earlier period remained on the demographic and economic fringe of the colonial world. Central America is a prime example: in the absence of large mineral resources, agriculture and cattle grazing became the only worthwhile economic activities, performed in farming establishments which were not conducive to high-density population concentrations (Webre 2022).

In 1700, the Spanish crown changed hands from the Austrian Hapsburgs to the French Bourbons, and the new kings instituted sweeping reforms. For instance, a regular standing military was instituted to defend Spain's territorial colonial claims from encroachment by other European powers. The new troops were formed via recruitment from among lower-class, ethnically diverse men. To sustain these reforms, the crown undertook measures to increase tax revenues from manufacturing and agriculture, and to foster transatlantic and intracolonial trade. Economic growth sustained the rise of a new class of wealthy, mostly urban, European-descent colony-born *criollos*, who began to demand a larger share of the institutional and social prominence hitherto held by Spain-born élites.

These geopolitical and economic transformations were felt not only in the cities of the central areas: borderland regions and their populations started to play an increasingly important role in the socioeconomic structure of the American colonies. In North America, as the British and French expanded their settlements, Spain moved to secure its territorial claims by establishing new missions, military garrisons, and towns (see Map 4.1). In these new foundations, ethnically diverse Hispanic American-born settlers mixed with other newcomers (for instance, Canary Islanders in the Louisiana settlements) (Weber 1992: 204–35).

Along the South American colonial fringe, geopolitical hostilities between Spain and Portugal over the area between current Argentina, Paraguay, and Brazil were settled in the Treaty of Madrid (1750), which placed much of the region under Portuguese control. This move had direct consequences for the Jesuit missions established in the previous century. Shortly after, in 1767, the Jesuits were expelled from the remaining missions, and the Indigenous Tupi-Guarani populations of the missions disbanded. Further south, an ill-defined border region (*pampas*), inhabited mostly by nomadic Indigenous groups, offered few

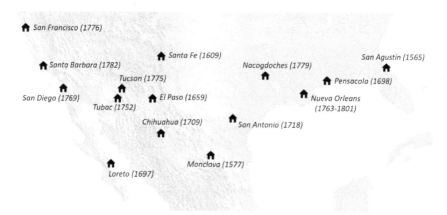

MAP 4.1. Select Spanish foundations (towns, garrisons, missions) across the northern colonial borderland and foundation year (map data by author; base map by Kaldari via Wikimedia Commons, license: https://creativecommons.org/licenses/by/4.0/deed.en)

economic incentives beyond cattle grazing. In these remote and sparsely populated frontiers on both ends of the Spanish colonial dominion, interactions among ethnically diverse individuals resulted in local forms of cultural and sociolinguistic hybridization. For instance, cattle herders of hybrid *mestizo* descent (*gauchos* in South America, *vaqueros* along the northern borderlands) laid the foundation for forms of economic and social organization that were instrumental in the economic development of these areas in the late eighteenth and early nineteenth centuries (§4.6 and §4.7).

The demographic evolution of the Indigenous populations was a particularly important environmental factor during this period. In some geographically marginal areas, demographic decimation continued well into the eighteenth century (e.g. the Paraguayan Guarani missions after the expulsion of the Jesuits and several smallpox epidemics, Jackson 2008: 125–67). By contrast, in the central areas, there was an overall reversal of the previous trend of population loss, aided by the gradual development of immunity to European pathogens (Lockhart and Schwartz 1983: 122–3). Indigenous demographic growth and the new economies of the late colonial period also resulted in increased transfers of population toward the cities, but Indigenous rural municipalities also incorporated more individuals of mixed European and Indigenous descent. As will be seen below (§4.7), increasingly dense networks connecting country and city favored the cultural and linguistic assimilation of Indigenous individuals, a process that intensified in the 1800s (§5.4).

As noted, the recovery of the Indigenous population in some areas and the new forms of production resulted in a general decline in the importation of slaves after the mid-seventeenth century (§4.2), but there were exceptions. For instance, as Cuba became the largest sugar cane producer in the Caribbean following the Haitian Revolution (1791–1804), slave arrivals from Africa and other European colonies increased dramatically. As a result, the proportion of population classified as Black surpassed that of other ethnic groups, Europeans included, until the mid-1800s (§5.6). The African population also rose sharply in the Río de la Plata area, reaching an estimated 40% in Buenos Aires and Montevideo at the turn of the nineteenth century (Lipski 2005: 100–1).

Over time, these demographic shifts caused the Spanish American colonies to look less and less like the ideal division into clear-cut phenotypical communities preconized by colonial authorities (§4.3). By the early 1800s, the proportion of *castas* (a generic label including anybody who was perceived as not phenotypically classifiable as Spaniard, Indigenous or Black) had surpassed an estimated 20% in Mexico and 30% in Peru (Lockhart and Schwartz 1983: 342) – a likely undercount given the well-documented tendency for individuals to self-identify as *españoles* if allowed by their physical appearance (Schwaller 2016). Early colonial classifications gave way to intricate casta taxonomies based on parental descent and reflected in late colonial paintings geared at helping colonial audiences navigate this increasingly complex ethnic landscape – an example is shown in Figure 4.5. Though legally disadvantaged, these racially diverse individuals claimed an increasingly important economic and social role (Lockhart and Schwartz 1983: 315–21). Thanks to their liminal position between recognized categories, they operated as transmission agents of social trends and, as seen in

FIGURE 4.5. *De mestizo y d[e] india, coyote* ('from a *mestizo* father and an Indigenous mother, a *coyote*'). Miguel Cabrera, Mexico, 1763 (TriniMuñoz via Wikimedia Commons, public domain)

the next section, contributed to the linguistic landscapes of this period in several significant ways.

4.6. Late colonial American language ecologies

During the late colonial period, the role of Spanish as the socially, economically, and institutionally dominant code solidified, but it was not necessarily everyone's language yet. For instance, at the time of Mexico's independence in 1821, about 60% of the population of the new republic did not speak it (Cifuentes 1998: 46), and widespread shift to Spanish did not start to take place until the nineteenth century in most areas (Cifuentes 1998: 46–7; Escobar 2001: 82–5; González Ollé 1996). Among the factors chipping away at the ecological niche of languages other than Spanish during the late colonial period, the increasing demographic exchanges between urban and rural areas were decisive.

The evolving economy of the Spanish colonies precipitated these changes. For instance, growing economic dependence between Lima and the nearby rural areas on the Andean foothills created 'a stepped system in which migrants from the minimally Hispanicized highland would move first to Indian towns in the foothills where Spanish language and ways were better known, then ... on to Lima's [Indian suburbs], and at last possibly into Lima itself' (Lockhart and Schwartz

1983: 168). Conversely, a humble Hispanicized population settled in formerly Indigenous areas to work in the expanding *haciendas*, thereby creating 'a Spanish community within the Indian one' (169). What ensued were new urban and rural communication contexts that presented the optimal conditions for multiple forms of linguistic negotiation. Art from this period gives witness to some of these contexts, depicting scenes where a racially diverse populace interacts in the same contexts: for instance, an anonymous painting from the late 1600s depicts phenotypically European, Afrodescendant and Indigenous residents sharing the public space of Lima's main square (*plaza mayor*) (see Figure 4.6). In the rural hinterlands of the colonial cities, ethnolinguistic contact and the spread of Spanish-speaking population offered an acquisition model that was largely detached from that of the urban areas. An example of this environment are the rural cattle estates (*ranchos*) that formed a network of loosely interconnected, low population density nuclei. In these networks, speakers of varied ethnic adscription, including both L1 and L2 speakers of Spanish, interacted across large geographical expanses and acted as a cultural and linguistic bridge between the more heavily Hispanicized urban areas and the Indigenous communities (Parodi 2001: 48–51).

Urban growth also favored the rise of institutions favoring linguistic homogenization. For instance, printing presses were established throughout the Spanish American colonies, and the first newspapers started circulating regularly (*Gaceta de Lima* in 1715, *Gaceta de México* in 1722) (Sánchez Méndez 2003: 181–2). Parochial and municipal schools opened in the cities, and additional universities were founded. Although only a minority of the population had access to these institutions, they are symptomatic of the emergence of a literate, American-born *criollo* socioeconomic élite with sufficient cultural and economic capital to shape discourses on linguistic performance and to contribute to the emergence of new local norms separate from the metropolitan models personified by Spain-born *peninsulares* (Lipski 2014).

FIGURE 4.6. Lima's *plaza mayor* in the late 1600s (anonymous painting) (Museo de América, Madrid, via Wikimedia Commons, public domain)

As the ecological embedding of many of these contacts underwent transformations, so did the speakers' motivations to incorporate innovative features into their traditional repertoires. Lockhart (1992) produced a detailed analysis of some of these ecologies of contact between Nahuatl and Spanish in central Mexico as well as their linguistic effects. In this account, demographic proportions and the overall power differential between populations operated as critical ecological motors determining the types (and direction) of linguistic accommodation. Contact effects were not unidirectional, but the socioeconomic structure of late colonial society did give the upper hand to Hispanic pools (note that Lockhart's use of 'Spaniard' is to refer to *españoles*, whether from Spain or the colonies):

> The Spaniards retained the basic settlement pattern the Nahuas had already established, their enterprises were permeated by Nahua labor mechanisms, they made increasing use of essentially Indigenous markets for everyday items of all kinds, they gradually adopted significant elements of Indigenous diet and material culture, and their language too was affected ... in much the same way as Nahuatl was affected by Spanish. [However], the overall process was far from symmetrical. It was conditioned ... by two factors above all: the general dominance of the Spaniards and the fact that they came in sufficient numbers to create a viable, partially self-contained society in no danger of being swallowed up by the local milieu' (1992: 435).

A salient sociolinguistic consequence of these environmental triggers was the emergence of a much larger group of Indigenous and *mestizo* bilinguals than in the early colonial period, who used Spanish to communicate with monolingual Spanish speakers and increasingly with each other. Bilingualism at the individual level and the lack of ideological mechanisms to uphold a strict separation between feature pools resulted in a variety of contact phenomena with can be seen to affect both the 'Nahuatl' and the 'Spanish' pools. Texts penned by bilingual speakers bear witness to these incorporations, including not just Spanish elements in Nahuatl (which Lockhart refers to as Stages 1, 2 and 3 of contact) but also Nahuatl influence on L2 Spanish (which he refers to as Stage 4, simultaneous with Stage 3 after about 1650). We will look at examples of the linguistic characteristics of these stages in §4.8.

Speakers of African descent continued to participate in many of these contacts. Although decreasing slave importation rates in the mid-1600s in several colonial areas (§4.2) contributed to the linguistic assimilation of the African population, African-based social networks persisted late into the colonial period. The mutual aid *cofradías* (brotherhoods) for recently arrived slaves recorded in cities like Lima and Buenos Aires as late as the early nineteenth century provide an example of these forms of cultural continuity (Lipski 2005: 96, 100–3). Spanish repertoires were not the slaves' only learning target, as shown by the cases of Nahuatl-dominant *negros* and *mulatos* recorded in central Mexico in the seventeenth century (Schwaller 2016: 111–45). Lipski (2007) describes the establishment of Africans in the *haciendas* of the Yungas region of Bolivia, where they resettled starting in the eighteenth century after the collapse of the mining complexes of the Andean highland (§4.5; see also Sessarego 2021). In these communities, generations of African slaves and Afrodescendants developed linguistic resources shaped by more frequent access to Aymara than Spanish. Another clear example of an environment where individuals of African descent constituted a majority can be found in the *palenques* formed by maroon ex-slaves, including San Basilio de Palenque, 30 miles southwest of Cartagena (present-day Colombia). By the early 1700s, there are metalinguistic records in this palenque of bilingual use of Spanish as well as a distinct code, likely an early form of the creole language used to this day (Klee and Lynch 2009: 97; §1.8).

4.7. Some contact outcomes in late colonial American ecologies

We just saw that demographic and sociolinguistic conditions after 1650 in most of the Spanish American colonies differed from those of the earlier period in significant ways. As a result, the linguistic pools in these late colonial populations were less affected by factors typical of a settlement stage, and more by processes of demographic and social consolidation (Schneider 2007; Trudgill 2004), especially in the central areas.

We can discern some of the linguistic effects of these late colonial sociolinguistic triggers in the progressive negotiation of Spanish features along metropolitan vs. colonial identities: recall (§4.5) that this period saw the social rise of colony-born *criollos* and *castas*, who vied for sociopolitical influence with the old ruling élite of European origin. The role of symbolic factors is clear in the preservation of options that evoked European norms. These features include the north-central Castilian phonemic distinction between /s/ and /θ/, which came to characterize the metropolitan varieties of this period in opposition to local *seseo* (§4.4). Guitarte (1983) quotes this phonemic contrast as a symbolic marker of allegiance to Spain among certain late colonial social élites (and see Caravedo 1992 for possible recent lexical retentions of /θ/ in the Andean area). By contrast, this was also the time when several variables that were to become characteristic of national varieties of Latin American Spanish began to exhibit regional distribution patterns, a pre-condition for their identification as indexical of post-colonial national identities in the nineteenth century (see *enregisterment*, §2.5; Company Company 2024; Lipski 2014), as will be explored in the next chapter (§5.5).

These emergent dialectal patterns are apparent in the evolution of 2nd-person non-deferential address. In the singular, we see alternation between two historical paradigms: *tú* forms, which by the late 1600s were favored in Spain, and *vos* forms, which continued to alternate with *tú* in many colonial areas in idiosyncratic combinations. Consider the example in (2), from a 1784 Buenos Aires family letter. In the fragment, *tú* forms are marked as T, and *vos* forms as V – note the combination of forms from both paradigms:

(2) Hermano Manuel, si te$_T$ quereis$_V$ aser cargo de las dos capellanias, la una de mil y doscientos pesos a favor de los señores Prevendados, podeis$_V$ aser el boleto firmado por vos$_V$ a ver si los que corren con otras capellanias quieren transpassar a tu$_T$ cargo (letter by Gabriela Basabilbaso to her brother Manuel, Buenos Aires, 1784, quoted in Fontanella de Weinberg 1989: 118).

'(My) brother Manuel, if you want to take charge of the two chaplaincies, one of which is for one thousand and two hundred pesos in favor of the prebendaries, you can write the bill, signed by you, to see if those who oversee the other chaplaincies want to transfer (them) to you'.

In the later colonial period, some areas (Mexico, parts of the Caribbean, coastal Peru) followed the metropolitan preference for *tú*, seemingly because of closer contact with European norms. By contrast, other areas (Central America, the Southern Cone) continued alternating between *vos* and *tú*, setting up the stage for subsequent negotiation in post-colonial dialectal norms (Moyna and Sanz-Sánchez 2023: 198–9; Sánchez Méndez 2003: 310–8; §5.5).

Along the borders of the late colonial realm, geographical and social isolation, coupled with the resettlement of new population contingents, resulted in innovative dialectal patterns. An example concerns *yeísmo*, the merger of medieval /ʎ/ with /j/ (as in *pollo* ['poʎo] > ['pojo] 'chicken'). While koinéization accounts (§4.4) have sometimes posited this merger as one of the outcomes of early colonial dialectal leveling, the archival record shows it spread gradually in most colonial areas throughout the sixteenth and seventeenth centuries (Kania 2010). Sanz-Sánchez (2013) has identified an exception to this pattern in New Mexico, a sparsely populated colony. Here, the spread of *yeísmo* was much more sudden, spanning only a few decades and showing the hallmarks of new dialect formation via koinéization (§2.6). The triggering event was the Hispanic resettlement of the colony in 1693 following an Indigenous uprising in 1680. In the resettlement, an older New Mexican population mixed with newcomers from central Mexico. Letters by pre-resettlement New Mexicans show few to no traces of *yeísmo* in spelling, but writings by same-age newcomers include frequent examples (for instance, *cabayo* instead of *caballo* 'horse', or *aller* instead of *ayer* 'yesterday'). The documentation also allows us to study the phonology of the first post-resettlement New Mexico-born generation.

Table 4.4. shows the distribution of spellings suggesting merger among a sample of members of these cohorts (a total of 31 writers were included

TABLE 4.4. Presence of *yeísmo* merger in spelling in selected writers from colonial New Mexico (Sanz-Sánchez 2013)

Writer	Year of birth	Place of birth	Merger in spelling?
Fernando de Chaves	1651	New Mexico	No
Antonio Lucero de Godoy	ca. 1656	New Mexico	No
Juan de Mestas Peralta	1661	New Mexico	No
Francisco Montes Vigil	1665	Zacatecas (central Mexico)	Yes
Juan de Atienza	1666	Puebla (central Mexico)	Yes
Francisco de Ribera	1673	Mexico City (central Mexico)	Yes
Domingo Vigil	ca. 1695	New Mexico	Yes
Juan Esteban García de Noriega	1696	New Mexico	Yes
Baltasar Abeita	1707	New Mexico	Yes

in this study). Note how writers born in New Mexico after 1693 exhibit non-etymological spellings suggesting merger, like the settlers from central Mexico and unlike those from pre-1693 New Mexico.

The contrast between the quick generalization of *yeísmo* in this fringe colony and its more gradual spread in other areas can be understood as the consequence of the very different sociolinguistic environments. In central Mexico, higher urbanization and population density appears to have favored a more progressive diffusion of this merger. By contrast, in New Mexico, the resettlement created the conditions for contact between non-merging and merging populations and the leveling out of this phonological contrast in as little as one generation, as seen in other situations of new dialect formation (Kerswill and Williams 2000a; Trudgill 2004; §2.6).

As we saw earlier in this chapter, increased contact among Hispanic and Indigenous populations is one of the key ecological traits of the second half of the Spanish colonial era in the Americas. Therefore, the debate about the degree of influence of Indigenous pools on colonial Spanish is especially relevant for our understanding of the sociolinguistics of this period. The literature has often treated the attested outcomes of contact in current forms of Spanish as illustrative of the conditions of contact in the late colonial period. For instance, commentators have traditionally stressed the lack of evidence of interference from Indigenous languages in normative Mexican Spanish (Lope Blanch 2000: 193–7; Klee and Lynch 2009: 116–21); the few uncontroversial exceptions include the low-productivity suffix –*eca/o* from Classical Nahuatl -*ecatl* in demonyms: *guatemalteco* 'Guatemalan-MASC', *coahuilteca* 'Coahuilan-FEM', etc., and the retention of Nahuatl [tɬ] in some Nahuatl-origin lexical items (*tlacuache* 'possum'). The usual argument is that the incorporation of Indigenous population into Hispanicized communities was gradual enough to ensure the elimination of stigmatized interference features from the contact pools of the communities in transition (§4.4). In this line of thinking, in areas like Yucatan, Paraguay or the Andes, the later spread of Spanish and the continued historical use of Indigenous languages is credited as explaining the more conspicuous phonological and structural effects of L2 learning on local Hispanic pools seen today (Klee and Lynch 2009: 113–68; Michnowicz 2015).

Although obvious structural transfer effects are largely absent from many current varieties of Latin American Spanish, the sociodemographic information surveyed in the preceding sections confirms that many linguistic pools of the late colonial period must have included contact features originating in bi/multilingual learning (see *variantes híbridas* and *español mestizado*, Sánchez Méndez 2003: 210–22). Winford (2005: 144) has pointed out that interference phenomena that were once common in a multilingual population may disappear once shift is complete. Such intermediate stages in the process of language shift constitute part of the history of contact in a population and are therefore worthy of attention from an evolutionary perspective.

In this sense, understanding contact in both its linguistic and its social dimensions allows us to go beyond the canonical definition of *transfer* (Thomason and Kaufman 1988) or *imposition* (Van Coetsem 2000) of L1 features on an L2 (§2.2) as proof of the influence of bilingual learning strategies, in the manner discussed in Chapter 2 (§2.6; Muysken 2013). Remember that variants that may have presented processing advantages for both L1 and L2 learners of various ages allow us to investigate these learning-related effects (see §3.5 for some of these effects in late-spoken Latin). We can see an example in forms of analogical regularization in traditional varieties of Latin American Spanish. Some of these forms and their standard equivalents are presented in Table 4.5.

TABLE 4.5. Select analogical processes in traditional varieties of Latin American Spanish (Sanz-Sánchez 2011)

Analogical process	Examples	Standard equivalents
Analogical imperfects	*traer, caer, reír* 'bring, fall, laugh-INF' → *traiba, caiba, reiba* 'brought, fell, laughed-1/3SG.IMP', see regular 1st-conjugation imperfects: *amar* 'love.INF' → *ama<u>ba</u>* 'loved' 1/3SG.IMP	*traía, caía, reía*
Leveling of morphological alternations	*ha* 'have-1SG.PRES.IND.AUX,' *ha* 'have-3SG.PRES.IND.AUX'	*he, ha*
Regularization of stress in the 1PL of the present subjunctive	*váya* 'go-1SG.PRES.SUBJ' *váyamos~váyanos* 'go-1PL.PRES.SUBJ'	*váya, vayámos*

As pointed out by Parodi (2001), the presence of these forms in multiple traditional rural dialects correlates closely with the sociolinguistics of late colonial marginal areas. These offered opportunities for contact among native and non-native speakers with various degrees of proficiency, weak social networks (§2.6), and the absence of established linguistic norms in contexts like the rural *ranchos* (§4.6). In other words, these formal coincidences are not due to geographical diffusion, but to ecological commonalities across these populations (Sanz-Sánchez 2011; §2.5) and seem to owe their selection to the application of universal acquisition principles that favor more learnable forms and which were not overridden by consistent exposure to alternative features or by social motivations in these marginal populations (see *vernacular universals*; Chambers 2004, §2.5).

Contact in this period seems to have also resulted in even less salient effects of non-native learning. These include semantic calques, accentual and prosodic patterns, pragmatic strategies, or discourse conventions, which can fly under the radar of prescriptive discourses to eventually become indexical of post-colonial linguistic identities (Schneider 2007: 21–70). For instance, the possibility of influence of Indigenous intonational contours on the speech of monolingual Latin American Spanish communities has been posited (Lipski 2014: 52–3), although, when examined in present-day dialects, the evidence in some cases (Pešková 2024 for Guarani) is more conclusive than others (Velázquez Patiño 2016 for Nahuatl; see §5.7 for an argument regarding the influence of L2 prosodic patterns on the emergence of some dialectal norms in the post-colonial period).

Along similar lines, Company Company (2007) has analyzed the increase in frequency of a series of grammatical features as part of the emergence of a

Mexican Spanish norm in the eighteenth century. These constructions include dative clitic *le* (see §3.8 for historical antecedents) instead of *lo* in accusative function; the reduplicated possessive construction *su* + N + PP phrase as in *su casa de usted*, lit. 'your-2SG.POSS.DEF house of you-2SG.POSS.DEF', and higher frequency of diminutives than in other variants (*cuchillo* 'knife' → *cuchillito* 'little knife'). She interprets the spread of these options against the backdrop of the social changes that shaped urban life in late colonial Mexico (§4.5 and §4.6): at a time of increasing hierarchization following the demographic recovery of the Indigenous population, mass migration of Indigenous workers to urban centers, and growing participation of bilinguals in many social spheres, these features were interpreted as negative politeness devices that made it easier for speakers to navigate an increasingly complex social space (see also Company Company 2024). Even though these elements do not fit canonical definitions of contact features via L2 learning, Company Company's analysis shows that, from an ecological standpoint, such selections are clearly a consequence of the local sociolinguistic dynamics of contact.

In bilingual communities, alternation between resources of Indigenous and European origin could be exploited actively as a device to signal bicultural identities. An interesting (even puzzling) product of this alternation is the Güegüense, an orally transmitted satirical drama about colonial political corruption probably composed originally in the late seventeenth or the early eighteenth century. It is still performed in rural Nicaragua and was added to UNESCO's list of Intangible Cultural Heritage in 2008 (UNESCO 2023; see Figure 4.7). This text combines Spanish and Central American Nahuatl (with possible Pipil influence; for a discussion of the difference between Pipil and other forms of Central American and Mexican Nahuatl in this period, see Romero 2014). This combination is illustrated in the fragment in (3) (from the edition of the text in Mántica 2020). Nahuatl elements are underlined.

(3) *Gobernador*. <u>Matateco</u> Dio <u>miscuales quilis no pilce</u> Capitán Alguacil Mayor: <u>no pilces, simocagüe</u> campamento Señores Principales, sones, mudanzas, velancicos <u>necana</u> y <u>paltechua linar mo</u> Cabildo Real. En primer lugar <u>tecetales seno</u> mesa de oro, <u>seno</u> carpeta de bordado, <u>seno</u> tintero de oro, <u>seno</u> pluma de oro, <u>seno</u> salvadera de oro, y no mas hemo papel blanco y <u>paltechua</u> sentar <u>mo</u> Cabildo Real.

'*Governor*. I pray that God may protect you, my son, Captain Chief Alguacil: my son, suspend in the quarters where the leading men live the music, dances, songs, ballets, and such matters that please the Royal Court. Firstly, it is a shame that we have no golden table, no embroidered tablecloth, no golden inkstand, no golden pen, no golden trays. We only have white paper and other things needed to record a session of the Royal Court' (translation adapted from Mántica 2020: location 761).

Spanish features are predominant in this fragment, especially in reference to colonial administration (*Capitán Alguacil Mayor* 'main local sheriff', lit. 'Captain Chief Alguacil'; *Cabildo Real* 'town council', lit. 'Royal Court') or Hispanic colonial culture (*sones, mudanzas, velancicos* 'music, dances, songs', *papel blanco* 'white paper'). Present-day syncretic practices that combine features from Hispanic and Indigenous pools (§6.3) have been proposed as potential parallels for similar hybrid practices in the colonial period (Sánchez Méndez 2003: 213). However, it is more likely that the type of mixture used in the Güegüense was never meant as a realistic representation of a spoken mixed code or of everyday hybrid conversational strategies (Romero 2024, p.c.): as a matter of fact, the authenticity of some of the Nahuatl elements in the text as recorded since the late 1800s has been called into question (Balmaseda Maestu 2004: 297). Most of these Nahuatl elements are repeated formulae that exhibit the effects of oral transmission of theatrical language in the community centuries after shift to Spanish had been complete. But even if this text is not a valid representation of everyday conversational bilingual practices in the colonial period, it is clear that its origins are anchored in a context where forms of bilingual proficiency could be actuated for ritual or aesthetic purposes.

Besides increasing contact among 'Spanish' and 'Indigenous' pools, the late colonial sociohistorical archive also gives witness to Afrodescendants' linguistic practices. As earlier in the colonial period, however, the sociolinguistic representativeness of this record is not to be taken for granted. The few available representations from the late colonial period generally perpetuate the conventions of the literary *habla de negros* by *bozal* slaves typical of earlier centuries (§4.3, §4.4), including not just clear departures from attested L1 models, but also elements of Portuguese origin. Legal documents recording brief utterances by African slaves verbatim provide sporadic and seemingly more authentic representations, as in

FIGURE 4.7. Present-day participants in a Güegüense performance in Nicaragua (Roberto Zuniga via Pexels)

(4) and (5), two examples from Cartagena (present-day Colombia) from 1693 (adapted from Lipski 2005: 188):

(4) Señó   tené   razón, decí   bien
    Master to have-INF reason to say-INF well
    'The master is right, he tells the truth'.
(5) Blanco hablá
    White   to speak-INF
    'The white (person) speaks'.

These brief fragments exhibit features found in other non-native forms of Spanish, most notably the loss of syllable-final /r/ (*señó* < *señor*, *tener* > *tené*), uninflected infinitives (*decí* 'he says, he tells', see st. Sp. *dice*), and the lack of articles (*blanco* 'the white (person)', see st. Sp. *el blanco / un blanco*). Occasionally, we also find references to forms of learning beyond the mere non-native approximation of L1 Spanish models. For instance, in a short play from Ayacucho in the Peruvian highlands, dated 1797, a Black female character (*negra*) combines non-native Spanish features and Quechua (Lipski 2005: 132–3), in what appears to be a realistic representation of the hybrid repertoires developed by Africans in many of these late colonial contexts.

Unfortunately, the archival record is quiet about the linguistics of other Afrohispanic pools during this period that we do have sociohistorical evidence of, such as the maroon *palenques*. This is the case of Palenquero in northern Colombia (§1.8), where (besides a few scattered metalinguistic comments; §4.6) the linguistics of the historical population must be reconstructed from forms attested in recent decades. In a recent example of this line of research, Raynor (2024) explains the dialectally idiosyncratic use of *mano* 'hand' and *pie* 'foot' for 'arm, leg' in the Spanish of Antioquia (Colombia) alongside standard *brazo* and *pierna*, respectively, as a consequence of the local colonial sociolinguistics of language learning. This included high proportions of speakers of African (Niger-Congo) languages, as well as Amerindian (Chocoan and Chibchan) languages, all of which happen to exhibit the same semantic pattern. Raynor interprets this feature as an example of L1 imposition (Van Coetsem 2000; §2.2) of a semantic frame via the L2 acquisition of Spanish by both African and Indigenous speakers during the colonial period – another example of the ecological importance of multiple causation in language change, as argued in Chapter 2 (§2.5).

4.8. Colonial osmoses: Spanish influence on Indigenous repertoires

The recombination of language features in these colonial pools did not only go in the direction of Spanish features as a reflection of assimilation into Hispanic society. In this section, I summarize the evidence for the incorporation of Spanish elements into Indigenous languages throughout the colonial period. It should be noted that analogous incorporations into ethnic African repertoires may have taken place (as suggested, for instance, by Portuguese loanwords in West African languages via contact with slave traders, Lipski 2005: 226), but we have very little textual evidence for these selections. Situations of high demographic concentrations of speakers of African languages in contact with other languages (as in the case of Antioquian Spanish mentioned in the preceding section, or in other Afro-Hispanic enclaves, Lipski 2007; Sessarego 2021; §4.6) may have provided a favorable setting for recombination options beyond the historically more common scenario of shift/acquisition of Spanish features with limited lexical or grammatical interference.

The archival evidence for the incorporation of contact-related innovations into Indigenous pools is much more abundant, in great part because alphabetic literacy became important for at least some Indigenous groups since the early decades of the Spanish colonial period (§4.3). For instance, in the early seventeenth century, *mestizo* Quechua and Spanish bilingual poet Inca Garcilaso de la Vega decried the way in which other fellow *mestizos* spoke and wrote Quechua: 'they imitate [Spaniards] in their pronunciation and their way of writing so much, that almost every expression that they use in our language when they write looks Hispanicized ("españolizadas"), just like the Spaniards say them and write them' (Inca Garcilaso de la Vega 1609, quoted in Cerrón Palomino 2003: 89; see below for an example).

Direct evidence supporting De la Vega's metalinguistic assessment can be gleaned from documents authored by bilingual individuals whenever alphabetic writing was adapted to Indigenous languages. Besides the Andes, central Mexico provides the best documented example. For instance, the corpus of colonial Nahuatl, studied in Lockhart (1992), shows a cline of contact effects that directly correlates with degrees of bilingualism and the incorporation of Hispanic cultural institutions by the Indigenous populations. These effects on Indigenous pools are the sociolinguistic counterpart to the growing effect of contact on Spanish repertoires (see 'Stage 4', §4.6). Lockhart has identified three main stages in this process, each with associated features, as shown in Table 4.6.

TABLE 4.6. Stages of incorporation of Spanish elements in colonial Nahuatl texts and sample associated features (Lockhart 1992: 261–325)

Stage	Period	Sample linguistic features	Examples
Stage 1	1519–50	Nahuatl neologisms for new concepts, semantic extensions, few loans	*maçatl* 'horse', lit. 'deer', *tlatlapoloni* 'key', lit. 'instrument for opening something', *tlequiquiztli* 'firearm', lit. 'fire trumpet'
Stage 2	1550–1650	Noun loans with Nahuatl morphology, no verbal loans, verbal semantic calques	*camisatli* 'shirt' (Sp. *camisa* 'shirt' + Nah. absolutive suffix -*tli*), *pia* 'to have' (originally, 'to hold, to keep in one's custody') after Sp. *tener*.
Stage 3	1650–today	Productive verbal derivation on Spanish roots, loan particles	*arrendaroa, obligaroa* 'to rent', 'to force' (Sp. *arrendar, obligar* + Nah. -*oa* infinitive verbal suffix); *como* 'as', *desde* 'from', *sin* 'without' (see Sp. *como, desde, sin*).

These patterns of incorporation of Spanish elements appear to not be exclusive to Nahuatl. For instance, in the Andean region, coetaneous texts show similar patterns of incorporation of Spanish loanwords (*gracia* 'grace', *ayunar* 'to fast', *ánima* 'soul') and semantic extensions in Quechua lexicon (as *qillqa* 'stroke, engraving', which came to also designate 'writing' and 'letter') (Rivarola 2001: 149–50).

Additional information about levels of familiarity with Spanish features other than lexical and morphological borrowings can be obtained from spelling trends. Specifically for the colonial Nahuatl corpus, Lockhart notes that the spelling of these loanwords tended to become more 'Spanish-like' as time went by, including less evidence for phonological transfer from Nahuatl. For instance, loanwords including voiced stops /b, d, g/ in the Spanish source, which had often in the early decades of the colonial period been written to reflect the lack of voicing distinctions in Nahuatl plosives (e.g., Sp. *bachiller, don* or *gobernador* as *pachilel, ton* and *copelnatol* 'graduate, Mr., governor') came to be typically spelled as in Spanish in later decades. This evolution points at a higher degree of awareness about Spanish phonology among the authors of these documents (1992: 293–6, 315–8).

Both the linguistic typology of these contact effects and their social pervasiveness seem to have been shaped by local degrees of pressure to develop competence or at least familiarity with Spanish repertoires. Thus, the data we just saw in Table 4.6 reflect the continuation of predominantly Indigenous sociolinguistic networks in the municipalities of central Mexico up until about 1650 (§4.2), with more widespread bilingualism not becoming common until the eighteenth century (Karttunen and Lockhart 1976; Lockhart 1992). By comparison, in the Yucatan Peninsula, less intensive agricultural exploitation and the lack of mining enterprises meant that European settlers were less numerous than in the central Mexican plateau, which in turn delayed the spread of Mayan-Spanish societal bilingualism (and the contact effects described above) by about one hundred years (Lockhart 1992: 446–8).

Large diachronic written corpora authored by bilingual scribes in the central areas of the Spanish colonial dominion offer priceless real-time evidence of how Indigenous populations negotiated contact with the colonizers' repertoires. However, similar contact effects can also be found in other regions where more recent linguistic surveys have identified elements that can be hypothesized to have been adopted in colonial times. For instance, lexical traces of contact with Hispanic pools during the colonial period are attested in languages all over the Americas, from North America (Lake Miwok, Hopi) to Mesoamerica (K'iche') and South America (Aymara, Mapudungun) (Campbell 2004: 265; Coler and Benegas Flores 2013; Golluscio 2009; Hill 1997). Once incorporated into these Indigenous repertoires, some of these elements were adopted by yet additional Indigenous populations, rather than via direct contact with Hispanic cultures, as shown by Bright (2000) about Spanish loanwords in languages of the US Southwest (like Navajo, Pima, and O'odham) via Nahuatl. And the same as in Nahuatl, we see a cline of contact effects, from Spanish loanwords to loaned morphemes and even more functional categories resulting in forms of syntactic or semantic convergence (§2.5, §2.6) across the pools in contact. By way of illustration, Cerrón Palomino (2010: 378–9) has found antecedents of several Spanish-influenced morphosyntactic features of present-day Quechua and Aymara in the colonial metalinguistic evidence (by Garcilaso de la Vega and others) – for instance, -*s* as a nominal and verbal plural morpheme in Quechua, modelled on Spanish nominal plural -*s* but pivoting on pluralization morphemes already available in pre-contact Quechua (a recombination strategy reminiscent of the reinterpretation of Spanish morphology by bilingual Nahuatl-Spanish speakers presented in Chapter 1; Flores Farfán 2008; §1.8).

An intriguing aspect of the ecology of contact in some of these Indigenous communities concerns the possibility that high rates of borrowing may have resulted in regular structural hybridization along lexical/grammatical lines (see *mixed languages,* Thomason and Kaufman 1988; Thomason 2001; and *relexification,* Muysken 2013; and §2.2). The best-known example in the earlier Spanish colonial dominion, Ecuadorian Media Lengua, combines Spanish lexicon with Quechua morphology but is most likely a twentieth-century phenomenon (see §6.2 and §6.4 for further discussion). Significantly, the sociolinguistic conditions likely to have triggered the emergence of Media Lengua amid contact with Spanish by Quechua-dominant speakers in country-to-town rotary or cyclical labor patterns appear to have obtained in at least some colonial areas (Lockhart and Schwartz 1983: 138–40, 150–1). The possibility that such settings may have motivated speakers to create mixed codes during the colonial period is insinuated by other recently described cases of linguistic hybridization (such as Rincón Zapotec, Schrader-Kniffki 2008; or forms of Spanish-Nahuatl contact phenomena, Hill and Hill 1986; see also §6.3).

Beyond the Americas, the Spanish colonial enterprise also targeted areas of Europe, northern Africa, southeast Asia, and the western Pacific Rim. We will take a closer look at some of these contact settings in the next section.

4.9. Colonial contacts in Asia and the Pacific: A sociodemographic and ecological sketch

The Spanish arrived in the Philippines in 1521, permanently settling in 1565 in Cebu and in 1571 in Manila (see Map 4.2 for these and other locations mentioned in this section). Control of the largest north-central islands was secured several decades later, but in the southern islands, it was heavily opposed by local Muslim states. Until Mexico's independence (1821), the Philippines were administered as part of the Viceroyalty of New Spain. Spain's colonial rule ended with the Spanish-American War of 1898, when the archipelago was ceded to the United States (§5.1).

Spanish missionaries and colonists found here a very different political and social landscape from that of the Americas. With no large political units or cities, the Philippine population was ethnolinguistically diverse (mostly Austronesian), with a long history of economic and cultural contacts with Southeast Asia. Lacking the mining or agricultural possibilities afforded by the Americas, the colonial authorities used the islands initially as a stopover for trade with the Maluku Islands (Moluccas, present-day Indonesia). Eventually, the Philippines became instrumental in a regular shipping system between Manila and Acapulco (*galeón de Manila*) that brought Mexican silver to the Philippines in exchange for Chinese and Japanese trade products and southeast Asian slaves (Seijas 2018).

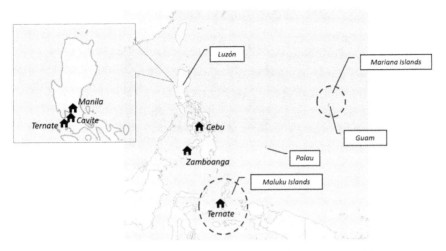

MAP 4.2. The Spanish colonial Philippines and the western Pacific area (map data by author; base map by Night w via Wikimedia Commons, license: https://creativecommons.org/licenses/by-sa/3.0/deed.en)

Because of this main role as a trade route node, the islands were never heavily settled by the Spaniards: a handful of soldiers, colonial officers, and missionaries from both Spain and the American colonies, concentrating in a few Hispanic settlements, made up the bulk of this contingent. As a result, the Indigenous sociodemographic structures were impacted less than in the Americas. Even so, in the Spanish towns, interethnic contacts among individuals of Hispanic, Philippine, east Asian and African descent quickly resulted in the emergence of a local *mestizo* group. Contacts with Spain increased somewhat in the nineteenth century following the introduction of steam-powered navigation and the opening of the Suez Canal (1863), but the demographic composition of the colony was not radically altered.

In addition to the Philippines, Spanish settlement in the Pacific included a short-lived military outpost in Taiwan (1626–42) and the more sociolinguistically consequential occupation of the Maluku Islands (Moluccas). Initially settled by Portugal, they came under Spanish control as per the dynastic union between both countries (1580–1640). A garrison on the island of Ternate was evacuated in 1662 to boost Spanish defenses against Chinese attacks in Manila. A contingent of Christian Moluccans (knowns as *mardicas*) who participated in this effort and settled on the outskirts of Manila have been claimed as one of the sources for the Iberian-based creoles of the Manila Bay (§4.10). Contact among Hispanic and Indigenous populations also occurred in other western Pacific archipelagoes like Palau, the Caroline Islands, and the Mariana Islands, including Guam. Only the latter was permanently settled by Spain as a stopover for the *galeón* connection with New Spain – scenes like the one in Figure 4.8 (from a late sixteenth-century illuminated manuscript describing the people and customs of the Spanish Asian colonies) acknowledge this role. The Marianas were ceded to the United States together with the Philippines in 1898 (§5.1).

FIGURE 4.8. Indigenous Mariana Islanders supplying food to the crew aboard a Spanish ship, Boxer Codex, late sixteenth century (Featous via Wikimedia Commons, public domain)

Despite the high social capital of Spanish in the colonial society of the Philippines, for much of this period motivation and opportunities for the Indigenous population to acquire Spanish features were to be found only in the few colonial towns and outposts. Here, presence of a diverse population favored a broad spectrum of contacts among individuals of Hispanic, Indigenous, African, Chinese, Japanese and other eastern Asian origins. Motivations for language learning varied: missionaries learned local Austronesian languages for preaching, Spaniards and other Hispanics learned them for trade, and Indigenous and east Asian individuals learned Spanish for a range of instrumental purposes. In the nineteenth century, as Spain began to pay more attention to the archipelago as one of the last remnants of its shrinking colonial domain, schools were instituted in rural areas, with Spanish as the language of instruction. These schools were dismantled after the American take-over in 1898, but they did contribute to an increase in the number of L2 Spanish speakers, from an estimated 2.46% of the Philippine population in 1870, to about 10% immediately after the end of the Spanish period (Lipski et al. 1996: 272; Quilis and Casado Fresnillo 2008: 69). Spanish also became an identity marker among upper-class *mestizos* – so much so that many of the foundational texts of the pro-independence movement by figures like Emilio Aguinaldo, Apolinario Mabini and José Rizal were written in Spanish.

Over time, a complex, evolving landscape of non-native Spanish recombinations resulted from these contacts. An example is the so-called *español de cocina* 'kitchen Spanish', a range of L2 Spanish repertoires among individuals employed in the service of the Spanish masters (Lipski 2010; see Lipski et al. 1996: 280 regarding *bamboo Spanish*, an approximation to Spanish by Japanese speakers settled in the Philippines). Others with more frequent access to native-like models developed high levels of proficiency in Spanish. As a telling example, some ethnically Philippine and Chinese witnesses are recorded in court proceedings as not requiring interpretation as early as the late 1600s (Kueh 2014: 131). This spectrum of repertoires, collectively conceived of as realizations of or approximations to Spanish, was the starting point for vestigial uses of Spanish in the mid-to-late twentieth century (Lipski 1987; §4.10).

In some locations, widespread non-native naturalistic learning in the absence of any consistent L1 model yielded several forms of structural recombination grouped under the collective label *Chavacano* (from Spa. *chabacano* 'unrefined, lowly') that have been studied as cases of creolization. In Ternate and Cavite, two towns in the vicinity of Manila, recombination was jumpstarted by the arrival of the Moluccan *mardicas,* who probably already spoke a Malay-influenced, Portuguese-based pidgin or creole (Clements 2009: 65). Here, *mardica* soldiers came into daily contact with Hispanic soldiers and the Indigenous population. Recombination continued as speakers from Ternate and Cavite resettled in the Manila suburb of Ermita starting in the 1600s, yielding early forms of the creole repertoires later known as *ternateño*, *caviteño*, and *ermitaño*. Further south, conditions for pervasive contact obtained in Zamboanga (on the island of Mindanao) in the early eighteenth century after the Spanish rebuilt an older garrison from the campaigns against Muslim *moros*. This resettlement brought together Hispanic soldiers, ethnic Tagalogs from Luzon, and Visayans from the central and southern islands, and possibly mercenaries from the Manila area creole-speaking communities (Lipski 2010). The result was yet another creole language (*zamboangueño*) that owes some of its structural characteristics to demographic and acquisitional parallels to the Manila Bay creoles. Lipski (2010) has proposed a model of gradual diachronic development of *zamboangueño* in several rounds of contact between the eighteenth and the twentieth centuries (§4.10). Modern forms of these repertoires have continued to be in use until the present, in various sociolinguistic conditions: *zamboangueño* is still transmitted and widely used, whereas the Manila Bay creoles are severely endangered (Lipski et al. 1996; Sippola 2020: 459). Additional similar creole varieties (or at least forms of contact Spanish featuring creole-like elements) may have been used in other areas of the Philippines (see Fernández Rodríguez 2011 for a late-1800s example from central Luzon).

In the many areas beyond the direct reach of Spanish authorities, contact with Iberian pools ranged from occasional to non-existent throughout most of the colonial period. However, the symbolic capital of Spanish as the language of a new institutional, religious, and cultural order was acknowledged far past the limits of the Hispanic enclaves, as demonstrated by the fact that speakers of many Indigenous Austronesian languages came to incorporate many (mostly lexical) elements to their local pools. Let's examine some of these contact effects.

4.10. East Asian and Pacific linguistic contact outcomes

The Spanish settlements in the Philippines seem like a good place to start exploring the outcome of colonial-era contacts in this region. Documents written by L1 Spanish speakers exhibit features that are also common in similar texts from the American colonies, including *seseo* (i.e. reduction to one voiceless sibilant; §4.4 and §7.2), merger of syllabic coda /l/ and /r/, aspiration or loss of syllable-final /s/, and variation between etymological and non-etymological use of 3rd-person clitics *lo, la, le* (Franco Figueroa 2010; see §3.8 for some background on the history of clitics in medieval Castilian, and §5.9 and §6.4 for some more recent contact effects on clitics in other ecologies). In the documentation produced by upper-class Filipino and *mestizo* élites, among whom the use of Spanish became a prominent social marker even following

FIGURE 4.9. Young Filipino and *mestizo* women reading pro-independence newspaper *La Independencia*, ca. 1898 (unknown photographer, The Huntington Library, Art Museum, and Botanical Gardens, public domain, source: https://huntington.org/verso/library-collectors-council-acquisitions-2024)

independence from Spain (see Figure 4.9 for a visually telling example), these non-standard features are less common. However, their everyday spoken performance encompassed a much broader repertoire, ranging from contact-influenced forms of spoken Spanish to local languages like Tagalog and even creoles (Fernández Rodríguez 2011).

By contrast, the record on the approximations to the language of the colonial masters by non-native speakers in everyday transactions is sparser. This was the case of the Spanish spoken by many Chinese immigrants in nineteenth-century Manila, a type of *español de cocina*. Such approximations included features like *mi/mia* ('my/mine-FEM') as a subject pronoun (see *yo* 'I' in st. Sp.), intervocalic /r/ as [l], and non-anaphoric object clitics (*mia quiele platical<u>o</u>* 'I want to talk') (Lipski 2010: 18–21), which are not typical of the imported pools from Spain or Spanish America (for additional examples, see Lipski 2010).

In the areas where creolized varieties emerged, linguistic selection departed significantly from what is found in other attested Philippine pools. Detailed descriptions of these varieties before the mid-1900s are lacking, so it is difficult to establish how close the current creole repertoires are to those of the Spanish colonial period. Recent changes like the replacement of normative European Spanish *nosotras/os* 'we' and *vosotras/os* 'you-PL' in *zamboangueño* with pronouns loaned from local Austronesian languages (Lipski 2012: 321–2; see Table 4.7 below) suggest a higher degree of similarity with non-creole varieties in the past. On the other hand, the influence of normative Spanish as used in nineteenth-century schools as the source of some of the similarities among the various Philippine creoles cannot be ruled out.

Among these formal commonalities, we find the combination of *ta* + verbal root (v.r.) to mark progressive/habitual aspect, *ya* + v.r. for past perfective (alternating with *a* in *ternateño*), and *di* + v.r. for future (*ay* in *zamboangueño*) (Lipski 2010, 2012; also §1.8 on the TMA particles of Palenquero). An example of the perfective structure in *ternateño* is presented in (6): note the alternation between *ya* and *a*.

(6) Ya   huntá   yo,   a   komprá   yo   ésti.
    PERF   gather   I   PERF   buy   I   this
    'I saved, I bought this' (Sippola 2020: 461).

In other respects, the northern varieties (*ternateño, caviteño, ermitaño*) differ from the southern varieties (*zamboangueño*). Table 4.7 presents the subject pronoun paradigms in three of these varieties. Note the difference between the northern creoles, where the pronouns transparently reflect Spanish forms (or original recombinations thereof, as in *ternateño* 'mihótroh' and 'lótroh', modelled after *vosotros*), and *zamboangueño* plural forms, derived from Cebuano and featuring the 1PL inclusive-exclusive distinction typical in Austronesian languages.

TABLE 4.7. Subject personal pronouns in three Philippine Spanish-based creole varieties (Lipski et al. 1996: 278; Lipski 2012)

	ternateño	caviteño	zamboangueño
1SG	yo	yo	yo
2SG	bos	tu	tu/bos
3SG	ele	ele	ele
1PL	mihótroh	nisós/nosos/nisotros	kamí (excl.), kitá (incl.)
2PL	buhótroh	busós/bosos/busotros	kamó
3PL	lótroh	ilos	silá

Such differences lay bare questions about the history of these creole repertoires, specifically whether *zamboangueño* is an offshoot of the northern varieties or whether it originated largely via L2 learning processes and post-colonial influence from local languages like Cebuano, with only marginal influence from northern relocated speakers (Lipski 2010, 2012). The use of *bos* for 2SG in some of these creoles is also revealing. It suggests that the Spanish repertoires that the earliest speakers of these creoles had access to featured abundant evidence of *vos* as the form for singular non-deferential address, either as a majority form or in alternation with *tú*. Recall (§4.7) that this was precisely the spoken address pattern reflected in texts from many Spanish American colonial areas in the early colonial period.

A fascinating aspect of the local ecology concerns the influence of the Manila *galeón* connection between the Philippines and New Spain. Linguistically, this connection surfaces in the widespread use of loanwords from Nahuatl (*atole* 'boiled rice meal', *mecate* 'rope', *zacate* 'grass') and Arawak or Taíno (such as *cabuya* 'pita, agave plant', *(e)naguas* 'skirt', *maíz* 'corn') (Lipski 1987: 37–8; §4.4). These items became entrenched in local pools and were still used by twentieth-century Spanish vestigial speakers (Lipski 1987: 44–5; Quilis and Casado Fresnillo 2008: 131–3). Conversely, the Spanish ships carried more than just porcelain, lacquerware, spices, or slaves back to the American colonies: the presence of southeastern Asian lexicon in Spanish (including Japanese loans *biombo* 'decorative movable wall' and *catana* 'sword', from 屏風 *byōbu* and 刀 *katana*, respectively) in colonial-era texts in the American colonies and even Spain, possibly filtered through Portuguese, can be connected to this trade route (Frago Gracia 1997).

Spanish loanwords in Philippine languages are among the most notorious contact effects from this period, and their adoption appears to have intensified in the nineteenth century in the wake of the spread of education in Spanish. As late as the mid-twentieth century, these loanwords accounted for 10–30% of the lexicon of Tagalog and Cebuano (Sippola 2020: 456). In addition to many of the items of Indigenous American origin mentioned above, other examples include Tag. *agwa* 'perfume' (see Sp. *agua* 'water'), Tag. *elektrisidad* (Sp. *electricidad*) 'electricity', and Ceb. *eskuela* (Sp. *escuela* 'school'). The adoption of loanwords also had consequences beyond the lexicon: for instance, languages like Tagalog, Cebuano and Ilocano developed a contrast between /o/~/u/ and /e/~/i/ in Spanish loanwords not originally present in their traditional lexicon (Steinkrüger 2008: 205–6), although this may have already been a change in progress in some Philippine languages, boosted by exposure to Spanish (Sippola 2020: 456) in true multicausational fashion. Socially limited bilingualism, however, seems to have put the brakes on the development of more substantial structural adaptations: Tagalog incorporated fewer discourse markers or function words from Spanish than many American Indigenous languages (§4.8) or Chamorro in Guam (see this section below) (Steinkrüger 2008: 213). But some function words and discourse markers were selected, including *pero* ('but'), *myientras* ('while', see Sp. *mientras*), and *bweno* ('so, ok, well then', see Sp. *bueno*) as conversational indicators of hybrid colonial identities and cultural dexterity (Sippola 2020: 457). Some of these functional elements were even embedded in hybrid (in ecological terms; §2.5) syntactic constructions combining Spanish and Austronesian elements, such as the *mas...* (< Sp.) *kaysa...* (<Tag.) comparative structure showcased in (7):

(7) Mas   maganda   si   Rosa   kaysa   sa   kapatid   niya.
     more   pretty   FOC   Rosa   than   POSS   sister   her
     'Rosa is prettier than her sister' (Sippola 2020: 456).

Contact conditions in the Philippines appear to have motivated at least some users to engage in even more hybrid conversational linguistic practices. An intriguing example is the code termed 'Malayo-Spanische', reported by Hugo Schuchardt (§2.2) as used in Vigan, north of Manila, in 1885. The excerpt in (8), provided by Schuchardt himself, shows incorporation of Spanish lexical items into a largely Ilocano grammatical base (Ilocano elements are underlined):

(8)   Mi estimado amigo: iparticipar<u>co</u> <u>qenca</u> á <u>na</u>nombrar<u>anac</u> á cabo del barrio <u>qet</u> sentir<u>ec</u> <u>unay ti caasanmo ditoy</u> porque convidar<u>enca</u> met comá á <u>maquipag</u>despachar <u>itoy bassit</u> á <u>na</u>preparar <u>ditoy balay</u>.

'My dear friend: I inform you that they appoint me chief of the district and I regret a lot your absence because I also wanted to invite you for the preparations I have at home' (from Steinkrüger 2008: 226).

This fragment features lexical colocations in Spanish (*mi estimado amigo* 'my dear friend', *cabo del barrio* 'chief of the district'), as well as Spanish lexical heads with Ilocano morphology, e.g. *sentirec* 'I regret', combining Sp. *sentir* 'to feel, to regret', and Ilocano morphemes *-e-* (transitive marker) and *-c* (1SG; for a complete morphosyntactic breakdown of this fragment, see Steinkrüger 2008: 226–7). The reliability of this attestation has been questioned (see, for instance, Fernández Rodríguez 2011: 199–200). But even if only partially modelled on actual communicative strategies of this period, together with archival and sociohistorical evidence for pidginized *español de cocina* and early creole varieties, this type of hybrid practices adds to the puzzle of contact effects in colonial Philippines.

Elsewhere in the Pacific Ocean, Indigenous pools in the Mariana Islands were also significantly reformulated via *relexification* (Muysken 2013; §2.2), consisting of the replacement of massive amounts of lexicon with Spanish forms (see §6.4 for another example in Ecuadorian Media Lengua). The result, termed *Chamorro* (locally *chamoru*) is classified as an Austronesian language containing as much as 50–60% of Spanish lexical material (Rodríguez-Ponga y Salamanca 1996: 247). There is no consensus as to the degree of Spanish grammatical influence on Chamorro (Lipski et al. 1996: 281–2). Some diachronic innovations motivated by contact with Spanish pools resemble those in the Philippine languages in having had at least some grammatical effects, such as the emergence of a five-vowel phonemic system (Rodríguez-Ponga y Salamanca 1996: 246) and the incorporation of some function words (like demonstrative *esti* < Sp. *este* 'this-MASC.SG' or article *un* < Sp. *un* 'a(n)-MASC.SG') (see Sippola 2020: 457–9 for these and other examples).

4.11. Conclusion

This chapter covered a wide range of sociolinguistic settings stemming from the geopolitical expansion of Spain over the Western Hemisphere and the Pacific Ocean. The available evidence on the linguistic, sociodemographic, and cultural conditions that followed Iberian settlement in the Americas shed light on the operation of multiple linguistic and social ecological mechanisms that shaped the emergence of feature pools often markedly different from those brought from the Iberian Peninsula. The linguistic results came to include elements that have traditionally been described as stemming from language contact and from dialect contact, whether originating directly in the contributing pools (= accommodation to dialectal features, interference due to L2 learning) or in more general learning strategies.

Speakers of various ethnic and linguistic adscriptions originating in four different continents participated in these pools to various degrees throughout the colonial period. Features of European origin, as symbolic of cultural and economic capital, were favored in many of these populations, resulting in linguistic and cultural assimilation. In other cases, however, the emerging repertoires exhibited the marks of local learning patterns, shaped by the undeniable action of speakers of non-European descent. In some of these settings, a clear-cut distinction between 'the influence of Spanish on other languages' vs. 'the influence of other languages on Spanish' is unfeasible, especially since, as in other language contact situations, the same bilingual individuals were often the agents of both directions of influence (Winford 2005).

Hundreds of years later, the historical and linguistic record of these contacts still challenges us to produce narratives of change that incorporate the actions of these various types of speakers. Unlike the imagined monsters and characters in the sixteenth-century European maps of the Americas that we started the chapter with, these speakers and their experiences were real. And, although usually silenced by the archival record and even more recent linguistic research, so were their voices and their cultural and linguistic practices.

Discussion questions

1. In the chapter, we have distinguished between 'early' and 'late colonial' ecologies based on several economic and sociocultural changes with sociolinguistic correlates, but this partition is, to some extent, arbitrary. In which ways are chronological partitions useful and in which ways are they unhelpful (or even detrimental) to our understanding of language history?

2. As we have seen in the chapter, besides written evidence in the form of letters or other types of documentation, materials such as metalinguistic evidence (i.e., explicit commentary on language use) and literary representations can assist us in reconstructing the sociolinguistic landscape of historically remote communities, especially minoritized ones. To which extent are these materials (un)representative of actual sociolinguistic realities, and how can we assess their reliability?

3. Besides the Spanish colonies, Romance features were also brought outside Spain to other contexts. Judeo-Spanish varieties (known as *ladino*, *haketía*, or *judezmo*, depending on the region) are an example (§6.1 and §6.9). Consult one of the available overviews of Judeo-Spanish (e.g. Penny 2000: 174–93) and read about several influential ecological factors in its development as reported in Kirschen (2018). How does the specific ecological embedding of Sephardic Jewish communities presented by Kirschen explain the linguistic selections that were recombined to give rise to Judeo-Spanish varieties?

5

Spanish in the Post-Colonial World: New Nations, New Citizens, New Contacts

5.1. Introduction: Questioning Spanish

In the summer of 1898, Spain's national pride took yet another blow: after a quick 16-week disastrous war, the peace treaty stipulated that Madrid was to cede the Philippines, Guam, Cuba, and Puerto Rico to the United States. 406 years after Columbus arrived in the Bahamas, the last remnants of Spain's once vast colonial empire were gone, and all the old metropolis could boast about were a few small possessions in Africa (§6.9). At a time when other powers like Britain and France still controlled millions of square miles beyond Europe, being replaced by a former European colony as the new colonial master of the Caribbean and the western Pacific must have felt to many in Spain like a cruel joke.

So, when Colombian philologist Rufino José Cuervo dared to invoke dialectal variation as a potential precursor to the break-up of Spanish into a host of Latin American national languages in 1899, he touched a nerve. Spanish novelist Juan Valera reacted to Cuervo's assessment in a newspaper editorial a few months later: Cuervo had failed to understand that the whole Hispanic world shared the same culture and spirit, expressed in a common language, so there was no risk that Spanish would follow the fate of Latin. Cuervo took the bait: in his response, he threw all his philological knowledge at Valera, charting the evolution of morphology and lexicon from Latin down to the current dialects and arguing that those same processes, if left to their own devices, would logically lead to linguistic fragmentation. Valera would not concede: how could a reputed linguist like Cuervo not realize that 'every living language, *the same as every natural organism*, carries in itself a force for preservation and regeneration' (quoted in Cuervo 2004: 109, my emphasis) that protects it from excessive changes? This back-and-forth went on for a few more rounds before dying down a few years later without either Cuervo nor Valera accepting defeat (more details are presented in Del Valle 2002, and the original texts are published in Cuervo 2004).

At first sight, the transatlantic disagreement between these two intellectuals reflects different views on the sociolinguistic diversity of Spanish. Cuervo, an expert dialectologist, was used to paying attention to the heterogeneous ways of talking that he heard in the streets of his hometown of Bogotá during the second half of the nineteenth century (see Figure 5.1 for a slightly earlier portrayal of some of the city's characters). For his part, Valera was an author and a diplomat with first-hand knowledge of classical Spanish literature and a deep-seated commitment to ensuring that, even though Spain had lost its colonies, it would not lose its place as the cultural beacon of the Hispanic world. But different as their backgrounds and motivations may seem, they both shared a fundamental belief that Spanish provided a common link for all Hispanic peoples, and that its status as a unified entity, perfected in the literary language, should be upheld. Their feud was ultimately less about language, and more about Hispanism as a viable system of beliefs and about Spanish as its symbol, at a time when Latin American nation-states were affirming themselves as geopolitical and cultural actors, and Spain's preeminence at both levels was more questionable than ever. Could this indeed be the downfall of Spanish that Nebrija (§3.1) had fretted about almost four centuries earlier?

These questions were not new and, unsurprisingly, they did not go away after Cuervo's and Valera's exchange. The end of the colonial period was a historically protracted process, spanning from the first armed uprisings against Spain in Latin America around 1810 to the 1898 defeat to the United States, and continuing well into the twentieth century up to Spain's de-colonization of Western Sahara in 1975. Throughout this process, the emergence of new nations triggered an ideological search for elements of cultural identification. In this search, language discourses played a central role – the activity of Madrid-based Real Academia

FIGURE 5.1. Early-independence Bogotá in the 1820s–1830s in Alcide D'Orbigny's *La relation du voyage dans l'Amérique méridionale pendant les années 1826 à 1833* (Fondo Antiguo de la Biblioteca de la Universidad de Sevilla via Flickr, public domain)

Española as an arbiter of language variation since its foundation in 1713 and the various reactions to this activity from various actors across the Spanish-speaking world are a particularly visible example of these ideological struggles (Del Valle 2002, 2013b). In fact, many of the linguistic changes stemming from post-colonial contacts in Hispanic societies may be conceptualized from this lens, as either conforming to discourses of cultural homogeneity or as enhancing linguistic divergence.

In this chapter, I focus on four areas where the linguistic consequences of these processes are particularly discernible. Three of these post-colonial settings selected in this chapter concern Latin America: new border communities (§5.2 and §5.3); the effects of country-to-city migration (§5.4 and §5.5); and the arrival of foreign populations (§5.6 and §5.7). The last two sections in the chapter concern Spain, showing how the sociolinguistics of the old metropolis during this period continued to be influenced by its relationship to its earlier colonies (§5.8 and §5.9). Several more recent post-colonial ecologies are covered in Chapter 6. As in previous chapters, I first present several key historical and demographic points, and I survey some important environmental triggers, before describing the local effects of contact.

5.2. New borders in the Spanish Americas: Historical and ecological context

The beginning of the end of Spain's colonial presence in the Americas can be connected to the Bourbon administrative and taxation reforms. As noted in Chapter 4 (§4.5 and §4.6), the *criollo* social élite claimed an increasingly prominent role in the socioeconomic structure of the Spanish colonies throughout the eighteenth century. Influenced by the ideals of free trade and personal freedom of the European Enlightenment (Villavicencio 2015), they opposed these reforms. Soon, economic demands turned into calls for political rupture, and the American (1776) and French (1789) revolutions offered a strategic roadmap. In addition, African slave and Indigenous uprisings during the colonial period (such as the New Mexico Pueblo Revolt in 1680, the Tupac Amaru Rebellion in Peru in 1780–3, and the Haitian Revolution in 1791–1804) presented an anti-colonial precedent for late colonial *castas*. These various ethnic groups did not necessarily share the same goals, but they coincided in seeing political independence from Spain as a necessary step toward social emancipation.

Napoleon's invasion of Spain in 1808 was the immediate catalyst for the widespread anti-colonial revolutions of the early nineteenth century. In a few years, Spain lost control of most of its American colonies (for instance, Mexico in 1821, Peru in 1824), and by the mid-1820s, Cuba and Puerto Rico were the only territories in the Western hemisphere still under Spanish control. A short-lived independent republic on Hispaniola was invaded by Haiti in 1822, declared independence in 1844, and reverted to Spanish control in 1861 before becoming independent again in 1865. Pro-independence uprisings in Cuba and Puerto Rico were initially squashed, but all-out war broke out in Cuba in 1895. American intervention brought the war to a quick end with Spain's defeat in 1898, as discussed (§5.1).

The most immediate geopolitical consequence of independence was the drawing of new borders. Short-lived nations (Republic of the Great Colombia, Republic of Central America) eventually split into smaller units. Territorial disputes led to conflicts among the new countries, as nations vied for natural resources (War of the Pacific between Chile, Bolivia, and Peru, 1879–84; Chaco War between Bolivia and Paraguay, 1932–5). The independence of the United States (1783), Haiti (1804), and Brazil (1825) also impacted the geopolitics, demography, and socioeconomics of the Western Hemisphere. Nowhere were the ecological consequences of these geopolitical shifts clearer than alongside these frontiers: here, hundreds of miles away from urban centers, the recently drawn borders overlapped with previously existing populations, whose linguistic repertoires differed markedly from those promoted as the emerging national standards (§4.7).

The Mexican borderlands exemplify some of the characteristics common to many of these areas. The new republic inherited the northern confines of the Viceroyalty of New Spain, from California and Sonora to the Gulf of Mexico (recall Map 4.1). Local economies were based on demographically undemanding activities, such as cattle grazing, small-scale agriculture, and trade. In this environment, an ethnically hybrid population developed local repertoires far away from the influence of the sociolinguistic models emanating from the late colonial cities (see the *rancho* settlement pattern, Parodi 2001; Santa Ana and Parodi 1998; §4.6). Institutions like the military also afforded these diverse populations more social mobility than elsewhere: '[o]n the frontier …, where record-keeping could be lax, mestizos, mulattos, and Hispanicized Indians found ample opportunities to transcend their official racial categories' (Weber 1992: 327–8).

After the declaration of the Republic of Texas (1836) and Mexico's defeat in the Mexican-American War (1846–8), the United States took control of much of the area. New economic opportunities attracted Anglo settlers, who had already started trickling in during the Mexican period, but this process exhibited regional differences. Thus, California saw a massive influx of English-speaking settlers after the discovery of gold in 1850. By contrast, areas like New Mexico or southern Arizona, with fewer opportunities for large-scale economic development, attracted much smaller numbers of newcomers: while the population increased by 184% in Texas and a staggering 310% in California between 1850 and 1860, in New Mexico the increase over the same period was a less impressive 52% (Sanz-Sánchez 2014: 223–4). The ethnolinguistic landscape of these border areas was further diversified by additional immigrants, including thousands of Chinese workers that were employed in gold mining or railroad construction.

These demographic upheavals and the symbolic capital of English as the new code of upward socioeconomic mobility had profound sociolinguistic consequences. In California, Spanish 'quickly became a politically subordinate language, spoken by an ever-decreasing minority and increasingly restricted in its social domains' (Moyna 2009a: 169). Motivation to acquire and use English did not present itself in the public arena only: marriage between Anglo newcomers and members of the local Hispanic élites encouraged contact even within the family. As a result, a shift to English was complete in as little as one generation in some areas. By contrast, in New Mexico, lower rates of Anglo immigration created less pressure for the Hispanic population to shift to English: as it turns out, it was Anglos that commonly learned Spanish as a precondition for their participation in the local ecologies, and bilingualism in English only became common several decades later (Moyna 2009a; Moyna and Coll 2008; Moyna and Decker 2005; Sanz-Sánchez 2014).

The unequal spread of English in these areas is captured in Table 5.1, which summarizes the percentage of population unable to speak English in 1890 and 1900 in four border areas as per decennial censuses. Note the stark difference between New Mexico and the other territories:

TABLE 5.1. Percentage of population age 10 and older unable to speak English in four US Southwest regions, 1890 and 1900 (Sanz-Sánchez 2014: 224)

	1890	1900
Arizona	5.53	4.03
California	0.85	0.34
Texas	0.66	0.69
New Mexico	69.93	51.17

New institutions and policies also altered the local conditions of language use, fostering assimilation to English – but here, too, sociolinguistic effects were variable. Thus, while English officially became the language of education in California as early as 1855 (Moyna 2009a: 168), schools in many areas of New Mexico continued education in Spanish until the early 1900s (Sanz-Sánchez 2014: 225). As late as 1914, Aurelio Espinosa, a native New Mexican, stated that about one third of New Mexican Hispanics were still monolingual in Spanish (1914: 245), especially outside the cities (243, 245).

The old northern borderlands of Mexico exemplify the new status of Spanish as a minority and/or symbolically disadvantaged language, but along the border between Uruguay and Brazil, the tables were turned in its favor. Since the 1600s, the area that is currently northern Uruguay was settled by farmers and ranchers of Portuguese origin, who encroached upon Tupi-Guarani Indigenous territory. Even decades after Uruguay's independence in 1828, a significant share of the population in the area spoke Portuguese (Moyna and Coll 2008: 110–1). Speakers here had little motivation to learn Spanish, as evidenced by the lack of metalinguistic comments in nineteenth-century everyday written documents – in contrast to frequent remarks on the spread of English in similar corpora from California and even New Mexico (Moyna 2009a; Moyna and Coll 2008; Sanz-Sánchez 2014). Things started to change in the late 1800s with the spread of universal schooling in Uruguay, the development of printed media, and the rise of national discourses on linguistic homogenization, which treated the linguistic continuities across the border with Brazil as a threat to national unity (Barrios 2013). But despite enhanced pressure to use Spanish, the area's isolation from the urban centers of southern Uruguay allowed local linguistic repertoires to continue exhibiting the marks of contact with Portuguese (Lipski 1994: 342; §5.3).

The ecological role of national antagonisms was even clearer on the border between the Dominican Republic and Haiti. Here, post-independence territorial frictions continued the colonial-area geopolitical disputes between Spain and France. The current border, drawn in 1844, has historically been porous: as a result, Haitians have been a prominent demographic component of the Dominican population since colonial times. These contacts have taken place against a tumultuous backdrop of invasions and aggressions. Between 1822 and 1844, the Dominican territory was occupied by Haiti, and French was implemented as the official language, with Haitian Kreyòl becoming common in many areas as Haitian ex-slaves occupied the estates vacated by the Spanish (Granda 1994: 206–55). The historical presence of Haitians along the western border area and in the north (Samaná Peninsula), coupled with the arrival of Afrodescendant English and English-based creole speakers from the United States and the West Indies, has given rise to a patchwork of linguistic influences on local Dominican varieties (Lipski 1994: 237–8; Poplack and Sankoff 1987; Ortiz López 2011), some of which will be exemplified below (§5.3). To this day, despite the undeniable evidence for cultural and linguistic influences across the two neighboring nations, linguistic features perceived to reflect Kreyòl influence are still targeted as anti-Dominican in official discourses. For example, the northern *cibaeño* dialect has traditionally been stigmatized under the belief that it is heavily influenced by Kreyòl, even though this perception is not accurate (Bullock and Toribio 2008).

5.3. The linguistics of the new Latin American borderlands

When studying the effects of contact along these frontier regions, we face many of the same methodological hurdles as in other historical settings. Much of the archival material from these areas was produced by government bureaucrats and reflects standard written norms. Fortunately, some writings by semiliterate individuals (§1.9) have also been preserved. These materials allow us to take a peek into at least some forms of variation closer to everyday communication in these populations at the geographical and cultural margins of the new Latin American nation-states.

The environmental conditions typical of these borderlands have left their imprint on these corpora. For instance, Moyna and Coll (2008) compared nineteenth-century texts from California and northern Uruguay and found similarities as well as differences. Among the similarities, we find intertextual mixing, with each participant in an exchange sticking to one language (for instance, in California, affidavits were often provided in Spanish, but the official court documents based on it were in English). Lexical insertions (including loanwords and phrase borrowings) are also common in both borders, as illustrated by the insertion of English 'on the strike' and Spanish 'palo,' respectively, in (1), from California, and (2), from Uruguay:

(1) Como los operarios del telégrafo están "on the strike" no sé si podré avisarle (1870; Moyna and Coll 2008, 117).

'Since telegraph operators are on the strike [sic], I don't know if I will be able to warn you'.

(2) Hum estabeliçimiento com casa de parede de pedra, mangueiras de palo, arvoredo fructales (1841; Moyna and Coll 2008: 119).

'A property with a house of stone walls, mango trees (?; lit. 'wooden mango trees'), fruit trees'.

But we also find differences. For instance, intersentential language mixing of the type illustrated in (3) is a lot more frequent in California than in Uruguay (note also the metalinguistic reference to the addressee's proficiency in each language):

(3) Aunque estoy bastante triste procuraré tener la cara lo menos desagradable que pueda cuando Ud. venga; no quiero nunca correr a mis visitas con miradas que matan de amargas. *Are you ready to read my letter in English? Remember, you told me you would translate into Spanish anything I should write in English* (1859; Moyna and Coll 2008: 118)

'Although I am quite sad, I will try to put on as pleasant a face as I can when you come. I would never want to kick out those who visit me with deadly bitter looks. Are you ready to read my letter in English? ...'

By contrast, bilingual hybrid lexicon is more frequent in Uruguay than in California (e.g. "naçón" 'nation', see Sp. *nación* and Port. *nação*). Syntactic contact features are particularly eloquent witnesses of the blurring of structural lines between the interacting repertoires. Such features include syntactic calques (as in the insertion of *a* for a personal direct object, which is uncharacteristic of Portuguese, shown in (4); see also §1.8 and §6.8) and the favoring of syntactic options in Spanish with a more frequent structural correlate in the other language, such as the passive voice in (5), possibly enhanced by the higher frequency of the passive in English.

(4) site a o meu filho Manoel Ylha (see Port. *cite o meu filho*; 1854; Moyna and Coll 2008: 120)

'so that he may summon my son Manuel Ilha'.

(5) Cuando salí de San Francisco mi sueldo era $150.00 al mes, luego que llegué fue subido a $175.00 (see Sp. *me lo subieron / se me subió*; 1883; Moyna and Coll 2008: 119)

'When I left San Francisco, my salary was $150.00 a month, after I arrived it was raised to $175.00'.

Moyna and Coll interpret these differences as outcomes of the local embedding of contact along each border. These included much more typologically similar contributing pools (Spanish and Portuguese) in northern Uruguay than in California (Spanish and English), and clearer, effective mechanisms of sociopolitical subordination for Spanish in California than for Portuguese in Uruguay. As a result, while in California we see the 'rapid ... replacement of one linguistic and social order by another,' in Uruguay 'the haphazard mixing reflects a [cultural and linguistic] continuum that could be interchangeably expressed in ... Spanish, Portuguese, or a combination of both' (121). In essence, these resources constitute yet another example of structural convergence by bilinguals, who, as discussed in Chapter 2 (§2.5, §2.6) typically take advantage of the grammatical overlaps across portions of their repertoires to create innovative combinations across named language boundaries.

The sociolinguistic embedding of language learning in these border areas also determined how quickly and in which direction local repertoires were recombined. Again, the United States-Mexico border provides an example. Recall (§5.2) that New Mexico exhibited much lower rates of Anglo immigration and more widespread use of Spanish than other areas along the northern side of the border well into the early twentieth century. These demographic differences are reflected in the archival record. Thus, texts written by Texas or California Hispanics born immediately after the 1848 annexation by the United States show attrition (Montrul 2022; §2.5) in traditional Spanish grammatical features, structural calques from English to Spanish, and (again) a preference for structural convergence across both languages (Martínez 2000 for Texas; Moyna 2009a for California) – an indication of a generational shift in language dominance in favor of English (see §6.7 for similar effects in recent bilingual heritage communities). Documents from New Mexico, by contrast, do not exhibit similar effects until at least half a century later (Sanz-Sánchez 2014). Examples of such features in these corpora include non-canonical verb agreement in (6) ("yo le escribe," see st. Sp. *yo le escribo*) or the elision of the complementizer (*que*) and the prenominal placement of adjectives ("bueno y grande solar," see more frequent Sp. *solar bueno y grande*) in (7):

(6) mas que yo le escribe cada dia (California, 1873; Moyna 2009a: 11)

'but that I write to you every day' (see st. Sp. *mas que yo le escribo cada día*).

(7) usted save ese es un bueno y grande solar (New Mexico, 1917; Sanz-Sánchez 2014: 236)

'you know that is a good and big lot' (see st. Sp. *usted sabe que ese es un solar grande y bueno*).

Documenting the linguistic contact history of border regions is particularly challenging whenever the local sociolinguistic dynamics were perceived as a danger to the new nations. As seen above, this was the case in the Dominican Republic, where we must rely on a scant documentary record largely in the form of literary representations and metalinguistic descriptions to study the stigmatized effects of contact between Spanish and Kreyòl (Lipski 2004). Although such representations were usually meant as stereotypes, they do seem to point at both the incorporation of Kreyòl elements by speakers of vernacular Dominican Spanish and approximations by Kreyòl speakers to local Dominican varieties. The lines in (8), from a parodic song written by Dominican author Juan Antonio Alix in 1874, illustrate some of these features in the speech of a hypothetical speaker of Haitian origin (Lipski 2005: 170). In the song, the name "Otrú" perhaps refers to the Haitian town of Trou-du-Nord. "Lajabón" is Dajabón, a town on the Haitian-Dominican border.

(8) Hier tard mu sortí Dotrú   Yesterday very late I left Otrú
    Pu beniro a Lajabón,   to come to Dajabón
    e yo jisa l'entención   and I had (lit. 'I did') the intention
    de biní cantá con tú.   to come sing with you.
    Manque yo tá lugarú   Although I am a trickster (lit. a devil/sorcerer),
    pañol no tenga cuidá,   you Spanish man should not be worried,
    deja tu macheta a un la   leave your machete to the side
    pasque yo no cante así   so that I do not sing like this,
    tu va blesé mun ici   you are going to hurt me here.

Several forms in this excerpt are attributable to the non-native learning of Dominican Spanish (such as non-canonical gender marking, as in "machete," marked as feminine with -*a*, see st. Sp. *machete* 'machete-MASC.SG,' or "jisa," with an ending in -*a* absent in st. Sp. *hice* 'did-1SG.PRET). Another acquisitionally significant form is "tá," an apocopated, uninflected form of *esta(r)* 'to be' that forms the basis of *ta* + infinitive, a common periphrasis in *bozal* texts, Afro-Hispanic varieties, and other forms of naturalistically learned L2 Spanish (§4.7 and §5.7). *Ta* also operates as an imperfective particle in Iberian-based creoles Palenquero and Papiamentu (Klee and Lynch 2009: 100, 102, and §1.8; remember, too, the use of *ta* as a habitual or progressive marker in Philippine creoles, §4.10). Here, however, *ta* is used with a noun ("lugarú," a loanword from Kreyòl *lougarou*), and its use appears to be more as a generic uninflected copula. This use is not typical of recorded Hispanic *bozal* speech, but it does occur in Papiamentu (Lipski 2004: 525–9).

Besides the application of bilingual acquisition strategies, we have evidence here of hybridization (§2.5) across various historical source feature pools: spoken Dominican Spanish (for instance, in "pañol" 'Spaniard-MASC.SG' and "cuidá" 'worry, care-MASC.SG', seemingly reflective of reduced Caribbean articulations of *español* and *cuidado* or more likely *cuidar* 'to take care of'); French (*hier* 'yesterday', see Kr. *ayè / yè*, Sp. *ayer*); and Kreyòl, most clearly illustrated by 1ST.SG forms *mu/mun*, which stem from older forms of current Kreyòl *mwen* (Lipski 2004: 15). In some forms, more than one process is at work: for instance, *biní cantá* shows a combination of Spanish lexical bases in a verbal periphrasis with non-canonical syntax: both "biní" (see st. Sp. *venir* 'come.INF') and "cantá" (see st. Sp. *cantar* 'sing.INF') show elision of word-final /r/, a common feature of both Caribbean Spanish and Afro-Hispanic texts (§4.7), but this combination does not include *a*, contrary to Spanish (*venir a cantar*) but as done in French (*venir chanter*) and Kreyòl (*vin chante*) (see Ortiz López 2011 for more recent contact effects).

The sociolinguistic dynamics of the post-independence era were not felt only along these emergent frontiers. More central areas also underwent profound demographic, social, and linguistic changes, as we will see next.

5.4. The internal historical ecological dynamics of the new Latin American republics

Political independence brought about significant sociodemographic changes across the new nations: anti-colonial wars took a heavy demographic toll among the urban and rural peasantry, which made up the brunt of the fighting armies. Hostilities also led many to seek refuge in the cities, and many loyalist families left for Europe. All these factors, coupled with infectious disease outbreaks, resulted in demographic stagnation immediately following independence in many countries. For instance, as much as 10% of Mexico's population was wiped away as a result of the war, and agricultural and mining production was disrupted, further contributing to the depopulation of rural areas (Romero Sotelo and Jáuregui 2003: 32).

Slowly, though, the population of many of the young Latin American republics rebounded, and starting in the late 1800s, basic public health improvements (such as smallpox vaccination), coupled with higher birth rates and foreign immigration (§5.6) led to population growth (Pérez Brignoli 2010: 15). These increases were sometimes dramatic: for instance, by the 1880s, the populations of Uruguay and Argentina had increased by a startling 1,300% and 311% respectively by comparison to pre-independence figures, owing mostly to foreign immigration, as we will see below. Other areas, like Central America, Mexico, or the Andes initially saw much more modest population increases, but growth intensified in the first decades of the twentieth century. Thus, by 1950, Mexico had more than doubled its late nineteenth-century population and Central America had more than tripled it (Pérez Brignoli 2010: 16–8).

During the first decades following independence, Hispanic Latin American societies continued to be primarily rural. The last quarter of the 1800s marked a reversal to this trend, and by the early 1900s, many countries started seeing a concentration of population in the urban areas (Almandoz 2008), spurred by industrialization and immigration (both internal and foreign; on this point, see §5.6). By way of illustration, Figures 5.2 and 5.3 show population estimates for Lima and Mexico City in this period. As can be seen, after sustained but slow growth throughout the 1800s, both cities grew exponentially in the first half of the twentieth century.

Economic changes also shaped the demographic evolution of this period. Along the Andean rim, migrants from the highlands relocated to the coast or the Amazonian lowlands to work in new exploitative industries: cacao bean harvesting in Ecuador, tin mining in Bolivia, and sugar and natural rubber production in Peru (Maguiña Salinas 2016; Yépez Martínez and Gachet Paredes 2014). Across the Southern Cone, the introduction of barbed wire in the 1880s allowed landowners to manage their estates with fewer laborers (Hora 2001), leading to a surplus of workers. The evolution of mining during this period in the desert area currently shared by Chile, Peru, and Bolivia offers a fascinating example of the interface between economic and demographic changes at a local level: the extraction of silver in the first half of the 1800s, followed by natural fertilizers (first guano, then *salitre* 'sodium nitrate'), drew rural population from the three countries to the region. After Chile's victory in the War of the Pacific (1879–83), the sodium nitrate mines attracted a higher proportion of arrivals from the center and south of the country. The prices of nitrate salt collapsed in the 1910s, leading many of these workers to abandon the area, but those who stayed contributed to the long-term demographic growth of northern Chile (Avilés 2016: 23–6).

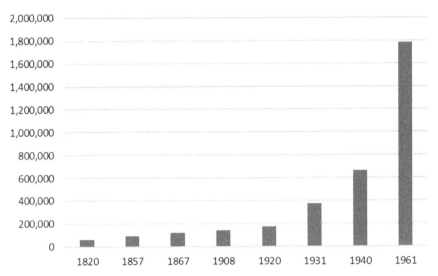

FIGURE 5.2. Population of Lima, 1820–1961 (figure by author, data from Córdova Aguilar 1989; Maguiña Salinas 2016)

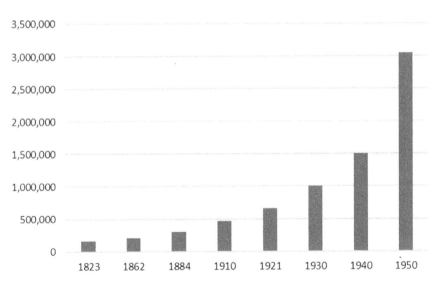

FIGURE 5.3. Population of Mexico City, 1824–1950 (figure by author, data from Kemper and Royce 1979; Dirección General de Estadística 1950)

One of the most obvious ecological consequences of urbanization and the redistribution of rural populations was the massive restructuring of Indigenous feature pools in favor of Spanish. Although the roots of this phenomenon can be located in the socioeconomic changes of the late colonial period (§4.5 and §4.6), the disruption of Indigenous ethnolinguistic networks intensified in the post-colonial era. The disappearance of the institutionalized legal and social marginalization of non-Hispanic individuals typical of the colonial period (see *república de indios*, §4.3) also had sociolinguistic implications: 'Indigenous people, who had once been members of separate legal divisions ["repúblicas"], were faced with navigating a new administrative system as citizens ... and monolingualism in an Indigenous language represented a major disadvantage' (Villavicencio 2015: 720–3). These legal changes worked in tandem with educational policies that enshrined Spanish as the national language and a cultural amalgamator, marking the spectrum of Indigenous linguistic repertoires as indexes of cultural backwardness, and enhancing the motivation for Indigenous speakers to favor Spanish in an ever-expanding range of social spheres.

Demographic growth and nation-state building also favored the creation of political, economic, and cultural institutions that promoted linguistic homogenization. These public institutions, in turn, required a new class of clerical workers (*funcionarios, empleados públicos*), versed in normative forms of Spanish. The authority of these institutions was legitimized in a growing number of venues, including newspapers, schools, and universities. These institutions played a role as harbors of new communities of practice (§1.4 and §2.6) based on corporate membership, where discourses on citizenship and national identity were embraced. As these institutions promoted an association between nation and language, they favored some local uses as indexes for the new nations, affirming their cultural independence from the old metropolis (Del Valle 2013b; see also Klee and Lynch 2009: 118). Ironically, by bringing cohorts of learners together, schools also provided a stage for forms of linguistic negotiation that clashed with the standard promoted by the teachers. The generalization of *voseo* for 2SG address against explicit prescription in Argentina and Uruguay in the early 1900s provides a well-documented case study (Narvaja de Arnoux 2013), as we will see below (§5.5). As standardizing and diversifying practices alternated, controversies about the legitimacy of Latin American vs. European Spanish norms became a staple of the academic debates of this period: the Cuervo-Valera showdown that opened this chapter (§5.1) is a clear instance.

The symbolic construction of Spanish as a pre-condition for socioeconomic and political agency is a hallmark of this period across Hispanic Latin America. But normative institutions (like schools and governmental agencies) were not the only avenues for the spread of Spanish. For instance, in Mexico, *arrieros* (muleteers), a highly mobile collective, became agents in the spread of rural repertoires, and *ferias* (town markets) attracted a sociolinguistically mixed crowd (Villavicencio 2015: 739–45). Similarly, the growing towns alongside railroad tracks allowed for everyday contact among an ethnolinguistically diverse population (see Figure 5.4), granting rural speakers access to urban areas but also favoring forms of linguistic negotiation that differed markedly from the practices promoted by school teachers and academic institutions. Some of the linguistic characteristics of these emergent contact pools can be partially gleaned from recent literature on communities currently undergoing shift to Spanish (Flores Farfán 2008; Schrader-Kniffki 2008) or which have preserved mostly rural social networks, as we saw in the case of ranchos and the emergence of traditional rural dialects of Spanish (§4.6 and §4.7). These situations provide a likely sociolinguistic analogue for what was once a much more socially widespread process in post-independence Mexico.

FIGURE 5.4. The *Ferrocarril Central Mexicano* at a stop in rural Mexico in the late 1800s (Library of Congress, public domain)

Peru offers another paradigmatic example of some of these processes (Clements 2009: 158–89; Escobar 2001; and Klee and Lynch 2009: 129–34). Throughout the nineteenth century, incipient industrialization, agricultural development, and economic instability following the country's defeat in the War of the Pacific resulted in increased internal migration, with Lima as the preferred destination (recall Figure 5.2). Demographic relocation and the symbolic value of Spanish as an instrument of political agency and socioeconomic mobility facilitated language shift – but even so, as of 1940, 35% of Peruvians were still tallied as monolingual in Quechua, Aymara, or other Indigenous languages (Klee and Lynch 2009: 133). In the cities, bilingual speakers gave rise to new urban vernaculars by combining canonical elements of standard Spanish with at least some features originating in spoken varieties of Andean Spanish and others due to various learning strategies, a phenomenon that continues today (§6.3 and 6.4).

Overall, these changes are typical of populations undergoing language shift: in these situations, the *verticalization* of the cultural structures of the minority group, with increasing orientation to hierarchical systems controlled outside the community (schools, economic institutions, health systems, etc.), bring about an increased preference for the repertoires of the majority or mainstream society (Brown 2022; see §5.6 below for examples among European immigrant communities, §6.2 for more recent examples, and §7.4 for an ecological discussion of this process).

5.5. The emergence of national varieties of Latin American Spanish

Lipski (2014: 44–5) has identified the urban growth of the post-independence period in Latin America as a critical factor allowing for the enregisterment (Johnston 2016; §2.5) of specific features as symbols of national identity. According to Lipski, these features first emerged as urban social markers in the late colonial period before spreading through the social landscape of the swelling cities of the 1800s and eventually across their rural hinterlands (see also Company Company 2024). These features included the articulation of /j/ as [ʒ] in Buenos Aires and Montevideo, the sibilant ('assibilated') articulation of phrase-final /r/ as [ɹ̝] in Mexico City (§6.3), and the palatalization of /x/ as [ç] in Santiago.

Sociohistorical cues lend support to Lipski's scenario. For instance, Fontanella de Weinberg (1987) recorded the spread of *yeísmo*, the merged articulation of the reflexes of medieval /ʎ/ and /j/ (§4.7), in eighteenth-century texts from Buenos Aires. Subsequently, the change whereby merged /j/ came to be articulated as voiced alveopalatal [ʒ] became a linguistic stereotype of the Argentinian capital and, by extension, the region. Initially stigmatized, this pronunciation must have first spread among the working classes and gained covert prestige as the 1800s progressed. By the 1930s, descriptions of Buenos Aires Spanish remarked on the trend toward devoicing ([ʒ]→ [ʃ]), showing that the alveopalatal articulation was already fully entrenched (§2.4) in the urban norm (Guitarte 1983: 147–65). But covert sociocultural allure was probably not the only factor in the spread of this innovation: it must also have been a learning target for those arriving from rural areas and, critically, for the hundreds of thousands of foreign immigrants resettling in the Río de la Plata region since the 1850s (§5.6).

A particularly revealing example of the linguistic effects of multiple simultaneous environmental triggers in post-colonial Buenos Aires is the spread of a new address norm based on *voseo*, that is, the use of historically plural forms for 2SG address. Recall (§4.7) that colonial pools featured widespread variation among several address forms and their associated paradigms, including non-deferential *tú* and *vos*. In Río de la Plata Spanish, two norms appear to have taken shape by the early nineteenth century: a rural norm, favoring *vos*, and an urban norm, modeled after European Spanish, which selected *tú* (Bertolotti 2016). Both, however, continued to alternate in everyday spoken language (Fontanella de Weinberg 1987: 110–20), as illustrated in (9–10) below, from letters written in the 1850s (from Fontanella de Weinberg 1987: 115). As in Chapter 4, forms historically belonging to the *vos* paradigm are marked as 'form$_V$,' and *tú* forms as 'form$_T$'. Only 2SG forms showing historical alternation in Río de la Plata Spanish have been labeled (for instance, by this point, possessive *tu* could be used for both *vos* and *tú* reference):

(9) Así, cuando hoy lo sois$_V$, debes$_{V/T}$ culpar solamente a tu maldita ingratitud

'Therefore, when you are so today, you must blame only your damn ingratitude'.

(10) Tú_T tienes_T conocimiento
    'You have knowledge'.

The ambiguousness of some spellings complicates our interpretation of this data (for instance, "debes" 'you must-2SG.PRES.IND' in (9), which in the absence of accent marks in the original texts could stand for either *tú* form *debes* /'debes/ or *vos* form *debés* /de'bes/). Be that as it may, it is clear that some of these uses depart markedly from those in current Río de la Plata Spanish: they include *vos* diphthongized forms ("sois" in 9, instead of current monophthongal *vos* form *sos*), *tú* forms in the present indicative ("tienes" in 10, instead of *vos* form *tenés*), and *tú* forms in subject position ("tu" in 11, instead of *vos*), none of which are part of the current dialectal norm. Remarkably, by the late 1800s, textual and metalinguistic evidence indicates that this alternation had been leveled in favor of *vos* forms (Moyna and Sanz-Sánchez 2023: 202–5). How did these centuries-long alternation disappear in just a few decades?

Moyna (2009b) and Moyna and Sanz-Sánchez (2023) have tackled this question, taking the chronological overlap between the explosive urban growth of the region (§5.4) and these linguistic changes as their starting point. In their account, several ecological factors conspired to yield this change. These factors included a highly diffuse pool of 2SG forms (combining L1 and L2 interpretations of the already highly variable traditional local norm); the acquisitional advantages presented by *vos* verbal forms (which do not present some of the morphological irregularities of *tú* forms, like diphthongization: p_o_der → compare *tú* form p_ue_des and *vos* form p_o_dés 'can-2SG.PRES.IND'); large cohorts of native and non-native learners of various ages; and the opportunity for scores of children to form social networks (§2.2, 2.6) in the booming working class slums and the new public schools at the turn of the twentieth century. They point out that the spread of *vos* forms in the archival record proceeded along a well-defined path (imperative > indicative > subjunctive) that coincides fully with the general sequence of verbal tense acquisition in child language. Putting all these pieces together, they attribute the generalization of the *vos*-based address paradigm to young children, who amidst a socially and linguistically unclear acquisition model, created their own norm in collaboration with their peers. Ironically, this selection occurred in the face of the *tú* forms preconized by the children's teachers and textbooks. Río de la Plata *voseo* epitomizes the linguistic consequences of the new patterns of communication that emerged in the growing urban areas of post-colonial Spanish Latin America. These consequences will become even clearer when we analyze the effects of large-scale foreign immigration (§5.6 and §5.7).

Contacts outside the cities provide an interesting counterpoint to the effects of urbanization on the emergence of new dialectal norms. Consider the case of the sodium nitrate mines of northern Chile, which as explained (§5.4) offered miners from the country's central and southern regions the opportunity to interact with Peruvian and Bolivian immigrant workers (see Figure 5.5). The result was a series of features now characterizing the northern Chilean variety (Avilés 2016: 69–72). One of these features is *vos* forms which, unlike in the Río de la Plata, remained in alternation with *tú*. This alternation is illustrated in (11), a fragment of a letter from 1928 written by a miner's wife to reproach her husband for having a lover:

(11) Hilario tu $_T$ no bas $_{V/T}$ a dejar nunca esa mujer porque tu$_T$ le escrive$_T$ a ella porque mi hermana la bisto lellendo las cartas porque ella se pone a leerlas afoera del correo i si es asi Hilario devis$_V$ aser honbre de desirmelo (Avilés 2016: 85).

'Hilario, you are never going to leave that woman because you still write to her, my sister has seen her reading the letters, because she stands outside the post office and reads them, and if that is the case, Hilario, you must be a man and tell me'.

Here, we see variation between *vos* forms ("devis") and *tú* forms ("tu," "escrive[s]") – a hybrid pattern reminiscent of the late colonial and early nineteenth-century Río de la Plata documentation, which continues to this day after being incorporated into a sociolinguistically and pragmatically complex Chilean 2SG address spoken norm (Rivadeneira Valenzuela 2016; §6.3). These letters between members of a mining family demonstrate that dialectal norms do not

FIGURE 5.5. Miners (*salitreros*) in a sodium nitrate mine in northern Chile, ca. 1900 (Biblioteca Nacional de Chile, public domain)

only emerge in urban areas: given the right circumstances, non-urban speakers can also play a critical role.

The sociohistorical record of this period is more opaque in connection to Indigenous feature pools. Available representations usually take the form of literary stereotypes with a comic intent. Joaquín Fernández de Lizardi's novel *El Periquillo Sarniento* ('the Mangy Parrot'), published between 1816 and 1831, offers an early post-independence portrayal of the Spanish of an L1 Nahuatl earthenware seller in Mexico City (Frago Gracia 2014: 44–5), as shown in (12) and (13).

(12) Agora lo veremos si me lo pagas mi loza, y páguemelo'sté de prestito, porque si no, el diablo nos ha de llevar horita horita.

'Now we will see if you (will) pay me for my earthenware, and pay me right now, because otherwise, the devil is going to take us both right away'.

(13) Tlacatecolo, mal diablo, ladrón jijo de un dimoño, agora lo veremos quién es cada cual.

'You demon, you bad devil, you thief, son of a demon, we will now see who's who'.

Noteworthy features here include a redundant or unlicensed *lo* clitic ("agora lo veremos si me lo pagas mi loza," see st. Sp. *ahora veremos si me pagas mi loza*) (§4.4), the combined use of 2SG deferential (*usted*) and non-deferential (*tú*) forms ("si me lo pagas$_T$ ... págue$_U$melo'sté$_U$," see st. Sp. deferential *si me lo paga... páguemelo usted* or non-deferential *si me lo pagas.... págamelo tú*) and emblematic loanwords ("tlacatecolo," see Nah. *tlacatecatl* 'demon'). Mexican colloquialisms ("de prestito" 'quickly, right now' and "horita horita" 'now, right away') and non-standard features traditionally available in rural L1 repertoires ("osté," "vías," "jijo," "agora," see st. Sp. *usted, veías, hijo, ahora*) are also used. Several of these elements can still be found in recently documented Nahuatl-Spanish bilingual pools (Flores Farfán 2008), making it legitimate to suspect that they really were heard by Fernández de Lizardi from early nineteenth-century Nahuatl-dominant speakers. These features confirm that, as in so many other ecologies in this book, Indigenous speakers in post-independence Mexico built individual repertoires by making selections that challenged the traditional boundaries between named language or dialect varieties.

In the next section, our attention turns to the ecological consequences of the massive arrival of foreign immigrants to post-colonial Hispanic Latin America, comprising free immigrants (mostly European) as well as forced labor (African slaves or Chinese indentured laborers).

5.6. Immigrants, indentured workers, and slaves

After independence, many of the new Latin American republics sought to foster demographic and economic growth. To that purpose, they relaxed restrictions on (mostly European) immigration, making it easy for immigrants to open businesses and own land. These measures did not always yield immediate results. For instance, in Peru, despite the government's efforts, the proportion of immigrants remained minuscule throughout the 1800s, peaking in 1876 at a meager 4% of the total population (Maguiña Salinas 2016: 83; but see this section below regarding Chinese immigration). On occasion, pro-immigration policies backfired. A well-known example is the secession of Texas from Mexico in 1836, led by Anglo settlers from the United States, many of whom the Mexican government had allowed to relocate to the country's northern border (Romero Sotelo and Jáuregui 2003: 39–42; §5.2).

The largest surge of foreign immigration occurred between the 1880s and the 1930s. At this time, the Southern Cone, particularly Argentina and Uruguay, became the second largest attractor of foreign immigration in the world after the United States (Moya 2006: 11), and with an even larger demographic weight: foreign immigration in Argentina contributed to 29% of the country's demographic growth between 1841 and 1940, compared to 10% for the same period in the United States (Pérez Brignoli 2010: 11–2). Table 5.2 shows the absolute and relative numbers of foreign arrivals in Argentina between 1857 and 1940 for the top seven countries of origin – as the data show, Italians and Spaniards were by far the largest contingents.

TABLE 5.2. Foreign immigration to Argentina, by nationality, 1857–1940 (Banfi 2018: 49)

Origin	Total number	Percentage of total
Italy	2,970,000	44.9%
Spain	2,080,000	31.5%
France	239,000	3.6%
Poland	180,000	2.7%
Russian Empire	177,000	2.7%
Ottoman Empire	174,000	2.6%
German Empire	152,000	2.3%
Total	6,611,000	100%

Some of these immigrants settled in rural areas to work in cattle grazing and agriculture (for instance, Germans from Russia and Danish immigrants, Fontanella de Weinberg 1978; Heegård Petersen et al. 2019). Most, however, settled in the cities, contributing to the urban boom at the turn of the twentieth century (§5.4). Nowhere in Latin America were foreign arrivals as abundant as in the Río de la Plata area, but immigrants arrived in other places too. For instance, in late-1800s Mexico, Porfirio Díaz's government attracted Americans and Greeks to Sinaloa, Koreans to Yucatan, and French, Chinese, Japanese, Russian and German immigrants to Baja California (Méndez Reyes 2013: 67; see §6.6 for a heritage Italo-Venetan community in central Mexico). German-descent Mennonites escaping assimilation pressures in Canada and the United States settled in northern Mexico, especially Chihuahua (Hansen 2005), as well as in the Paraguayan Chaco (Marqués Rodríguez 2017). A seldom-discussed case concerns arrivals from the Middle East, including Syrian and Lebanese immigrants, who settled in virtually every Latin American country since the late 1800s. Despite their small numbers, they were instrumental in the development of local socioeconomic networks as entrepreneurs and creditors, especially in marginal, poorer areas (Moya 2006: 20–6).

Other populations arrived in more disadvantaged conditions. Labor-intensive activities (agriculture, mining, railroad construction) demanded low-cost workers, and these became harder to come by once most European nations abandoned the Atlantic slave trade in the early 1800s (see this section below). Chinese indentured laborers filled this gap in many regions. In Peru, an estimated 90,000 arrived in the third quarter of the nineteenth century (Maguiña Salinas 2016: 73–4). In Cuba, still a Spanish colony until 1898, most of the estimated 114,000 Chinese workers arriving in this period were employed in the sugar cane plantations (Clements 2009: 103–5). They technically were on multi-year voluntary contracts, but dismal labor and living conditions caused high death rates among them. Still, many of them chose to stay in Cuba once their contracts expired, contributing to further diversify the local demographic landscape.

As legal restrictions to slavery were enacted, arrivals of African slaves stopped in many countries. Cuba, one of Spain's few remaining possessions in the Americas, was the most notable exception. As mentioned (§4.5), the island became a large importer of slaves since the late eighteenth century after the Haitian Revolution caused much of Haiti's sugar production to be displaced to other Caribbean islands. As a result, in the first half of the nineteenth century, Afrodescendants made up most of the Cuban population, as shown in Figure 5.6.

The Black population included recently arrived slaves from Africa and other European Caribbean colonies, as well as freed Black people born in Africa and on the island (Lipski 1994: 227–8; 2005: 103–7). White people were local *criollos*, Spanish loyalists that found refuge in Cuba during the Latin American

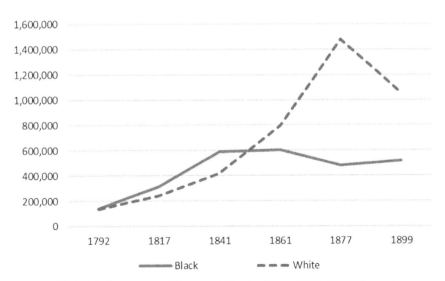

FIGURE 5.6. Black and white population in Cuba, 1792–1899 (figure by author, data from Clements 2009: 76)

independence wars, as well as newcomers from Spain (Galicians, Asturians, Canary Islanders, Catalans) and other Europeans. The local demographic mixture also included thousands of Haitians that settled in the eastern regions, and newly arrived Chinese indentured workers. The numerical predominance of the Afrodescendant population during much of the 1800s has fed conjectures about the possibility that processes of linguistic creolization similar to those observed in other Caribbean European colonies may have taken place here as well (§4.3). However, as will be seen below, other factors appear to have thwarted the emergence of creoles in nineteenth-century Cuba.

With incoming foreign contingents ranging from a handful of individuals to several millions, large immigrant groups were in principle better suited to exert more long-lasting influences on local feature pools. The varieties spoken by these immigrants were far from uniform even among individuals from the same country. For instance, Italian immigrants used many (often non-mutually intelligible) regional varieties; among Chinese workers, southeastern varieties like Min and Cantonese predominated (Clements 2009: 109). German-speaking migrants ranged from speakers of northern Plattdeutsch in Paraguay (Klee and Lynch 2009: 184) to Swiss German in Chihuahua (Hansen 2005: 9), among other varieties. Even Spaniards were not all monolingual Spanish speakers, especially those from bilingual areas like Galicia, Catalonia, and the Basque region.

The social dynamics of immigration were just as important as their demographics. Some groups came with an explicit goal *not* to assimilate, and whenever they were willing to inhabit undesirable areas, Latin American governments often did not mind. Mennonites, who secured explicit agreements with Paraguay and Mexico to have their way of life not interfered with, are a clear (though perhaps unusually extreme) example (Marqués Rodríguez 2017; Hansen 2005). Welsh immigrants in the inhospitable Argentine Patagonia are another case in point (Lublin 2013). Other immigrant groups in rural areas initially maintained tight-knit social networks for several decades, including practices and institutions that fostered language maintenance, like endogamy and community-based schools (for instance, Danish and Volga German immigrants to the southwest of Buenos Aires, Heegård Petersen et al. 2019; Hipperdinger and Rigatuso 1996). As these internal structures become reoriented to mainstream ones over the course of the twentieth century, shift to Spanish advanced, reproducing the pattern seen in other heritage communities (Brown 2022; §5.4 and §6.2).

In the cities, by contrast, the participation of immigrants in the local economies favored their social and linguistic assimilation. Integration also came as the consequence of state-sanctioned policies that promoted cultural homogenization. The Río de la Plata region again provides a paradigmatic example: here, public schooling was meant to expose children from immigrant families to Spanish and, through it, build a strong sense of belonging to their country of residence (Barrios 2013 for Uruguay; Narvaja de Arnoux 2013 and Ennis 2015 for Argentina). Classrooms soon became a key sociolinguistic environment where ethnically and linguistically diverse children interacted and negotiated standard and non-standard language features, as shown earlier in the case of local *voseo* (§5.5). Another example of a more informal institution that fostered contact were the *conventillos*, urban tenements housing as many as several hundred working-class newcomers of foreign and rural domestic origin, as in the example shown in Figure 5.7. In these communal living arrangements, immigrants and their children were exposed to highly heterogeneous repertoires, further contributing to the breakdown of pre-migration ethnolinguistic lines (Cravino 2016).

In these multiethnic settings, speakers could resort to several sources besides Spanish to navigate everyday communication. This first-hand description from 1901 of the linguistic ecology encountered by a recent Piedmontese immigrant in Buenos Aires underscores the diversity of the local sociolinguistic landscape:

> The language here is Castilian, quite similar to Spanish, but you cannot hear anyone speaking it. Wherever I go, either at the hotel or at work, everybody speaks either Piedmontese or Italian, including people from other countries, and even Argentinians themselves speak Italian (Sanhueza 2015: 191).

This description conjures up an environment where elements of foreign pools were in use well beyond the original immigrant communities. Although the assimilatory mechanisms worked as intended, with the immigrants' children growing up speaking Spanish, at least some linguistic features associated with immigrant populations became symbols for upwards social mobility and became incorporated in the emergent urban vernaculars, as we will see below (§5.7).

Indentured workers and slaves faced a very different sociolinguistic environment than immigrants in the urban areas. For many, living and working in conditions of

FIGURE 5.7. Buenos Aires *conventillo* in 1905 (Archivo General de la Nación, public domain)

isolation from the general population, there were few opportunities nor incentives to learn Spanish (Clements 2009: 109; Figures 5.8 and 5.9 illustrate some of these conditions). Others did have access to networks where they were exposed to Spanish repertoires. In late 1800s Cuba, for instance, some Chinese indentured workers

FIGURE 5.8. Chinese indentured workers in a rural settlement in Cienfuegos province, Cuba, ca. 1884, from Edwin Atkins *Sixty Years in Cuba* (1926) (public domain)

FIGURE 5.9. Afrodescendant sugar cane cutters in rural Cuba, late 1800s, from Robert Porter's *Industrial Cuba* (1899) (via Project Gutenberg, public domain)

fought alongside whites and Afro-Cubans in the insurgency against Spain. Many married Cuban women and their children grew up in direct contact with L1 Cuban Spanish (123). Even in the sugar plantations where many African slaves lived, social isolation from L1 and other L2 speakers was never complete, especially in the smaller agricultural enterprises. There are many indications that first-generation slaves (§4.3) spoke non-native varieties including elements from various sources: L2 acquisition-influenced features, transfer from their L1s (Yoruba, Kikongo, etc.), and even elements from Haitian Kreyòl and Papiamentu as spoken by slaves from Haiti and the Dutch Antilles. Their children, however, appear to have acquired repertoires indistinguishable from other forms of spoken Cuban Spanish – an indication that some Afrodescendants were able to access a certain degree of social mobility (Clements 2009: 88–91; Lipski 2005: 150–8).

5.7. Linguistic outcomes: Native and exogenous pools in contact

These fluid immigrant environments favored multiple forms of acquisition and linguistic recombination, constituting perfect examples of the multiple causation (§2.5) at the root of all forms of language change. Often, the action of non-native speakers was but one of several triggers motivating learners to select a specific option, as seen above for the emergence and spread of *voseo* in Río de la Plata Spanish (§5.5), where speakers of both local and foreign background seem to have collaborated. In the next paragraphs, I focus on two features for which research has identified non-native learners as critical ecological actors: the lexicon and intonation of Río de la Plata Spanish, and the morphosyntax of contact Spanish varieties among African slaves and Chinese workers in Cuba.

Recall that Italians were the largest immigrant contingent in the Río de la Plata (§5.6). Their non-native approximations to local pools resulted in a set of features that were represented collectively in local literature as a variety termed *cocoliche* (see Conde 2011; Ennis 2015; Fontanella de Weinberg 1987). Recurring *cocoliche* features include the stop articulation [k] of velars /x, g/ (*trabaco* < *trabajo* 'work.1SG.PRES.IND'; *nieco* < *niego* 'deny.1SG.PRES.IND'); the raising of /o/ as [u] (*vistu* < *visto* 'seen.PART'); verbal analogies (*queriba* < *quería* 'want.1ST.IMP.IND'); and Italian syntax, such as *article+possessive+noun* order in noun phrases (*il su color* 'its color', see Sp. *su color*) (Ennis 2015: 134–9). Many of these features appear to have been symbolic of unassimilated immigrant identities and were not selected in the emergent sociolinguistic norms. Italian loanwords are an exception: together with Quechua and Guarani items, many were incorporated into *lunfardo*, a lexical repertoire among the working classes of Buenos Aires and Montevideo partly originating in the argot of local criminals (Fontanella de Weinberg 1987: 142–4). Among these items, we find *chapar* 'to take, to grab' (see Genovese *ciappâ*, Sp. *agarrar, tomar*), *domani* 'tomorrow' (see st. Italian *domani*, Sp. *mañana*), *faso* 'cigarette' (see Venetian *fassu* 'bundle', Sp. *cigarrillo*), and *laburar* 'to work' (see Calabrese *lavurarë*, Sp. *trabajar*) (Conde 2011).

Other consequences of learning among and from Italian immigrants were less obvious but socially pervasive. The prosody of Río de la Plata Spanish offers an example. Most varieties of Spanish are traditionally described as displaying so-called *late peak alignment* in pre-nuclear accents in declarative statements (that is, the fundamental frequency (F0) of an intonational unit reaches its highest point toward the end of the tonic syllable or even in the post-tonic syllable). By contrast, Río de la Plata Spanish exhibits *early peak alignment*, with the highest F0 value fully within or in the beginning of the stressed syllable, and a more pronounced fall in the intonational contour of declarative sentences than other Spanish dialects. A comparison (Colantoni and Gurlekian 2004) between these patterns and those of Italian varieties has yielded significant similarities. Available sociohistorical evidence suggests that these prosodic patterns were not typical in the Río de la Plata in the mid-nineteenth century. Therefore, the authors argue that their origin lies in the demographics of contact among speakers of Italian and other speakers at the turn of the twentieth century. Originally a consequence of non-native dialect and language learning, these intonational patterns spread throughout the community once they became symbolic of socially mobile urban identities, as in the case of lunfardo lexicon (see also Ennis 2015: 138–9; and §4.7 for similar contact effects on prosody dating back to the colonial period in other varieties).

But local sociolinguistic conditions were not always as conducive to selection outside the foreign-origin population. As seen in §5.6, Chinese indentured workers in Cuba lived in a situation of exploitation and social isolation. Their approximations to Cuban Spanish, therefore, were primary targets for elimination by their children, who had more consistent access to local feature pools than their parents. Evidence of these non-native approximations can be gleaned from literary and historical sources (Clements 2009, 2016; Figueroa Arencibia 2008). The exchange in (14), a literary dialogue between a Spanish army commander (A) and a Chinese worker (B), illustrates some of these features (only B's turns have been glossed):

(14) (A) Tú chino, ¿no ha pasado alguien anoche por aquí?
  'You, Chinaman, did anyone pass by here last night?'

  (B) No señó Capitán, pa mi no sentí   gente   pasá.
    No sir   Captain   for me no hear-UNINF people pass-UNINF
    'No, my (lit. 'sir') captain, I did not hear people pass by.'

  (A) ¿Tú viste un grupo de insurrectos armados esta mañana que venían de Varadero?
    'Did you see a group of armed insurgents this morning that were coming from Varadero?'

  (B) Yo   no   mila   gente   suleto   tiene
    I   no   look-3SG.PRES.IND people   insurrect   have-3SG.PRES.IND
    arma   por   la   mañana. No señó, pa   mi
    weapon in   the   morning no sir   for me
    no   sabe,   ta   trabaja,
    no   know-3SG.PRES.IND be-UNINF   work-3SG.PRES.IND
    quema   carbón.
    work-3SG.PRES.IND coal.
    'I didn't see armed insurgent people in the morning. No sir, I don't know, I was working, burning coal.'

(Clements 2009: 114–5)

(B) turns reveal several features uncharacteristic of monolingual varieties of Spanish: various phonological adaptations, most notably [l] instead of syllable-initial /ɾ/ and /r/ ('mila', st. Sp. *mira*), morphosyntactic features including prepositional phrases instead of subject pronouns ('pa mi', see st. Sp. *yo* 'I'), present indicative (or uninflected) forms ('mila', 'quema') for past reference (see st. Sp. preterite *miré* 'I looked/saw', imperfect *quemaba* or past progressive *estaba quemando* 'I was burning'), and lack of subject-verb agreement ('pa mi no sabe', st. Sp. *(yo) no sé*) and gender agreement ('gente suleto', st. Sp. *gente insurrecta*).

Another notable feature here is the combination of the particle *ta* with the present indicative or uninflected form *trabaja* ('I was working', see st Sp. *estaba trabajando*), which is reminiscent of similar constructions in Iberian-based creoles Papiamentu and Palenquero (see §5.3 on *ta* in nineteenth-century Dominican Spanish-Kreyòl contact varieties). However, *ta* + infinitive in Papiamentu or Palenquero (§1.8) does not encode past reference, as in our example, but is instead a marker of present tense and imperfective aspect (Klee and Lynch 2009: 100, 102). If this construction is indeed representative of real contact features in these non-native Chinese-Cuban repertoires, its presence could be due to a variety of factors. Lipski (1999: 226–8) interprets it as a remnant of contact with Macao Creole prior to arrival in Cuba or a consequence of contact with Afro-Cuban speakers. Clements invokes universal learning principles (§2.6), with Chinese speakers reanalyzing frequent and perceptually prominent *estar* 'to be.INF' as an aspectual or tense marker (2009: 115). From a multi-causational perspective, all these hypotheses are not contradictory: instead, they underscore different aspects of the rich ecology of historical contacts giving rise to non-native Chinese repertoires in rural Cuba.

In comparison to the documentary record on Chinese workers or Afro-Hispanics elsewhere, the evidence of Afro-Cuban repertoires in the 1800s is more detailed, thanks to the work of contemporary commentators who described many of their features to contribute to the emergent academic conversation on Caribbean creoles. Clements (2009: 81–100) has summarized several of these traits. In addition to elements occurring in other Afro-Hispanic corpora (such as the lack of canonical subject-verb or noun-adjective agreement, or double negation as in *no quiere no* 'he does not want', see st. Sp. *no quiere*), the Cuban corpus includes other phenomena, illustrated in (15–7).

(15) Non-distinction of case or word categories:

> No   tiene   enfermo
> No   have-3SG.PRES.IND   sickness
> 'He is not sick', lit. 'he doesn't have sick' (see st. Sp. *no tiene enfermedad / no está enfermo*).

(16) Reanalysis of certain words:

> Él   no   entiende   ninguno
> He   no   understand-3SG.PRES.IND   no/no one
> 'He does not understand anything', lit. 'he does not understand no one' (see st. Sp. *él no entiende nada*).

(17) Non-use of function words:

No está barriga de su madre
Neg be.3SG.PRES.IND womb of his mother
'He is not in the womb of his mother', lit. 'he is not womb of his mother' (see st. Sp. *no está en la barriga de su madre*).

Clements notes that most of these features are common in L2 speech in other ecologies and can be explained as outcomes of adult acquisition (2009: 97–8) rather than as remnants of a stable pidgin or fully creolized variety, as sometimes argued (§4.3 and §5.6). Evidence for possible L1 transfer effects can be found in features like double negation, which exhibit structural equivalents in several West African languages and in Papiamentu. Interestingly, Afro-Cubans contributed to the emergence of the same spoken forms of Cuban Spanish as other populations – for instance, the *ta* + INF combinations recorded in the Chinese-Cuban corpus could still be found in rural Afro-Cuban speech in the early twentieth century (Ortiz López 1998).

Overall, the sociohistorical archive shows immigrant and other exogenous populations playing a critical role in the emergence of the new diverse repertoires of the post-colonial period – an ironic turn of events in light of Latin American state planners' efforts to promote cultural and linguistic homogenization.

5.8. New contacts in the old metropolis: The language ecology of post-colonial Spain

As we end this chapter on post-colonial ecologies, turning our attention to the colonial metropolis might seem contradictory. But, as we will see below, Spain remained connected to its previous colonies demographically, socially, and economically during this period. In this sense, the 'post-colonial' also applies to the old colonial master, and paying attention to the sociolinguistics of Spain will yield a more complete picture of the environmental dynamics of this time.

The political history of Spain in the nineteenth and early twentieth centuries was shaped not only by the loss of much of its colonial power, but also by internal political tensions. The period spanning the Napoleonic invasion of the Iberian Peninsula (1808–13) and the Spanish Civil War (1936–39) saw the beginning of modern parliamentary regimes, the first political constitutions, and the emergent articulation of citizen rights. These changes took place against a backdrop of political and institutional instability, with frequent coup-d'états, one dictatorship and two failed republics. Economically, some regions became heavily industrialized (especially the Basque Country and Catalonia), but Spain continued to be largely an agricultural country, with smaller properties in the north and large estates (*latifundios*) in the south. During the mid-1800s, official expropriations (*desamortizaciones*) were introduced to force the nobility and the Catholic Church to bequeath their properties to the state for their sale and foster a middle class of landowners. However, most properties were bought by aristocrats and the urban bourgeoisie, who favored non-intensive forms of agriculture requiring fewer workers. The growing availability of industrially manufactured products also put many craftspeople out of work (Nicolau 2005: 110–4).

Spanish in the Post-colonial World 153

As the productive structure of the country changed, so did its demographic landscape. During this period, the population experienced moderate, yet continued growth. The economic changes described above resulted in country-to-city migration, especially starting in the early 1900s. Figures 5.10 and 5.11 show the evolution of the population in this period in Madrid and Barcelona, the country's two largest cities.

Not everybody was able to find a job in the city, and starting in the 1880s, emigration rose: in the 1905–14 period, an estimated 1.5–2 million Spaniards left the country (Nicolau 2005: 92, 103). Most headed to Latin America, especially Cuba,

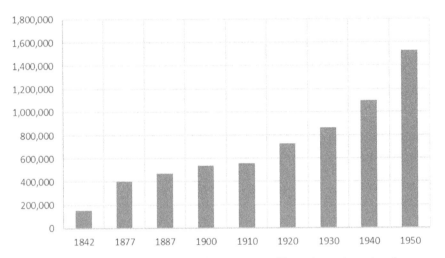

FIGURE 5.10. Population of Madrid, 1842–1950 (figure by author, data from INE 2023a)

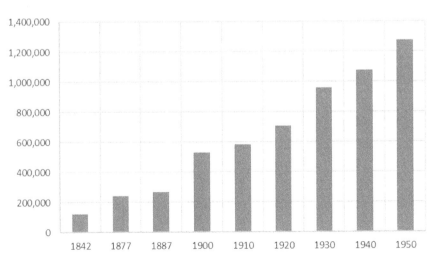

FIGURE 5.11. Population of Barcelona, 1842–1950 (figure by author, data from INE 2023a)

Argentina, and Venezuela. More Spanish emigrants chose Argentina than any other destination, even overtaking Italian arrivals in the early twentieth century (§5.6). Spanish immigrants contributed to various economic areas (Catalan sugar cane plantation owners in Cuba and Puerto Rico, Galician and Asturian small business owners and craftsmen in the Río de la Plata, Canary Islander agricultural laborers in Venezuela) (Castillo Martos 2001). Because relocating to another country was expensive, external migration tended to include more professionally skilled and literate individuals than internal country-to-city movements (Silvestre 2005: 241–2).

These demographic flows not only modified the social landscape in the regions of destination, but also in the areas that the emigrants came from. By way of illustration, Figure 5.12 displays the evolution of the population in Mondoñedo, in an area of rural Galicia with strong out-migration in this period (Castillo Martos 2001: 46). Mondoñedo's demographic stagnation stands in sharp contrast to the growth recorded by the largest cities on both sides of the Atlantic around the same time.

As agricultural properties became concentrated in the hands of a smaller group of people and city factories employed ever larger contingents of workers, awareness about socioeconomic differences grew, leading to the emergence of labor unions and political parties (for instance, the Spanish Socialist Workers' Party in 1879). Increasing confrontation between the political left and conservative forces set the stage for the collapse of the Second Republic and Francisco Franco's fascist coup-d'état in 1936.

Tensions also took the form of increased demands for political devolution from peripheral regions. As Spain begrudgingly faced the end of its colonial era (§5.1) and organized itself as a nation-state, political centralization was contested in areas with a sense of ethnolinguistic differentiation from the Castilian center, especially the Basque Country, Catalonia, and Galicia. New political

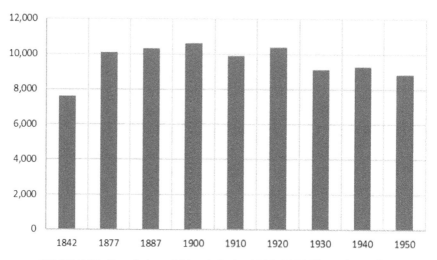

FIGURE 5.12. Population of Mondoñedo, 1842–1950 (figure by author, data from INE 2023a)

organizations emerged that advocated for autonomy or even independence for these regions (e.g. *Lliga de Catalunya* 1887 in Catalonia, *Euzko Alderdi Jeltzalea* 1895 in the Basque Country). Their emergence was accompanied by the development of cultural movements (Basque *Pizkundea*, Catalan *Renaixença*, Galician *Rexurdimento*) that promoted literature in languages other than Spanish. Calls for linguistic standardization became more frequent and led to the foundation of normative bodies (Galician: *Real Academia Galega* 1906, Catalan: *Institut d'Estudis Catalans* 1907, Basque: *Euskaltzaindia* 1919). In 1931, the new Republican constitution explicitly recognized several of these regional languages. Most of these steps were reverted when Francisco Franco seized power in 1939 and imposed Spanish-only policies in the following decades, but Galician, Basque, and Catalan regained regional official status in the Spanish Constitution of 1978.

These political, economic, demographic, and cultural changes had profound sociolinguistic consequences. For instance, growing social stratification favored indexical associations between specific speech features and socioeconomic strata, and competition among linguistic norms became a symbol of class-based and ethnolinguistic rivalries. Madrid exemplifies these changes. Internal migration to Spain's capital was geographically diverse: arrivals from the central regions (especially Old and New Castile) predominated in the late nineteenth century and the early twentieth century, but migrants also came from the south (Andalusia, Extremadura) and the north (Asturias, Galicia). In this sense, Madrid was more like Barcelona and less like other growing urban areas of this period, like Seville, Valencia, or Bilbao, which tended to attract migration mostly from their surrounding rural hinterlands (Silvestre 2005: 240). Most of these internal migrants resettled in a ring of working-class suburbs, particularly around the city's southern edge (De Miguel 1982: 56), where they mixed with speakers from other areas: Madrid's *corralas*, tenements housing families of varied provenance (as illustrated in Figure 5.13), are reminiscent of Río de la Plata *conventillos* (§5.6). Contemporary observers remarked on some of the emerging symbolic values of the features that were negotiated in this sociolinguistic mixture, as captured in this colorful description of everyday life in one of these neighborhoods in Benito Pérez Galdós's novel *Fortunata y Jacinta* (1887):

> Through the narrow windows one could hear, mixed with the smell of cheap fried food and a dingy, closed-up ambiance, a murmur of accented conversations, full of the clumsy sound of dragged final syllables. This manner of speech has emerged in Madrid from a blend of the Andalusian drawl, made fashionable by soldiers, and the Aragonese accent, which is picked up by all who want to act manly (Molina Martos 2006: 133).

Country-to-city migration was not the only factor fostering contact in Spain at this time. As was the case in Latin America (§5.4), a significant sociocultural development was the implementation of universal public schooling, codified into law in 1857. The linguistic effects of public schools, however, were hampered by their irregular spread: between 1880 and 1906, the population with no schooling actually increased (from 50.6% to 58.1%) (Núñez 2005: 232–33). During the Second Republic (1931–39), authorities prioritized educational reform by opening 7,000 schools just in the first year (Garrido Palacios 2005: 104). As in

FIGURE 5.13. A *corrala* in the Madrid neighborhood of Puente de Vallecas, early 1900s (Luis Torres via Pinterest, public domain)

post-colonial Latin America, schooling had a double effect: it exposed students to homogenizing discourses and standard language models, but it also gave whole cohorts of children of varied provenance the opportunity to form age-based networks. Military conscription, established in 1912 for periods of three years, was another institution that provided opportunities for the emergence of new contact repertoires, especially among poor and working-class men (Molina Luque 2012).

In the peripheral bilingual areas, the ecologies of this period showcase the effects of centuries-long contact processes, and the growing perception of Spanish as an instrument of socioeconomic mobility. As an example, Table 5.3 shows the proportions of population that could speak Basque in the mid-1800s. We can see a sharp difference between the southern region (Navarre, Araba), where shift to Spanish was more advanced, and the northern region (Bizkaia, Gipuzkoa), where Basque was still widespread.

Despite the resilience of languages other than Spanish in the rural areas, homogenizing forces gained the sociolinguistic upper hand as the 1800s progressed, especially in the cities. The result in the Basque region and other bilingual areas is usually described as one of diglossia (§3.7), with Spanish as the high

TABLE 5.3. Estimated percentage of speakers of Basque by province, 1866–8 (Madariaga 2014: 735)

Province	Percentage of speakers
Gipuzkoa	96.42%
Bizkaia	81.43%
Navarre	19.97%
Araba	9.95%

code and a symbol of socioeconomic mobility (see also Enrique Arias 2012 for Majorca, and Hawkey and Langer 2016 for Catalonia).

Around the turn of the twentieth century, migration from monolingual Spanish regions and the symbolic promotion of Spanish favored repertoires where obvious non-Spanish features were disfavored. Shift was more pervasive in contexts that were sensitive to explicit language discourses, as exemplified by the widespread use of Castilian in rural Catalan bureaucracy in the mid-nineteenth century, despite low spoken Spanish proficiency among the local population (Fullana 2017). In the cities, motivation to use Spanish was enhanced by the growing presence of monolinguals from other regions, as well as by social, economic, and institutional factors. Donostia (San Sebastián), in the Basque area, illustrates the influence of these factors in the generational progression of language shift:

> Between 1875 and 1925, economic progress, the strengthening of administrative bonds with central authorities, a progressive opening to Spanish and European culture, and the spread of literacy [favored] access to Spanish and the neglect of Basque. [Census data] show that a [large] part of the children born in San Sebastián in the last decade of the nineteenth century already had no other language but Spanish… Approximately forty per cent of them considered themselves monolingual in Spanish (Camus Bergareche and Gómez Seibane 2010: 231).

These developments were not always met with acquiescence, as shown by calls from Galician, Basque, and Catalan intellectuals and politicians to embrace local languages. However, the advent of Franco's fascist regime and the explicit institutionalization of monolingualism in Castilian Spanish in all state-related policies and practices galvanized the social and political disadvantages of non-Castilian repertoires, increasing the pressure toward assimilation.

5.9. The linguistics of early post-colonial Spain

The growing city of Madrid offers a paradigmatic example of the multidialectal contact pools typical of many Peninsular urban areas in this period. Molina Martos (2006) has studied changes in the distribution of three phonological variants across the sociolinguistic space of the city in the second half of the twentieth century, and explicitly traces back the onset of these patterns to the demographic shifts of the late 1800s (§5.8). These variants include the *yeísmo* merger of lateral palatal /ʎ/ and fricative palatal /j/ (§4.7 and §5.5), the aspiration or loss of syllable-final /s/, and the loss of intervocalic /d/. Metalinguistic evidence reveals that these features were initially perceived as 'southern' or 'unpolished.' Again, Pérez Galdós's novels illustrate these attitudes. In the example below, a character of well-to-do origins but with an inclination to associate with people of much humbler background is described as follows in *Fortunata y Jacinta* (1887):

> His savvy mother perceived a significant change in his son's habits and friendships outside the home, and she figured it out from her observation of certain very peculiar modifications in his voice and language. *He would give his* ll *the same dragged tone that low-class people use for consonant* y, and he had also picked up a variety of eccentric idioms and offensive expressions that she did not find the least funny (quoted in Molina Martos 2006: 133, my emphasis).

This passage is clearly referring to *yeísmo*, presented as a stigmatized index of low socioeconomic status that was seemingly gaining covert prestige. In Molina Martos's analysis, the critical trigger in the social diffusion of these three variants was the new demographic mix in the working-class suburbs. Feature pools in Madrid's micro-ecologies at this time also included north-central alternatives, which still retained prestige among the middle and upper classes. These features were reinforced by some migrant strains – for instance, women from the northern provinces (Asturias, Cantabria) gained a reputation among Madrid's bourgeoisie as reliable nannies, wet nurses, and domestic workers (De Miguel 1982: 61). Alternation among these features in the changing sociolinguistic landscapes of Spain's capital continued well into the mid-twentieth century, when some of these variants (most notably syllable-final /s/ aspiration [h] and deletion [Ø], and the loss of intervocalic /d/) started to be met with explicit disapproval as symbolic of working class or otherwise unsophisticated identities (Molina Martos 2006: 148).

Increasing social stratification had particularly transparent effects on speakers' pragmatic choices. A good example can be found in forms of address, which are particularly prone to change in sociolinguistically unstable environments, as seen elsewhere in this book (§4.7, §5.5, §6.7). At this time, we see changes in the pragmatic value of the paradigms associated to the two 2SG address forms used in Spain, non-deferential *tú* and deferential *usted*. In the early 1800s, the distribution of the paradigms associated with these two forms appears to have favored *usted* as the unmarked form, with *tú* restricted to familiar, non-symmetrical exchanges (for instance, from parents to children). Starting in the 1870s, Molina Martos (2021) has registered a spread of *tú* along two social vectors: top-down, as a marker of increased familiarity among the upper classes (with children using it to address parents), and bottom-up, as an index of solidarity in extrafamilial, symmetrical exchanges (i.e. among friends) among the lower classes. Around the turn of the twentieth century, industrialization, urbanization, and the spread of schooling (§5.8) all brought about a desire to signify upwards mobility among the urban middle classes, as well as solidarity among the working classes, and *tú* became the form of choice to symbolize these social aspirations. Later, social ideologies in vogue during Franco's regime also favored *tú* as the unmarked form for all sorts of symmetrical exchanges as it was seen to aid in keeping class-based conflicts at bay. Still, local environmental differences gave rise to dialectal differences, as shown by the regional persistence of some nineteenth-century uses, such as children's use of *usted* to address parents, which survived in rural areas well into the following century (Granados Romero 2018).

The linguistic effects of communication in these new urban contact environments were particularly innovative wherever contact pools included frequent access to non-Castilian Spanish features. Literary portrayals of the repertoires of rural or socioeconomically disadvantaged bilingual speakers are common throughout the 1800s (for instance, Basque-dominant individuals, Echenique Elizondo 1997). But sociohistorical evidence confirms that some contact effects were also pervasive among speakers of higher status, providing a sociolinguistic model for upwards mobility in which at least some contact features were not stigmatized. For instance, Camus Bergareche (2015) and Gancedo Negrete and Isasi Martínez (2015) have located some of these contact features in letters written by educated nineteenth-century Basque-Spanish bilingual speakers, as illustrated in (18–22):

(18) Merger of /s/ and /θ/, as indicated by non-canonical uses of *s* and *c/z*:

tropieso 'stumble', *perciana* 'window shutters'

(19) Null objects:

Estoy haciendo colección de sellos$_i$ y quisiera que se empeñara [usted] en recogerme Ø$_i$ pero que sean todos diferentes.

'I am collecting stamps$_i$, and I would want that you would make sure to get Ø$_i$ for me but [make sure] they are all different'.

(20) Non-canonical clitic marking:

[to the writer's mother] y sabe que *le* quiere muchísimo su hijo del centro del corazón muchísimo.

'and you [=his mother] know that your son loves *you* a lot from the center of his heart, a lot'.

(21) Assertive *ya*:

Ayer vino el hijo de Martín. Cuando me dijo que no tenía carta, *ya* me dio que pensar.

'Yesterday Martín's son came. When he told me that he did not have [a] letter, he *certainly* made me wonder'.

(22) OV word order:

Tu carta han leído todas
'They all have read your letter'.

In (18), non-canonical spellings suggest that the contrast between /s/ and /θ/, typical of all north-central Castilian Spanish varieties, has been neutralized as /s/ (see st. Sp. *tropie<u>z</u>o, per<u>s</u>iana*). In (19), the object clitic that is unmarked in most Spanish varieties has been omitted (see st. Sp. *recogérme<u>los</u>*). In (20) a single direct object clitic (*le*) is used with a feminine referent, instead of canonical Spanish *la* (see st. Sp. *la quiere*). In (21), *ya*, usually a temporal adverb ('already'), is used as an assertive particle ('definitely, indeed'). In (22), OV order, unmarked in Basque, is used instead of VO, unmarked in Spanish (see st. Sp. *todas han leído tu carta*). It should be noted that every single one of these elements has been identified in the recent literature about contact between Basque and Spanish (Klee and Lynch 2009: 39–56), which demonstrates that these innovations have been a part of Basque contact pools historically.

The sociolinguistic complexity of Spain's peripheral regions at this time is also reflected in the double directionality of contact-based replications, including the spread of Castilian Spanish features (or elements otherwise favored by contact) into traditional non-Castilian pools. At a time when cultural and political discourses increasingly called for the promotion and codification of standardized forms of Galician, Basque, and Catalan (§5.8), perceived Castilian linguistic influences were faced with opposition. For instance, in 1924, Catalan language scholar Pompeu Fabra bemoaned the effects of syntactic convergence (§2.5 and §2.6) with Spanish:

> Spanish influence can be felt in the use of verbal tenses, it has caused changes in grammatical gender, it has produced the substitution of all the expressions used by the Catalan classical writers for the expression of neuter concepts ... Catalan syntax has become an obsequious copy of Spanish syntax (quoted in Arnal i Bella 2007: 17).

There is evidence that Fabra's pessimistic assessment was not altogether inaccurate, as shown by sociohistorical evidence from various Catalan-speaking areas in the 1800s and early 1900s indicating at least some level of convergence with Castilian (Enrique Arias 2012). Fabra saw Castilian Spanish influence in two types of choices: the substitution of Castilian variants for traditional Catalan ones, as in (23), and the increase in the frequency of one variant historically present in Catalan over another in cases when the favored variant is also favored in Castilian, as in (24) (examples by Pompeu Fabra himself, quoted in Arnal i Bella 2007: 23):

(23) En aquell moment no *érem* a casa. – En aquell moment no *estàvem* a casa.
'At that moment, we were not at home'.

(24) Si *era* més alt no hi passaria. – Si *fos* més alt no hi passaria.
'If he was taller, he would not pass through'.

In (23), the copula *érem* (< *ésser* 'be.INF') is replaced by *estàvem* (< *estar* 'be.INF'), following the Spanish model in which *estar* (not *ser*) is the copula in locative contexts. In (24), the first option, with the indicative in the protasis of the conditional (*era* 'be.3SG.IMP.IND'), is replaced by the subjunctive (*fos* 'be.3SG.IMP.SUBJ'), as typically done in most varieties of Spanish (*si fuera más alto...*).

While this evidence shows that these features were current in early twentieth-century Catalan, it is also likely that their frequency varied widely across social groups, geographical areas, and levels of exposure to Spanish. Fabra himself acknowledged that Castilian influence was much less pervasive in the spoken language (Arnal i Bella 2007: 19), suggesting that the written language was the channel via which many of these contact effects spread. This contrasts with the situation in recent decades, where syntactic convergence with Spanish in Catalan has been attributed to the action of L1 Spanish or Spanish-dominant bilinguals (Blas Arroyo 2011).

5.10. Conclusion

As Spain's vast transoceanic empire crumbled, the sociopolitical and economic organization of the newly born Hispanic Latin American republics brought about tangible changes to the sociolinguistic landscapes of millions of speakers: borders were drawn, new sources of economic activity were promoted, political, socioeconomic and intellectual élites emerged and asserted their authority, and the demographic profile of many of the incipient nations was thoroughly rearranged via immigration. Many of the sociolinguistic correlates of these changes continued trends already initiated during the colonial period, as in the spread of Hispanic repertoires as the demographically and symbolically prominent codes of the post-colonial Hispanic Latin American societies, at the expense of Indigenous languages or other ethnolinguistically marked repertoires. Other factors were new. These included the growing flows of country-to-city migration, and especially the arrival of millions of immigrants, indentured laborers and (in some cases) even slaves. Together, these factors conspired to give rise to language repertoires and practices that challenged ideals of cultural homogeneity and shaped the new local vernaculars at the urban, regional, and national level, both in the emancipated colonies and in the old metropolis.

As this once vast colonial domain underwent these sweeping demographic, linguistic and ideological transformations, the overarching question posed in the heated exchange between Rufino José Cuervo and Juan Valera that we started this chapter with began to resonate even more strongly: how much diversity could Spanish take before its users would cease seeing each other as speakers of the same language? What did they still have in common? What is Spanish, after all? As we will see in the next chapter, this question continues to ring as loudly as ever.

Discussion questions

1. Discourses on nationality fostered by high social capital institutions (governments, education systems, the printing press) can be an influential top-down factor encouraging speakers to select specific elements. However, features enregistered as symbolic of a specific national identity can also emerge bottom-up from speaker networks. Which examples of both influences can you find in Chapter 5? Are those mechanisms still active in an increasingly globalized world, and if so, how?

2. According to Schneider (2007), post-colonial English varieties emerged as they went through predictable stages, from an original transplantation of the metropolitan language to distinctive local varieties with clear norms and possibly some contact influence from Indigenous languages. Based on what you have read in Chapters 4 and 5, does this model work for Latin American and other post-colonial varieties of Spanish, and if so, to which extent? Can you think of any exceptions?

3. As we get closer to the present, we find more and more tangible evidence of the role that minoritized populations (Indigenous, working-class or rural

speakers, slaves, immigrants) have played in the emergence of new sociolinguistic norms. Besides discussing their sociolinguistic importance (in the manner proposed in Chapter 5), in what other ways or by using which materials could language histories in Spanish and other languages be more acknowledging of this role?

6

Recent Contacts: New Language Ecologies in a Transnational World

6.1. Introduction: Glocalizing Spanish

It seems like everybody wants a piece of Spanish these days. Over the past two decades, news on initiatives to try and describe, legislate, or promote specific visions of what Spanish is and how it should be used keep coming. Just a few examples: in 2009, Bolivia approved a new constitution that gave over thirty Indigenous languages official status alongside Spanish; in 2015, the Spanish Parliament granted citizenship to descendants of Sephardic Jews expelled from Spain in 1492, explicitly acknowledging *ladino* or *haketía* (i.e. Judeo-Spanish) as one of the criteria to prove Sephardic ancestry; in 2017; *Despacito*, a song in Spanish by Puerto Rican artists Luis Fonsi and Daddy Yankee featuring reggaeton and Latin pop beats topped music charts in 47 countries (Cobo 2022); in 2022, Buenos Aires officials prohibited non-binary language (*lenguaje inclusivo*) in the city's schools to prevent it from interfering (as they put it) with the students' reading comprehension. In all these events, 'Spanish' is understood as an indicator of something else: colonial imposition, historical heritage, global pop culture, or gender ideology. This dialogic tug-of-war is, ultimately, a struggle to voice and access specific types of sociopolitical agency. In other words: deciding who has a right to define Spanish has become as important as determining what it is and how it should be used (Lynch 2018; Mar-Molinero and Paffey 2011; Villa and Del Valle 2015).

Studying recent forms of contact amid this multiplicity of voices is challenging, but being able to access present-day speaker behavior and attitudes affords us a vantage point from which to observe the action of specific environmental triggers on language variation and change. Recent and current populations offer abundant proof of the *heteroglossic* (§1.7) operation of homogenizing and diversifying motivations in the process of feature selection. On the one hand, factors such as education systems and testing protocols (Artamonova et al. 2017; Barrett et al. 2023), nationality and citizenship ideologies (Lipski 2011), and economic and cultural globalization discourses (Lynch 2018) privilege a reduced range of monolingual competencies or instrumental forms of bilingualism as a passport for political and socioeconomic agency (§5.4 for historical antecedents). On the flipside, intranational and transnational migration (Gugenberger and

Mar-Molinero 2018; Klee and Caravedo 2005; Zimmermann and Morgenthaler García 2007), digitally mediated communication (Lynch 2018; Wentker and Schneider 2022) and new cultural products (such as music genres like reggaeton, trap, or rap in Indigenous languages) (Balam and Shelton 2023; Mar-Molinero 2008) often foster hybrid, non-standard or stigmatized linguistic options as symbolic of cultural divergence and resistance.

In reality, most of these environmental triggers can operate to promote homogenization *and* diversification simultaneously, depending on the setting. For instance, over the past several decades, migrants have contributed to the emergence of markedly heterogeneous linguistic pools, as exemplified visibly in the linguistic landscapes of immigrant neighborhoods in many cities (see Figure 6.1). Similarly, recent travel and communication technologies also allow migrants to be connected to their places of origin more frequently and via more channels than ever before in diverse transnational global networks. At the same time, speakers in these settings are subject to sociolinguistic pressures to acquire specific resources, a process that contact literature has conceptualized in terms of *dialectal leveling* or *koinéization* (Martín Butragueño 2016, 2020; Parodi 2011) or *language shift* (Brown 2022; Canuto Castillo 2015; Silva-Corvalán 1994; Zentella 1997), but which often transcends and questions dialect and/or language boundaries (Mar-Molinero 2020).

In these diverse settings, speakers are presented with multiple competing rationales to adopt or reject specific features and their sociolinguistic meanings.

FIGURE 6.1. A trilingual (Chinese, Spanish, English) store sign in Madrid (courtesy of Aída Cajaravile, Elena González, Jasmín Soto and Raquel Oviedo with EquiLing, https://www.equiling.eu/es/)

For instance, Spanish-language media in the United States oscillate between embracing the sociolinguistic diversity of their multinational audience and promoting an assumedly neutral and homogeneous linguistic norm (*español neutro*, Lynch 2018: 28–30). This norm is in turn used to standardize media content and to construct an ideal Hispanic media consumer, projecting assumptions about linguistic correctness and subordinating the communicative practices of bilingual, multidialectal Latinxs (Mendoza-Denton and Gordon 2011: 557–9; Valencia and Lynch 2020). In this context, heteroglossic practices in public media, like code-switching in digital environments (Wentker and Schneider 2022) or bilingual pop music (Balam and Shelton 2023) are not merely aesthetic strategies. Rather, they reflect claims of sociopolitical agency from speakers whose linguistic practices are customarily delegitimized by standard discourses on linguistic appropriateness, socioeconomic success, and cultural legitimacy (§7.3).

Direct observation of these fluid and heterogeneous present-day linguistic ecologies has spurred a focus on *mobility* in recent approaches to contact. From this perspective, language use is not bound to specific localities (§1.4). Instead, speakers share linguistic resources as they move across national and sociolinguistic boundaries, whether in face-to-face or digitally mediated exchanges (Blommaert 2010; Canagarajah 2017: 2). In turn, new theoretical paradigms have emerged to capture the elusive sociolinguistic dynamics of these hyperdiverse settings. For instance, some authors (Zimmerman and Morgenthaler García 2007) have proposed the *linguistics of migration* as its own area of research. Others (Mar-Molinero 2020) have embraced the construct of *super-diversity*, stressing the 'dynamic interplay of variables among an increased number of new, small and scattered, multiple-origin, transnationally connected, socio-economically differentiated and legally stratified immigrants' (Vertovec 2007: 1024). Besides foregrounding the inherent diversity of every language population, these proposals question the ability of previous sociolinguistic models to describe and analyze the dynamics of language variation and change in twenty-first-century linguistic ecologies.

If sociolinguistic hyperdiversity is the new norm for many speakers, defining a language (§1.4) becomes an even more fleeting goal than ever. Over the past two decades, Spanish has been imagined as a 'global language' (Mar-Molinero 2008), a 'polycentric language' (Morgenthaler García 2007; Zimmerman and Morgenthaler García 2007), or a highly cohesive 'dialect continuum' (Moreno-Fernández and Ueda 2018). Although sociolinguistic heterogeneity is acknowledged as a basic trait in these theorizations, many still share in at least some of the underlying premises of the essentialist and monoglossic view of language typical of Western linguistics since the nineteenth century (§1.2). For instance, complexity is still often understood as reflecting some overarching structure, with sociolinguistic variation organized according to predictable constraints. From this perspective, multilingual practices might be common but do not ultimately challenge the status of languages as objects whose essential traits are somehow external to their speakers (see Del Valle 2014: 90–1 for this critique).

Taking the mid-twentieth century as a chronological threshold, this chapter covers a selection of sociolinguistic environments that challenge some of these assumptions. To organize this chapter, and at the risk of backgrounding other factors, I take national borders as a starting point, classifying contacts as *intranational* or *transnational*. This division is certainly questionable: in an increasingly mobile world, many ecological factors operate at both levels. At the same time, though, nation-state borders and policies still shape the way in which at least some speakers communicate with each other: migrants, refugees, and asylum seekers, for instance, are keenly aware of how national boundaries can impact one's everyday lived experience. As commonly noted in the literature on globalization, a defining trait of the age of mobility is the interaction between the local and the global: 'the local continues to thrive, although it must increasingly be seen as *glocal*, that is, enmeshed in transnational processes' (Eriksen 2007: 10, emphasis in original). This chapter explores some of these glocal interactions, stressing the need to both study the effect of national boundaries and transcend them in order to understand the environmental dynamics of many present-day populations.

The chapter is organized as follows. I first survey a selection of intranational ecologies (§6.2), overviewing some prominent linguistic effects of intranational contacts not involving migration (§6.3) and others that involve significant demographic movements (§6.4). I then discuss transnational contexts, exploring their main demographic (§6.5) and ecological characteristics (§6.6) as well as their linguistic consequences, both in settings of international migration (§6.7) and in cross-border contacts (§6.8). The remainder of the chapter focuses on settings beyond this national/transnational divide, including some recent manifestations of de-colonization in Africa (§6.9) and digital communication as an expanding setting for contact and change (§6.10), before concluding the chapter.

6.2. Intranational Hispanic ecologies: Contacts within national borders

As seen in Chapter 5 (§5.4), production concentration in the cities since the nineteenth century has led to significant nation-internal demographic transfers. In some countries, internal migration has been intensified by the loss of rural land following international trade deals, but the push from multinational companies to control natural resources has further disrupted many rural and Indigenous communication landscapes: Ecuador's recent agreements to allow Chinese holdings to extract crude oil in the Amazonian jungle as payment for the country's debt, a move with disastrous consequences for the environment and local Indigenous communities (Einhorn and Andreoni 2023), are a case in point. Armed conflicts have also resulted in forced internal migration. For instance, in Colombia, the conflict between the government and the FARC armed group (1964–2017) resulted in an estimated 6.8 million displaced people (UN High Commissioner for Refugees 2023: 26–7). Significant population displacements following economic or political instability have also plagued Cuba, Central America, and Venezuela, causing both internal and transnational migration (see §6.5 for figures).

Many of these demographic movements have taken the form of country-to-city migrations. Table 6.1 shows the evolution of the population of four large cities since the mid-twentieth century, generally exhibiting marked growth during this period (these data correspond to the respective municipalities and not to their whole metropolitan areas). Since cities cannot absorb all the incoming population, a part of this migration feeds transnational population movements (§6.5).

TABLE 6.1. Population for select dates in Bogotá, Lima, Madrid, and Mexico City, in thousands (Bogotá: DANE 2023; Lima: INEI 2023; Madrid: INE 2023b; Mexico City: INEGI 2023)

Bogotá		Lima		Madrid		Mexico City	
Year	Population	Year	Population	Year	Population	Year	Population
1964	1,697	1961	1,784	1950	1,527	1950	3,050
1985	4,236	1971	3,308	1970	3,120	1970	6,874
1999	6,276	1993	6,434	1990	2,909	1990	8,235
2005	7,185	2005	7,363	2011	3,198	2010	8,851
2020	7,743	2022	10,004	2022	3,280	2020	9,209

The share of the population living in urban areas has increased significantly over the last several decades in many parts of the world. In Spain, between 1960 and 2021, the urban population share increased from 56.5% to 77.17%. In the whole Latin America and Caribbean region, it grew from 50.58% to 81.37% respectively (World Bank 2022).

Internal migration is connected to social and economic triggers that frequently operate internationally, and nowhere is this clearer than along border areas. For example, lower production costs in Mexico than in the US have spurred industrialization in the form of manufacturing plants (*maquiladoras*) on the southern side of the border since the 1970s, a trend that has been recently enhanced by trade agreements among the US, Canada, and Mexico (NAFTA in 1994, USMCA in 2020). This process has attracted workers from other parts of Mexico, leading to marked population growth: for instance, Tijuana's population grew from just under a half a million in 1980 to almost 2 million in 2020 (INEGI 2023). Not all internal migration patterns imply movement to urban areas, especially when non-urban areas provide opportunities for agricultural, mining, or industrial development (for instance, Albertí 2015 in northern Argentina).

As earlier in history, growing urban areas continue to provide opportunities for exposure to new feature pools. Neighborhoods with high immigrant concentrations, commonly referred to as *ciudades dormitorio* (commuter towns, lit. 'bedroom cities'), are often located on the outskirts of the large cities, as in the case of Getafe and Alcalá de Henares outside Madrid or Ecatepec outside Mexico City (Martín Butragueño 2016; Molina Martos 2006; see Figure 6.2). In these intranational immigrant settings, frequency of contacts in individual social networks operates as an important predictor for the spread of linguistic innovations (§2.6), often in a hierarchical pattern, that is, from larger to smaller towns (for instance, in the Murcia region of Spain, Hernández-Campoy 2011: 708–19, or in central Chile, Rivadeneira Valenzuela 2016).

Frequency of communication is not the only factor driving the adoption of features: internal migrants participate in multiple contact environments, which are not just physical or demographic, but also symbolic (Morgenthaler García 2007).

FIGURE 6.2. Neighborhood on the outskirts of Ecatepec, Mexico (Gzzz via Wikimedia Commons, license: https://creativecommons.org/licenses/by-sa/4.0/deed.en)

Generational differences provide a window into the interplay between symbolic factors and deterministic triggers (like frequency of contact). For instance, first-generation migrants often establish tight social networks with other same-origin speakers in the first generation, but their children typically participate in more mobile, open networks. These weaker networks then become the vehicle for the adoption of new features and the values they symbolize (§2.6). Generational differences thus create a variety of environmental conditions even within the family (e.g. Caravedo and Klee 2012; Klee and Caravedo 2005 for intergenerational differences in the distribution of contact features in Lima, and Canuto Castillo 2015 for intergenerational patterns of language shift in Indigenous Otomi-speaking communities in Mexico City; see also §6.6 and §6.7 below about similar effects in transnational contacts).

Internal migrants interact in multiple micro-ecologies that call for complex acts of identity construction and language use: within one's own family, within existing local networks, and within extended networks (work, school, friendship, leisure). In these settings, language use is determined by a combination of deterministic and non-deterministic factors. For instance, in an analysis of a social network of high school friends in the southern coastal Spanish city of Málaga, Villena-Ponsoda (2005) found that much of their linguistic behavior correlated with their degree of participation in the network. However, specific individuals exhibited a less predictable use of some features, which appeared to be deployed situationally to perform non-urban personas. More recently, Díaz-Dávalos (2018) has described the emergence since the 1960s of a group identity centered around Ciudad Satélite, an American-style middle-class residential development on the outskirts of Mexico City. Here, group membership is indexed not just by one's status as a neighborhood resident, but also by institutional participation (boy scout groups, golf clubs), concurrence to shared spaces (fast-food restaurants, church functions) and personal style choices (pet ownership, manicured front yards) that are symbolic of a non-traditional lifestyle.

By contrast to the locations that migrants move to, triggers for the rapid rearrangement of feature pools are less pervasive in the communities that migrants come from. However, via travel, media, and exposure to formal education, speakers in these communities also come to negotiate the features used in urban repertoires and their symbolic values, sometimes resulting in a layering of speech community norms. Santa Ana and Parodi (1998) studied the rural area around Zamora (Michoacán, in southwestern México). They observed that, in this population, familiarity with local, regional, and national norms of use was gained through participation in specific social networks. Thus, individuals participating in networks with contacts outside the region were more capable of assessing the values assigned to local, rural, or otherwise non-standard forms, and better equipped to navigate the stylistic landscapes associated to each norm than less mobile speakers (see §2.5 and the next section for examples).

The ecological effects of the ideologies and institutions promoted by nation-states are particularly noticeable in Indigenous populations, which have historically been the source of country-to-city migration (see §5.4 for precedents). In many such settings, Indigenous languages and Spanish features perceived as the consequence of L2 learning are disfavored as indicators of socioeconomic stagnation. By contrast, proficiency in Spanish is seen as a tool for social and economic empowerment (Marr 2011; Messing 2007). From a generational point of view, inter-generational language shift is often identified as the result. For instance, in contexts of country-to-city migration, everyday use of the Indigenous language is typically sustained only by the first generation, with children and adolescents growing up as Spanish dominant (Canuto Castillo 2015; Martín Butragueño 2020).

Besides the generational patterning of language shift, attention to the contextual values that specific features gain in everyday communication also sheds light on the process of shift in Indigenous populations. For instance, in their study of Nahuatl and Spanish in the rural hinterland of Puebla (Mexico), Hill and Hill (1986) noted a progressive restriction of the settings in which Nahuatl was accepted or unmarked. In this process, frequency of participation in specific networks interfaced with the values attached to each of the languages in everyday communication events, with Spanish progressively encroaching on an ever-broader range of social functions:

> Spanish-speaking priests pronounce the liturgy and take confessions only in Spanish. The increasing influence of the national parties in community government means that even the most local decisions will be taken in consultation with monolingual speakers of Spanish. Municipal judges align themselves with the Spanish-speaking world and insist on Spanish in local courts. The exclusive use of Spanish in the classroom has thrust the language into the family home itself, as parents struggle to prepare their children for school… Wage workers meet friends, ritual kin, and even wives through workmates in

the factory, not neighbors in the town, so that much of their social and even family life may take place in Spanish (1986: 404).

As the practical and symbolic advantages of using Spanish in each of these contexts expand, the social spheres of Nahuatl shrink, becoming more and more restricted to a handful of ritualistic settings where speakers perform a traditional *mexicano* identity (as in the drinking of fermented agave, known as *pulque*). As in other contexts of shift, language change is a function of socioeconomic and cultural change, brought about by the radical upheaval of the ancestral ecology of communication in the community (Brown 2022; §5.4, §5.6 and §7.4). Similar processes have been described for other Indigenous communities across Latin America (see Zapotec, Schrader-Kniffki 2008; Tojol-ab'al, Brody 2018; Mapudungun, Lagos et al. 2017).

In sharp contrast to more permanent contexts of internal migration or less mobile rural populations, cyclical or temporary movements between urban and rural areas allow for alternative patterns of feature recombination. The emergence of *medias lenguas* (mixed languages) in the Ecuadorian Andes is a striking example. Lipski (2020b: 414) reviews the literature according to which the medias lenguas used in rural areas of the Imbabura province (see Figure 6.3) originated in the mid-twentieth century as adult Kichwa-speaking men started working in Quito and other nearby cities for weeks or months at a time, coming into intermittent contact with Spanish speakers. Usage of Spanish features in these men's home communities eventually became symbolic of modernity and upward social mobility. As these contacts increased, more and more lexical and phrasal elements from Spanish were incorporated, giving rise to these new repertoires. In recent years, more frequent contacts with surrounding areas and the increase in schooling and outward migration are chipping away at the motivation

FIGURE 6.3. The rural foothills of Cerro Imbabura in Ecuador (David C. S. via Wikimedia Commons, license: https://creativecommons.org/licenses/by-sa/4.0/deed.en)

to maintain these codes, and younger speakers are shifting to Spanish, abandoning both Media Lengua and Kichwa (Lipski 2020b; Shappeck 2011). Some of the linguistic effects of these contacts are examined below (§6.4).

While pressures in favor of Spanish features are mounting in many populations, Indigenous responses to these pressures cannot be reduced to the relinquishing of traditional repertoires. One possible alternative is the articulation of *purist* discourses geared at shielding Indigenous pools from Spanish influence (Brody 2018; Hill and Hill 1986; Schrader-Kniffki 2008; §6.3). Other approaches emphasize the possibility of new contexts of use of Indigenous languages and more positive attitudes toward them. For instance, Makihara (2013) has analyzed new hybrid language uses and positive attitudes toward hybridization among younger Rapa Nui speakers on Easter Island (Chile) as the potential beginning of a turn-around in the historical shift to Spanish. Activism in support of official recognition for Indigenous languages (as in Bolivia's new constitution, §6.1) offers further proof that Indigenous speakers are not indifferent to these pressures and their linguistic effects.

The interactions among acquisitional, socioeconomic, and ideological triggers in these intranational environments have equally diverse linguistic results. In the next two sections, I organize these effects by whether they are characteristic of ecologies shaped by significant internal migration, reiterating that a clear-cut distinction between internal non-migratory and migratory contexts is ultimately unfeasible.

6.3. Outcomes of contact in non-migration-based intranational ecologies

Let's start by assessing some of the effects observed in situations where large-scale permanent internal migration is not present. A commonly observed pattern in these settings is the adoption of specific variants in hierarchical patterns (§6.2), from cities to rural areas. In many cases, the direction of change is toward features considered mainstream. For instance, the phonemic contrast between /ʎ/ and /j/ has recently eroded away in urban areas of northeastern Argentina along age and educational lines (with younger and formally educated speakers leading the change) in the direction of the Buenos Aires-based standard, where the remaining segment is articulated as an alveopalatal fricative [ʃ ~ ʒ] (Abadia de Quant 1996; see §4.7 and §5.5 for some historical background on this feature). Along similar lines, Ceballos Domínguez (2006) has documented the recent expansion of syllable-final full [s] articulations in urban areas of the eastern coast of Mexico, with young people moving away from the local [h] articulation. In Mexican Spanish, full articulations are considered distinctive of the national norm.

In this process, the symbolic values of specific features are always up for grabs. An example is the assibilated articulation of syllable-final /r/ as [ɹ], which became iconic of the urban upper-middle class of Mexico City and started spreading in the 60s: it has since been reinterpreted as a marker of affectation and started receding socially in the early 2000s (Lastra and Martín Butragueño 2006; §5.5). Individual selections adopted in local social networks via face-to-face interactions may also be enregistered (§2.5) to express geographical or social meanings: for instance, Rivadeneira Valenzuela (2016) describes a recent dialectal split in the Chilean use of 2SG address forms: counteracting strong historical prescription against the local use of *vos* forms (§5.5), they now irradiate from Santiago as part of a vernacular national norm. However, their adoption is stronger toward the north of the capital (Valparaíso, Iquique) than toward the south (Temuco, Coyhaique). The author attributes these differences both to the geographical proximity between Santiago and cities like Valparaíso and to the symbolic value of *vos* forms, which in the south are still more commonly perceived as rural or unsophisticated. In all these cases, we see speakers reacting to the symbolic associations of 'mainstream,' 'national,' or 'standard' features, sometimes embracing them, other times proposing local alternatives. In addition, these choices remind us that speakers do not necessarily attach iconic values to 'accents' or 'varieties,' but instead negotiate and select individual features piecemeal, in full ecological fashion (§2.5).

Rural ecologies are more infrequently studied than urban areas, but they exhibit local patterns of sociolinguistic negotiation that do not always involve dialectal convergence toward urban norms. The study of the effect of social networks on the use of specific features by Santa Ana and Parodi (1998) in rural Michoacán (México) offers an example. A more recent sociophonetic study (Barajas 2022) in a small town in the same area of Mexico has confirmed the effect of social networks on a specific stigmatized feature (the raising of unstressed vowels, as in *grande* 'big' [grã̄ɳde ~ grã̄ɳdi]), with less mobile male speakers favoring raising and using it as a marker of membership in the local community.

Whenever intranational ecologies harbor contact with Indigenous pools, speakers have access to typologically very different options, and may rely on bilingual acquisition strategies (Aalberse et al. 2019; Muysken 2013; §2.6) to reconcile these differences. A well-researched example is *castellano andino* (Cerrón Palomino 2003; Clements 2009; Escobar 2001, 2011; Klee and Lynch 2009: 129–52), typically described as a contact variety in the central Andes with a historical Quechua (or Aymara) substrate taking shape since the colonial period (§4.4). In this variety, we see Spanish lexical material in syntactic and semantic recombinations that reflect Indigenous structural frames – another form of linguistic hybridization via syntactic convergence by bilinguals (§2.6). Some examples are shown in (1–3).

(1) De-   me   cerrando   la   puerta
    Give-3SG.PRES.SUBJ   me   close-GER   the   door
    'Please, close the door' (Klee and Lynch 2009: 149).

(2) De   mi   mamá   en   su   casa   estoy   yendo
    Of   my   mum   in   her   house   be-1SG.PRES.IND   go-GER
    'I am going to my mum's house' (Clements 2009: 176).

(3) Mi   hija   había creído   que   le
    My   daughter   had believed-3SG.PST.PERF.IND   that   to her
    estaban   tirando   con   piedra
    be-1SG.IMP.IND   throw-GER   with   stone
    'My daughter (said that she) believed (lit. 'had believed') that they were throwing stones at her' (Klee and Ocampo 1995: 59).

In (1), *dar* 'to give' as an auxiliary in combination with a gerund form ("cerrando") appears to be a reproduction of a softened imperative structure in Quechua that combines *cara-* 'to give' and a gerund (*-shpa*); in (2), the double possessive (*de mi... su...*) mirrors a Quechua structure where both the possessor (marked with a possessive postposition *–pa*) and the possessed (marked as such with a possessed suffix *–n*) are expressed; and in (3), the repurposing of the Spanish past perfect ("había creído") as an evidential ('she said') has been explained as a reproduction of Quechua evidentiality to indicate that, in this case, the reported event was not witnessed by the speaker (for instance, Babel and Pfänder 2014; see also §2.2). The contact hypothesis is confirmed by studies that show that these features are more common among bilinguals and socioeconomically lower speakers, whose pools have historically included less exposure to normative monolingual models (Klee and Ocampo 1995).

Paraguay is another long-term contact context resulting in structurally idiosyncratic features (Estigarribia 2015; Gynan 2011; Klee and Lynch 2009: 153–66). Here, in sharp contrast with *castellano andino*, less marked sociolinguistic hierarchization has caused features originating in Guarani/Spanish bilingual learning to be socially pervasive. One of the outcomes is the frequent use of structures that were common in historical Spanish pools but have since all but disappeared from most other forms of Spanish, as in (4–6) (from Gynan 2011: 365).

(4)   Nadie   no   vino
      Nobody   not   come-3SG.PRET.IND
      'Nobody came' (see st. Sp. *nadie vino/no vino nadie*).

(5)   Un   mi   hermano   vive   en   Asunción
      A   my   brother   live-3SG.PRES.IND in   Asunción
      'One of my brothers lives in Asunción' (see st. Sp. *uno de mis hermanos vive en Asunción*).

(6)   Voy   en   el   mercado
      Go-1SG.PRES.IND   in   the   market
      'I go to the market' (see st. Sp. *voy al mercado*).

These structures are historically significant because speakers of Paraguayan Spanish have access to analogous Guarani options, including a double negative structure for (4), a nominal structure with determinant and possessive premodifiers for (5), and the marking of the goal of movement with *–pe*, which in Guarani also encodes location, reflected in (6) by Sp. *en* 'in' instead of *a* 'to'. In all these cases, therefore, Paraguayan bilingual speakers have selected features that were present locally in the historical Spanish pools but with Guarani parallels, a typical example of multiple causation (§2.5) rooted in bilingual processing strategies.

These features are but a small sample of the hybridizing practices applied by Paraguayan speakers, who customarily combine grammatical and lexical elements of historical Guarani and Spanish pools to yield a range of conversational strategies locally known as *jopará* (Estigarribia 2015), as in (7). Guarani elements are underlined:

(7) Menda   niko   e(s) jodido   porque   cuando
    Marriage EMPH   is   screwed   because when
    salís   la iglesia-gui, o-je-creé   tu   dueño, y
    2SG.go.out the church-from 3.REFL.believe your owner and
    te   trata como cualquier cosa,   ha   o-ka'ú-rõ,   katu-ete
    you   treat like any   thing   and   3.drunk-if   just-very
    ne-nupã
    2SG-hit

'To be married, I say, is difficult because when you walk out of the church he believes he is your owner, and he treats you like a thing, and when he is drunk, he always beats you up' (Estigarribia 2015: 185).

These practices are part of a sociolinguistic continuum of integration of Spanish and Guarani features that is sensitive to social and contextual factors (Estigarribia 2015). The widespread use of such hybrid repertoires in spoken communication across all social groups of this South American nation confirms that they are assessed positively as iconic of Paraguayan national identity (Lipski 2011). Use of Guarani (or Spanish and Guarani) in at least some high registers (as in governmental campaigns, see Figure 6.4) illustrates this emblematic role even in official language discourses.

FIGURE 6.4. Spanish and Guarani in a Paraguayan governmental campaign about a pregnancy subsidy (Administración Nacional de la Seguridad Social via Flickr, license: https://creativecommons.org/licenses/by-sa/2.0/deed.en)

Contexts of intense sociolinguistic pressure favoring shift to Spanish exemplify how speakers navigate these pressures in socially meaningful ways by resorting to elements from each of the 'languages,' as well as innovative recombinations. The Hill and Hill (1986) study of a traditionally Nahuatl-speaking region in central Mexico introduced above (§6.2) offers a richly documented and telling example. Here, speakers have created various registers of language ('frames') with associated linguistic features. These registers include the monolingual use of Spanish; the incorporation of Spanish elements into an otherwise mostly Nahuatl matrix; monolingual spoken Nahuatl; and a purist Nahuatl code. Critically, language shift in this community does not merely involve the substitution of one language by another. On the contrary, it implies the continuation of centuries-long hybrid communicative practices whereby speakers combine elements of Indigenous and non-Indigenous provenance.

Let's examine some of these linguistic strategies. Spanish lexical heads with Nahuatl morphology as shown in (8) are particularly common, but it is also possible to find Spanish affixes on Nahuatl heads, such as *-ero/a* for professions and trades in (9), and Spanish functional loanwords, as in the incorporation of *hasta* 'until, even' with an adverbial function and *bueno* as a discourse marker in (10). Nahuatl material in these examples is underlined. All examples are from Hill and Hill (1986):

(8) no-madrináh-tzin
     my-godmother-HON
     'my dear/revered godmother' (167)

(9) tlahchiqu-ero
     collect maguey sap-AGNT
     'person who collects maguey sap' (197)

(10) Hasta división o:yec. Hasta o:quitlatilihqueh ni:almía:l. Bueno, tonterías o:quichi:hualtihqueh.
     'Even there was disagreement. They even burned his haystack. Well, they did foolish things to him' (191).

As in other settings involving typologically distinct pools, like the Andes or Paraguay, speakers exploit structural junctures where the two pools happen to be equivalent or similar, that is, congruent (see discussion of 'Hispanicized Nahuatl' in Flores Farfán 2008 in §1.8). We can see an example in relative clauses, where speakers increasingly opt for head-initial orders (as in 11, with *tlaxcal* as the head) over head-final orders, once the preferred option in Nahuatl (as in 12, where *profesora* is the head), thus privileging the head-initial arrangement typical in Spanish (both examples from Hill and Hill 1986: 248–9).

(11) in   tlaxcal   den   mitzmacaz
     ADJ   tortilla   de-ADJ   give.3SG.FUT-it-to-you
     'the tortilla that she will give you'

(12) in   te:machtia   profesora
     ADJ   teach-3SG.PRES.people   teacher
     'the teacher who teaches people'

A fascinating convergence strategy in this population is *stress shift*, whereby Spanish lexical items carrying word-final stress are stressed on the second-to-last syllable as per the stress pattern of Nahuatl: Sp. *mamá* 'mom', *lugár* 'place', *corrál* 'livestock pen' > Nah. *máma:, lúga:r, córra:l*. At first sight, this might simply seem a straightforward non-native transfer or imposition effect (§2.2, §2.6), where non-dominant Spanish speakers map L1 accentual patterns onto their L2 lexicon. However, Hill and Hill's data reveals no correlation with age, a strong predictor of levels of Spanish dominance in many bilingual communities. Instead, stress shift in this population operates as a stylistic emblematic device allowing speakers to perform an 'authentic' Nahuatl-speaking persona regardless of Nahuatl proficiency (1986: 212–22; a partially analogous discourse strategy on the basis of Quechua stress in a variety of Bolivian Spanish is described in Babel 2014). Similar forms of manipulation of linguistic resources for symbolic purposes can be found in Rincón Zapotec (Oaxaca, Mexico). Here, rather than relinquishing the ancestral language altogether, bilinguals have applied similar syncretic strategies to those in the Nahuatl case, creating a 'mixed' register via the intertwining of Hispanic and Indigenous linguistic resources (Schrader-Kniffki 2008: 71).

An important ecological corollary from these studies is that the application of hybridizing mechanisms where speakers draw simultaneously across named language varieties (§2.5) is not necessarily a temporary anomaly in populations undergoing language shift. While the Nahuatl speakers studied by Hill and Hill currently find themselves under strong pressure to adopt Spanish monolingualism, at least some of the same effects can be seen in communities featuring more long-term bilingualism with other languages. Examples seen in this section range from cases where Spanish is the majority language promoted by the nation-state (Quechua) to situations where societal and individual bilingualism has historically been accepted (Paraguay). As argued since the beginning of this book, this range of sociolinguistic situations proves that speakers may draw from their local linguistic pools to create innovative repertoires, regardless of sociopolitical definitions of language competence.

6.4. Outcomes of contact in intranational ecologies based on internal migration

We can now survey some contact effects in intranational settings shaped by significant levels of internal migration. Speakers resettling in the increasingly diverse urban areas of the late twentieth and early twenty-first centuries provide a primary test case (Lynch 2020). Many of these effects have been described as the function of dialectal accommodation (§2.3 and §2.6). For instance, Serrano Moreno (2008) has studied a series of phonetic variables among speakers from the northwestern Mexican state of Sonora living in Mexico City. These variables include the spirantization of /tʃ/→ [ʃ], the aspiration and loss of syllable-final /s/, and the erosion and loss of intervocalic /d/. After just a few years in the capital, most newcomers accommodate to their linguistic environment by significantly reducing their use of 'Sonoran' variants, especially [ʃ], a socially salient northwestern linguistic stereotype in Mexico.

Country-to-city migration also allows for the negotiation of the symbolic value of specific features in the emergence of new urban vernaculars. For instance, in one of the earliest variationist studies in the Hispanic world, López Morales (1983) studied several sociolinguistic variables in San Juan (Puerto Rico). These variables included features widespread in all Puerto Rican Spanish varieties, such as the full elision of syllable-final /s/ and the lateralization of coda /r/ → [l], and others more common in rural repertoires, such as the uvularization of /r/→ [ʀ], the elision of intervocalic /d/ and the spirantization of /tʃ/ → [ʃ]. Rather than rejecting the rural forms, young San Juan residents have combined both rural and urban features, giving rise to a new local norm. These choices illustrate (again) the ecological emergence of new varieties via feature-by-feature negotiation, rather than from unidirectional dialect shift to an already established norm.

The liminal sociolinguistic position of *ciudades dormitorio* (§6.2) on the edge of larger metropolitan areas makes these towns interesting settings to explore the effects of dialectal accommodation in migratory intranational contexts. Ecatepec, one of Mexico City's largest suburbs (1.6 million people, INEGI 2023) with a high percentage of residents from across Mexico, is an example. Here, Martín Butragueño (2016) has analyzed the distribution of several variables, including two morphosyntactic features: non-standard number agreement in existential *haber* 'there is/there are', exemplified in (13) by the 3PL ending in *hubieran*, and *lo que es*, an informative discourse marker, 'that is / this means', shown in (14):

(13) la cuestión es de que pues yo ya no quise seguir este estudiando ¿no? No porque no *hubieran los medios* ¿no? (see st. Sp. *hubiera (los) medios*) (151)

'the thing is, I did not want to continue studying, right? Not because *there were no means*, right?'

(14) en El Olivar viví hasta los ocho años, ya después ya me fui para allá, Chimalhuacán Estado de México, o sea sí, *lo que es* la avenida Chimalhuacán (154)

'I lived in El Olivar until I was eight, after that I moved to that area, Chimalhuacán [in the] state of Mexico, I mean, that'd be Chimalhuacán Avenue'.

General change trends for these variables in Ecatepec are the same as elsewhere across the metropolitan area, but their sociolinguistic patterning is local. For instance, while middle-aged speakers exhibit the highest rates of *haber* agreement in other neighborhoods, adolescents lead this change in Ecatepec. Similary, *lo que* exhibits a more gender-specific pattern, with men producing virtually every example in the Ecatepec data. The author attributes these differences to the social position of the Ecatepec informants, mostly working-class individuals who are connected to metropolitan networks but are not as socially mobile as other speakers. Ecatepec residents index their local identity by selecting specific options among the available features in the larger Mexico City pool but using them in idiosyncratic ways.

In other cases, internal migrants enter markedly different linguistic environments from those of their areas of origin. Bilingual internal migrants' agency in these contexts is transparently illustrated again by *castellano andino*: besides being used in the historically bilingual Peruvian highlands (§6.3), many of its features have also become part of urban sociolinguistic landscapes via internal migration. Klee and Caravedo (2005) and Caravedo and Klee (2012) have investigated several of these variants among migrants in Lima and their children. These features include the assibilation of /r/ → [ɹ], several non-normative clitic uses (including dative *le* for direct object functions (*leísmo*), accusative *lo* for indirect object functions (*loísmo*), uninflected *lo* as a general direct object clitic, and clitic omission), and the present perfect to signal the conclusion of a narrative, illustrated in (15). The preterite is italicized, and the present perfect is underlined.

(15) [t]tengo bien así presente que una ropa se le *escapó*, ¿no? y entonces el agua se lo estaba llevando y entonces la señora por querer agarrar su ropa se *cayó* ... y la señora se iba, así se iba, entonces todas las que estaban lavando la ropa gritaban ¡Auxilio! ven pa salvar, total que entre todas la <u>han sacado</u>, la <u>han agarrado</u> y la <u>han sacado</u>.

'I remember clearly that she *dropped* a piece of clothing, right?, and then the water started to carry it away, and then the lady, trying to grab her clothes, *fell in*, and the lady started to get carried away, she was getting carried away, so all the ladies that were washing clothes were yelling 'help! Someone come save her', somehow they all <u>got</u> her out, they <u>grabbed</u> her and they <u>got</u> her out' (Caravedo and Klee 2012: 15).

The results reveal an intricate sociolinguistic pattern. On the one hand, there is general accommodation toward the coastal features typical of Lima and away from stigmatized elements, including assibilation and *loísmo*. At the same time, the migrants' children (who are typically monolingual in Spanish) appear to develop hybrid repertoires characterized both by accommodation to the Lima norm and by variable use of uninflected *lo*, *leísmo*, and the narrative present perfect. These contact effects signal the emergence of a new 'migrant hybrid culture' (Klee and Caravedo 2005: 20) expressed creatively through language and cultural outlets like music, theater, and other forms of art in Lima and other growing metropolitan areas of the twenty-first century.

Speakers' agency in the mediation of the linguistic and symbolic relation between Hispanic and Indigenous pools is conspicuous in other internal settings, as in the case of *medias lenguas* in the Ecuadorian highlands. Recall (§6.2) that these codes emerged around the mid-twentieth century in the context of gender-based cyclical labor patterns among rural Indigenous populations. The resulting repertoires have been studied as examples of relexification (§2.2) via the massive incorporation of Spanish lexicon into a Kichwa matrix (see §4.10 for a somewhat less pervasive case in Chamorro). They differ from canonical situations of borrowing in that lexical incorporation is defined as massive ('a case of lexical borrowing gone wild,' Thomason 2001: 90), with lexical replacement estimated at around 90% of the Kichwa lexicon (Shappeck 2011: 37). Spanish loans are adapted phonologically to Kichwa and take on the semantic value of equivalent Kichwa items. The following comparison between spoken Ecuadorian Spanish (16a), Kichwa (16b) and the local Media Lengua of Salcedo (16c) illustrates this equivalence (examples from Stewart 2011: 38). In these data, Sp. *guagua* 'small child' is a Kichwa loanword. Note the incorporation of Spanish lexical roots for 'to cook' and 'to knit' in (16c):

(16a) Ecuadorian Spanish
 el guagua cocin-a y tej-e
 the child cook-3SG.PRES.IND and knit-3SG.PRES.IND

(16b) Kichwa
 wawa-ka janu-tak awan-tak
 child-TOP cook-CONJ knit-CONJ

(16c) Salcedo Media Lengua
 wawa-ka kuzin-tak i tixa-tak
 child-TOP cook-CONJ and knit-CONJ

 'the child cooks and knits'.

Contact situations such as Ecuadorian Media Lengua, Nahuatl in central Mexico and *castellano andino* in Peru complexify one-dimensional narratives of shift from Indigenous languages to Spanish. While these Indigenous populations are clearly under mounting pressure to assimilate to the Spanish linguistic majority, speakers still exercise agency as they navigate this sociolinguistic environment by recombining (§2.5) features of varied provenance to express new forms of identity in both urban and rural settings (specifically for Media Lengua, see Lipski 2020b: 429–32).

6.5. The sociodemographics of transnational Hispanic ecologies

As stated in the introduction to this chapter (§6.1), today's contacts are increasingly transnational. Among the prime drivers of transnational contacts, cross-border migration has become a global phenomenon. The number of people worldwide living in a country other than that of their birth increased from 79 million in 1960 to 281 million in 2022, as estimated by the United Nation's International Organization for Migration (McAuliffe and Triandafyllidou 2022: 3). Transnational migration is not uniformly distributed: some countries exhibit a positive net demographic migrant balance and others a negative balance. Table 6.2 displays the balance between emigrating and immigrating populations for select countries in 2020. The relative migration balance column shows the proportion of immigrating to emigrating population for each country (for instance, in the United States, the immigrating contingent is 16.89 times larger than the emigrating population).

These data show that some countries (the US, Canada, Spain, Chile, and Argentina) have become net migration *receivers*, while others (Peru, Dominican Republic, Mexico, Honduras, El Salvador, and Cuba) are net migration *senders*. An additional important factor is the relative weight of these migration flows in relation to the population of each country: while many more Mexicans than people from each of the other six net emigrating countries on the table have left their country of birth, the proportion of Mexicans living abroad in relation to the total national population (8.82%) is much lower than that of

TABLE 6.2. Emigrants and immigrants, absolute balance (in thousands), and relative balance for select countries in 2020 (UN Department of Economic and Social Affairs 2020)

	Emigrants	Immigrants	Absolute balance	Relative balance
United States	2,996	50,632	47,632	16.89
Canada	1,292	8,049	6,757	6.23
Spain	1,489	6,842	5,353	4.59
Chile	643	1,645	1,002	2.55
Argentina	1,076	2,281	1,205	2.12
Peru	1,519	1,224	−295	−1.24
Dominican Republic	1,608	603	−1,005	−2.66
Mexico	11,185	1,197	−9,988	−9.34
Honduras	985	39	−946	−25.25
El Salvador	1,599	42	−1,557	−38.07
Cuba	1,757	3	−1,754	−585.66

Cubans (15.60%) or Salvadorans (25.32%) (as per 2021 country population estimates, World Bank 2022). Migratory patterns are also dynamic. For instance, Hispanic countries were once the largest origin of yearly immigrant arrivals to the United States, but by 2009 Asian countries had surpassed them (Budiman 2020). Immigrant contingents are not only multinational, but also linguistically diverse. For instance, in Spain, Moroccans, Romanians, and Ecuadorians are the largest immigrant groups (UN Department of Economic and Social Affairs 2020).

As was the case for intranational movements, some forms of cross-border migration are cyclical or temporary. An early example in this period was the Bracero Program, a temporary visa agreement between Mexico and the United States that resulted in the arrival of over 4 million Mexican workers in the US between 1942 and 1964. Mexican and Central American cyclical migrants continue to work in the United States yearly for months at a time (Rosales Sandoval 2014). Puerto Ricans, who can travel back and forth between the island and the mainland as American citizens freely, are not technically international migrants, but have often participated in cyclical movements (Hinojosa 2018). Return forms of migration by immigrants who go back to their place of origin either cyclically of permanently add to the sociolinguistic complexity of transnational migratory movements (Gugenberger and Mar-Molinero 2018).

Besides the economic trigger typically associated with transnational migration, violence or political instability also push migrants to cross borders. According to the United Nations, the number of 'people of concern' (refugees, asylum seekers, internally displaced and stateless people) reached 108.4 million globally in 2022 (UN High Commissioner for Refugees 2023). Central America has become a prime example, due to several factors: the killing and displacement of Indigenous populations by local governments and multinational companies (most notably in Guatemala and El Salvador), armed conflicts between the 1970s and the 1990s (e.g. Salvadoran Civil War, Sandinista Revolution in Nicaragua), food shortages due to drought, and insecurity as cartels supplying drugs to North American and European markets have spread their activity to the region. A combination of political and economic triggers is also at the root of the waves of Cuban arrivals in the United States following the 1959 revolution, and the estimated 5.5 million Venezuelans that have left their country since the early 2000s (UN High Commissioner for Refugees 2023).

Cross-border movements also include more ephemeral forms of contact. For instance, every day thousands of Moroccan women (*porteadoras* 'carriers') cross the border with the North African Spanish enclave cities of Ceuta and Melilla to bring European goods into Morocco, taking advantage of tax exemptions granted by the European Union to these two cities (Irídia - Centre Per la Defensa dels Drets Humans 2017: 56–8; §6.9). Similarly, many residents of Mexican border cities like Tijuana, Nogales, and Ciudad Juárez cross in and out of the United States daily: in June 2023, the San Ysidro-Tijuana border checkpoint alone (depicted in Figure 6.5) registered 2.8 million crossings of people into the US, an average of almost 100,000 daily (Bureau of Transportation 2023). In addition, international tourism provides yet another source of short-term transnational contact. Among Hispanic countries, in 2019 (the last year before COVID-related travel restrictions), Spain stood out as the second most popular destination worldwide after France with over 84 million tourists, and Mexico was seventh with over 45 million (UN World Tourism Organization 2023). These shorter-term

FIGURE 6.5. Vehicles crossing from Mexico into the United States at the Tijuana-San Ysidro checkpoint (Magnus Manske via Wikimedia Commons, license: https://creativecommons.org/licenses/by-sa/3.0/deed.en)

movements are usually not studied as forms of migration, but they add to the demographic porousness of many borders around the world.

6.6. Transnational environmental complexities across and beyond borders

Transnational contacts in this age of mobility (§6.1) are particularly challenging to categorize ecologically. Thanks to developments in transportation and communication technologies, an individual's communication network may now include face-to-face everyday interactions in their location of residence, periodic physical border crossings that renew ties between migrants and their places of origin, as well as digitally mediated exchanges with friends, relatives, coworkers or even strangers down the hallway, around the block, or across the planet.

Farr (2006), a study of a network of rural Mexican migrants (*rancheros*) with ties to both Michoacán (western Mexico) and Chicago, offers a paradigmatic portrait of the simultaneous anchoring of transnational communication in two nations, and of the motivations and mechanisms that speakers rely on to participate in them:

> In this established transnational community ... somebody is virtually always on the move between the rancho and Chicago. Every few months people retired in Mexico visit Chicago, young people make it across the border to join friends and family there, families in Chicago decide to return to Mexico to retire, to start businesses, or to raise children in the safer context of the rancho, and other communities reluctantly decide to return to Chicago because the continuing economic crisis in Mexico constrains their abilities to support their families. Communication by telephone, and for some by e-mail (formerly letters), is now a regular part of their lives (2006: 24).

Members of this binational network effectively live in 'Chicagoacán': a physical and symbolic space, constructed around the *rancho* as a central reference of community membership, and continuously recreated by means of shared and evolving traditions, values, and communicative routines. Chicagoacán reflects the dynamics of current transnational contacts, where mobility implies participation in communicative spaces at local and global levels.

Many of the sociological and sociolinguistic theoretical paradigms proposed to analyze communication and language use in this transnational age of mobility are best exemplified by the mega-cities of the late twentieth and early twenty-first centuries (Lynch 2018, 2020; Martín Butragueño 2020; Smakman and Heinrich 2018; and §6.2). From a transnational perspective, the environmental effects of foreign immigration are both *centrifugal* and *centripetal*: foreign immigration diversifies pre-contact linguistic landscapes, but also immerses recently arrived speakers in the sociolinguistic dynamics of their new country of destination. These dynamics often include the expectation that migrants will assimilate to the surrounding majority, especially when the communicative repertoires they bring with them are associated with foreignness or low socioeconomic status.

Spanish in the United States illustrates these sociolinguistic dynamics. In this context, large-scale shift to English has occurred for decades, despite the presence of at least 42 million Spanish speakers as of 2022 (US Census Bureau 2023), the continued arrival of Spanish-speaking immigrants, the growing use of Spanish in media and education, and the generally favorable attitudes among first-generation immigrants toward bilingualism (Mora and Lopez 2023). Any positive effects of these triggers on the ethnolinguistic vitality of the language are cancelled out by the influence of monoglossic beliefs that favor the monolingual use of English in many social domains (Barrett et al. 2023). Immigrants experience these beliefs everywhere: in public discourse, at work, in the classroom, even within their own families. An illustration of the pervasive effects of the push toward assimilation can be seen in Figure 6.6, showing self-reported levels of proficiency in spoken Spanish ('Can you carry on a conversation in Spanish?') by generational group (G1 = foreign born, G2 = at least one foreign-born parent, G3 = two US-born parents) in an August 2022 survey among 3,000 US Latinxs. Note the clear decrease by the third generation.

Although such shifts to the majority language are attested among multiple immigrant linguistic minorities, specific environmental conditions may nuance the progression of assimilation. This is the case, for instance, whenever bilingualism is perceived as a key to socioeconomic advancement. For instance, in south Florida, Spanish is associated with formally educated, internationally mobile upper-middle class immigrants more commonly than elsewhere in the United States. Miami is also a global economic hub for many media, trade, and manufacturing companies that target Latin American markets, further contributing to the perceived socioeconomic usefulness of bilingual repertoires. Consequently, Spanish (or at least English-Spanish bilingualism) exhibits higher symbolic

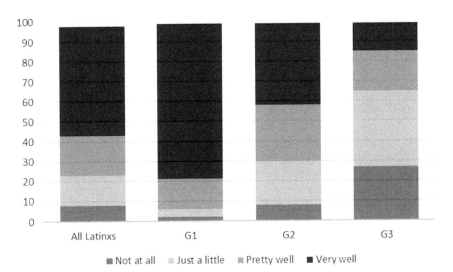

FIGURE 6.6. Levels of self-reported conversational Spanish proficiency across three generations of US Latinxs (figure by author, data from Mora and López 2023)

capital here by comparison to other Hispanic ecologies in the United States (Carter and D'Alessandro Merii 2023; Valencia and Lynch 2020). While these factors do not ensure the intergenerational maintenance of Spanish in the city, they do favor higher rates of use among at least some US-born Latinxs than in other North American urban areas.

Transnational migration does not always lead to generational language shift. For instance, cyclical migration (see §6.2 for intranational examples) may also lead to results other than generational assimilation. Senegalese immigrants in Buenos Aires, another global city, are a case in point (Kleidermacher 2014). This contingent consists of mostly young male immigrants that often work as street merchants, electricians, or cab drivers, and who speak languages like Wolof and French. Their goal is rarely to remain abroad, but rather to secure a job that will allow them to send remittances to their families. Many of them arrive in Argentina from surrounding countries (Brazil, Bolivia) having accrued some familiarity with Hispanic repertoires. Once in Buenos Aires, participation in Senegalese confraternities ensures communication with other fellow Senegalese immigrants. Those with legal status go back home periodically and contribute to maintain the ties between those in Senegal and those abroad, in true transnational fashion. In this situation, Spanish is learned naturalistically and without the large-scale generational shift typical of more established immigrant groups. Upon occasion, immigrant languages are preserved by virtue of the positive assessment of bilingualism in the population, sometimes with strict differentiation of social functions for each of the repertoires. This situation has been described for speakers of *chipileño*, a heritage variety of Venetan Italian used in central Mexico since the 1860s (Tararova 2017).

Interactions among immigrant populations are also an important ecological trigger. We can see an example in immigrant neighborhoods: here, new sociolinguistic hierarchies are negotiated that not only reflect the demographics of the immigrant continent, but also their attitudes about the value of specific features. These symbolic values are in turn enacted in a variety of contexts, starting from one's own family. This is the case with speakers growing up in mixed Mexican and Puerto Rican families (*MexiRicans*) in Chicago, whose linguistic choices reflect very conscious acts of identity as 'Mexican,' 'Puerto Rican,' or both (Potowski and Torres 2023; Rosa 2019). As children and adolescents go on to build their own social networks, they bring these values with them for further negotiation. For instance, in a study of language attitudes among Canada- and foreign-born Hispanic adolescents in Montreal, Pérez Arreaza (2016) found that participants were very aware of dialectal diversity among various national norms, and this awareness guided how they accommodated to each other linguistically. The combination of deterministic factors (for instance, one's degree of exposure to specific features throughout the lifespan) and psychological factors (the meaning of these features as expressions of ethnic or national identity) has been shown to drive patterns of variation and change in many Hispanic transnational contexts (Escobar and Potowski 2015: 157–77; Fernández-Mallat 2018; Lara Bermejo 2018; Mar-Molinero 2020). Speakers participating in cyclical migration routines offer additional proof of immigrants' ability to navigate multiple linguistic and symbolic landscapes. For instance, in southeastern Pennsylvania, temporary migrant agricultural workers from Guanajuato (Mexico) assess the same phonological feature (specifically, assibilation of phrase-final /r/ as [ɹ̝], §5.5 and §6.3) in different ways depending on whether they happen to find themselves in the United States or back home (Matus Mendoza 2004).

The ecological complexity typical of transnational communication is epitomized by multilingual situations that question the traditional dichotomy between 'language maintenance' and 'language shift.' Chicanx speakers in the US Southwest offer an example. In this population, speakers access a broad range of linguistic resources, from native and non-native realizations of spoken Mexican Spanish and English (and their respective standardized versions), to African American English and Chicanx English. Dexterity in the combination of elements from these historical pools constitutes a key part of the speakers' communicative range, enacted to symbolize membership in the local community (Fought 2003). Chicanx English, routinely classified as an ethnic variety of English, bears the marks of decades-long contact with Spanish in Mexican American communities in the US Southwest (see Figure 6.7). As we will see below (§6.7 and §7.4), its description as a mere result of shift to English obscures the environmental dynamics of language use, learning and change in this community.

Nowhere are these transnational sociolinguistic triggers more discernible than along national borders, which not only provide opportunities for demographic and linguistic contact, but also for the explicit confrontation of ethnolinguistic

FIGURE 6.7. Mural with Latinx, Chicanx, and Mexican Catholic and Indigenous references in Barrio Logan, San Diego, California (teddeady via Flickr, license: https://creativecommons.org/licenses/by-nc-nd/2.0/deed.en)

rivalries. In a general sociolinguistic overview of several Hispanic border areas, Lipski (2011) has distinguished between situations where contacts across the borderline are shaped by overtly oppositional national ideologies (*back-to-back borders*), and cases where contacts are favored by frequent communication and the general ideological ambiance of the binational region (*face-to-face borders*). An example of the first scenario can be found along the border between Haiti and the Dominican Republic (§5.2). By contrast, less confrontational border environments can foster positive attitudes toward bilingualism and motivate speakers to embrace hybrid repertoires symbolizing local frontier identities. Contact varieties of Portuguese in northern Uruguay (Carvalho 2014; §5.3) and along the border between Spain and Portugal (Clements 2009: 190–209) reflect this situation. Some linguistic outcomes of these border ecologies are explored below (§6.8).

In some circumstances, transnational dynamics become a central ingredient in the emergence of new national sociolinguistic identities. Belize Spanish offers a paradigmatic example: a former British colony, this country is the product of three centuries of border redrawing, most recently between Mexico, Guatemala, and British Belize. Its demography has been historically characterized by interactions among African slaves, British settlers, ethnic Mayans, *mestizo* immigrants from Mexico and Honduras, and Garifuna speakers. These contacts have led to a markedly diffuse sociolinguistic situation (Balam et al. 2014: 245) motivating most Belizeans to develop multilingual competence in various repertoires (including Belizean Kriol, standard English, Spanish, and Garifuna) and creating opportunities for everyday heteroglossic communicative practices, as will be seen below (§6.8).

In the next two sections, I review some of the observed results of contact in these transnational environments. These include both migration-based contacts (§6.7) and contacts along national borders (§6.8). As was the case intranationally, this division does not imply a clear-cut distinction between both settings.

6.7. Migration-based transnational contact outcomes

As seen throughout this chapter, immigrants (whether internal or transnational) are often pressured to assimilate to the surrounding majorities. Linguistically, assimilation typically brings about the favoring of features characteristic of the majority and away from those brought in by the migrant contingent, as described in studies of *dialectal accommodation* (if contact is seen from the perspective of dialect contact) or *language shift* (from the lens of language contact).

Pressures to assimilate to the surrounding majority are particularly apparent whenever features operate as indexes of geographical origin. Consider, for instance, the various forms of assimilation among internal immigrants to Mexico City (§6.4): transnational immigrants often exhibit similar effects. For instance, Rodríguez Cadena (2005) has studied the choices among options for syllable-final /r/ and /l/ by Cubans living in the Mexican capital. Their original dialect includes variation between standard (full) articulations, shared with normative Mexican Spanish, as well as a range of dialectal variants that are common in Cuba but much less so in central Mexico, including elision, assimilation to the following segment, and lateralization of /ɾ/ as [l]. The study shows that the frequency of the options perceived as non-Mexican decreases sharply among these immigrants after a few years in Mexico City, especially in the case of the (highly stigmatized) lateralized /ɾ/.

But, as we may expect, the ecological story is often more complex than a simple unidirectional move toward dialectal assimilation. Instead, transnational migrants weigh multiple triggers as they decide whether and how much to accommodate. This negotiation has been explored by Pesqueira (2008) in a study of how Buenos Aires-born migrants living in the Mexican capital articulate /j/ either as [ʃ] or [ʒ] (typical of their original dialect; §5.5) or as [j] (the Mexican variant). The likelihood that a speaker favored the Mexican option was determined by a host of linguistic and sociolinguistic factors, including the token frequency of each lexical item, length of residence in Mexico, degree of contact with Mexicans or Argentinians in each speaker's social networks, attitudes toward Mexican Spanish, and long-term prospects to stay abroad; as a result, some speakers accommodate very intensely, while others resist accommodation.

As was the case with intranational migration, transnational immigrants negotiate their repertoires on a feature-by-feature basis, rather than as part of externally defined dialectal packages. For instance, Bolivian immigrants in northern Chile (Fernández-Mallat 2018; see Figure 6.8) have been shown to disfavor some Bolivian features (such as present perfect in narratives, see §6.4 for this same

FIGURE 6.8. A Bolivian confraternity parading in the streets of Arica, Chile, in 2012 (Andrea021, via Wikimedia Commons, license: https://creativecommons.org/licenses/by-sa/3.0/deed.en)

feature in Peruvian *castellano andino*) but they tend to retain others, including double possessive constructions (*su hermana de mi mamá*, see st. Sp. *la hermana de mi mamá* 'my mom's sister') and *en* with location adverbs (*en allá* 'there, over there', see st. Sp. *allá*). The author explains these differences as the function of a combination of structural and social factors. These include whether the feature in question is syntactically embedded in the speakers' variety (disfavoring accommodation), whether they are undergoing change in the original varieties in Bolivia (favoring accommodation), and the degree to which each is consciously deployed situationally in the performance of immigrant identities.

Similar results have been yielded by a study of dialectal accommodation across three generations of Ecuadorian immigrants in Madrid (Lara Bermejo 2018) that focused on 2SG address forms, which (as we have seen before in this book) have historically exhibited pervasive variation in Spanish (§4.7, §5.5). In this case, the immigrant pool includes dialectally specific forms (namely, singular non-deferential *vos, sumercé* in Ecuador, plural non-deferential *vosotras/os* in Spain) as well as shared forms with cross-dialectal pragmatic differences (including non-deferential singular *tú*, deferential singular *usted*, and plural *ustedes*). The immigrants in this study show a generational accommodation trend toward the European Spanish pattern, with third-generation speakers using it consistently. By contrast, second-generation speakers alternate between Ecuadorian and European uses, depending on the communicative context and their on-site construction of identity.

Studies of contact *among* Hispanic immigrant communities (a common occurrence in transnational settings, as seen in §6.6), also challenge simple narratives of assimilation to majority features. For instance, Hernández (2009) studied the articulations of word-final /n/, namely velar [ŋ] and alveolar [n], among Salvadorans in Houston (§2.5), where the largest group of Latinxs is of Mexican origin. In El Salvador, speakers typically exhibit higher rates of velarization than in Mexican Spanish. The author collected data in two neighborhoods where immigrants from both countries interact, Holly Springs and Segundo Barrio (with the latter having a higher proportion of Salvadoran residents), and then compared these data to a rural community in El Salvador. Overall, Houston Salvadorans exhibited lower rates of velarization than their compatriots back home, which the author interprets as the outcome of conscious accommodation to Mexican Spanish via the suppression of stigmatized [ŋ]. The author also found a significant difference between the two Houston neighborhoods, with the lowest velarization rates in Holly Springs, where Salvadorans' personal networks include more frequent contact with Mexicans.

Equally complex effects as those seen in contact among similar feature pools can be observed in transnational bilingual or multilingual contacts. In this area, contact between Spanish and English in the United States is arguably the best studied case (Carter and D'Alessandro Merii 2023; Escobar and Potowski 2015; Fuller and Leeman 2020; Otheguy and Zentella 2012; Potowski and Torres 2023; Zentella 1997). A foundational reference in this area is Silva-Corvalán (1994), an exploration of the relationship between generation and language use in the Spanish verbal systems across several generations of Mexican Americans in Los Angeles, comprising Mexico-born speakers and bilingual heritage speakers of Spanish.

Silva-Corvalán's data showed a clear recombination of the tense-mood-aspect verbal categories typical of monolingual varieties, with each successive generational cohort using fewer categories and compensating this reduction by extending the semantic value of the remaining ones. Examples (17–9) illustrate these strategies (from Silva-Corvalán 1994: 40–1); relevant forms are underlined.

(17) Pluperfect indicative > preterite:

Y estábamos esperando a mi amá, porque ella fue (see st. Sp. *había ido*) a llevar a mi hermano a la dentista.

'And we were waiting for my mom, because she had gone to take my brother to the dentist'.

(18) Past subjunctive > imperfect:

Se comunicó con el police department a ver si tenían uno que estaba (see st. Sp. *estuviera*) interesado en ser teacher, so me llamaron a mí.

'He called the police department to see if they had anyone who might be interested in being a teacher, so they called me'.

(19) Conjugated verb form > infinitive:

Y no quería que otras personas hacer (see st. Sp. *hicieran*) cosas por ella.

'And she didn't want other people to do things for her'.

Additional forms of reduction in this heritage speaker corpus affect the semantic distribution of specific verbs. An example is the distribution of the two Spanish copulas, *ser* and *estar* (both 'to be'), with the latter historically expanding over the former even in monolingual varieties (*es lleno* > *está lleno* '(it) is full'). Revealingly, Silva-Corvalán's bilinguals in Los Angeles presented a higher proportion of innovative *estar* uses than monolinguals, enhancing this diachronic trend, rather than merely simplifying the system by eliminating the contrast between both copulas (1994: 92–132).

Silva-Corvalán observed that these reductions across verbal categories, often treated as forms of heritage language attrition or incomplete acquisition in bilingual speakers (Montrul 2022; Polinsky 2018; §2.5 and §7.4), followed a predictable path: the first categories to be lost were those that are acquired late, are less frequent in discourse, tend to occur in subordination, and/or require an anchoring outside the speakers' immediate world (for instance, in hypotheses and contra-factual information, rather than description or narration) (1994: 20–55). Note, however, that this reduction implies the continuation of tendencies already present in the input Spanish varieties – even some first-generation speakers participated in some of these reductions, although less frequently than US-born speakers. Here, again, we find evidence of bi/multilingual speakers' preference for cognitively economical options, in this case a reduced set of verbal categories, rather than the simple mapping of characteristics of their dominant language onto their weaker language (§2.6).

So far, we have seen that transnational migration-based ecologies have often been interpreted from an assimilatory lens, with linguistic minorities losing their traditional repertoires via 'dialect contact' or 'language contact.' However, the sociolinguistic dynamics of immigrant communities often transcends this dichotomy (§2.3). Again, Spanish in the United States offers some of the best researched examples. In Orozco's (2018) comparison between Colombian Spanish in New York City and non-migrant Colombian Spanish, a prominent question is whether the observed differences should be attributed to bilingualism, to contact among users of various Spanish pools ('dialects') in the city, or to both. The study focuses on several features where the prototypical grammars of Spanish and English differ sharply either formally or in terms of frequency, which should in principle make it easier to distinguish between 'language contact' and 'dialect contact' effects. One of these features is the expression of futurity, which in Spanish offers three main options: a morphological future (*cantaré* 'I will sing'); the present tense (*canto* 'I sing'); and a periphrastic future with *ir* 'to go' as an auxiliary (*voy a cantar* 'I am going to sing'). Contrastive frequency data for Colombia and New York (NYC) are shown in Table 6.3. Note the marked reduction in the morphological form, and the increase in the periphrasis in the NYC data.

TABLE 6.3. Relative frequency of variants for the expression of futurity in Barranquilla and NYC Colombian Spanish (Orozco 2018: 35)

	Barranquilla (Colombia)	NYC
Morphological future	18.2%	7.2%
Simple present tense	35.9%	30.3%
Periphrastic future	45.9%	62.5%
Total	100%	100%

To explain these differences, Orozco appeals to a combination of environmental triggers. These include the surface similarities between Spanish and English periphrastic future forms (e.g. both *will* + INF and *be going to* + INF in Eng.), contact with speakers of other Spanish varieties where periphrastic constructions are frequent (most notably, Caribbean varieties like Puerto Rican and Dominican Spanish), as well as the same cognitive bias for transparent and convergent constructions that we have seen in other situations of contact. Critically, all these triggers operate simultaneously on the same speakers to shape their grammars (see Otheguy and Zentella 2012 for similar observations about NYC Spanish). As argued in Chapter 2 (§2.3), the overlapping effects of 'dialect contact' and 'language contact' are yet another manifestation of the sociolinguistic dynamics of contact settings, where speakers select and recombine features in communicatively effective and cognitively advantageous ways, cutting across socioculturally established boundaries among named varieties.

An ecological contact-based approach can also help us reassess situations that have been described as straightforward cases of language loss. An example is Chicanx English, a variety of English in the US Southwest that, as advanced above (§6.6), feeds from multiple linguistic pools. Traditionally studied as an L1 ethnic variety of English resulting from shift from Spanish, its features suggest a more complex process of selection than mere reconfiguration toward

English monolingual models. Fought (2003) lists several characteristic features in Los Angeles Chicanx English. Many clearly reproduce L1 English sources (for instance, invariable *be* from African American English, or the fronting of /u/ and quotatives *be like* and *be all*, shared with California Anglo English). Yet some elements are either absent or extremely infrequent in L1 English, and can be hypothesized to stem from L2 English, especially at the phonological level, where Chicanx English 'bears the imprimatur of Spanish throughout the sound system' (81). For instance, by comparison with other forms of L1 English, this variety exhibits less frequent reduction of unstressed vowels; more phonetic realizations of [i] in cases for phonemic /ɪ/ (especially in morphemic /ɪŋ/, that is, *-ing*) and intonation contours intermediate between non-Latinx English and Mexican Spanish, among other features (62–92). L2 sources can also be invoked for some syntactic and semantic features: for instance, uses of *on* and *in* different from other English varieties, as in *he was in a beer run* or *must have been on the fifth grade*, reveal the influence of *en*, the only situational preposition in Spanish (93–110).

From an evolutionary perspective, the fact that elements originating in Spanish continue to operate as linguistic models in Chicanx English questions one-dimensional narratives of language loss in this population. In a similar vein, recent research on Miami English (Carter and D'Alessandro Merii 2023) has shown that calqued expressions from Spanish (such as *get down from the car*, *invite me a drink* and *it's not for anything*, modelled on Spanish *bajar del carro*, *invitarme a un trago* and *no es por nada*, as alternatives for more cross-dialectally general *get out of the car*, *buy me /treat me to a drink* and *for no good/special reason*) have become frequent in the speech of English-dominant Latinxs and are deemed acceptable even by some local non-Latinx English speakers. Evidence from Chicanx and Miami English confirms the critical role that bilingual speakers play as agents of change in many transnational communities.

Besides exploring these patterns of selection and reinterpretation of specific features, research on transnational communities has also explored the potential for bilingual conversational strategies to contribute to language change. Code-switching (§2.3), where speakers alternate between two named varieties in conversation, is a common strategy in the performance of bilingual and bicultural identities (recall Paraguayan *jopará* in §6.3, which has been described as a form of socially pervasive code-switching in a non-transnational environment). Code-switching has been identified as a potential trigger for some changes (Muysken 2013; Thomason 2001: 131–6). Specifically for Spanish in the US, Toribio (2011: 534–6) discusses some possible linguistic effects of code-switching on patterns of phonetic and morphosyntactic selection among Spanish-English bilinguals. These effects include VOTs (voice onset times) in voiceless stops /p, t, k/ that are intermediate between Spanish and English, and higher proportions of overt subject pronouns than in both monolingual Spanish and non-switched speech by the same speakers. She hypothesizes that these realizations may become learning targets at the population level whenever code-switching is a frequent social practice: '[i]n this way, Latinos who engage in Spanish-English code-switching may be active agents in the promotion of new varieties of US Spanish and US English' (536). Historically, therefore, code-switching is not just an ephemeral, on-the-spot practice. On the contrary, it operates as a site for linguistic negotiation with possible long-term consequences for the reconfiguration of communal repertoires.

Examples (20–22) illustrate some of the switches found by Zentella in her classical study of Spanish-English code-switching among Puerto Rican children in *el bloque*, in New York City's East Harlem (examples below adapted from Zentella 1997: 118–9).

(20) Full sentence:

Pa, ¿me vas a comprar un jugo? It costs 25 cents.
'Dad, are you going to buy me a juice? It costs 25 cents'.

(21) Noun phrase:

Tú estás metiendo your big mouth.
'You are butting in'. (lit. 'you are sticking your big mouth')

(22) Independent clauses:

My father took him to the ASPCA y lo mataron.
'My father took him to the ASPCA and they killed him'.

The fact that the most frequent switches in this study involved full sentences, clauses, and phrases (i.e. intersentential and intrasentential switches, as in 20 and 21/22 respectively) indicates that these children had acquired the grammatical patterns typical of both source repertoires and could juggle them effortlessly in conversation. As it turns out, most switches identified by Zentella were not of the 'crutch'-type to fill in a lexical gap (1997: 98–9). Instead, speakers switched strategically to fulfill a plethora of conversational purposes, including clarifications, direct speech quotations, requests, or changes in footing or narrative frame. In the context of monoglossic ideologies promoting one-to-one matches between languages and national ethnicities, code-switching emerges as a quintessentially transnational, translingual practice (§1.4).

6.8. The linguistics of transnational contacts along borders

We now turn our attention to some prominent linguistic consequences of contact along national borderlines, which as advanced (§6.6) offer a testing ground for the combined role of transborder movements and national ideologies on language use. In Lipski's (2011) survey of the dialectal makeup of various Latin American border regions, cases range from those where borderlines do not appear to correlate with linguistic variation to areas where linguistic isoglosses (§2.3) coincide with international boundaries. For instance, although syllable-final /s/ is typically aspirated as [h] or deleted by most Honduran speakers, Hondurans along the border with Guatemala (Figure 6.9) exhibit much lower rates of erosion, close to those typical in the neighboring country. By contrast, on the Paraguayan side of the border with Argentina, the alveopalatal articulation of /j/ as [ʃ ~ ʒ] increasingly common in northeastern Argentina (§6.3) is not

FIGURE 6.9. Currency exchangers on the Guatemalan side of the border with Honduras (Frans-Banja Mulder via Wikimedia Commons, license: https://creativecommons.org/licenses/by/3.0/deed.en)

typically heard. Lipski attributes these different outcomes to a complex range of ecological factors specific to each border, including the local demographics, how easily residents may cross the border and sustain transnational communication networks, the presence of Indigenous communities, and historical national rivalries (44–6; see 'back-to-back' borders, §6.6).

This layering of historical transborder contact effects can be witnessed along the Spain-Portugal *raya/raia* 'border' (for contact along the Uruguay-Brazil border, see Carvalho 2014, and §5.2, §5.3). Clements (2009: 190–209) and Clements et al. (2011) have studied various forms of linguistic hybridization in the small Portuguese town of Barrancos, a short two-mile drive from the border with Spain. Here, speakers have historically had access to forms of spoken southern European Spanish and Portuguese through family connections, work, and everyday travel, as well as to the standard Portuguese promoted in the schools. The town's residents have tapped into all these pools to create repertoires (*barranquenho*) that blur traditional classifications of Spanish and Portuguese as separate languages. Examples (23–24) illustrate some of the overlaps between the prototypical forms of both languages (a-b) and their interpretation in Barrancos (c) (all examples from Clements et al. 2011: 406, forms of interest are underlined):

(23a) Portuguese
   Tenho-o visto

(23b) Spanish
   Lo he visto

(23c) Barranquenho
O tenho visto
'I have seen/have been seeing him'.

(24a) Portuguese
Quando a tiver toda pronta, chame-me

(24b) Spanish
Cuando la tenga toda lista, llámeme

(24c) Barranquenho
Quando a tenha toda pronta, me chama
'When you have all of it ready, call me'.

In (23c), Barranquenho occupies an intermediate position between Portuguese and Spanish – although the lexicon is fundamentally Portuguese, the position of the clitic *o* is pre-verbal, as in Spanish (23b). In (24c), the present subjunctive form *tenha* coincides formally with Portuguese (rather than Spanish *tenga*), but its use instead of future subjunctive *tiver* in canonical Portuguese (24a) betrays the influence of the Spanish present subjunctive in future irrealis contexts shown in (24b). By profiting cognitively from the structural and lexical overlap among these historical pools, speakers in Barrancos or along the Uruguay-Brazil border have created novel repertoires that can be mobilized to perform bicultural identities (Carvalho 2014; Clements 2009: 414–5).

The Central American nation of Belize provides an even more striking illustration of the linguistic effects of the sociohistorical heterogeneity typical of border areas. As noted (§6.6), the local landscape has historically involved a rich web of contacts among typologically different pools (Mayan languages, Garifuna, Mexican and Central American Spanish, Kriol, and standard English). Balam et al. (2014) have studied verbal compounds of the type *hacer* 'to do' + INF among multilingual, ethnically Hispanic (*mestizo*) speakers in the Orange Walk town of northern Belize, about 35 miles from the Mexican border. This structure is illustrated in (25–26) (examples from Balam et al. 2014: 254):

(25) Nunca   he   hecho   witness   un   girls' fight
     Never   have.1SG.AUX   do.PART   witness.INF   a   girls' fight
     'I have never witnessed a girls' fight'.

(26) Hay   un   program   que   hace   allow
     There is   a   program   that   do.3SG.PRES.IND. allow.INF
     hacer   chat
     do.INF   chat.INF
     'There is a program that allows chatting'.

In these examples, *hacer* + INF constructions coexist with English lexicon ('witness', 'girl's fight', 'program'), and reveal the combined effect of various factors. Acquisitionally, they are 'a strategic means of maximizing lexical resources in [the] bilingual/multilingual speakers' repertoire' (Balam et al. 2014: 262), allowing speakers to bypass the morphological complexity of Spanish verbal inflection in low-frequency verbs (262). Sociolinguistically, their use is linked to code-switching as a regular conversational practice, which is expected as part of the communicative proficiency of Belizeans (257). Although these types of constructions have been attested in other situations of contact (for instance, Southwest US Spanish, Toribio 2011: 538), in Belize they have local historical sources: as it turns out, *hacer* + INF constructions have also been reported among Yucatán Mayan-Spanish bilinguals, and analytic constructions in Kriol provide yet another possible cognitive pivot (Balam et al. 2014: 258–9). As in other situations examined in this book, Belizean speakers' choices cannot be ascribed to one single ecological trigger and should instead by analyzed as the outcome of multiple diachronic sources operating across named language varieties.

6.9. Twenty-first-century post-colonial continuities in the Maghreb

Chapters 4 and 5 have covered several colonial and post-colonial settings in the Americas and Asia. Spain's colonial expansion also encompassed Africa, bringing about various forms of contact among Iberian and African repertoires. These are exemplified by Jewish and Muslim populations forcibly expelled from Spain or escaping religious prosecution starting in the late fifteenth century (§3.1); Christian captives sold into slavery in northern Africa between the sixteenth and eighteenth centuries; rural populations from southeastern Spain settling in French Algeria in the late nineteenth and early twentieth centuries; Spanish military serving in the Spanish protectorate in northern Morocco (1912–1956); and missionaries, teachers, and government officials in Equatorial Guinea, a Spanish colony between 1778 and 1968.

Spanish is still a sociolinguistically prominent component of two African regions. In Equatorial Guinea, Spanish continues to be learned as an L2 as one of the country's official languages amid a complex sociolinguistic landscape also including, among other varieties, several Niger-Congo languages and Pichinglis, an English-lexified creole (Gomashie 2019; Yakpo 2016). The other region is the Maghreb, where besides *haketía* (the now-endangered, historical Judeo-Spanish variety of north African Sephardic Jews; Bürki 2016), Spanish is still used among ethnic Spaniards and L1 Arabic speakers in cities like Tangiers and Tetouan. In the Maghreb, the local sociolinguistic environment includes Arabic and Berber, French as the preferential language of education, widespread access to Spanish media in Morocco's north, frequent cross-border contacts in Ceuta and Melilla (see *porteadoras*, §6.5), transnational cyclical movements between both countries by Moroccan immigrant families, and the use of Spanish in foreign language instruction.

As of the 2010s, fewer than 3,000 ethnic Spaniards remained in northern Morocco (compared to around 200,000 at the end of Spain's protectorate; Sayahi 2011: 478). These are mostly elderly individuals who speak forms of Andalusian Spanish and who are often not dominant in Arabic, besides high-frequency emblematic loanwords (481). For at least some speakers, personal networks do include frequent access to Spanish, French, and Arabic, with frequent code-switching among the three, as shown in the intersentential switches in (27). Sequences between brackets are in Arabic, and underlined material is in French (from Sayahi 2011: 481).

(27) [il waːlid ʒawiʒ ihna, fi kaːza ʒawiʒ ʒa esɣiːr ʒa mʕa walidih]. Quince años tenía mi padre cuando vino aquí con su padre. Ils ne trevaillaient que les carrières [xaddamiːn ɣir fil lahʒar], des types de carrières. Ils travaillaient dans les carrières et des trucs.

'My father got married here, in Casablanca he got married. He came while still young with his parents. My father was 15 years old when he came here with his father. They worked in rock quarries. They only worked [with] rocks, some type of quarries. They worked in rock quarries and stuff'.

Most Spanish in northern Morocco, however, is currently heard not from ethnic Spaniards, but among L1 Arabic speakers, who learn it naturalistically from Spanish speakers or as a language of instruction. They exhibit a broad range of personal repertoires, determined by age and context of exposure, opportunities for interaction in Spanish, and motivation to approximate L1 models. Besides Spanish lexicon, these repertoires include the articulation of /ɲ/ as [nj] (*año* [anjo]; see st. Sp. [aɲo] 'year'); alternation between [θ] and [s] (*cinco* [θinko ~ sinko] 'five'); alternation in [e~o] and [i~u], especially in unstressed position (*primero* as [pɾemeɾo]; st. Sp. [pɾimeɾo]); non-canonical stress shift in some words (*película* as [peliku'la]; st. Sp. [pe'likula] 'movie'); and blurring of standard Spanish verbal categories, such as indicative/subjunctive (*espero que él viene para decirme,* see st. Sp. *espero que él venga para decirme* 'I hope that he's coming to tell me') or copulas *ser* and *estar* (*él también era en la misma situación,* st. Sp. *él también estaba en la misma situación* 'he was also in the same situation') (Sayahi 2005: 202–4). Some of these features stem from the application of common non-native learning strategies (like the merger of phonological and grammatical categories; §2.6), while others (such as [nj] or stress shifts) are most likely due to transfer (§2.2) from Arabic. As is the case among ethnic Spaniards, code-switching with Arabic and French is common.

Further south, in the former colony of Western Sahara, Spanish features also continue to be a part of the local contact landscapes (Candela Romero 2007; Morgenthaler García 2011). During the colonial period (1886–1975) whole generations of Sahrawis were exposed to instruction in Spanish. Occupation of most of the territory by Morocco in 1975 resulted in two markedly different sociolinguistic areas. In the areas controlled by Morocco, speakers came to be exposed to Moroccan linguistic policies and to thousands of Moroccan settlers. Consequently, French and standard Arabic are now the languages of media and education, with forms of spoken Arabic used in informal interactions. Conversely, in the areas controlled by the Sahrawi Arab Democratic Republic (SADR) and in the refugee encampments of Tindouf (Algeria), home to about 170,000 Sahrawis, Spanish is recognized as an official language alongside Arabic, and is used in media, education, and bureaucracy. Spanish is also instrumental in interactions with Spain-born aid and medical personnel in the refugee camps (see Figure 6.10). Many older children and adolescents travel to Spain as students or are hosted by Spanish families during the summer, and health workers are often trained in Cuba.

The Spanish features used by Sahrawis exhibit many of the same contact effects described above for L2 speakers in Morocco. But the local conditions of

FIGURE 6.10. A bilingual Arabic-Spanish dental clinic sign in a Sahrawi refugee camp in Tindouf, Algeria (Loïc Alejandro via Pexels)

contact are apparent in the widespread use of Spanish loanwords in lexical fields like machinery (*estorniador* 'screwdriver', see Sp. *destornillador*; *muiyi* 'spring', see Sp. *muelle*), automotion (*bulante* 'steering wheel', see Sp. *volante*; *ruida* 'wheel', see Sp. *rueda*), food (*bera* 'pear', see Sp. *pera*; *hiladu* 'ice cream', see Sp. *helado*) and healthcare (*bumada* 'ointment', see Sp. *pomada*; *resita* 'prescription', see Sp. *receta*). Conversationally, bilingual and bicultural knowledge is actuated via emblematic and tag switches, as illustrated in the exchange in (28) between two speakers (SP1 and SP2) (Morgenthaler García 2011: 114):

(28) SP1. ma ʕəndu *cochi gasulina*.
           'The car has no gas'.
     SP2. emnīn kuntum?
           'Where were they?'
     SP1. ehðe Aousserd
           'Close to Aousserd'.
     SP2. yāḷḷāh mʕāya bāš nǧību *gasulina, ¿vale?*
           'Let's go, then! Come with me to bring the gas, ok?'
     SP1. *Vale* yāḷḷāh! *¡No pasa nada!*
           'Ok, let's go! It's all good!'

In this sequence, we can see inserted Spanish loanwords ("cochi" 'car', "gasulina" 'gas') and set phrases and discourse markers ("vale" 'ok?', "no pasa nada" 'it's all good'). These practices exemplify how Sahrawi speakers mobilize Spanish features as an index of post-colonial sociolinguistic identities, a practice with clear political motivations in this context of anti-colonial confrontation with Morocco.

6.10. Beyond borders: Contacts in the digital world

In an increasingly transnational world, the internet stands as *the* global ecology par excellence. The de-localized nature of digital communication allows individuals to participate in networks regardless of geographical space or chronological simultaneity, a hallmark of ecologies in the age of transnational mobility (§6.1, §6.6). The sociolinguistic role of digitally mediated communication is two-fold: digital platforms offer a site for the promotion of normative and homogenizing discourses, but also for the expression of linguistic dissidence. It is therefore no coincidence that the presence of Spanish on the internet is central to its recent articulation as a 'world language' or a 'global language' (Lynch 2018; Mar-Molinero 2008; Villa and Del Valle 2015) (§6.1). At the same time, socioeconomic inequalities create vast regional differences in internet access and frequency of use. Thus, among Hispanic countries as of 2021, the share of the population with frequent internet access ranged from 94% in Spain and 90% in Chile to 51% in Guatemala and 48% in Nicaragua (International Telecommunication Union 2021). These differences suggest that the internet may still, after all, not be as global an ecology as often assumed. Nevertheless, researchers have started to pay attention to how digital communication may offer a channel for the spread of linguistic innovations (Bryden et al. 2018; Efrat-Kowalski 2021; Laitinen et al. 2020).

The environmental role played by digitally mediated communication for many speakers has not gone unheeded by prescriptive bodies, which now strive to chart and quantify it. For instance, since 2012, the Instituto Cervantes yearbooks have included updated tallies on the use of Spanish on a variety of internet platforms (Facebook, Twitter, Wikipedia, etc.) and comparisons with other languages (see, for instance, Instituto Cervantes 2022). In these quantifications, the presence of Spanish on the internet is taken as an indication of its ethnolinguistic vitality in the geopolitical competition among world languages (Moreno Fernández 2015b; Moreno Fernández and Otero Roth 2007). These quantifications are accompanied by declarations on the importance of ensuring that Spanish remains among the most used languages on the internet. Together with the monoglossic and homogenizing language practices characterizing many educational or academic settings (§1.3), the focus on the digital use of the language is a key part of the discourse on Spanish as a global resource, but (ironically) it also reveals some of the same anxieties and distrust about its assumed global destiny that we have seen since Nebrija's *Gramática* (§3.1).

This anxiety also takes the form of qualitative concerns about linguistic practices in digital environments, legitimizing various forms of prescriptive intervention. The creation of FundéuRAE, a non-profit public-private partnership between Real Academia Española, news agency EFE and BBVA bank charged with the promotion of normative Spanish in the media, is an example. Pledging to keep a close watch over how the language is used in public spaces, this organization warns of the dangers of allowing non-normative practices to go unchecked. These attitudes are apparent in the following excerpt from a 2019 interview with journalist Mario Tascón during his term as director of FundéuRAE, where he answers a question as to whether Spanish needs to be shielded on the internet from contact effects like loanwords:

Since many new [technological] concepts stem from the English-speaking world, it is easier for other languages to just incorporate the corresponding loanwords. At the same time, it does create a comprehension problem for non-experts who may not necessarily understand these terms until they are established ..., so there is a risk, yes, a risk that people won't understand each other (interview with Manuel Tascón, March 30, 2019, *Infobae.es*).

Tascón's framing of contact as a problem is not just symptomatic of the linguistic purism typical of monoglossic ideologies. It also rests on the assumption that communication can only be efficient in the absence of contact-based linguistic selections, with speakers staying within normative language boundaries (note that, as he puts it, it is 'languages' that find it 'easier' to borrow words, not actual language users).

Considering these assumptions, it is legitimate to wonder whether this trepidation about language contact in digital contexts is justified, or whether speakers do in fact refrain from transgressing linguistic boundaries in their digital interactions to avoid these assumed pitfalls. As it turns out, they do not seem to – on the contrary, digital environments allow for hybrid linguistic practices that may be censored or suppressed in other environments. For instance, Alba Niño (2015) has studied the online use of *amestáu,* an umbrella term for colloquial forms of Asturian (northern Spain) (§2.3) in contact with Castilian Spanish. In the exchange in (29), extracted from a popular worldwide social platform, seven participants (A-G) play with the structural and semantic differences and overlaps among three typologically similar feature pools: Catalan (CAT), Asturian (AST), and Castilian Spanish (SPA).

(29) 1A. Estic mayat (*CAT + AST*)
   CAT + AST
   'I'm exhausted-MASC'.
 2B. toy mayá (*AST*)
   'I'm exhausted-FEM'.
 3C. Toy frayá (*AST*)
   'I'm beaten up-FEM'.
 4A. Mayats y frayats, units per el cansanci (*CAT + AST*)
   'The exhausted and the beaten up, united by tiredness'.
 5D. Estic feta pols! (*CAT*)
   'I'm worn out-FEM'. (lit. 'I've turned into dust')
 6E. feta també es un formatge grec (*CAT*)
   '*Feta* is also a Greek cheese'.
 7A. 'T'estimo locament' no era una cançó de Les Grecs també?: P
   Toy fechu una llaceria ho! (*CAT + SPA + AST*)
   'Wasn't 'I love you like crazy' a song by the 'Grecas' (music band) too?
   :P I'm feeling miserable'.
 8B. Estic fet una llacereta (*CAT +AST*)
   'I'm in misery'.
 9F. Por favor que algún catalán nos ayude a resolver esto (*SPA*)
   'Please, can a Catalan help us clear this up?'

10G. Després de treballar tot el dia el millor es anar-se al llit.
Suena mal, pero es el mejor remedio:) (*SPA + CAT*)
'After working all day, the best thing is to go to bed. (Anar-se) may sound awful, but it is the best remedy:)'.

(from Alba Niño 2015: 241).

The starting point in this exchange is a statement by one of the participants ("estic mayat" 'I'm exhausted-MASC') where a common colloquial Asturian expression (*tar mayáu* 'to be exhausted', lit. 'to be beaten up') is given Catalan morphology ("estic" 'I am', see Ast. *toi~to*, and Catalan adjectival masculine singular ending –*t* in "mayat"). This blend kickstarts a series of responses where participants negotiate the formal similarities among the three pools via several strategies: (a) structures that stick to the canonical borderlines of normative versions of each language (that is, 'monolingual' statements, as in 6E, 9F); (b) code-switched statements (as in 10G, where the first sentence ("Després de treballar ...") is Catalan, and the second ("Suena mal ...") is Castilian Spanish; (c) and blends where the structure matches more than one language, or elements of both are morphologically blended (e.g. 8B "estic fet una llacereta", where the Asturian expression "toi fechu una llacería" 'I am feeling miserable', lit. 'I am turned into a misery' is given Catalan morphology with Catalan nominal suffix –*et(a)* 'little x' to replace the nominal ending –*ia* of Asturian "llacería"). The participants manipulate the lexical and structural features available to them to build solidarity by using puns and cultural double entendres, as in E's recasting of "feta," originally used by D as the feminine singular participle of Cat. *fer* 'to do, to make', as the homonymous name of the Greek cheese, and Cat. "Grec" 'Greek' by A as a pivot to refer to a Spanish Flamenco-rock duo (las Grecas) from the 1970s.

Throughout this conversation, participants display an awareness of the conceptual linguistic boundaries between these codes, consciously transgressing them for pragmatic purposes (humor, solidarity, etc.). This exchange illustrates how digital platforms provide a medium to challenge the linguistic and symbolic boundaries promoted by monoglossic discourses, embracing the formal and expressive possibilities of linguistic hybridity (much to the dismay of prescriptivists!). Twenty-first-century digital communication has emerged as yet a new contact ecology – the diachronic effects of which will surely continue to be a prominent area of linguistic inquiry in the coming decades.

6.11. Conclusion

As the twenty-first century unfolds, questions about what Spanish is and who gets to decide it continue to be posed. Some of this questioning comes from historically familiar actors: governments, language planning institutions, or speakers with socioeconomic capital. Other voices are newer or ring louder today than ever before: immigrants, refugees, multinational companies, heritage and bi/multilingual speakers, language learners, language assessment professionals, non-binary and non-gender conforming individuals, and linguists. The scene for this confrontation of ideas and practices has also expanded beyond face-to-face spoken interactions and written language to encompass audiovisual media and cultural products, digital platforms, and social networks. The more actors partake in this collective negotiation, the harder it becomes to converge on one single definition of Spanish. This is not quite the unified language community that Antonio de Nebrija, Rufino José Cuervo, Juan Valera or Menéndez Pidal envisioned: or is it? Whatever our answer to this question may be, millions of speakers continue to affirm and question this dream in everyday communication.

In this chapter we have reviewed a selection of recent contact settings where speakers have enacted or departed from previous definitions of Spanish in ways that are simultaneously local and global, old and new. These include intranational and transnational situations, frequently rooted in permanent or cyclical migratory movements; post-colonial spaces; and digital communication. The abundant data from these settings, collected by sociolinguists and other contact-minded researchers, grants us a first-row seat to the multilayered nature of contact and provides us with a much richer perspective on the dynamics of language use and variation than in more historically remote contexts. In turn, this data can be used to advance new theories on language change and refine available ones. The speakers in the ecologies in this chapter sometimes coalesce around shared choices in social networks, emerging new dialects, or contexts where homogenized linguistic practices are valued (such as educational institutions or the job market). Other times, they express forms of linguistic dissidence as they recombine features from their respective pools into new combinations via universal processing and bilingual acquisition strategies. Most often, they do both.

In all these cases, as elsewhere in this book, speakers keep doing what they have done since language emerged as a tool for communication over 100,000 years ago: communicating with each other in their respective populations as allowed by their cognitive capabilities, exchanging and confronting linguistic and symbolic resources, and creating repertoires that transcend the mythical boundaries of named language varieties.

Discussion questions

1. Generational partitions have become popular in many countries (e.g. 'silent' generation, 'baby boomers,' 'Generation X,' 'millennials,' and 'Gen Z' in the US). Researchers have tested whether these classifications are sociologically real, and linguists are no exception (e.g., for Spanish, see Roels et al. 2021). On the other hand, these classifications are clearly rooted on understandings of society and age that are anything but universal. Are these or other generational classifications used where you live? And are they useful to understand how individuals come to participate in or reject specific changes?

2. Throughout the book, we have reflected on the historical role played by cities as ecological sites. Some of the dynamics of contact in the megacities of the twenty-first century have clear antecedents in the cities of the colonial period, or even of earlier periods. Which ecological factors can be seen to operate historically in urban ecologies, and which are new?

3. L2 Spanish education is an increasingly important ecological setting that Chapter 6 has not explored. What ecological factors shape language acquisition in these settings? What expectations about language proficiency and performance do L2 students and teachers negotiate, and are these expectations accepted or resisted?

7

Toward New Ecological Narratives in Language Histories

7.1. What have we learned?

Throughout this book, we have explored the history of Spanish not as an ancestral genealogy of linguistic inheritance, but as a constellation of contact events. To do so, we have stepped away from the idea of languages as organic categories or types (§1.4) and closer to their members, i.e. the idiolects, socially embedded in the cognition of individual speakers (§2.4). Readers might by now feel like languages are a little bit like those strips of sand we see along coastal areas, as in Figure 7.1. Everybody can name them ('beach,' 'playa,' or whatever); we can see them, and we feel we can describe them (how wide they are, what color the sand is, etc.). We also assign meanings to them that we can share with other kindred spirits (fun in the sun if you are a tourist; a place to land your boat if you make a livelihood fishing; a fragile ecosystem if you are a coastal biologist). In short, these sandy strips are a familiar part of our experience.

But if we try to categorize what they are and study how they were formed, things become less clear. Does a beach need to have sand to be one? How about pebbly or rocky beaches? Is the sand right under the water also part of a beach? We also know that the action of different elements (wind, tides, animal and human activity) will create visible patterns in the sand that may be ephemeral or last for years. Sand particles also have diverse origins: some (most) are tiny pieces of various minerals, others are organic (fragments of seashell and coral skeletons, bits of rotten wood or seaweed). As humans, we abstract away from all this diversity and instability, and we create a concept ('beach') that we feel serves us well and expresses our experience.

Granted, idiolects are unlike grains of sand in several important ways. For one, humans are aware of themselves and of each other. And unlike sand, language features have a purpose. But we can use this partial analogy (or others – recall the language-as-parasite metaphor in §1.6 and §2.4) to emphasize the *emergent* nature of language as a complex adaptive system (§1.5). This does not mean that human beings cannot deploy linguistic features consciously: as we have seen repeatedly in the preceding chapters, they often do, attaching social meanings to specific linguistic resources, giving rise or disrupting the shared patterns that we

FIGURE 7.1. Waves, sea foam, grains of sand, seaweed ... or a beach?
(source: author)

classify as 'languages,' 'dialects,' or 'norms.' But these choices are not entirely predictable, because they are subject to multiple factors besides speakers' awareness or their willingness to contribute to shared behaviors. Just like grains of sand on a beach, speaker repertoires in a population are real, as are the effects of various environmental forces that make these repertoires coalesce into specific languages or dialects; but these formations are never static, nor endowed with any ulterior entity.

In this book, I have covered only a few of the historical settings where populations of speakers in contact with each other have given rise to linguistic formations that, like grains of sand on a beach, we have come to categorize conventionally as an object, 'Spanish' in this case. Despite my best effort to offer a representative sample of these contact environments, this book leaves many sociohistorical spaces and their speakers unexplored. Just as an example, I have not discussed the environmental role of sign languages, but Deaf individuals have existed and formed communities since the beginning of human history, and their communicative practices are an increasingly visible part of the ecology of Spanish (Morales López 2019). I also have not elaborated on instructional contexts (including the teaching of Spanish as an L2 or 'foreign' language), which have emerged as yet another battleground for the competition among alternative constructions of Spanish (Mar-Molinero 2008; Rosa 2019; Schwartz 2023; Villa and Del Valle 2015). Also, even though everybody seems to be talking about it as I write these lines in late 2023, I have consciously refrained from exploring the emerging effects of artificial intelligence. As a rapidly evolving technology, its role is still not clear (at least to me), but language software companies, language planners, and even some linguists (for instance, Muñoz Basols et al. 2024) are certainly paying close attention to it. Lastly, as I stated in the beginning of the book (§1.9), I have focused on the formal features traditionally covered in language histories, even though these resources are but a small part of our communicative repertoires.

Despite these limitations, this overview of contact events has confirmed that the history of Spanish is as much a history of commonalities as it is a history of differences. Ecologically, the commonalities are not necessarily the ones that language historians are used to talking about – elements of phonology, grammar, or lexicon perpetuated across generations. Like sand on a beach, these things may be here one day, gone the next: just ask the speakers of early Iberian Romance varieties, whose phonology departed significantly from that of spoken Latin (§3.6); the speakers of Philippine Iberian-based creoles, who generated grammatical innovations modeled on local Austronesian languages or via L2 acquisition (§4.10); the children who produced a new address norm in the immigrant neighborhoods of the Río de la Plata by repurposing old morphology with new semantic and pragmatic values (§5.5); or the users of *castellano andino*, many of whose grammatical selections are only partially intelligible to non-Andean speakers (§6.3 and §6.4). In all these cases, speakers introduced noticeable changes in the areas of language that historical linguists usually work with (phonology, morphology, syntax, lexicon) as they write genealogical narratives of continuity and descent (Ennis 2015: 139).

Instead, as I have argued throughout this book, we can locate more robust diachronic continuities by focusing on the contact *processes* whereby speakers learn, negotiate, and modify language features in communication. Sure enough, these acts of communication take place amid vastly different circumstances, contributing to the emergence of population-wide patterns at different scales (a family; a social network of friends or coworkers; a heritage community; a regional dialect; a national variety). From this perspective, an Ecuadorian immigrant family in twenty-first-century Madrid (Lara Bermejo 2018) looks very different from a convent inhabited by European and *mestizo* nuns, African slaves, and Indigenous servants in sixteenth- and seventeenth-century Mexico (Sierra Silva 2018) or a band of fourth-millennium BC horse riders on the Pontic Steppes (Anthony and Ringe 2015). And yet, all these speakers were doing the same thing, using their age-specific cognitive dispositions to process the linguistic features they had access to, and reinterpreting them in ways that were communicatively and socially effective. There are no qualitative differences in the underlying processes applied by all these speakers, only environmental differences causing some of them to make different selections from others (§2.5).

Embracing this way of looking at language change (and I hope by now readers will at least be willing to consider it!) has several important implications for how we research and tell the story of a language. Below I sketch some of the most prominent ones.

7.2. What is language change? Put yourself in the speakers' shoes!

Incorporating an ecological contact-based perspective in language change narratives means adopting a bottom-up rather than a top-down approach. Questions of language change are not just questions about the bundles of features that we call 'Spanish,' 'English,' 'Malagasy,' etc. They are also (and primarily) questions about how speakers actively contributed to dynamic patterns of variation and change. In other words, environmentally informed language histories should ultimately be as much about people as they are about language.

In some ways, this approach complicates things. It's certainly easier to pose a sequence of phonological changes to go from, say, proto-Indo-European *pénkʷe to Spanish *cinco* [ˈs/θiŋko] 'five' than it is to reconstruct the environmental factors that led speakers to make those selections over millennia (especially when, for most of these settings, the social and linguistic record is essentially non-existent; §3.2). But thinking ecologically also encourages us to reach deeper and more broadly into the data that we *do* have, capitalizing on multiple vantage points (articulatory, acquisitional, cognitive, sociolinguistic, anthropological, sociopolitical, etc.) in order to sketch a fuller picture of how and why speakers may have selected specific forms (on this point, see §7.4). After all, deep-time reconstructions also rely on our knowledge of people, as when we posit that proto-Indo-European /p/ velarized as /k/ in Latin before palatalizing as /kʲ/ in early Romance and then evolving into /ts/ and eventually /s/ or /θ/ in Spanish (§1.9), all of which are plausible steps based on our knowledge of human phonation. The richer our ecological scenario, the more complete and true-to-life accounts of change we will be able to outline.

An example of what's to be gained by adopting a speaker-focused perspective on language history narratives concerns the phonological evolution of colonial Latin American Spanish, which involved (among other changes) the merger of several sibilants to /s/ (*seseo*), as discussed in Chapter 4 (§4.4). Recall that these mergers have been traditionally interpreted as the product of the transplantation of specific varieties of Spanish to the American colonies. In this story, Spain-born speakers, most notably Andalusians, carried these patterns to the Western Hemisphere, where they eventually generalized as part of new colonial dialectal norms (Lapesa 1981; Hidalgo 2016). One major shortcoming of these accounts is that, regardless of how we define Spanish in the colonial context, most of its speakers were soon to be not Spaniards, but speakers of Indigenous, African, or multiethnic descent, many of them non-native.

For decades, research on these changes in colonial Spanish has told us about the action of Spain-born settlers, the importance of innovative or conservative norms from Spain, the structure of transplanted European society in the colonies … but where's everybody else in this picture? Elsewhere (Sanz-Sánchez 2013, 2019; Sanz-Sánchez and Tejedo Herrero 2021; Sanz-Sánchez and Moyna 2023) I have addressed the phonological history of colonial Spanish by appealing to a combination of acquisitional and sociolinguistic factors, and incorporating the action of speakers other than Spain-born L1 Spanish speakers – in other words, of the majority of the population in these colonial settlements (§4.2). To summarize this argument, speakers of non-European descent didn't just learn this new dialectal norm from the colonists: they actively participated in its creation, interpreting a diffuse input, and producing a cognitively more economical phonology. The result is a more sociolinguistically comprehensive and historically veridical account that combines the archival, sociohistorical and acquisitional information to explain these linguistic changes based on what we know about the people that carried them out. As our knowledge of early colonial Spanish continues to evolve, aspects of this account may have to be refined, and if so, good: it will mean that our knowledge of the ecology of these changes continues to improve, and so will the resulting explanations.

An important take-away from this discussion is that there is *always* room to incorporate the ecological, whether talking about present-day speakers whose behavior we can access directly or speakers in chronologically distant environments. In either situation, a reliable account of language change always has to be relatable, at some level, to the socially situated behavior of speakers in contact. In this endeavor, our knowledge of the human brain as a critical element of the speakers' cognition is our ally. From this perspective, an environmental take on language evolution is rooted in a *uniformitarian* approach to at least some aspects of language change (Walkden 2019), where local demographic, social and ideological aspects operate upon a universal mental basis (Aboh 2015; DeGraff 2009; Efrat-Kowalski 2021; Winford 2017, 2020) to result in specific patterns of feature selection.

7.3. Who can change language? Everybody!

Another implication of an ecological approach to the writing of language histories is that their scope will always be determined by how we define a *population*. In Chapter 2 (§2.4), I defined this concept as a group of communicating individuals (or, to be precise, their idiolects, housed in the cognition of speakers in contact), in full agreement with the evolution-based, environmental perspective on language change (Aboh and Vigouroux 2021; Mufwene 2001, 2008). From this perspective, it becomes hard to speak of the history of named language varieties: after all, not all Spanish speakers communicate with each other (or, historically, we can be pretty sure that present-day speakers do not communicate face-to-face with past speakers!).

But what if the members of different non-communicating populations come to share similar beliefs about the symbolic value of specific resources, as can be seen in the promotion of standard Spanish as symbolic of socioeconomic mobility and cultural capital (Valencia and Lynch 2020)? How useful is the contact-based definition of a population then? Defining a population is particularly challenging in recent communication settings, where migration, media, technology, and other processes (§6.1) force us to think beyond face-to-face spoken communication. At the same time, a population-based lens generates exciting opportunities to consider language change in various types of settings, allowing for the inclusion of experiences that may not appear to be meaningful from a 'top-down' perspective (at least not at first sight), but which were meaningful to the people who inhabited and co-constructed those spaces.

To illustrate this point, we can compare present-day sociolinguistics and language historiography. Current sociolinguists are very much interested in language variation and communication among bi/multilingual speakers, heritage speakers, rural speakers, speakers of color, minoritized speakers, or immigrants (for instance, the chapters in Díaz-Campos 2022; Lynch 2020; or Potowski 2018).

But when one considers the historiography of Spanish, this focus is still far from the norm. As I argued in the beginning of this book (§1.3), histories of Spanish are still largely histories of the standard language. And from this perspective, only some changes (and some speakers) are of interest. A metaphor that expresses this idea is the *language funnel*, where only the features that have been selected as part of the standard language filter down through the spout to become part of the historical narrative (Watts 2012), as shown in Figure 7.2.

In the historiography of Spanish, we have often ignored or not paid much attention to populations and linguistic practices that were not seen as feeding into the main trends of change in the standard language. Sure, we knew there were other speakers and other forms of Spanish – but we could afford to not spend too much time on them, since, after all, we didn't feel they left any lasting marks on the standard. Even a cursory reading of history of Spanish manuals and textbooks demonstrates that the Spanish of rural speakers, immigrants, Indigenous populations, slaves, or the working classes (in other words, most speakers) is typically not reflected or only acknowledged when including them to some extent is unavoidable (for instance, when discussing patterns of lexical borrowing from the Indigenous languages of the Americas, as in Cano 2005; Penny 2002; Pharies 2015). These acts of filtering what counts and does not count as Spanish (or, as per the discussion in Chapter 1, what deserves to be remembered; §1.3) do not fall into an ideological vacuum: elsewhere, present-day constructions on what counts as 'Spanish' often rationalize forms of exclusion in very explicit ways, sometimes invoking historical research as an argument.

For instance, current public discourse in the Spanish-speaking world often derides (or openly ridicules) language alternatives by at least some LGBTQ+

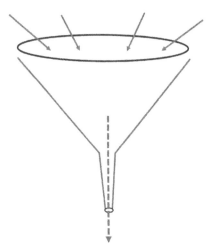

Diversity and variation in sociohistorical data

Streamlined and homogenized language histories

FIGURE 7.2. The funnel view in language histories (adapted from Watts 2012: 586)

speakers and their allies that question the traditional divide between masculine and feminine morphological markers (masculine -*o*, feminine -*a*, and masculine plural -*os* for collective reference) in reference to people. In this majority discourse, non-canonical gender marking alternatives (e.g. -*x* in written Spanish or -*e(s)* for non-binary or collective reference) (Papadopoulos 2024) are rejected because they are not used by most people (recall the explicit prohibition of some of these options by Buenos Aires educational authorities in 2022, §6.1). Similarly, institutions like the Real Academia Española invoke historical arguments to brand gender-neutral morphological markers as pragmatically unnecessary or grammatically disruptive (Real Academia Española 2020). But for some speakers, these forms do have a purpose, and that's why they use them. After all, one could just as easily interpret language standards as sets of features enforced by sociolinguistic minorities with socioeconomic capital going against what most speakers would have otherwise selected (Barrett et al. 2023). Historical linguistic narratives that center standard Spanish are thus mobilized to brand some linguistic practices and the identities they symbolize as central, and others as marginal, with or without the consent of historical linguists.

A population-based ecologically mindful historical sociolinguistic approach allows us to explicitly treat the repertoires of minoritized speakers as products of speaker agencies and as worthy objects of study rather than as mere linguistic deviations or historical footnotes. In this sense, this stance offers us a chance to democratize language history narratives, incorporating perspectives beyond those that may be felt to be relevant in traditional or predominant discourses on what language change is, how it happens and who drives it (Elspass 2007; Namboodiripad and Henner 2022).

7.4. Final words: On not throwing the baby out with the bathwater

Over the past two decades, ecologically informed scholars have joined a growing number of linguists who are dissatisfied with many of the traditional categories of linguistic description and analysis that some (although certainly not all) research on language continues to take for granted. These categories include, for instance, the notion of nativeness, bilingualism as the competence in separate linguistic systems, or language transmission in communities of monolingual speakers as the default mechanism of language change (see Hackert 2012 about the emergence of the *native speaker* idea as a sociopolitical construct in the history of English, or Otheguy et al. 2019 for a critique of the *dual correspondence theory* of bilingualism; see also §1.9 for a similar critique). This criticism is often coupled with a questioning of many of these constructs (and the methodologies that rely on them) as representative of Western assumptions on language (Canagarajah 2014, 2017; García and Wei 2014; Higby et al. 2023; Namboodiripad and Henner 2022). But, as I argued at the very beginning of this book (§1.9), approaching language environmentally and thinking beyond some of the traditional categories in diachronic linguistics does not mean that we should discard the knowledge accumulated over decades of research on language acquisition, variation, and change. We just need to rethink or recontextualize what this previous literature is telling us.

For instance, while not explicitly articulated as an ecological framework, the *verticalization* model (Brown 2022; see §5.4, §5.6 and §6.2 for earlier applications of this model in this book) proposes that language shift is not only a sociolinguistic process, with speakers giving up their language after a phase of bilingualism. Instead, language shift in this paradigm is the outcome of the interface among multiple cultural and institutional triggers, as internally oriented (horizontal) structures are substituted by externally oriented (vertical) ones (such as schools, churches, production mechanisms, marriage patterns). This substitution triggers interconnected changes at the sociolinguistic level (which languages are used when) as well as the symbolic level (what does it mean to use specific languages in specific contexts). From this perspective, language shift can be interpreted as the function of environmental changes in the embedding of language use in the heritage population.

With this model in mind, an ecological lens allows us to reinterpret not just the sociolinguistic progression of language shift, but also its linguistic correlates, i.e. which selections speakers make in the shifting environment and what comes *after* the shift. In principle, we could expect verticalization to lead to the replacement of one feature pool by another (the linguistic correlate to sociocultural change), with speakers in intermediate stages exhibiting features typical of bilingual heritage acquisition (Aalberse et al. 2019). An example discussed above (§2.4, §6.7) is heritage Spanish in the US, which exhibits patterns of morphological simplification of the verbal categories of monolingual systems, with Latinxs past the 3rd generation usually self-identifying as English-dominant or monolingual. This kind of situation is usually taken to imply that the shift away from Spanish is complete.

But as seen repeatedly in this volume, language shift hardly ever leads to the outright substitution of one feature pool by another, even in cases of extreme sociocultural and demographic pressure (e.g. Taíno/Arawak lexical items in Caribbean Spanish, §4.4). Instead, we usually see speakers in shifting populations navigate sociocultural changes by making selections that are cognitively and socially advantageous (Mufwene 2022). This process of recombination implies not just substitution, but also innovation and even retention. In the specific case of Spanish in the US, repertoires such as Chicanx English (§6.7) are a powerful reminder that there must be more to this shift story than the replacement of one language with another: critically, the emergence of these pools involved the retention and reinterpretation of elements of Spanish phonology or semantics which, although not matching external definitions of proficiency in Spanish, are still linguistically salient and symbolically meaningful.

Acknowledging the dynamics of feature selection in heritage populations does not mean we should ignore the evidence of sociocultural and sociolinguistic change in these settings (or the models that, like verticalization, have been proposed to study these changes): in the case of Chicanx communities, by any collective definition of what it means to 'speak Spanish,' shift to English is surely taking place. But treating individual speakers as agents of language change that negotiate multiple motivations in contact situations, rather than just as vehicles of broader sociolinguistic processes, can help us gain a more nuanced view of the linguistic dynamics of shift and its outcomes at both the individual and the collective level.

Another important implication of this perspective has to do with the materials that we work with to study language change. Often throughout this book, we have been faced with the difficulty in reconstructing the sociolinguistic landscapes of many historical settings. But precisely because all ecologies are complex (§7.2), historical sociolinguistic approaches to language change can benefit from data and methodological promiscuity. Lauersdorf (2018) encourages us to 'use all the data,' and offers the following recommendations:

(1) Identify all possible sources of language data – data may be 'hiding' where you don't expect it, in unexplored physical locations and in unexplored textual locations.
(2) Consult the entirety of the language data available to you – avoid selective sampling (inclusion or exclusion) of language data based on a priori notions of what kind of data you need, how much data you need, where it should come from, etc.
(3) Language data isn't the only data – use all the socio-historical data! (Lauersdorf 2018: 211–12).

There are also caveats that we should keep in mind: because data are, as Lauersdorf points out, filtered through history, the representativeness (whose linguistic practices are being reflected) and validity (how close to actual sociolinguistic patterns the evidence is) of historical records are always a concern (Schneider 2002). Whoever collected, curated, or edited the archive that we now call 'data' always did so under some assumption of what was informative, relevant, or significant, that is, some judgment on what (and who!) matters and should be remembered (§1.3 and §7.3). Even this book, which has picked several 'representative' ecologies, is an example of this selection. So it's not only that data can be used to construct a limited version of history – the data *is* a limited version of history. Therefore, as we use all the data, we should also mistrust all the data, and question the ways in which it may be creating socioculturally biased 'blind spots' in our vision of history.

For historical sociolinguists, this is a familiar feeling, captured in the by now common adage that historical sociolinguists must rely on 'bad data' (Auer et al. 2015; Labov 1994: 11). But data are only so bad as our inability to recognize their limitations. If we are realistic about what the data are telling us, we can build from that. What is missing from the record? Who is missing? What could we use to fill in the gaps? Whose perspective on what and who matters am I getting from the data? And by relying on this data, how am I contributing to perpetuate or disrupt assumptions about linguistic and cultural normalcy? These questions are admittedly not just historical sociolinguistic questions: they are also sociopolitical questions about how and why we do research on language, and not everybody may recognize the same need to engage with them as they research language history. At minimum, however, an ecological approach should encourage us to get as many perspectives on sociolinguistic phenomena as possible and should remind us that the stories we tell could always be told from a different perspective.

I hope this book will inspire readers to not only think about the history of Spanish, and possibly other languages, as a constellation of contact events, but (most importantly) about the people who shaped these events as linguistic and sociopolitical agents, both in the past and today. Doing so will yield a more comprehensive, socially inclusive and, ultimately, more accurate picture of human history, and of language change as a key part of it.

Discussion questions

1. Few current language features in Spanish elicit so many reactions from speakers as non-binary language (*lenguaje inclusivo, lenguaje no binario*; see Papadopoulos 2024; §6.1, §7.3). Do an internet search to locate some of these reactions. What do they reveal about the ideas on language use upheld by different groups of speakers, and about the kinds of environmental triggers that may favor or disfavor linguistic innovations in twenty-first-century language ecologies?

2. Throughout this book, we have seen many linguistic actors (authors, academic institutions, governments) expressing forms of *anxiety* about the purported effects of language change on the very integrity of Spanish as a language. And yet, centuries after Nebrija, hundreds of millions continue to self-identify as Spanish speakers. To which extent are these language ideologies effective in upholding linguistic boundaries? Do we still speak Spanish because we have been taught to be its stewards, or are these ideas on what counts as Spanish pliable throughout history?

3. What areas (time periods, geographical or social settings, speakers) has this book left uncovered? Which should be treated in future ecological explorations of language change in Spanish? And what kinds of assumptions about language use, language change and speakers has this book left unquestioned?

References

Aalberse, Suzanne (2024), 'Multilingual acquisition across the lifespan as a sociohistorical trigger for language change', in *Lifespan Acquisition and Language Change: Historical Sociolinguistic Perspectives*, ed. Israel Sanz-Sánchez, Amsterdam: John Benjamins, pp. 104–6.

Aalberse, Suzanne, Ad Backus and Pieter Muysken (2019), *Heritage Languages: A Language Contact Approach*, Amsterdam: John Benjamins.

Abadía de Quant, Inés (1996), 'Sistemas lingüísticos en contacto y sus consecuencias en el área palatal del español de dos capitales del Nordeste argentino: Corrientes y Resistencia', *International Journal of the Sociology of Language* 117, 11–25.

Aboh, Enoch (2015), *The Emergence of Hybrid Grammars: Language Contact and Change*, Cambridge: Cambridge University Press.

Aboh, Enoch and Cécile Vigouroux, eds. (2021), *Variation Rolls the Dice: A Worldwide Collage in Honour of Salikoko S. Mufwene*, Amsterdam: John Benjamins.

Adamou, Evangelia (2013), 'Change and variation in a trilingual setting: Evidentiality in Pomak (Slavic, Greece)', in *The Interplay of Variation and Change in Contact Settings*, eds. Isabelle Léglise and Claudine Chamoreau, Amsterdam: John Benjamins, pp. 229–52.

Adamou, Evangelia (2021), *The Adaptive Bilingual Mind: Insights from Endangered Languages*. Cambridge: Cambridge University Press.

Adams, James (2003), *Bilingualism and the Latin Language*, Cambridge: Cambridge University Press.

Adams, James (2007), *The Regional Diversification of Latin: 200BC–AD600*, Cambridge: Cambridge University Press.

Adams, James (2013), *Social Variation and the Latin Language*, Cambridge: Cambridge University Press.

Aikhenvald, Alexandra (2012), *Languages of the Amazon*, Oxford: Oxford University Press.

Alatorre, Antonio (1979), *Los 1001 años de la lengua española*, México City: Fondo de Cultura Económica.

Alba Niño, María (2015), 'Switching, mixing and choosing languages online: The case of Asturian and Castilian (Spanish)', in *Medien für Minderheitensprachen:*

Mediensprachliche Überlegungen zur Eintwicklung von Minderheitensprachen, eds. María Alba Niño and Rolf Kailuweit, Freiburg: Rombach, pp. 211–51.

Albertí, Alfonsina (2015), 'Migraciones temporarias, ciclos laborales y estrategias de reproducción social: El caso de las unidades domésticas del área rural de Bernardo de Irigoyen (Misiones, Argentina)', *Mundo Agrario* 16 (33), http://www.mundoagrario.unlp.edu.ar/article/view/MAv16n33a04 (last accessed 15 July 2023).

Aldrete, Bernardo de (1674 [1606]), *Del origen y principio de la lengua castellana o romance que oi se usa en España*, Madrid: Melchor Sánchez.

Almandoz, Arturo (2008), 'Despegues sin madurez. Urbanización, industrialización y desarrollo en la Latinoamérica del siglo XX', *Eure* 34(102), 61–76.

Anthony, David and Don Ringe (2015), 'The Indo-European homeland from linguistic and archaeological perspectives', *Annual Review of Linguistics* 1, 199–219.

Arnal i Bella, Antoni (2007), 'La convergència sintàctica', in *Entorn i vigència de l'obra de Fabra*, eds. Anna Montserrat and Olga Cubells, Valls: Cossetània, pp. 15–25.

Artamonova, Tatiana, Maria Hasler-Barker and Edna Velásquez (2022), 'Heritage language learners' experiences with TExES LOTE – Spanish: Is there bias?', *Journal of Latinos and Education*, doi: 10.1080/15348431.2022.2144862.

Ascoli, Graziadio (1881), *Una lettera glottologica*, Torino: Ermanno Loescher.

Auer, Anita, Catharina Peersman, Simon Pickl, Gijsbert Rutten and Rik Vosters (2015), 'Historical sociolinguistics: The field and its future', *Journal of Historical Sociolinguistics* 1(1), 1–12.

Auer, Peter (2015), 'Reflections on Hermann Paul as a usage-based grammarian', in *Hermann Paul's 'Principles of Language History' Revisited: Translations and Reflections*, eds. Peter Auer and Robert Murray, Berlin: De Gruyter, pp. 177–208.

Auer, Peter and Frans Hinskens (2005), 'The role of interpersonal accommodation in a theory of language change', in *Dialect Change: Convergence and Divergence in European Languages*, eds. Frans Hinskens, Peter Auer and Paul Kerswill, Cambridge: Cambridge University Press, pp. 335–57.

Avilés, Tania (2016), *Letras del desierto: Edición de un corpus epistolar para su estudio lingüístico, Región de Tarapacá, Chile, 1883–1937*, Santiago: Cuarto Propio.

Babel, Anna (2014), 'Time and reminiscence in contact: Dynamism and stasis in contact-induced change', *Spanish in Context* 11(3), 311–34.

Babel, Anna, and Stefan Pfänder (2014), 'Doing copying: Why typology doesn't matter to language speakers', in *Congruence in Contact-induced Language Change: Language Families, Typological Resemblance, and Perceived Similarity*, eds. Juliane Besters-Dilger, Cynthia Dermarkar, Stefan Pfänder, and Achim Rabus, Berlin: De Gruyter, pp. 239–57.

Backus, Ad (2021), 'Usage-based approaches', in *The Routledge Handbook of Language Contact*, eds. Evangelia Adamou and Yaron Matras, London: Routledge, pp. 110–26.

Bakhtin, Mikhail (1981), *The Dialogic Imagination: Four Essays*, ed. Michael Holquist, Austin: University of Texas Press.

References

Bakker, Peter and Yaron Matras (2013), 'Introduction', in *Contact Languages: A Comprehensive Guide*, eds. Peter Bakker and Yaron Matras, Berlin: De Gruyter Mouton, pp. 1–14.

Balam, Osmer, Ana de Prada Pérez and Dámaris Mayans (2014), 'A congruence approach to the study of bilingual compound verbs in Northern Belize contact Spanish', *Spanish in Context* 11(2), 243–65.

Balam, Osmer and Jacob Shelton (2023), 'The use of Spanglish in Latin rap music: An analysis of inter- and intraclausal code-switching', *Bilingual Review/Revista Bilingüe* 35(1), 32–52.

Balmaseda Maestu, Enrique (2004), 'El español americano de *El Güegüence o Macho-Ratón*', in *Memoria de la palabra: Actas del VI Congreso de la Asociación Internacional Siglo de Oro*, eds. María Luisa Lobato and Francisco Domínguez Matito, Madrid: Iberoamericana/Vervuert, pp. 295–305.

Banfi, Cristina (2018), 'Heritage languages in Argentina', in *Heritage Language Policies around the World*, eds. Corinne Seals and Sheena Shah, London: Routledge, pp. 48–66.

Barajas, Jennifer (2022), 'Vocalic variation: A sociolinguistic analysis of atonic vowel raising in rural Michoacán, México', in *The Routledge Handbook of Variationist Approaches to Spanish*, ed. Manuel Díaz-Campos, London: Routledge, pp. 9–22.

Barrett, Graham (2024), 'Conservatism in language: Framing Latin in late antique and early medieval Iberia', in *Languages and Communities in the Late-Roman and Post-Imperial Western Provinces*, eds. George Woudhuysen and Alex Mullen, Oxford: Oxford University Press, pp. 85–126.

Barrett, Rusty, Jennifer Crammer, and Kevin McGowan (2023), *English with an Accent: Language, Ideology and Discrimination in the United States*, London: Routledge.

Barrios, Graciela (2013), 'Language diversity and national unity in the history of Uruguay', in *A Political History of Spanish: The Making of a Language*, ed. José del Valle, Cambridge: Cambridge University Press, pp. 197–211.

Bauer, Brigitte (2009), 'Word order', in *Syntax of the Sentence*, vol.1., eds. Philip Baldi and Pierluigi Cuzzolin, Berlin: De Gruyter Mouton, pp. 241–316.

Baxter, Gareth and William Croft (2016), 'Modeling language change across the lifespan: Individual trajectories in community change', *Language Variation and Change* 28, 129–73.

Beale-Rivaya, Yasmine (2011), 'Maintaining a language of culture: Outcomes of medieval Iberian shift as a predictor for Spanish in the American Southwest', *American Speech* 86(4), 415–40.

Beltrán Llorís, Francisco (2005), 'El latín en la Hispania romana: Una perspectiva histórica', in *Historia de la lengua española*, ed. Rafael Cano, Barcelona: Ariel, pp. 83–106.

Bentz, Christian and Morten Christiansen (2015), 'Linguistic adaptation: The trade-off between case marking and fixed word orders in Germanic and Romance languages', in *Eastward Flows the Great River: Festschrift in Honor of Professor William Wang on his 80th birthday*, eds. Peng Gang and Shi Fen, Hong Kong: City University of Hong Kong Press, pp. 45–61.

Bertolotti, Virginia (2016), 'Voseo and tuteo, the countryside and the city: Voseo in Río de la Plata Spanish at the beginning of the 19th century', in *Forms of Address in the Spanish of the Americas*, eds. María Irene Moyna and Susana Rivera-Mills, pp. 15–33.
Biblioteca Digital Hispánica (2023a), Antonio de Nebrija, *Gramática castellana*, https://bdh-rd.bne.es/viewer.vm?id=0000174208&page=1 (last accessed 15 July 2023).
Biblioteca Digital Hispánica (2023b), Juan de Valdés, *Diálogo de la lengua*, https://bdh-rd.bne.es/viewer.vm?id=0000048928 (last accessed 15 July 2023).
Bickerton, Derek (1981), *Roots of Language*, Ann Arbor, MI: Karoma Publishers.
Blas Arroyo, José Luis (2011), 'Spanish in contact with Catalan', in *The Handbook of Hispanic Sociolinguistics*, ed. Manuel Díaz-Campos, Malden MA: Wiley, pp. 374–94.
Blommaert, Jan (2010), *The Sociolinguistics of Globalization*, Cambridge: Cambridge University Press.
Blythe, Richard and William Croft (2021), 'How individuals change language', *PLoS ONE* 16(6), e0252582.
Bodleian Library (2023), Codex Mendoza, MS. Arch. Selden. A. 1, https://digital.bodleian.ox.ac.uk/objects/2fea788e-2aa2-4f08-b6d9-648c00486220/ (last accessed 15 July 2023).
Borucki, Alex, David Eltis and David Wheat (2015), 'Atlantic history and the slave trade to Spanish America', *American Historical Review* 120(2), 433–61.
Boyd-Bowman, Peter (1976), 'Patterns of Spanish Emigration to the Indies until 1600', *The Hispanic American Historical Review* 56(4), 580–604.
Boyd-Bowman, Peter (1988), 'Brotes de fonetismo andaluz en México hacia fines del siglo XVI', *Nueva Revista de Filología Hispánica* 36(1), 75–88.
Brain, Cecilia (2010), 'Aprendizaje de lenguas indígenas por parte de españoles en Nueva España en los primeros cien años después de la conquista', *Colonial Latin American Review* 19(2), 279–300.
Bright, William (2000), 'Hispanisms in Southwest Indian languages', *Romance Philology* 53(2), 259–88.
Britain, David (2016), 'Dialect contact and new dialect formation', in *The Handbook of Dialectology*, eds. Dominic Watt, John Nerbonne and Charles Boberg, Oxford: Wiley, pp. 143–58.
Brody, Jill (2018), 'A comparison across three generations of Tojol-ab'al (Mayan) speakers', *Language Variation and Contact-Induced Change: Spanish Across Space and Time*, eds. Jeremy King and Sandro Sessarego, Amsterdam: John Benjamins, pp. 111–25.
Brown, Josh, ed. (2022), *The Verticalization Model of Language Shift: The Great Change in American Communities*, Oxford: Oxford University Press.
Bryden, John, Shaun Wright, Vincent Jansen (2018), 'How humans transmit language: horizontal transmission matches word frequencies among peers on Twitter', *Journal of the Royal Society Interface* 15: 20170738.
Budiman, Abbi (2020), 'Key findings about U.S. immigrants', Washington, DC: Pew Research Center, https://www.pewresearch.org/?p=290738 (last accessed 15 July 2022).

Bullock, Barbara and Jacqueline Toribio (2008), 'Kreyol incursions into Dominican Spanish: The perception of Haitianized speech among Dominicans', in *Bilingualism and Identity: Spanish at the Crossroads with Other Languages*, eds. Mercedes Niño-Murcia and Jason Rothman, Amsterdam: John Benjamins, pp. 175–98.

Bureau of Transportation (2023), Border Crossing Entry Data, https://data.bts.gov/Research-and-Statistics/Border-Crossing-Entry-Data/keg4-3bc2/data (last accessed 15 July 2023).

Bürki, Yvette (2016), 'Haketia in Morocco. Or, the story of the decline of an idiom', *International Journal of the Sociology of Language* 239, 121–55.

Bybee, Joan (2010), *Language, Usage and Cognition*. Cambridge: Cambridge University Press.

Campbell, Lyle (2004), *Historical Linguistics: An Introduction*, Cambridge, MA: MIT University Press.

Camus Bergareche, Bruno (2015), 'El castellano del País Vasco en el siglo XIX: Las cartas del Archivo Zavala', in *Actas del IX Congreso Internacional de la Historia de la Lengua Española*, Madrid: Iberoamericana/Vervuert, pp. 1775–89.

Camus Bergareche, Bruno and Gómez Seibane (2010), 'Basque and Spanish in 19th century San Sebastián', *Ianua. Revista Philologica Romanica* 10, 223–39.

Canagarajah, Suresh (2014), *Translingual Practice: Global Englishes and Cosmopolitan Relations*, London: Routledge.

Canagarajah, Suresh (2017), 'Introduction: The nexus of migration and language', in *The Routledge Handbook of Migration and Language*, ed. Suresh Canagarajah, London: Routledge, pp. 1–28.

Candela Romero, Pilar (2007), 'El español en los campamentos de refugiados saharauis (Tinduf, Argelia)' in *Enciclopedia del español en el mundo: Anuario del Instituto Cervantes 2006–2007*, Madrid: Instituto Cervantes, pp. 48–52.

Cano, Rafael, ed. (2005), *Historia de la lengua española*, Barcelona: Ariel.

Canuto Castillo, Felipe (2015), 'Otomíes en la ciudad de México: La pérdida de un idioma en tres generaciones', *Lengua y migración* 7(1), 53–81.

Caravedo, Rocío (1992), '¿Restos de la distinción /s/ y /θ/ en el español del Perú?', *Revista de Filología Española* 72(3), 639–54.

Caravedo, Rocío and Carol Klee (2012), 'Migración y contacto en Lima: El pretérito perfecto en las cláusulas narrativas', *Lengua y migración* 4(2), 5–24.

Carter, Phillip and Kristen D'Alessandro Merii (2023), 'Spanish-influenced lexical phenomena in emerging Miami English', *English World-Wide* 44(2), 219–50.

Carvalho, Ana Maria (2014), 'Linguistic continuity along the Uruguayan-Brazilian border: Monolingual perceptions of a bilingual reality', in *Spanish and Portuguese across Time, Place, and Borders*, ed. Laura Callahan, London: Palgrave Macmillan, pp. 183–99.

Castillo Martos, Manuel (2001), 'Mano de obra española en la industria argentina', *Llull* 24(1), 33–58.

Ceballos Domínguez, Rubí (2006), 'La (s) implosiva: hacia un mayor consonantismo en la zona conurbada Veracruz – Boca del Río', in *Líderes lingüísticos. Estudios de variación y cambio*, ed. Pedro Martín Butragueño, Mexico City: El Colegio de México, pp. 13–36.

Cerrón Palomino, Rodolfo (2003), *Castellano andino: Aspectos sociológicos, pedagógicos y gramaticales*, Lima: Pontificia Universidad Católica.

Cerrón Palomino, Rodolfo (2010), 'El contacto inicial quechua-castellano: la conquista del Perú con dos palabras', *Lexis* 34(2), 369–81.

Chambers, Jack K. (2004), 'Dynamic typology and vernacular universals', in *Dialectology Meets Typology: Dialect Grammar from a Cross-Linguistic Perspective*, ed. Bernd Kortmann, Berlin: De Gruyter Mouton, pp. 127–45.

Chambers, Jack K. and Peter Trudgill (1998), *Dialectology*, Cambridge: Cambridge University Press.

Chang, Will, David Hall, Chundra Cathcart and Andrew Garrett (2015), 'Ancestry constrained phylogenetic analysis supports the Indo-European steppe hypothesis', *Language* 91(1), 194–244.

Chappell, Whitney and Bridget Drinka, eds. (2021), *Spanish Socio-Historical Linguistics: Isolation and Contact*, Amsterdam: John Benjamins.

Chomsky, Noam (1986), *Knowledge of Language: Its Nature, Origin, and Use*, New York: Praeger.

Cifuentes, Bárbara (1998), *Letras sobre voces: Multilingüismo a través de la historia*, Mexico City: Comisión Nacional de la Cultura y las Artes.

Clackson, James (2016), 'Latin as a source for the Romance languages', in *The Oxford Guide to the Romance Languages*, eds. Adam Ledgeway and Martin Maiden, Oxford: Oxford University Press, pp. 3–13.

Clackson, James and Geoffrey Horrock (2007), *The Blackwell History of the Latin Language*, Malden, MA: Wiley-Blackwell.

Clements, Joseph Clancy (2009), *The Linguistic Legacy of Spanish and Portuguese: Colonial Expansion and Language Change*, Cambridge: Cambridge University Press.

Clements, Joseph Clancy (2016), 'Chinese-Spanish Contact in Cuba in the 19th Century', in *Multilingualism in the Chinese Diaspora Worldwide*, ed. Li Wei, London: Routledge: 87–107.

Clements, Joseph Clancy (2018), 'Speech communities, language varieties, and typology', *Journal of Pidgin and Creole Languages* 33(1), 174–92.

Clements, Joseph Clancy, Patrícia Amaral, and Ana Luís (2011), 'Spanish in Contact with Portuguese: The Case of Barranquenho', in *The Handbook of Hispanic Sociolinguistics*, ed. Manuel Díaz Campos, Oxford: Blackwell, pp. 395–417.

Cobo, Leila (2022), '5 ways "Despacito" changed Latin music forever', *Billboard* 1 June 2022 https://www.billboard.com/music/latin/despacito-changed-latin-music-1235079900/ (last accessed 15 July 2023).

Colantoni, Laura and Jorge Gurlekian (2004), 'Convergence and intonation: Historical evidence from Buenos Aires Spanish', *Bilingualism: Language and Cognition* 7(2), 107–19.

Coler, Matt and Edwin Benegas Flores (2013), 'A descriptive analysis of Castellano loanwords in Muylaq' Aymara', *Liames* 13(1), 101–13.

References

Company Company, Concepción (2007), *El siglo XVIII y la identidad lingüística de México*, Mexico City: Universidad Nacional Autónoma de México.

Company Company, Concepción (2024), 'El español en América (II): de la colonia a las independencias (ca. 1680–1830)', in *Lingüística histórica del español: The Routledge Handbook of Spanish Historical Linguistics*, eds. Steven Dworkin, Gloria Clavería Nadal and Álvaro Octavio de Toledo y Huerta, London: Routledge, pp. 522–31.

Conde, Óscar (2011), *Diccionario etimológico del lunfardo*, Buenos Aires: Penguin Random House Argentina.

Contreras Carranza, Carlos (2020), 'La crisis demográfica del siglo XVI en los Andes: Una discusión acerca de sus dimensiones y consecuencias', *Diálogo Andino* 61(1), 7–25.

Córdova Aguilar, Hildegardo (1989), 'La Ciudad de Lima: Su evolución y desarrollo metropolitano', *Revista Geográfica* 110(1), 231–65.

Cravino, Ana (2016), 'Historia de la vivienda social. Primera Parte: Del conventillo a las casas baratas', *Vivienda y Ciudad* 3(1), 7–24.

Croft, William (2000), *Explaining Language Change: An Evolutionary Approach*, London: Longman.

Croft, William (2008), 'Evolutionary linguistics', *Annual Review of Anthropology* 37(1), 219–34.

Croft, William (2021), 'A sociolinguistic typology for languages in contact', in *Variation Rolls the Dice: A Worldwide Collage in Honour of Salikoko S. Mufwene*, eds. Enoch Aboh and Cécile Vigouroux, Amsterdam: John Benjamins, pp. 23–56.

Cuervo, Rufino José (2004), *El castellano en América: Polémica con Juan Valera*, ed. Mario Germán Romero, Bogotá: Instituto Caro y Cuervo.

DANE (2023), Censo nacional de población y vivienda, https://www.dane.gov.co/index.php/estadisticas-por-tema/demografia-y-poblacion/censo-nacional-de-poblacion-y-vivenda-2018/cuantos-somos (last accessed 15 July 2023).

De Bot, Kees and Lars Bülow (2021), 'Cognitive factors of language contact', in *The Routledge Handbook of Language Contact*, eds. Evangelia Adamou and Yaron Matras, London: Routledge, pp. 168–84.

De Miguel, Amando (1982), 'La población en Madrid en los primeros años del siglo', *Revista Española de Investigaciones Sociológicas* 19(1), 55–71.

DeGraff, Michel (2009), 'Language acquisition in creolization and, thus, language change: Some cartesian-uniformitarian boundary conditions', *Language and Linguistics Compass* 3/4, 888–971.

Del Valle, José (2002), 'Historical linguistics and cultural history: The polemic between Rufino José Cuervo and Juan Valera', in *The Battle over Spanish between 1800 and 2000: Language Ideologies and Hispanic Intellectuals*, ed. Luis Gabriel-Stheeman and José del Valle, London: Routledge, pp. 64–77.

Del Valle, José (2013a), 'Language, politics, and history: An introductory essay', in *A Political History of Spanish: The Making of a Language*, ed. José del Valle, Cambridge: Cambridge University Press, pp. 3–20.

Del Valle, José (2013b), 'Linguistic emancipation and the academies of the Spanish language in the twentieth century: The 1951 turning point', in *A*

Political History of Spanish: The Making of a Language, ed. José del Valle, Cambridge: Cambridge University Press, pp. 229–45.
Del Valle, José (2014), 'Lo político del lenguaje y los límites de la política lingüística panhispánica', *Boletín de Filología* 49(2), 87–112.
Del Valle, José (2016), 'La lengua como lugar de memoria (y olvido). Reflexión glotopolítica sobre el español y su historia', *Estudios de Lingüística del Español* 37(1), pp. 17–26.
Díaz Ariño, Borja, María José Estarán and Ignacio Simón (2019), 'Writing, colonization, and Latinization in the Iberian Peninsula', in *Palaeohispanic Languages and Epigraphies*, eds. Alejandro Sinner and Javier Velaza, Oxford: Oxford University Press, pp. 396–416.
Díaz-Campos, Manuel, ed. (2022), *The Routledge Handbook of Variationist Approaches to Spanish*, London: Routledge.
Díaz-Dávalos, Gabriela (2018), Creating and re-creating political discourse through government texts in an urban Mexican community: A case study of Ciudad Satélite, PhD dissertation. Temple University.
Diessel, Holger (2007), 'Frequency effects in language acquisition, language use, and diachronic change', *New Ideas in Psychology* 25(2), 108–27.
Dirección General de Estadística (1950), *Séptimo censo general de población*. Mexico City: Secretaría de Economía.
Dörnyei, Zoltán, Peter MacIntyre and Alastair Henry, eds. (2015), *Motivational Dynamics in Language Learning*. Bristol: Multilingual Matters.
Drinka, Bridget (2013), 'Phylogenetic and areal models of Indo-European relatedness: The role of contact in reconstruction', *Journal of Language Contact* 6(2), 379–410.
Drinka, Bridget (2020), 'Contact and early Indo-European in Europe', in *The Handbook of Language Contact*, ed. Raymond Hickey, Malden, MA: Wiley, pp. 304–21.
Drinka, Bridget (2022), 'Populations in contact: Linguistic, archaeological, and genomic evidence for Indo-European diffusion', in *The Cambridge Handbook of Language Contact*, vol. 1, eds. Salikoko Mufwene and Anna María Escobar, Cambridge: Cambridge University Press, pp. 122–51.
Dworkin, Steven (2012), *A History of the Spanish Lexicon. A Linguistic Perspective*, Oxford: Oxford University Press.
Dworkin, Steven, Gloria Clavería Nadal and Álvaro Octavio de Toledo y Huerta, eds. (2024), *Lingüística histórica del español: The Routledge Handbook of Spanish Historical Linguistics*, London: Routledge.
Echenique Elizondo, María Teresa (1997), 'Castellano y lengua vasca en contacto: ¿Hubo una lengua criolla a fines del siglo XIX en Bilbao?', *Analecta Malacitana* 20(1), 59–71.
Echenique Elizondo, María Teresa (2003), 'Substrato, adstrato y superestrato y sus efectos en las lenguas románicas: Iberorromania', in *Romanische Sprachgeschichte*, eds. Gerhard Ernst, Martin-Dietrich Gleßgen, Christian Schmitt und Wolfgang Schweickard, Berlin: De Gruyter Mouton, pp. 607–421.
Eckert, Penelope (2000), *Language Variation as Social Practice: The Linguistic Construction of Identity in Belten High*, Malden, MA: Wiley.

Eckert, Penelope (2019), 'The individual in the semiotic landscape', *Glossa: A Journal of General Linguistics* 4(1), doi: 10.5334/gjgl.640.
Eckkrammer, Eva Martha, ed. (2021), *Manual del español en América*, Berlin: De Gruyter.
Efrat-Kowalski, Nour (2021), 'Learnability and ecological factors as motivators of language change', in *Variation Rolls the Dice: A Worldwide Collage in Honour of Salikoko S. Mufwene*, eds. Enoch Aboh and Cécile Vigouroux, Amsterdam: John Benjamins, pp. 289–305.
Einhorn, Catrin and Manuela Andreoni (2023), 'Ecuador trató de frenar la extracción de petróleo y proteger la Amazonía, pero sucedió lo contrario', *New York Times*, 15 January 2023, https://www.nytimes.com/es/2023/01/15/espanol/ecuador-petroleo-amazonia.html (last accessed 15 July 2023).
Ellis, Nick (2005), 'At the interface: Dynamic interactions of explicit and implicit language knowledge', *Studies in Second Language Acquisition* 27(2), 305–52.
Ellis, Nick and Diane Larsen-Freeman, eds. (2009), *Language as a Complex Adaptive System*. Special issue of *Language Learning* 59.
Elspass, Stephan (2007), 'A twofold view "from below": New perspectives on language histories and language historiographies', in *Germanic Language Histories 'From Below' (1700–2000)*, eds. Stephan Elspass, Nils Langer, Joachim Scharloth and Wim Vandenbussche, Berlin: De Gruyter, pp. 3–9.
Ennis, Juan Antonio (2015), 'Italian-Spanish contact in early 20th century Argentina', *Journal of Language Contact* 8, 112–45.
Enrique Arias, Andrés (2012), 'Retos del estudio sociohistórico del contacto de lenguas a través de un corpus documental. El caso del castellano en contacto con el catalán en Mallorca', *Revista de Investigación Lingüística* 15, 23–46.
Eriksen, Thomas (2007), *Globalization: The Key Concepts*, Oxford: Berg.
Erker, Daniel (2017), 'The limits of named language varieties and the role of social salience in dialectal contact: The case of Spanish in the United States', *Language and Linguistics Compass* 11, doi: 10.1111/lnc3.12232.
Escandón, Patricia (2014), '"Esta tierra es la mejor que calienta el sol": La emigración española a América, siglos XVI–XVII', in *Historia comparada de las migraciones en las Américas*, ed. Patricia Galeana, Mexico City: Universidad Nacional Autónoma de México, pp. 19–31.
Escobar, Anna María (2001), 'Contact features in Colonial Peruvian Spanish', *International Journal of the Sociology of Language* 149, 79–93.
Escobar, Anna María (2011), 'Spanish in contact with Quechua', in *The Handbook of Hispanic Sociolinguistics*, ed. Manuel Díaz Campos, Oxford: Blackwell, pp. 321–52.
Escobar, Anna María and Kim Potowski (2015), *El español de los Estados Unidos*, Cambridge: Cambridge University Press.
Espinosa, Aurelio Macedonio (1914), 'Studies in New Mexican Spanish. Part III: The English Elements', *Révue de Dialectologie Romane* 6, 24–117.
Estigarribia, Bruno (2015), 'Guaraní-Spanish Jopara mixing in a Paraguayan novel', *Journal of Language Contact* 8(2), 183–222.
Farr, Marcia (2006), *Rancheros en Chicagoacán: Language and Identity in a Transnational Community*. Austin: University of Texas Press.

Fernández-Mallat, Víctor (2018), 'Mantenimiento y desplazamiento de rasgos lingüísticos no indexados socialmente: Migrantes de los Andes bolivianos en el norte chileno', *Lengua y migración* 10(1), 33–56.

Fernández Ordóñez, Inés (2012a), 'Dialect areas and linguistic change. Pronominal paradigms in Ibero-Romance dialects from a cross-linguistic and social typology', in *The Dialect Laboratory: Dialects as a Testing Ground for Theories of Language Change*, eds. Gunther De Vogelaer and Guido Seiler, Amsterdam: John Benjamins, pp. 73–106.

Fernández Ordóñez, Inés (2012b), 'La gestación compleja del español', Presentation at the Universidad Autónoma de Madrid, 3 September 2012. https://www.uam.es/FyL/documento/1446774243378/2012_LA%20gestaci%C3%B3n%20compleja.pdf (last accessed 15 July 2023).

Fernández Ordóñez, Inés (2015), 'Dialectos del español peninsular', in *Enciclopedia de Lingüística Hispánica*, ed. Javier Gutiérrez Rexach, London: Routledge, 387–404.

Fernández Rodríguez, Mauro (2011), 'Chabacano en Tayabas: Implicaciones para la historia de los criollos hispano-filipinos', *Revista Internacional de Lingüística Iberoamericana* 9(1), 189–218.

Figueroa Arencibia, Jesús (2008), 'Aproximación al estudio del español chino hablado en Cuba', *Revista Internacional de Lingüística Iberoamericana* 6(11), 185–204.

Fill, Alwin and Hermine Penz (2018), *The Routledge Handbook of Ecolinguistics*, London: Routledge.

Flores Farfán, José Antonio (2008), 'The Hispanicization of modern Nahuatl varieties', in *Hispanisation: The impact of Spanish on the Lexicon and Grammar of the Indigenous Languages of Austronesia and the Americas*, eds. Thomas Stolz, Dik Bakker, Rosa Salas Palomo, Berlin: De Gruyter, pp. 27–48.

Fontanella de Weinberg, María Beatriz (1978), 'Algunos aspectos de la asimilación lingüística de la población inmigratoria en Argentina', *International Journal of the Sociology of Language* 18(1), 5–36.

Fontanella de Weinberg, María Beatriz (1987), *El español bonaerense: cuatro siglos de evolución lingüística (1580–1980)*, Buenos Aires: Hachette.

Fontanella de Weinberg, María Beatriz (1989), 'Los usos de segunda persona singular en el período colonial', *Anuario de Lingüística Hispánica* 5(1), 109–24.

Fontanella de Weinberg, María Beatriz (1992), 'Nuevas perspectivas en el estudio de la conformación del español americano', *Hispanic Linguistics* 4(2), 275–99.

Font-Santiago, Cristopher, Mirva Johnson, Joseph Salmons (2022), 'Reallocation: How new forms arise from contact', *Language and Linguistics Compass*, doi: https://doi.org/10.1111/lnc3.12470.

Fought, Carmen (2003), *Chicano English in Context*, New York: Palgrave MacMillan.

Frago Gracia, Juan Antonio (1997), 'Japonesismos entre Acapulco y Sevilla: sobre biombo, catana y maque', *Boletín de Filología* 36(1), 101–18.

Frago Gracia, Juan Antonio (2014), 'Estampas sociolingüísticas del español de México en la Independencia, I: el indio bilingüe, el marginal, la mujer', *Boletín de Filología* 49(1), 37–57.

Franco Figueroa, Mariano (2010), *El español de Filipinas: Documentos coloniales*, Cádiz: Universidad de Cádiz.
Fullana, Olga (2017), 'Fe de lengua: El català dels notaris catalans als inicis de l'època contemporània', *Ianua. Revista Philologica Romanica* 17, 49–60.
Fuller, Janet and Jennifer Leeman (2020), *Speaking Spanish in the US: The Sociopolitics of Language*, Bristol: Multilingual Matters.
Gal, Susan and Judith Irvine (1995), 'The boundaries of languages and disciplines: How ideologies construct difference', *Social Research* 62(4), 967–1001.
Galmés de Fuentes, Álvaro (1994), *Las jarchas mozárabes: Forma y significado*, Barcelona: Crítica.
Gancedo Negrete, María Soledad and Carmen Isasi Martínez (2015), 'Manifestaciones del contacto de lenguas en unas cartas guipuzcoanas del siglo XIX', in *Actas del IX Congreso Internacional de la Historia de la Lengua Española*, Madrid: Iberoamericana/Vervuert, 1813–30.
García de Diego, Vicente (1961), *Gramática histórica española*, Madrid: Gredos.
García, Ofelia and Li Wei (2014), *Translanguaging: Language, Bilingualism, and Education*, London: Palgrave MacMillan.
Garrett, Andrew (2006), 'Convergence in the formation of Indo-European subgroups: Phylogeny and chronology', in *Phylogenetic Methods and the Prehistory of Languages*, eds. Peter Forster and Colin Renfrew, Cambridge: McDonald Institute for Archaeological Research, pp. 139–51.
Garrido Palacios, Manolo (2005), 'Historia de la educación en España (1857–1975): Una visión hasta lo local', *Contraluz* 2, 84–146.
Giménez-Eguíbar, Patricia (2024), 'La contribución del árabe al hispanorromance', in *Lingüística histórica del español: The Routledge Handbook of Spanish Historical Linguistics*, eds. Steven Dworkin, Gloria Clavería Nadal and Álvaro Octavio de Toledo y Huerta, London: Routledge, pp. 362–71.
Golluscio, Lucía (2009), 'Loanwords in Mapudungun, a language of Chile and Argentina', in *Loanwords in the World's Languages: A Comparative Handbook*, eds. Martin Haspelmath and Uri Tadmor, Berlin: De Gruyter, pp. 1036–71.
Gomashie, Grace (2019), 'Language vitality of Spanish in Equatorial Guinea: Language use and attitudes', *Humanities* 8(1), 33, doi: 10.3390/h8010033.
Gonzalbo Aizpuru, Pilar (2001), *Educación y colonización en la Nueva España 1521–1821*, Mexico City: Universidad Pedagógica Nacional.
González Ollé, Fernando (1996), 'La precaria instalación del español en la América virreinal', *Anuario de lingüística hispánica* 12/13, 327–60.
Gooskens, Charlotte and Vincent Van Heuven (2020), 'How well can intelligibility of closely related languages in Europe be predicted by linguistic and non-linguistic variables?', *Linguistic Approaches to Bilingualism* 10(3), 351–79.
Granados Romero, Isabel (2018), 'Formas de tratamiento en una comunidad rural: Rute (Córdoba)', *Alfinge* 30, 73–106.
Granda, Germán de (1994), *Español de América, español de África y hablas criollas hispánicas: cambios, contactos y contextos*, Madrid: Gredos.
Grant, Anthony (2021), 'Contact-induced linguistic change: An introduction', in *The Oxford Handbook of Language Contact*, Oxford: Oxford University Press, pp. 1–48.

Gugenberger, Eva and Clare Mar-Molinero, eds. (2018), *El impacto lingüístico de la migración transnacional y la migración de retorno en, desde y hacia el espacio iberorrománico*, special issue of *Revista Internacional de Lingüística Iberoamericana* 16(1).

Guitarte, Guillermo (1983), *Siete estudios sobre el español de América*, Mexico City: Universidad Nacional Autónoma de México.

Gumperz, John (1980), *Discourse Strategies*, Cambridge: Cambridge University Press.

Gynan, Shaw (2011), 'Spanish in contact with Guaraní', in *The Handbook of Hispanic Sociolinguistics*, ed. Manuel Díaz-Campos, Malden MA: Wiley, pp. 353–73.

Hackert, Stephanie (2012), *The Emergence of the English Native Speaker: A Chapter in Nineteenth-Century Linguistic Thought*, Berlin: De Gruyter Mouton.

Haffner, Ildikó (2009), 'Investigação histórica do bilinguismo na Península Ibérica a partir do século XV até ao século XVII', *Études romanes de Brno* 30(1), 225–33.

Hall-Lew, Lauren, Patrick Honeybone and James Kirby (2021), 'Individuals, communities, and sound change: An introduction', *Glossa: A Journal of General Linguistics* 6(1): 67, doi: 10.5334/gjgl.1630.

Hansen, Lawrence (2005), 'Las migraciones menonitas al norte de México entre 1922 y 1940', *Migraciones Internacionales* 3(1), 6–31.

Haugen, Einar (1950), 'The analysis of linguistic borrowing', *Language* 26(2), 210–23.

Haugen, Einar (1966), 'Dialect, language, nation', *American Anthropologist* 68(4), 922–35.

Haugen, Einar (1971), 'The ecology of language', *The Linguistic Reporter Supplement* 25 (1), 19–26.

Havinga, Anna and Nils Langer, eds. (2015), *Invisible Languages in the Nineteenth Century*, Frankfurt: Peter Lang.

Hawkey, James and Nils Langer (2016), 'Language policy in the long nineteenth century: Catalonia and Schleswig', in *Current Trends in Historical Sociolinguistics*, ed. Cinzia Russi, Berlin: De Gruyter Mouton, pp. 81–107.

Heegård Petersen, Jan, Gert Foget Hansen and Jacob Thøgersen (2019), 'Correlations between linguistic change and linguistic performance among heritage speakers of Danish in Argentina', *Linguistic Approaches to Bilingualism* 10(5), 690–727.

Heeringa, Wilbert, Jelena Golubovic, Charlotte Gooskens, Anja Schüppert, Femke Swarte and Stefani Voigt (2013), 'Lexical and orthographic distances between Germanic, Romance and Slavic languages and their relationship to geographic distance', in *Phonetics in Europe: Perception and Production*, eds. Charlotte Gooskens and Renée van Bezooijen, Frankfurt: Peter Lang, pp. 99–137.

Heggarty, Paul, Cormac Anderson, Matthew Scarborough, Benedict King, Remco Bouckaert, Lechosław Jocz, Martin Joachim Kümmel, Thomas Jügel, Britta Irslinger, Roland Pooth, Henrik Liljegren, Richard Strand, Geoffrey Haig, Martin Macák, Ronald Kim, Erik Anonby, Tijmen Pronk, Oleg Belyaev, Tonya Kim Dewey-Findell, Matthew Boutilier, Cassandra Freiberg, Robert

Tegethoff, Matilde Serangeli, Nikos Liosis, Krzysztof Stroński, Kim Schulte, Ganesh Kumar Gupta, Wolfgang Haak, Johannes Krause, Quentin Atkinson, Simon Greenhill, Denise Kühnert and Russell Gray (2023), 'Language trees with sampled ancestors support a hybrid model for the origin of Indo-European languages', *Science* 381(6656), doi: 10.1126/science.abg0818.

Hekking, Ewald & Dik Bakker (2010), 'Tipología de los préstamos léxicos en el otomí queretano: una contribución para el estudio sistemático y comparativo de diversas lenguas representativas del mundo desde un enfoque interlingüístico', *CIENCIA@UAQ* 3, 27–47.

Hendriks, Jennifer (2024), 'The dynamics of lifelong acquisition in dialect contact and change', in *Lifespan Acquisition and Language Change: Historical Sociolinguistic Perspectives*, ed. Israel Sanz-Sánchez, Amsterdam: John Benjamins, pp. 84–103.

Hernández, José Esteban (2009), 'Measuring rates of word-final nasal velarization: The effect of dialect contact on in-group and out-group exchanges', *Journal of Sociolinguistics* 13(5), 583–612.

Hernández-Campoy, Juan Manuel (2011), 'Variación and identity in Spain', in *The Handbook of Spanish Sociolinguistics*, ed. Manuel Díaz-Campos, Malden MA: Wiley, pp. 704–27.

Hickey, Raymond (2010), 'Language contact: Reconsideration and reassessment', in *The Handbook of Language Contact*, ed. Raymond Hickey, Oxford: Blackwell, pp. 1–28.

Hidalgo, Margarita (2001), 'Sociolinguistic stratification in New Spain', *International Journal of the Sociology of Language* 149, 55–178.

Hidalgo, Margarita (2016), *Diversification of Mexican Spanish: A Tridimensional Study in New World Sociolinguistics*, Berlin: De Gruyter.

Higby, Eve, Evelyn Gámez and Claudia Holguín Mendoza (2023), 'Challenging deficit frameworks in research on heritage language bilingualism', *Applied Psycholinguistics* 44, 417–30.

Hill, Jane and Kenneth Hill (1986), *Speaking Mexicano: Dynamics of Syncretic Language in Central Mexico*, Tucson: The University of Arizona Press.

Hill, Kenneth (1997), 'Spanish loanwords in Hopi', in *The Life of Language: Papers in Linguistics in Honor of William Bright*, ed. Jane Hill, P. J. Mistry and Lyle Campbell, Berlin: De Gruyter, pp. 19–23.

Hinojosa, Jennifer (2018), 'Two sides of the coin of Puerto Rican migration: Depopulation in Puerto Rico and the redefinition of the diaspora', in *Centro Journal* 30(3), 230–53.

Hipperdinger, Yolanda and Elizabeth Rigatuso (1996), 'Dos comunidades inmigratorias conservadoras en el sudoeste bonaerense: Dinamarqueses y alemanes del Volga', *International Journal of the Sociology of Language* 117(1), 39–61.

Hopper, Paul (1987), 'Emergent grammar', in *Proceedings of the Thirteenth Annual Meeting of the Berkeley Linguistics Society*, pp. 139–57.

Hora, Roy (2001), *The Landowners of the Argentine Pampas: A Political and Social History, 1860–1945*, Oxford: Clarendon.

Hundt, Marianne and Daniel Schreier (2013), 'Introduction: Nothing but a contact language', in *English as a Contact Language*, eds. Daniel Schreier and Marianne Hundt, Cambridge: Cambridge University Press, pp. 258–82.

INE (2023a), Cifras de población: Alteraciones de los municipios en los Censos de Población desde 1842. https://www.ine.es/intercensal/inicio.do (last accessed 15 July 2023).

INE (2023b), Cifras de población y censos demográficos, https://www.ine.es/dyngs/INEbase/es/categoria.htm?c=Estadistica_P&cid=1254735572981 (last accessed 15 July 2023).

INEGI (2023), Censo de Población y Vivienda 2020, https://www.inegi.org.mx/programas/ccpv/2020/ (last accessed 15 July 2023).

INEI (2023), Perú: Compendio estadístico 2023, https://www.inei.gob.pe/media/MenuRecursivo/publicaciones_digitales/Est/Compendio2023/COMPENDIO2023.html (last accessed 15 July 2023).

Instituto Cervantes (2022), 'El español en el mundo 2022: Anuario del Instituto Cervantes', https://cvc.cervantes.es/lengua/anuario/anuario_22/ (last accessed 15 July 2023).

International Telecommunication Union (2021), Digital Development Dashboard, https://www.itu.int/en/ITU-D/Statistics/Dashboards/Pages/Digital-Development.aspx (last accessed 15 July 2023).

Irídia: Centre Per la Defensa dels Drets Humans (2017), *La frontera sur: Accesos terrestres*, https://iridia.cat/es/Publicaciones/frontera-sur-accesos-terrestres (last accessed 15 July 2023).

Isac, Daniela and Charles Reiss (2013), *I-Language: An Introduction to Linguistics as Cognitive Science*, Oxford: Oxford University Press.

Jackson, Robert (2008), *The Bourbon Reforms and the Remaking of Spanish Frontier Missions*, Leiden: Brill.

Jahr, Ernst Håkon (1999), 'Sociolinguistics in historical language contact: The Scandinavian languages and Low German during the Hanseatic period', in *Language change: Advances in historical sociolinguistics*, ed. Ernst Håkon, Berlin: De Gruyter Mouton, pp. 119–39.

Jacobs, Auke (1995), *Los movimientos migratorios entre Castilla e Hispanoamérica durante el reinado de Felipe III, 1598–1621*, Amsterdam: Rodopi.

Jakobs, Marlena and Matthias Hüning (2022), 'Scholars and their metaphors: On language making in linguistics', *International Journal of the Sociology of Language* 274(1), 29–50.

Johnstone, Barbara (2016), 'Enregisterment: How linguistic items become linked with ways of speaking', *Language and Linguistics Compass* 10(11), 632–43.

Kania, Sonia (2010), 'Documenting 'yeísmo' in medieval and colonial Spanish texts', *Romance Philology* 64(2), 223–34.

Karttunen, Frances and James Lockhart (1976), *Nahuatl in the Middle Years: Language Contact Phenomena in Texts of the Colonial Period*, Berkeley: University of California Press.

Kemper, Robert and Anya Royce (1979), 'Mexican urbanization since 1821: A macro-historical approach', *Urban Anthropology* 8(3), 267–89.

Kerswill, Paul and Ann Williams (2000a), 'Creating a new town koine: Children and language change in Milton Keynes', *Language in Society* 29(1), 65–115.

Kerswill, Paul and Ann Williams (2000b), Salience. as an explanatory factor in language change: Evidence from dialect levelling in urban England, *Reading Papers in Linguistics* 4, 63–94.

Kinsbruner, Jay (2005), *The Colonial Spanish-American City: Urban Life in the Age of Atlantic Capitalism*, Austin: University of Texas Press.
Kirschen, Bryan (2018), 'Sociolinguistics of Judeo-Spanish', *Language and Linguistics Compass* 12, doi: https://doi.org/10.1111/lnc3.12274.
Klee, Carol and Alicia Ocampo (1995), 'The expression of past reference in Spanish narratives of Spanish-Quechua bilingual speakers', in *Spanish in Four Continents: Studies in Language Contact and Bilingualism*, ed. Carmen Silva-Corvalán, Washington DC: Georgetown University Press, pp. 52–70.
Klee, Carol and Andrew Lynch (2009), *El español en contacto con otras lenguas*, Washington, DC: Georgetown University Press.
Klee, Carol and Rocío Caravedo (2005), 'Contact-induced language change in Lima, Peru: The case of clitic pronouns', in Selected Proceedings of the 7th Hispanic Linguistics Symposium, ed. David Eddington, Somerville, MA: Cascadilla, pp. 12–21.
Kleidermacher, Gisele (2014), 'Migraciones africanas subsaharianas hacia la Argentina: Pasado y presente', in *Historia comparada de las migraciones en las Américas*, ed. Patricia Galeana de Valades, Mexico City: Universidad Nacional Autónoma de México, pp. 279–94.
Kloss, Heinz (1967), 'Abstand languages and Ausbau languages', *Anthropological Linguistics* 9(7), 29–41.
Kremer, Dieter (2005), 'El elemento germánico y su influencia en la historia lingüística peninsular', in *Historia de la lengua española*, ed. Rafael Cano, Barcelona: Ariel, pp. 133–48.
Kretzschmar, William (2015), *Language and Complex Systems*, Cambridge: Cambridge University Press.
Kroll, Judith and Fengyang Ma (2018), 'The bilingual lexicon', in *The Handbook of Psycholinguistics*, eds. Eva Fernández and Helen Smith Cairns, Malden MA: Wiley, pp. 249–319.
Kueh, Joshua (2014), The Manila Chinese: Community, Trade, and Empire, c. 1570-c.1770. PhD dissertation, Georgetown University.
Kühl, Karoline and Kurt Braunmüller (2014), 'Linguistic stability and divergence: An extended perspective on language contact', in *Stability and Divergence in Language Contact: Factors and Mechanisms*, eds. Kurt Braunmüller, Steffen Höder and Karoline Kühl, Amsterdam: John Benjamins, pp. 13–38.
Labov, William (1994), *Principles of Linguistic Change. Volume 1: Internal Factors*, Oxford: Blackwell.
Labov, William (2001), *Principles of Linguistic Change. Volume 2: Social Factors*, Oxford: Blackwell.
Labov, William (2007), 'Transmission and diffusion', *Language* 83(2), 344–87.
Lagos, Cristián, Felipe Pérez de Arce, Verónica Figueroa (2017), 'The revitalization of the Mapuche language as a space of ideological struggle: the case of Pehuenche communities in Chile', *Journal of Historical Archaeology and Anthropological Science* 1(5), 197–207.
Laitinen, Mikko, Masoud Fatemi and Jonas Lundberg (2020), 'Size matters: Digital social networks and language change', *Frontiers in Artificial Intelligence* 3, 46, doi: 10.3389/frai.2020.00046.
Lapesa, Rafael (1981), *Historia de la lengua española*, Madrid: Gredos.

Lara Bermejo, Víctor (2018), 'Acomodación en los pronombres de tratamiento de ecuatorianos en España', *Lengua y migración* 10(1), 7–31.

Larsen-Freeman, Diane (2007), 'Reflecting on the cognitive-social debate in second language acquisition', *The Modern Language Journal* 91(1), 773–87.

Lastra, Yolanda and Pedro Martín Butragueño (2006), 'Un posible cambio en curso. El caso de las vibrantes en la ciudad de México', in *Estudios sociolingüísticos del español de España y América*, ed. Isabel Molina Martos, Ana María Cestero Mancera and Florentino Paredes García, Madrid: Arco Libros, pp. 35–68.

Lathrop, Thomas (1980), *The Evolution of Spanish: An Introductory Historical Grammar*, Newark, DE: Juan de la Cuesta.

Lauersdorf, Mark Richard (2018), 'Historical (standard) language development and the writing of historical identities: A plaidoyer for a data-driven approach to the investigation of the sociolinguistic history of (not only) Slovak', *V zeleni drželi zeleni breg: Studies in Honor of Marc L. Greenberg*, eds. Stephen Dickey and Mark Richard Lauersdorf, Bloomington: Indiana, pp. 199–218.

Leather, Jonathan and Jet van Dam (2003), 'Towards an ecology of language acquisition', in *Ecology of Language Acquisition*, eds. Jonathan Leather and Jet van Dam, Dordrecht: Springer, pp. 1–29.

Levaggi, Abelardo (2001), 'República de indios y república de españoles en los reinos de Indias', *Revista de Estudios Histórico-Jurídicos* 23(1), 419–28.

Library of Congress (2023), Georg Braun, *Civitates Orbis Terrarum*, https://www.loc.gov/resource/g3200m.gct00128a/?st=gallery (last accessed 15 July 2023).

Lightfoot, David (2006), *How New Languages Emerge*, Cambridge: Cambridge University Press.

Lipski, John (1987), 'Contemporary Philippine Spanish: Comments on vestigial usage', *Philippine Journal of Linguistics* 17(2), 37–48.

Lipski, John (1994), *Latin American Spanish*, London: Longman.

Lipski, John (1999), 'Chinese-Cuban pidgin Spanish: Implications for the Afro-Creole debate', in *Creole Genesis, Attitudes and Discourse*, eds. John Rickford and Suzanne Romaine, Amsterdam: John Benjamins, pp. 215–33.

Lipski, John (2004), 'Nuevas perspectivas sobre el español afro-dominicano', in *Pensamiento lingüístico sobre el Caribe insular hispánico*, ed. Sergio Valdés Bernal, Santo Domingo: Academia de Ciencias de la República Dominicana, pp. 505–52.

Lipski, John (2005), *A History of Afro-Hispanic Language: Five Centuries, Five Continents*. Cambridge: Cambridge University Press.

Lipski, John (2007), 'Afro-Yungueño speech: The long-lost "black Spanish"', *Spanish in Context* 4(1), 1–43.

Lipski, John (2008), *Varieties of Spanish in the United States*, Washington, D.C.: Georgetown University Press.

Lipski, John (2010), 'Chabacano y español: resolviendo las ambigüedades', *Lengua y Migración* 2(1), 5–41.

Lipski, John (2011), 'Dialects and borders: Face-to-face and back-to-back in Latin American Spanish', *International Journal of the Linguistic Association of the Southwest* 30(2), 33–54.

Lipski, John (2012), 'Características lingüísticas del español filipino y del chabacano', in *Historia cultural de la lengua española en Filipinas: ayer y hoy*, ed. Isaac Donoso Jiménez, Madrid: Verbum, pp. 307–23.

Lipski, John (2014), 'The many facets of Spanish dialect diversification in Latin America', in *Iberian Imperialism and Language Evolution in Latin America*, ed. Salikoko Mufwene, Chicago IL: University of Chicago Press, pp. 38–75.

Lipski, John (2015), 'Palenquero and Spanish: What's in the mix?', in *The Iberian Challenge: Creole Languages beyond the Plantation Setting*, eds. Armin Schwegler, John McWhorter and Liane Ströbel, Madrid: Iberoamericana/Vervuert, pp. 153–80.

Lipski, John (2020a), *Palenquero and Spanish in Contact: Exploring the Interface*, Amsterdam: John Benjamins.

Lipski, John (2020b), 'Reconstructing the life-cycle of a mixed language: An exploration of Ecuadoran Media Lengua', *International Journal of Bilingualism* 24(2), 410–36.

Lipski, John (2022), 'The emergence and evolution of Romance languages in Europe and the Americas', in *The Cambridge Handbook of Language Contact, Vol. 1*, eds. Salikoko Mufwene and Anna María Escobar, Cambridge: Cambridge University Press, pp. 427–58.

Lipski, John, Peter Mühlhäusler and F. Duthin (1996), 'Spanish in the Pacific', in *Atlas of Languages of Intercultural Communication in the Pacific, Asia, and the Americas*, eds. Stephen Wurm, Peter Mühlhäusler, Darrell Tryon, Berlin: De Gruyter Mouton, pp. 271–98.

Lleal, Coloma (1990), *La formación de las lenguas romances peninsulares*, Barcelona: Barcanova.

Llody, Paul (1987), *From Latin to Spanish: Historical Phonology and Morphology of the Spanish Language*, Philadelphia: American Philosophical Society.

Lockhart, James (1992), *The Nahuas after the Conquest: A Social and Cultural History of the Indians of Central Mexico, Sixteenth through Eighteenth Centuries*, Stanford, CA: Stanford University Press.

Lockhart, James and Stuart Schwartz (1983), *Early Latin America: A History of Colonial Spanish America and Brazil*, Cambridge: Cambridge University Press.

Lope Blanch, Juan (2000), *Español de América y español de México*, Mexico City: Universidad Nacional Autónoma de México.

López Izquierdo, Marta (2024), 'Latín e hispanorromance durante la Edad Media (1200–1450)', in *Lingüística histórica del español: The Routledge Handbook of Spanish Historical Linguistics*, eds. Steven Dworkin, Gloria Clavería Nadal and Álvaro Octavio de Toledo y Huerta, London: Routledge, pp. 372–82.

López Morales, Humberto (1983), *Estratificación social del español de San Juan de Puerto Rico*, Mexico City: Universidad Nacional Autónoma de México.

Lorrio, Alberto and Joan Sanmartí (2019), 'The Iberian peninsula in pre-Roman times: An archaeological and ethnographical survey', in *Palaeohispanic Languages and Epigraphies*, eds. Alejandro Sinner and Javier Velaza, Oxford: Oxford University Press, pp. 25–55.

Lublin, Geraldine (2013), 'La identidad en la encrucijada: La comunidad galesa del Chubut y las conmemoraciones del Centenario y Bicentenario de la Revolución de Mayo', *Identidades* 5(3), 115–30.

Luján, Eugenio (2024), 'La influencia de las lenguas prerromanas como consecuencia del contacto lingüístico', in *Lingüística histórica del español: The Routledge Handbook of Spanish Historical Linguistics*, eds. Steven Dworkin, Gloria Clavería Nadal and Álvaro Octavio de Toledo y Huerta, London: Routledge, pp. 328–38.

Lynch, Andrew (2018), 'Spatial reconfigurations of Spanish in postmodernity: The relationship to English and minoritized languages', in *Language Variation and Contact-Induced Change: Spanish across space and time*, eds. Sandro Sessarego and Jeremy King, Amsterdam: John Benjamins, pp. 11–34.

Lynch, Andrew, ed. (2020), *The Routledge Handbook of Spanish in the Global City*, London: Routledge.

MacSwan, Jeff (2017), 'A multilingual perspective on translanguaging', *American Educational Research Journal* 54(1), 167–201.

Madariaga Orbea, Juan (2014), *Sociedad y lengua vasca en los siglos XVII y XVIII*, Bilbao: Euskaltzaindia.

Maguiña Salinas, Ernesto (2016), 'Un acercamiento al estudio de las inmigraciones extranjeras en el Perú durante el siglo XIX y las primeras décadas del siglo XX', *Tierra Nuestra* 8(1), 65–96.

Maians i Siscar, Gregori (1737), *Orígenes de la lengua española*, Madrid: Juan de Zúñiga.

Makihara, Miki (2013), 'Language, competence, use, ideology, and community on Rapa Nui', *Language & Communication* 33(1), 439–49.

Makoni, Sinfree and Alastair Pennycook (2006), 'Disinventing and reconstituting languages', in *Disinventing and Reconstituting Languages*, ed. Sinfree Makoni and Alastair Pennycook, Clevedon: Multilingual Matters, pp. 1–41.

Mallory, J. P. and Douglas Adams (2006), *The Oxford Introduction to Proto-Indo European and the Proto-Indo-European World*, Oxford: Oxford University.

Mancini, Marco (2021), 'Does Prenestinian fe:faked actually exist?', *Journal of Latin Linguistics* 20(1), 75–108.

Mántica, Carlos (2020), *El Güegüence, un desconocido*, Managua: Hispamer. Amazon Kindle edition.

Mar-Molinero, Clare (2008), 'Subverting Cervantes: Language authority in Global Spanish', *International Multilingual Research Journal* 2(1), 27–47.

Mar-Molinero, Clare, ed. (2020), *Researching Language in Superdiverse Urban Contexts: Methodological and Theoretical Concepts*, Bristol: Multilingual Matters.

Mar-Molinero, Clare and Darren Paffey (2011) 'Linguistic imperialism: Who owns Global Spanish?', in *The Handbook of Hispanic Sociolinguistics*, ed. Manuel Díaz-Campos, London: Blackwell, pp. 747–64.

Marqués Rodríguez, Iñaki (2017), 'Menonitas 1927–1935. Colonización y evangelización en el Chaco paraguayo', *Revista Latino-Americana de História* 6(17), 176–91.

Marr, Tim (2011), '"Ya no podemos regresar al quechua": Modernity, identity and language choice among migrants in urban Peru', in *History and Language in the Andes*, eds. Paul Heggarty and Adrian Pearce, London: Palgrave Macmillan, pp. 215–38.

Martín Butragueño, Pedro (2016), Inmigración y reconstrucción de la identidad lingüística: El caso de Ecatepec, *Cuadernos AISPI* 8(1), 145–70.

Martín Butragueño, Pedro (2020), 'Building the megalopolis: Dialectal leveling and language contact in Mexico City', in *The Routledge Handbook of Spanish in the Global City*, ed. Andrew Lynch, London: Routledge, pp. 234–74.

Martín Butragueño, Pedro, and Nadiezdha Torres Sánchez (2022), 'Lexical borrowing and variation: The case of Amerindian words in Latin American Spanish', in *The Routledge Handbook of Variationist Approaches to Spanish*, ed. Manuel Díaz-Campos, London: Routledge, pp. 546–58.

Martinet, André (1952), 'Celtic lenition and Western Romance consonants', *Language* 28(2), 192–217.

Martínez, Glenn (2000), 'A sociohistorical basis of grammatical simplification: The absolute construction in nineteenth-century Tejano narrative discourse', *Language Variation and Change,* 12(1), 251–66.

Matras, Yaron (2020), *Language Contact*. Cambridge: Cambridge University Press.

Matus Mendoza, María de la Luz (2004), 'Assibilation of /-r/ and migration among Mexicans', *Language Variation and Change* 16(1), 17–30.

McAuliffe, Marie and Anna Triandafyllidou, eds. (2022), *World Migration Report 2022*, Geneva: International Organization for Migration.

McWhorter, John (2000), *The Missing Spanish Creoles: Recovering the Birth of Plantation Contact Languages*, Berkeley: University of California Press.

McWhorter, John (2015), 'The missing Spanish creoles are still missing: Revisiting Afrogenesis and its implications for a coherent theory of creole genesis', in *The Iberian Challenge: Creole Languages beyond the Plantation Setting*, eds. Armin Schwegler, John McWhorter and Liane Ströbel, Madrid: Iberoamericana/Vervuert, pp. 39–66.

Meisel, Jürgen (2018), 'Bilingual acquisition: A morphosyntactic perspective on simultaneous and early successive language development', in *The Handbook of Psycholinguistics*, eds. Eva Fernández and Helen Smith Cairns, Malden MA: Wiley, pp. 635–52.

Meisel, Jürgen, Elsig Martin and Rinke Esther (2013), *Language Acquisition and Change: A Morphosyntactic Perspective*, Edinburgh: Edinburgh University Press.

Melis, Chantal and Agustín Rivero Franyutti (2008), *Documentos lingüísticos de la Nueva España: Golfo de México*, Mexico City: Universidad Nacional Autónoma de México.

Méndez Reyes, Jesús (2013), 'Alemanes en el noroeste mexicano: Notas sobre su actividad comercial a inicios del siglo XX', *Estudios de historia moderna y contemporánea de México* 46, 55–86.

Mendoza-Denton, Norma and Bryan Gordon (2011), 'Language and social meaning in bilingual Mexico and the United States', in *The Handbook of Hispanic Sociolinguistics*, ed. Manuel Díaz-Campos, Malden MA: Wiley, pp. 553–78.

Menéndez Pidal, Ramón (1950), *Orígenes del español: estado lingüístico de la Península Ibérica hasta el siglo XI*, Madrid: Espasa-Calpe. First published in 1926.

Menéndez Pidal, Ramón (1958), *Manual de gramática histórica española*, Madrid: Espasa-Calpe. First published in 1904.

Messing, Jacqueline (2007), 'Multiple ideologies and competing discourses: Language shift in Tlaxcala, Mexico', *Language in Society* 36(4), 555–77.

Mesthrie, Rajend (2008), 'Pidgins/creoles and contact languages: An overview', in *The Handbook of Pidgin and Creole Studies*, eds. Silvia Kouwenber and John Singler, Malden, MA: Wiley, pp. 263–86.

Michnowicz, Jim (2015), 'Maya-Spanish contact in Yucatán, Mexico: Context and sociolinguistic implications', in *New Perspectives on Hispanic Contact Linguistics in the Americas*, eds. Sandro Sessarego and Melvin González Rivera, Madrid: Iberoamericana/Vervuert, pp. 21–42.

Michnowicz, Jim, Rebecca Ronquest, Sarah Chetty, Georgia Green, and Stephanie Oliver (2023), 'Spanish in the Southeast: What a swarm of variables can tell us about a newly forming bilingual community', *Languages* 8, 168, doi: 10.3390/languages8030168.

Milroy, James and Lesley Milroy (1985), 'Linguistic change, social network and speaker innovation', *Journal of Linguistics* 21, 339–84.

Milroy, Lesley and James Milroy (1992), 'Social network and social class: Toward an integrated sociolinguistic model', *Language in Society* 21(1), 1–26.

Minervini, Laura (2024), 'Aspectos sociolingüísticos del contacto entre cristianos, judíos y musulmanes', in *Lingüística histórica del español: The Routledge Handbook of Spanish Historical Linguistics*, eds. Steven Dworkin, Gloria Clavería Nadal and Álvaro Octavio de Toledo y Huerta, London: Routledge, pp. 372–82.

Molina Luque, Fidel (2012), *Servicio militar y conflicto: Historia y sociología de las quintas en España (1878–1960)*, Lleida: Milenio.

Molina Martos, Isabel (2006), 'Innovación y difusión del cambio lingüístico en Madrid', *Revista de Filología Española* 86(1), 127–49.

Molina Martos, Isabel (2021), 'Cambio lingüístico y transformación social: Formas y fórmulas de tratamiento en España (1860–1940)', *Revista Internacional de Lingüística Iberoamericana* 19(2), 173–95.

Montrul, Silvina (2013), *El bilingüismo en el mundo hispanohablante*, Malden, MA: Wiley-Blackwell.

Montrul, Silvina (2022), *Native Speakers, Interrupted: Differential Object Marking and Language Change in Heritage Languages*, Cambridge: Cambridge University Press.

Montrul, Silvina and Carmen Silva-Corvalán (2019), 'The social context contributes to the incomplete acquisition of aspects of heritage languages', *Studies in Second Language Acquisition* 41(2), 269–73.

Montrul, Silvina and Kim Potowski (2007), 'Command of gender agreement in school-age Spanish heritage speakers', *International Journal of Bilingualism* 11(3), 109–32.

Mora, Lauren and Mark Hugo Lopez (2023), 'Latinos' views of and experiences with the Spanish language', Washington, DC: Pew Research Center, https://www.pewresearch.org/race-and-ethnicity/2023/09/20/latinos-views-of-and-experiences-with-the-spanish-language/ (last accessed 15 July 2023).

Morales López, Esperanza (2019), 'Bilingüismo intermodal (lengua de signos / lengua oral)', *Revista de Estudios de Lenguas de Signos REVLES* (1), 340–65.
Moreno de Alba, José (1988), *El español de América*, Mexico City: Fondo de Cultura Económica.
Moreno Fernández, Francisco (2015a), *La maravillosa historia del español*, Barcelona: Espasa.
Moreno Fernández, Francisco (2015b), 'La importancia internacional de las lenguas', Harvard: Instituto Cervantes de la Facultad de Artes y Ciencias de la Universidad de Harvard, https://cervantesobservatorio.fas.harvard.edu/en/reports/international-importance-languages (last accessed 15 July 2023).
Moreno Fernández, Francisco and Jaime Otero Roth (2007), *Atlas de la lengua española en el mundo*, Barcelona: Arial.
Moreno Fernández, Francisco and Jaime Otero (2008), 'The status and future of Spanish among the main international languages: Quantitative dimensions', *International Multilingual Research Journal*, 2 (1), 67–83.
Moreno-Estrada, Andrés, Simon Gravel, Fouad Zakharia, Jacob McCauley, Jake Byrnes, Christopher Gignoux, Patricia Ortiz-Tello, Ricardo Martínez, Dale Hedges, Richard Morris, Celeste Eng, Karla Sandoval, Suehelay Acevedo-Acevedo, Paul Norman, Zulay Layrisse, Peter Parham, Juan Carlos Martínez-Cruzado, Esteban González Burchard, Michael Cuccaro, Eden Martin and Carlos Bustamante (2013), 'Reconstructing the population genetic history of the Caribbean', *PLoS Genetics* 9(11): doi: https://doi.org/10.1371/journal.pgen.1003925.
Moreno-Fernández, Francisco and Hiroto Ueda (2018), 'Cohesion and particularity in the Spanish dialect continuum', *Open Linguistics* 4, 722–42.
Morgenthaler García, Laura (2007), 'Migraciones y economía del español actual: Procesos de estandarización entre inmigrantes y población receptora', *Revista Internacional de Lingüística Iberoamericana*, 5(2), 47–68.
Morgenthaler García, Laura (2011), 'Aspectos sociolingüísticos del contacto español-árabe en el Sahara Occidental: Primer acercamiento', *Revista Internacional de Lingüística Iberoamericana* 9(2), 101–19.
Moya, José (2006), 'A continent of immigrants: Postcolonial shifts in the Western Hemisphere', *Hispanic American Historical Review* 86(1), 1–28.
Moyna, María Irene (2009a), 'Back at the rancho: Language maintenance and shift among Spanish-speakers in post-annexation California (1848–1900)', *Revista Internacional de Lingüística Iberoamericana* 7(2), 165–84.
Moyna, María Irene (2009b), 'Child acquisition and language change: Voseo evolution in Río de la Plata Spanish', in *Proceedings of the 2007 Hispanic Linguistics Symposium*, Somerville MA: Cascadilla, pp. 131–42.
Moyna, María Irene and Wendy Decker (2005), 'A historical perspective on Spanish in the California borderlands', *Southwest Journal of Linguistics*, 24(1), 145–67.
Moyna, María Irene and Magdalena Coll (2008), 'A tale of two borders: 19th century language contact in southern California and northern Uruguay', *Studies in Hispanic and Lusophone Linguistics* 1(1), 105–38.
Moyna, María Irene and Wendy Decker (2008), 'How the California girls (and boys) lost their accents', in *Recovering the U.S. Hispanic Linguistic Heritage:*

Sociohistorical Approaches to Spanish in the United States, ed. Alejandra Balestra, Glenn Martínez and María Irene Moyna, Houston: Arte Público, pp. 163–90.

Moyna, María Irene and Israel Sanz Sánchez (2023), 'Out of the mouths of babes: The role of children in the formation of the Río de la Plata address system', *Journal of Historical Sociolinguistics*, 9(2), 189–220.

Mufwene, Salikoko (2001), *The Ecology of Language Evolution*, Cambridge: Cambridge University Press.

Mufwene, Salikoko (2008), *Language Evolution: Contact, Competition, and Change*, London: Continuum.

Mufwene, Salikoko (2010), 'SLA and the emergence of creoles', *Studies in Second Language Acquisition*, 32(1), 359–400.

Mufwene, Salikoko (2014), 'Latin America: A linguistic curiosity from the point of view of colonization and the ensuing language contacts', in *Iberian Imperialism and Language Evolution in Latin America*, ed. Salikoko Mufwene, Chicago IL: University of Chicago Press, pp. 1–37.

Mufwene, Salikoko (2018), 'Language evolution from an ecological perspective', in *The Routledge Handbook of Ecolinguistics*, eds. Alwin Fill and Hermine Penz, London: Routledge, pp. 73–88.

Mufwene, Salikoko (2022), 'The verticalization model of language shift from a population-structure perspective: A commentary', in *The Verticalization Model of Language Shift*, ed. Joshua Brown, Oxford: Oxford University Press, pp. 166–94.

Mufwene, Salikoko, and Cécile Vigouroux (2017), 'Individuals, populations, and timespace: Perspectives on the ecology of language revisited', *Language Ecology* 1(1), 75–102.

Muñoz Basols, Javier, Mara Fuertes Gutiérrez and Luis Cerezo, eds. (2024), *La enseñanza del español mediada por tecnología: De la justicia social a la Inteligencia Artificial (IA)*, London: Routledge.

Muysken, Pieter (2013), 'Language contact outcomes as the result of bilingual optimization strategies', *Bilingualism: Language and Cognition* 16(4), 709–30.

Nadeau, Jean-Benoît and Julie Barlow (2013), *The Story of Spanish*, New York: St. Martin's Griffin.

Namboodiripad, Savithry and Jonathan Henner (2022), 'Rejecting competence: Essentialist constructs reproduce ableism and white supremacy in linguistic theory', *Language Learning* 73(2), 321–24.

Narvaja de Arnoux, Elvira (2013), 'Grammar and the state in the Southern Cone in the nineteenth century', in *A Political History of Spanish: The Making of a Language*, ed. José del Valle, Cambridge: Cambridge University Press, pp. 152–66.

Navarro Tomás, Tomás (1962), *Atlas lingüístico de la península ibérica, I: Fonética*, Madrid: CSIC.

Negrão, Esmeralda and Evani Viotti (2014), 'Brazilian Portuguese as a transatlantic language: Agents of linguistic contact', *InterDISCIPLINARY Journal of Portuguese Diaspora Studies* 3, 135–54.

Nevalainen, Terttu, Tanja Säily, Turo Vartiainen, Aatu Liimatta and Jefrey Lijffijt (2020), 'History of English as punctuated equilibria? A meta-analysis

of the rate of linguistic change in Middle English', *Journal of Historical Sociolinguistics* 6(2), doi: 10.1515/jhsl-2019-0008.
Nicolau, Roser (2005), 'Población, salud y actividad', in *Estadísticas Históricas de España*, eds. Albert Carreras and Xavier Tafunell, Bilbao: Fundación BBVA, pp. 77–154.
Nölle, Jonas Riccardo Fusaroli, Gregory Mills and Kristian Tylén (2020), 'Language as shaped by the environment: Linguistic construal in a collaborative spatial task', *Palgrave Communications* 6(27), doi: 10.1057/s41599-020-0404-9.
Núñez, Clara Eugenia (2005), 'Educación', in *Estadísticas Históricas de España*, eds. Albert Carreras and Xavier Tafunell, Bilbao: Fundación BBVA, pp. 155–244.
Núñez Méndez, Eva (2012), *Fundamentos teóricos y prácticos de historia de la lengua española*. New Haven, CT: Yale University Press.
Núñez Méndez, Eva, ed. (2019), *Biculturalism and Spanish in Contact: Sociolinguistic Case Studies*, London: Routledge.
Nycz, Jennifer (2013), 'Changing words or changing rules? Second dialect acquisition and phonological representation', *Journal of Pragmatics* 52(1), 49–62.
Orduña, Eduardo (2019), 'The Vasco-Iberian theory', in *Palaeohispanic Languages and Epigraphies*, eds. Alejandro Sinner and Javier Velaza, Oxford: Oxford University Press, pp. 219–39.
Orozco, Rafael (2018), *Spanish in Colombia and New York City: Language Contact Meets Dialectal Convergence*, Amsterdam: John Benjamins.
Ortega, Lourdes, Andrea Tyler, Hae In Park and Mariko Uno, eds. (2016), *The Usage-based Study of Language Learning and Multilingualism*, Washington, DC: Georgetown University Press.
Ortiz López, Luis (1998), *Huellas etnolingüísticas bozales y afrocubanas*, Madrid: Iberoamericana/Vervuert.
Ortiz López, Luis (2011), 'Spanish in contact with Haitian Creole', in *The Handbook of Spanish Sociolinguistics*, ed. Manuel Díaz-Campos, Malden MA: Wiley, pp. 418–45.
Ortiz López, Luis, Rosa Guzzardo Tamargo and Melvin González-Rivera, eds. (2020), *Hispanic Contact Linguistics: Theoretical, Methodological and Empirical Perspectives*, Amsterdam: John Benjamins.
Osthoff, Hermann and Karl Brugmann (1878), *Morphologische Untersuchungen auf dem Gebiete der indogermanischen Sprachen*, Leipzig: S. Hirzel.
Otheguy, Ricardo and Ana Celia Zentella (2012), *Spanish in New York: Language Contact, Dialect Leveling and Structural Continuity*, Oxford: Oxford University Press.
Otheguy, Ricardo, Ofelia García and Wallis Reid (2015), 'Clarifying translanguaging and deconstructing named languages: A perspective from linguistics', *Applied Linguistics Review* 6(3), 281–307.
Otheguy, Ricardo, Ofelia García and Wallis Reid (2019), 'A translanguaging view of the linguistic system of bilinguals', *Applied Linguistics Review* 10(4), 625–51.
Otheguy, Ricardo, Naomi Shin and Daniel Erker (2022), 'On the idiolectal nature of lexical and phonological contact: Spaniards in contact with Nahuas

and Yorubas in the New World', in *The Cambridge Handbook of Language Contact*, vol. 2, eds. Salikoko Mufwene and Anna María Escobar, Cambridge: Cambridge University Press, pp. 370–400.

Oxford English Dictionary (2023), 'History' (last accessed 15 July 2023).

Papadopoulos, Ben (2024), 'Identifying gender in gendered languages: The case of Spanish', in *Redoing Linguistic Worlds: Unmaking Gender Binaries, Remaking Gender Pluralities*, eds. Kris Knisely and Eric Russell, Bristol: Multilingual Matters.

Parodi, Claudia (2001), 'Contacto de dialectos y lenguas en el Nuevo Mundo: La vernacularización del español de América', *International Journal of the Sociology of Language* 149, 33–53.

Parodi, Claudia (2011), 'El otro México: español chicano, koineización y diglosia en los Angeles, California', in *Realismo en el análisis de corpus orales*, ed. Pedro Martín Butragueño, Mexico City: El Colegio de México, pp. 217–43.

Paul, Hermann (1920), *Prinzipien der Sprachgeschichte*. Halle: Max Niemeyer. First published in 1880.

PBS Learning Media (2015), 'The Stages of the Spanish Reconquista', https://whyy.pbslearningmedia.org/resource/social-studies-034-mg-r1-grades-6-12/the-stages-of-the-spanish-reconquista/ (last accessed 15 July 2023).

Penny, Ralph (2000), *Variation and Change in Spanish*, Cambridge: Cambridge University Press.

Penny, Ralph (2002), *A History of the Spanish Language*, Cambridge: Cambridge University Press. First published in 1991.

Penny, Ralph (2006), 'What did sociolinguistics ever do for language history? The contribution of sociolinguistic theory to the diachronic study of Spanish', *Spanish in Context* 3(1), 49–62.

Pérez Arreaza, Laura (2016), 'Las actitudes lingüísticas de los jóvenes hispanos de Montreal', *Language and Migration* 8(2), 105–32.

Pérez Brignoli, Héctor (2010), 'América Latina en la transición demográfica, 1800–1980', *Población y Salud en Mesoamérica* 7 (2), https://revistas.ucr.ac.cr/index.php/psm/article/view/1090/1151 (last accesssed 15 July 2023).

Pešková, Andrea (2024), 'In the echoes of Guarani: Exploring the intonation of statements in Paraguayan Spanish', *Languages* 9(1), 12, doi: 10.3390/languages9010012.

Pesqueira, Dinorah. 2008. 'Cambio fónico en situaciones de contacto dialectal: el caso de los inmigrantes bonaerenses en la ciudad de México', in *Fonología instrumental. Patrones fónicos y variación*, eds. Esther Herrera and Pedro Martín Butragueño, Mexico City: El Colegio de México, pp. 171–89.

Pharies, David (2015), *Breve historia de la lengua española*, Chicago IL: University of Chicago Press.

Plag, Ingo (2008), 'Creoles as interlanguages: Inflectional morphology', *Journal of Pidgin and Creole Languages* 24(1), 109–30.

Poch Olivé, Dolors, ed. (2016), *El español en contacto con las otras lenguas peninsulares*, Madrid: Iberoamericana/Vervuert.

Polinsky, Maria (2018), *Heritage Languages and their Speakers*, Cambridge: Cambridge University Press.

Pons Rodríguez, Lola (2016), *Una lengua muy larga*. Barcelona: Arpa Editores.

Poplack, Shana (1980), 'Sometimes I'll start a sentence in Spanish Y TERMINO EN ESPAÑOL: Toward a typology of code-switching', *Linguistics* 18(7), 581–618.

Poplack, Shana and David Sankoff (1987), 'The Philadelphia story in the Spanish Caribbean', *American Speech* 62(4), 291–314.

Potowski, Kim and Lourdes Torres (2023), *Spanish in Chicago*. Oxford: Oxford University Press.

Potowski, Kim, ed. (2018), *The Routledge Handbook of Spanish as a Heritage Language*, London: Routledge.

Pratt, Marie Louise (1987), 'Linguistic utopias', in *The Linguistics of Writing*, eds. Nigel Fabb, Derek Attridge, Alan Durant and Colin MacCabe, Manchester: Manchester University Press, pp. 48–66.

Quilis, Antonio and Celia Casado Fresnillo (1995), *La lengua española en Guinea Ecuatorial*, Madrid: UNED.

Quilis, Antonio and Celia Casado Fresnillo (2008), *La lengua española en Filipinas: Historia, situación actual, el chabacano, antología de textos*, Madrid: CSIC.

Ragsdale, Corey, Cathy Willermet and Heather Edgar (2019), 'Changes in indigenous population structure in colonial Mexico City and Morelos', *International Journal of Osteoarcheology* 29(1), 501–12.

Ranson, Diana and Margaret Quesada (2018), *The History of Spanish: A Student's Introduction,* Cambridge: Cambridge University Press.

Raynor, Eliot (2024), 'The contact origin(s) of 'hand' and 'foot' > 'limb' in Antioquian Spanish: Tracing historical adult L1 transfer', in *Lifespan Acquisition and Language Change: Historical Sociolinguistic Perspectives*, ed. Israel Sanz-Sánchez, Amsterdam: John Benjamins, 264–93.

Real Academia Española and Asociación de Academias de la Lengua Española (2009), *Nueva gramática de la lengua española*, Madrid: Espasa-Calpe.

Real Academia Española (2020), *Informe de la Real Academia Española sobre el lenguaje inclusivo y cuestiones conexas*, https://www.rae.es/sites/default/files/Informe_lenguaje_inclusivo.pdf (last accessed 15 July 2023).

Real Academia Española (2023), Corpus Diacrónico del Español (CORDE). 'lúa' http://corpus.rae.es/cordenet.html, (last accessed 15 July 2023).

Renfrew, Colin (1987), *Archaeology and Language: The Puzzle of Indo-European Origins*. London: Jonathan Cape.

Requena, Pablo E. (2022), 'Variation versus deviation: Early bilingual acquisition of Spanish differential object marking', *Linguistic Approaches to Bilingualism*. doi: https://doi.org/10.1075/lab.21001.req

Resnick, Melvyn and Robert Hammond (2011), *Introducción a la historia de la lengua española*, Washington, DC: Georgetown University Press.

Ripoll López, Gisela (1989), 'Características generales del poblamiento y la arqueología funeraria visigoda de Hispania', *Espacio, Tiempo y Forma: Prehistoria y Arqueología* 2, 389–418.

Rivadeneira Valenzuela, Marcela (2016), 'Sociolinguistic variation and change in Chilean voseo', in *Forms of Address in the Spanish of the Americas*, eds. María Irene Moyna and Susana Rivera-Mills, pp. 87–117.

Rivarola, José Luis (2001), *El español de América en su historia*, Valladolid: Universidad de Valladolid.

Robledo, Juan (2019), 'Mario Tascón: "Hay un problema con la calidad del uso del español en general en Internet"', *infobae.es* 30 March 2019, https://www.infobae.com/america/cultura-america/2019/03/30/mario-tascon-hay-que-un-problema-con-la-calidad-del-uso-del-espanol-en-general-en-internet/ (last accessed 15 July 2023).

Rodríguez Cadena, Yolanda (2005), 'Variación y cambio en la comunidad de inmigrantes cubanos en la ciudad de México: las líquidas en coda silábica', in *Líderes lingüísticos: estudios de variación y cambio*, ed. Pedro Martín Butragueño, Mexico City: El Colegio de México, pp. 61–88.

Rodríguez-Ponga y Salamanca, Rafael (1996), 'Islas Marianas', in *Manual de dialectología hispánica: El español de América*, ed. Manuel Alvar López, Barcelona: Ariel, pp. 244–8.

Roels, Linde, Fine De Latte and Renata Enghels (2021), 'Monitoring 21st-century real-time language change in Spanish youth speech', *Languages* 162, doi: 10.3390/languages6040162.

Roeper, Tom (2016), 'Multiple grammars and the logic of learnability in Second Language Acquisition', *Frontiers in Psychology* 7, doi: 10.3389/fpsyg.2016.00014.

Rohlfs, Gerhard (1954), 'Die lexicalische Differenzierung der romanischen Sprachen: Versuch einer romanischen Wortgeographie', *Sitzungsberichte der Bayerischen Akademie der Wissenschaften* 4.

Romero, Sergio (2014), 'Grammar, dialectal variation, and honorific registers in Nahuatl in seventeenth-century Guatemala', *Anthropological Linguistics* 56(1), pp. 54–77.

Romero, Sergio (2024), personal communication.

Romero Sotelo, María Eugenia and Luis Jáuregui (2003), 'México 1821–1867. Población y crecimiento económico', *Iberoamericana* 3(12), 25–52.

Rosa, Jonathan (2019), *Looking like a Language, Sounding like a Race: Raciolinguistic Ideologies and the Learning of Latinidad*. Oxford: Oxford University Press.

Rosales Sandoval, Isabel (2014), 'Historia reciente de las políticas migratorias en Centroamérica', in *Historia comparada de las migraciones en las Américas*, ed. Patricia Galeana, Mexico City: Universidad Nacional Autónoma de México, pp. 204–25.

Rosas Mayén, Norma (2007), Afro-Hispanic Linguistic Remnants in Mexico: The Case of the Costa Chica region of Oaxaca. PhD dissertation, Purdue University.

Rothman, Jason and Roumyana Slabakova (2018), 'The generative approach to SLA and its place in modern second language studies', *Studies in Second Language Acquisition* 40(1), 417–42.

Rys, Kathy (2007), Dialect as a second language: Linguistic and non-linguistic factors in secondary dialect acquisition by children and adolescents. PhD dissertation, Universiteit Gent.

Salmons, Joe (1992), *Accentual Change and Language Contact: Comparative Survey and a Case Study of Early Northern Europe*, Stanford, CA: Stanford University Press.

References

San Juan, Esteban and Manuel Almeida (2005), 'Teoría sociolingüística y red social: datos del español canario', *Revista Internacional de Lingüística Iberoamericana* 3(1), pp. 133–50.

Sánchez Méndez, Juan (2003), *Historia de la lengua española en América*, Valencia: Tirant lo Blanch.

Sánchez-Prieto Borja, Pedro and Delfina Vázquez Balonga (2018), 'Toledo frente a Madrid en la conformación del español moderno: El sistema pronominal átono', *Revista de Filología Española* 98(1): 157–87.

Sanhueza, María Teresa (2015), 'Inmigrantes italianos en Argentina: La correspondencia entre Oreste, Abele y Luigi Sola (1901–1922)', *Zibaldone: Estudios Italianos* 3(1), 183–205.

Sankoff, Gillian (2018), 'Language change across the lifespan', *Annual Review of Linguistics* 4, 297–316.

Santa Ana, Otto and Claudia Parodi (1998), 'Modeling the speech community: Configuration and variable types in the Mexican Spanish setting', *Language in Society* 27(1), 23–51.

Sanz-Sánchez, Israel (2011), 'Analogical imperfects and the fate of Iberian verbal morphology in Latin American Spanish', *Southwest Journal of Linguistics* 30(2), 55–99.

Sanz-Sánchez, Israel (2013), 'Diagnosing dialect contact as the cause for dialect change: Evidence from a palatal merger in colonial New Mexican Spanish', *Diachronica* 30(1), 61–94.

Sanz-Sánchez, Israel (2014), 'Como dicen los americanos: Spanish in contact with English in territorial and early statehood New Mexico', *Spanish in Context* 11(2), 221–42. doi: 10.1075/sic.11.2.04san.

Sanz-Sánchez, Israel (2019), 'Documenting feature pools in language expansion situations: Sibilants in early colonial Latin American Spanish', *Transactions of the Philological Society* 117(2), 199–233.

Sanz-Sánchez, Israel and Fernando Tejedo-Herrero (2021), 'Adult language and dialect learning as simultaneous environmental triggers for language change', in *Spanish Socio-Historical Linguistics: Isolation and Contact*, eds. Whitney Chappell and Bridget Drinka, Amsterdam: John Benjamins, pp. 104–37.

Sanz-Sánchez, Israel and María Irene Moyna (2023), 'Children as agents of language change: Diachronic evidence from Latin American Spanish phonology', *Journal of Historical Linguistics* 13(3), 327–74.

Saussure, Ferdinand de (1986), *Course in General Linguistics*, Chicago IL: Open Court. First published in 1916.

Sayahi, Lotfi (2005), 'El español en el norte de Marruecos: Historia y análisis', *Hispanic Research Journal* 6(3), 195–207.

Sayahi, Lotfi (2011), 'Spanish in contact with Arabic', in *The Handbook of Hispanic Sociolinguistics*, ed. Manuel Díaz Campos, Oxford: Blackwell, pp. 473–89.

Schleicher, August (1853), 'Die ersten Spaltungen des indogermanischen Urvolkes', *Allgemeine Monatsschrift für Wissenschaft und Literatur*, 3(1), 786–7.

Schmidt, Johannes (1872), *Die Verwandtschaftsverhältnisse der indogermanischen Sprachen*, Weimar: Hermann Böhlau.

Schneider, Edgar (2002), 'Investigating variation and change in written documents', in *The Handbook of Language Variation and Change*, eds. J. K. Chambers, Peter Trudgill and Natalie Schilling-Estes, Oxford: Blackwell, pp. 67–96.

Schneider, Edgar (2007), *Postcolonial English: Varieties around the World*, Cambridge: Cambridge University Press.

Schrader-Kniffki, Martina (2008), 'From language mixing to mixed language via purism? Spanish in contact with Zapotec (Oaxaca/Mexico)', in *Hispanisation: The Impact of Spanish on the Lexicon and Grammar of the Indigenous Languages of the Americas*, eds. Thomas Stolz, Dik Bakker and Rosa Salas Palomo, Berlin: De Gruyter, pp. 49–76.

Schreier, Daniel (2016), 'Super-leveling, fraying-out, internal restructuring: A century of present *be* concord in Tristan da Cunha English', *Language Variation and Change*, 28, 203–24.

Schuchardt, Hugo (1917), 'Sprachverwandtschaft', in *Sitzungsberichte der Königlich Preussischen Akademie der Wissenschaften zu Berlin* 37(1), 518–29.

Schwaller, Robert (2012), 'The importance of mestizos and mulatos as bilingual intermediaries in sixteenth-century New Spain', *Ethnohistory* 59(4): 713–38.

Schwaller, Robert (2016), *Géneros de Gente in Early Colonial Mexico: Defining Racial Difference*, Norman: University of Oklahoma Press.

Schwaller, Robert (2018), 'Creating monstrosity in colonial Spanish America', in *Monsters and Borders in the Early Modern Imagination,* eds. Jana Byars and Hans Peter Broedel, London: Routledge, pp. 21–34.

Schwartz, Adam (2023), *Spanish so White: Conversations on the Inconvenient Racism of a 'Foreign' Language Education*, Bristol: Multilingual Matters.

Schwegler, Armin (1999). 'Monogenesis revisited: The Spanish perspective'. In *Creole Genesis, Discourse and Attitudes: Studies Celebrating Charlene Sato*, eds. John Rickford and Suzanne Romaine, Amsterdam: John Benjamins, pp. 235–62.

Schwegler, Armin (2011), 'Palenque (Colombia): Multilingualism in an extraordinary social and historical context', in *The Handbook of Hispanic Sociolinguistics*, ed. Manuel Díaz-Campos, Malden MA: Wiley, pp. 446–72.

Seijas, Tatiana (2018), *Asian Slaves in Colonial Mexico: From Chinos to Indians*, Cambridge: Cambridge University Press.

Serrano Moreno, Julio (2008), 'Habla sonorense en la ciudad de México: procesos de variación y cambio lingüístico', in *Estudios Lingüísticos y Literarios del Noroeste*, eds. Everardo Mendoza Guerrero, Maritza López Berríos and Ilda Elizabet Moreno Rojas, Culiacán: Universidad Autónoma de Sinaloa, pp. 49–76.

Sessarego, Sandro (2017), 'The Legal hypothesis of creole genesis: Presence/absence of legal personality, a new element to the Spanish creole debate', *Journal of Pidgin and Creole Languages* 32 (1), 1–47.

Sessarego, Sandro (2020), 'Not all grammatical features are robustly transmitted during the emergence of creoles', *Humanities and Social Sciences Communications* 7(1), 130.

Sessarego, Sandro (2021), *Interfaces and Domains of Contact-Driven Restructuring: Aspects of Afro-Hispanic Linguistics*, Cambridge: Cambridge University Press.

Shappeck, Marco (2011), Quichua-Spanish language contact in Salcedo, Ecuador: Revisiting Media Lengua syncretic language practices. PhD dissertation. University of Illinois Urbana-Champaign.

Shin, Naomi, Alejandro Cuza and Liliana Sánchez (2023), 'Structured variation, language experience, and crosslinguistic influence shape child heritage speakers' Spanish direct objects', *Bilingualism: Language and Cognition* 26(2), 317–29.

Siegel, Jeff (2010), *Second Dialect Acquisition*, Cambridge: Cambridge University Press.

Sierra Silva, Pablo Miguel (2018), *Urban Slavery in Colonial Mexico: Puebla de los Ángeles, 1531–1706*, Cambridge: Cambridge University Press.

Silva-Corvalán, Carmen (1994), *Language Contact and Change: Spanish in Los Angeles*, Oxford: Clarendon.

Silvestre, Javier (2005), 'Internal migrations in Spain, 1877–1930', *European Review of Economic History* 9(2), 233–65.

Sinner, Alejandro and César Carreras (2019), 'Methods of palaeodemograpy: The case of Iberian oppida and Roman cities in northeastern Spain', *Oxford Journal of Archaeology* 38(3), 302–24.

Sippola, Eeva (2020), 'Contact and Spanish in the Pacific', in *The Handbook of Language Contact*, ed. Raymond Hickey, Malden, MA: Wiley, pp. 453–68.

Smakman, Dick and Patrick Heinrich, eds. (2018), *Urban Sociolinguistics: The City as a Linguistic Process and Experience*, London: Routledge.

Smith, John Charles (2020), 'Contact and the Romance languages', in *The Handbook of Language Contact*, ed. Raymond Hickey, Malden, MA: Wiley, pp. 425–52.

Sorace, Antonella and Ludovica Serratrice (2009), 'Internal and external interfaces in bilingual language development: Beyond structural overlap', *International Journal of Bilingualism*, 13(2), 195–210.

Spaulding, Robert (1943), *How Spanish Grew*, Berkeley: University of California Press.

Steinkrüger, Patrick (2008), 'Hispanisation processes in the Philippines', in *Hispanisation: The impact of Spanish on the Lexicon and Grammar of the Indigenous Languages of Austronesia and the Americas*, eds. Thomas Stolz, Dik Bakker, Rosa Salas Palomo, Berlin: De Gruyter, pp. 203–36.

Tagliamonte, Sali and Alexandra D'Arcy (2009), 'Peaks beyond phonology: Adolescence, incrementation, and language change', *Language* 85(1), 58–108.

Tagliamonte, Sali and Sonja Molfenter (2007), 'How'd you get that accent? Acquiring a second dialect of the same language', *Language in Society*, 36(5), 649–75.

Tararova, Olga (2017), 'Language is me: Language maintenance in Chipilo, Mexico', *International Journal of the Sociology of Language* 248, 25–48.

Thomason, Sarah (2001), *Language Contact*, Edinburgh: Edinburgh University Press.

Thomason, Sarah and Terrence Kaufman (1988), *Language Contact, Creolization, and Genetic Linguistics*, Berkeley: University of California Press.

Toribio, Almeida Jacqueline (2011), 'Code-switching among US Latinos', in *The Handbook of Hispanic Sociolinguistics*, ed. Manuel Díaz-Campos, Malden MA: Wiley, pp. 530–52.

Trudgill, Peter (1986), *Dialects in Contact*, Oxford: Blackwell.

Trudgill, Peter (2004), *New-Dialect Formation: The Inevitability of Colonial Englishes*, Oxford: Oxford University Press.

Trudgill, Peter (2008), 'Colonial dialect contact in the history of European languages: On the irrelevance of identity to new-dialect formation', *Language in Society* 37(2), 241–80.

Trudgill, Peter (2011), 'Social structure, language contact and language change', in *The SAGE Handbook of Sociolinguistics*, eds. Ruth Wodak, Barbara Johnstone and Paul Kerswill, Los Angeles: SAGE, pp. 236–48.

Tuten, Donald (2003), *Koinéization in Medieval Spanish*, Berlin: De Gruyter.

Tuten, Dworkin (2024), 'La formación de nuevas variedades: koineización y criollización', in *Lingüística histórica del español: The Routledge Handbook of Spanish Historical Linguistics*, eds. Steven Dworkin, Gloria Clavería Nadal and Álvaro Octavio de Toledo y Huerta, London: Routledge, pp. 123–33.

UN Department of Economic and Social Affairs (2020), *International Migrant Stock* https://www.un.org/development/desa/pd/content/international-migrant-stock (last accessed 15 July 2023).

UN High Commissioner for Refugees (2023), Global Trends: Forced Displacement in 2022. https://www.unhcr.org/global-trends-report-2022 (last accessed 15 July 2023).

UN World Tourism Organization (2023), UNWTO Tourism Data Dashboard, https://www.unwto.org/tourism-data/unwto-tourism-dashboard (last accessed 15 July 2023).

UNESCO (2023), Intangible Heritage: El Güegüense. https://ich.unesco.org/en/RL/el-gueguense-00111 (last accessed 15 July 2023).

US Census Bureau (2023), *American Communities Survey. 2022 Language Spoken at Home Estimate*, https://data.census.gov/table/ACSST1Y2022.S1601?q=Language (last accessed 15 July 2023).

Valencia, Marelys and Andrew Lynch (2020), 'The mass mediation of Spanish in Miami', in *The Routledge Handbook of Spanish in the Global City*, ed. Andrew Lynch, London: Routledge, pp. 73–104.

van Coetsem, Frans (2000), *A General and Unified Theory of the Transmission Process in Language Contact*, Heidelberg: Winter.

Velázquez Patiño, Eduardo (2016), 'Stability of Nahuatl and Spanish intonation systems of bilingual Nahuatl speakers from the Mexican Veracruz Huasteca region', in *Proceedings of Speech Prosody 2016*, pp. 1148–52.

Velázquez Soriano, Isabel (2004), *Las pizarras visigodas: Entre el latín y su disgregación, la lengua hablada en Hispania s. VI–VIII*, Burgos: Instituto Castellano y Leonés de la Lengua.

Velázquez, Isabel (2024), 'El estadio lingüístico de la época visigótica', in *Lingüística histórica del español: The Routledge Handbook of Spanish*

Historical Linguistics, eds. Steven Dworkin, Gloria Clavería Nadal and Álvaro Octavio de Toledo y Huerta, London: Routledge, pp. 362–71.

Venâncio, Fernando (2014), 'O castelhano como vernáculo português', *Limite: Revista de Estudios Portugueses y de la Lusofonía*, 8(1), 127–46.

Vertovec, Steven (2007), 'Super-diversity and its implications', *Ethnic and Racial Studies* 30(6), 1024–54.

Vigil Escalera-Guirado, Alfonso and Juan Quirós Castillo (2012), 'Arqueología de los paisajes rurales altomedievales en el noroeste peninsular', in *Visigodos y omeyas: El territorio*, eds. Luis Caballero Zoreda, Pedro Mateos Cruz and Tomás Cordero Ruiz, Mérida: Instituto de Arqueología, pp. 79–95.

Villa, Laura and José del Valle (2015), 'The politics of Spanish in the world', in *The Routledge Handbook in Hispanic Applied Linguistics*, ed. Manel Lacorte, London: Routledge, pp. 571–87.

Villavicencio, Frida (2015), 'Entre una realidad plurilingüe y un anhelo de nación: Apuntes para un estudio sociolingüístico del siglo XIX', in *Historia sociolingüística de México: Volumen 2*, eds. Rebeca Barriga Villanueva and Pedro Martín Butragueño, Mexico City: Colegio de México, pp. 713–94.

Villena-Ponsoda, Juan (2005), 'How similar are people who speak alike? An interpretive way of using social networks in social dialectology research', in *Dialect Change: Convergence and Divergence in European Languages*, eds. Frans Hinskens, Peter Auer and Paul Kerswill, Cambridge: Cambridge University Press, pp. 303–34.

Walkden, George (2019), 'The many faces of uniformitarianism in linguistics', *Glossa: A Journal of General Linguistics* 4(1): 52, doi: 10.5334/gjgl.888.

Warren, Michelle (2003), 'Post-philology', in *Post-colonial Moves: Medieval through Modern*, eds. Patricia Clare Ingham and Michelle Warren, pp. 19–45. New York: Palgrave.

Watts, Richard (2012), 'Language myths', in *The Handbook of Historical Sociolinguistics*, eds. Juan Hernández-Campoy and Juan Camilo Conde-Silvestre, Malden MA: Wiley, pp. 584–606.

Weber, David (1992), *The Spanish Frontier in North America*, New Haven CT: Yale University Press.

Webre, Stephen (2022), 'Central America under Spanish colonial rule', in *The Oxford Handbook of Central American History*, ed. Robert Holden, Oxford: Oxford University Press, pp. 167–90.

Weinreich, Uriel (1953), *Languages in Contact: Findings and Problems*, The Hague: Mouton.

Weinreich, Uriel, William Labov and Marvin Herzog (1968), 'Empirical foundations for a theory of language change', in *Directions for Historical Linguistics*, eds. Winfred Lehmann and Yakov Malkiel, Austin: University of Texas Press, pp. 95–195.

Wentker, Michael and Carolin Schneider (2022), 'And she be like 'Tenemos frijoles en la casa': Code-switching and identity construction on YouTube', *Languages* 7(3), 219, doi: 10.3390/languages7030219.

Wiemer, Björn (2021), 'Convergence', in *The Routledge Handbook of Language Contact*, eds. Evangelia Adamou and Yaron Matras, London: Routledge, pp. 276–99.

Wilson, James (2010), *Moravians in Prague. A Sociolinguistic Study of Dialect Contact in the Czech Republic*, Frankfurt: Peter Lang.

Winford, Donald (2005), 'Contact-induced changes: Classification and types of processes', *Diachronica* 22(2): 373–427.

Winford, Donald (2017), 'The ecology of language and the New Englishes: Toward an integrative framework', in *Changing English: Global and Local Perspectives*, eds. Markku Filppula, Juhani Klemola, Anna Mauranen and Sveltana Vetchinnikova, Berlin: De Gruyter Mouton, pp. 25–55.

Winford, Donald (2020), 'The New Spanishes in the context of contact linguistics: Toward a unified approach', in *Hispanic Contact Linguistics: Theoretical, Methodological, and Empirical Perspectives*, eds. Luis Ortiz-López, Rosa Guzzardo Tamargo and Melvin González-Rivera, Amsterdam: John Benjamins, pp. 11–41.

Woolard, Kathryn (2007), 'La autoridad lingüística del español y las ideologías de la autenticidad y el anonimato', in *La lengua: ¿patria común? Ideas e ideologías del español*, ed. José del Valle, Madrid: Iberoamericana/Vervuert, pp. 129–42.

World Bank (2022), *World Bank Open Data*, https://data.worldbank.org/ (last accessed 15 July 2023).

Wright, Roger (2016), 'Latin and Romance in the medieval period: A sociophilological approach', in *The Oxford Guide to the Romance Languages*, eds. Adam Ledgeway and Martin Maiden, Oxford: Oxford University Press, pp. 14–23.

Yakpo, Kofi (2016), '"The only language we speak really well": The English creoles of Equatorial Guinea and West Africa at the intersection of language ideologies and language policies', *International Journal of the Sociology of Language* 239, 211–33.

Yépez Martínez, Natalia and Francisco Gachet Paredes (2014), 'Migración interna en la región andina: Tendencias históricas y y problemas actuales', *Andina Migrante* 18, 2–13.

Zentella, Ana Celia (1997), *Growing up Bilingual: Puerto Rican Children in New York*. Malden MA: Wiley.

Zimmermann, Klaus and Laura Morgenthaler García (2007), 'Introducción: ¿Lingüística y migración o lingüística de la migración?: De la construcción de un objeto científico hacia una nueva disciplina', *Revista Internacional de Lingüística Iberoamericana* 5(2), 7–19.

Index of Languages and Language Families

African American English, 185, 191
Arabic, 43, 46, 73, 80, 85–6, 195–7
Aragonese, 78, 81, 83, 155
Arawak, 95, 123, 210
Asturian (*and* Astur-Leonese, Leonese) 39, 81, 83, 84, 199–200
Austronesian, 118, 122–3, 125, 205
Aymara, 99, 109, 117–18, 139, 172

Bantu, 99
Barranquenho, 193–4
Basque, 37, 43, 59, 63–4, 73, 79, 81, 155–7, 159–60
Belizean Kriol, 186
Berber, 43, 72, 80, 195

Calabrese, 149
California Anglo English, 191
Cantonese, 146
Cape Verdean Creole, 19
Castellano andino *see* Spanish: Andean Spanish
Castilian; *see also* Spanish, 3, 7, 43, 57–9, 74, 78, 80–7, 90, 96, 101, 121, 147, 154, 157, 160, 199–200
Catalan, 10, 38, 59, 80–1, 146, 155, 160, 199–200
Caviteño, 121, 123
Cebuano, 46, 123–4
Celtiberian, 63–4
Celtic, 61–3, 69–70, 86
Chabacano (*and* Chavacano), 121
Chamorro (*and* Chamoru), 124–5, 178
Chibchan, 99, 115
Chicanx English, 185, 190–1, 210

Chinese, 12, 46, 118, 120, 143–5, 148, 150, 164
Chipileño, 184
Chocoan, 115
Czech, 60

Danish, 146

English, 7, 12, 16–17, 27, 37, 40–1, 47, 51, 60, 75, 86, 130–4, 161, 164, 183, 185–6, 188, 190–2, 194–5, 199, 206, 209–10
Ermitaño, 121, 123
Etruscan, 62

Faliscan, 62
French, 12, 19, 37, 59, 68, 132, 135, 184, 195–6

Galician, 10, 39, 81, 146, 154–5, 157, 160
Gallo-Romance, 80
Garifuna, 186, 194
Germanic (*and* Proto-Germanic), 37, 61–2, 72, 74–5, 78, 86
Gothic, 37, 59, 62, 74–5
Greek, 60, 63, 65–6, 70, 80, 144
Guarani; *see also* Tupi-Guarani, 95, 112, 149, 173–4

Haketía *see* Judeo-Spanish
Hawaiian Pidgin, 19
Hebrew, 80
Hopi, 117

Iberian Romance (*and* Ibero-Romance), 37–8, 43, 74, 59, 68, 80
Ilocano, 124
Indo-European; *see also* Proto-Indo-European, 4, 26, 28, 30, 37, 58, 60–2, 86
Inga Quechua, 52
Italian, 38, 59, 68, 146–7, 149–50, 184
Italic, 61, 64, 69

Japanese 120, 124
Judeo-Spanish (haketía, judezmo, ladino), 126, 163, 195
Judezmo *see* Judeo-Spanish

Kartvelian (*and* Proto-Kartvelian), 61
K'iche, 117
Kichwa; *see also* Quechua, 36, 52, 178–9
Kikongo, 19, 99, 149
Kinyarwanda, 48
Korean, 12
Kreyòl, 19, 132, 132–5, 149
Kriol, 194–5

Ladino *see* Judeo-Spanish
Lake Miwok, 117
Latin, 4–5, 7, 25, 27–8, 36–7, 39, 48–9, 57–72, 74–5, 77–8, 80–1, 84, 127, 205
Leonese *see* Asturian
Lusitanian, 63

Macao Creole, 151
Malagasy, 206
Malayo-Spanische, 124
Mapudungun, 99, 117, 170
Mayan, 99, 117, 186, 194–5
Media Lengua; *see also* Salcedo Media Lengua, 22, 36, 118, 125, 170–1, 178–9
Miami English, 191
Min, 146
Mozarabic (*and* Romanandalusí), 43, 80–1, 86

Nahuatl, 19, 22–4, 97, 99, 108, 111–12, 116–17, 123, 169–70, 175–6
Navajo, 117
Nenets, 16
Niger-Congo, 95, 115, 195
Norwegian, 32

Old English, 62
Old Irish, 62
O'odham, 117
Oscan, 62, 69

Palenkero (*and* Palenquero), 19–24, 36, 115, 135, 151
Papiamentu, 135, 149, 151–2
Piedmontese, 147
Pima, 117
Pipil, 113
Plattdeutsch, 146
Portuguese; *see also* Barranquenho, 10, 19, 23, 41, 53, 59, 75, 80–1, 95, 131, 133, 186, 193–4
Portuguese-based creoles, 53
Portuguese-based pidgin, 121
Proto-Finno-Ugric, 62
Proto-Indo-European (PIE), 58, 60–2, 86, 115, 206
Proto-Uralic, 61
Provençal, 68
Punic, 63, 65

Quechua, 52, 99, 115–16, 99–100, 118, 139, 149, 173, 176

Rapa Nui, 171
Romanandalusí *see* Mozarabic
Romance; *see also* Iberian Romance, Gallo-Romance, 39, 49, 59, 68–9, 71–5, 80–1
Romanian, 37
Russian, 144

Salcedo Media Lengua, 179
Sanskrit, 60
Sardinian, 68
Semitic (*and* Proto-Semitic), 61
Spanish
    Afro-Hispanic varieties, 116, 135, 151
    Andalusian Spanish, 101, 195
    Andean Spanish (*and* castellano andino), 36, 139, 172–3, 177, 179, 188, 205
    Belize Spanish, 186
    Bolivian Spanish, 176, 187–8
    Buenos Aires Spanish, 109–10, 140, 149–50
    Caribbean Spanish, 190, 210
    Central American Spanish, 194
    Chilean Spanish 141–2, 167, 171–2
    Cibaeño Spanish, 132

Index of Languages and Language Families 247

Colombian Spanish, 190
Costa Chica Spanish, 99
Cuban Spanish, 149–50, 152
Dominican Spanish, 134–5, 190
Ecuadorian Spanish, 178–9
European Spanish, 138, 140
Latin American Spanish, 26, 98–101, 109, 111–12, 140
Mexican Spanish, 111, 113, 138–43, 171, 185–8, 191
Montevideo Spanish, 140
New York City Spanish, 40–1, 190, 192
North African Spanish, 181
North Carolina Spanish, 49, 51
Paraguayan Spanish, 95–6, 99, 111, 173–4, 191–2
Puerto Rican Spanish, 184, 177, 190, 192
Río de la Plata Spanish 91, 140–2, 146, 149–50, 205
Southwest United States Spanish, 195
Tegucigalpa Spanish, 16
Unites States Spanish, 37, 49
Swedish, 37
Swiss German, 146

Tagalog, 122, 124
Taíno, 95, 99, 123, 210
Tartessian, 63
Ternateño, 121, 123
Tojol-ab'al, 170
Tok Pisin, 19
Tupi-Guarani, 99

Umbrian, 62, 69
Uralic, 61
US English, 191

Vedic Sanskrit, 60
Venetan Italian, 184; *see also* Chipileño
Volga German, 146

Welsh, 62, 146
Wolof, 184

Yoruba, 99, 149

Zamboagueño, 46, 121–3
Zapotec (*and* Rincón Zapotec), 118, 170, 176

Index of Subjects

Abstand (language), 10, 23, 38
accommodation, 40–1, 97, 100, 108, 125, 176–8, 186–8
accusative, 71, 78, 84–5, 178
acquisition (adult, biases, bi/multilingual, child, dialect, incomplete, language, non-native), 14–15, 17, 19, 23–4, 33, 39–40, 43, 46–7, 49, 51, 53, 66, 72, 85, 102, 112, 115, 141, 152, 189, 205, 209
actuation, 33, 49, 102
address (second person) *see tú, usted, vos, vosotras/os*
adolescents, 34, 54, 169, 177, 184, 196
adstrate; *see also* stratum, 59
adults, 36, 46, 53, 57, 81, 96
Africa, 88, 90, 105, 127, 145, 166
Afro-Cubans, 149, 152
Afrodescendants, 96, 108, 114–15, 145, 149
age (as a factor in language change); *see also* adolescents, adults, children, 33, 40, 46, 48, 50, 112, 141, 171, 176, 196, 201
Al-Andalus, 80
Algeria, 195–7
Amazonian region, 136, 166
analogical forms (*and* analogy), 16, 30, 43, 70, 112
Anatolian hypothesis, 60
Andalusia, 67, 85, 91, 155
Andalusians, 85
Andes, 109, 111, 116, 136, 170, 172, 175
anthroponyms, 64, 68, 74–5, 78
archival data, 8, 60, 74, 79–80, 98–9, 110, 115, 126, 134, 141

Argentina, 104, 136, 138, 144, 146, 154, 179–80, 184, 192
Arizona, 131
Armenian hypothesis, 60
Asia, 88, 90, 118, 120, 195, 229
aspiration, 101, 121, 157–8, 176
assertive *ya*, 159
assibilation, 178, 185
assimilation (linguistic, sociolinguistic), 64, 67, 105, 108, 115, 131, 146, 152, 157, 183, 186, 188
Asturias (*and* Asturias-Leon), 78–9, 85, 155, 158
Asunción, 173
asylum seekers, 166, 180
attrition, 46–7, 134
Ausbau (language), 10, 23, 38–9
authority (educational, linguistic), 7, 28, 138, 155, 161, 209

Bahamas, 56, 127
Baja California, 144
Barcelona, 153, 155
Basque region, 73, 84, 146, 156, 152–7
Belize, 186, 194–5
bilingual acquisition strategies, 51–2, 98, 111, 135, 172, 201
bilingualism (heritage, individual, long-term, sequential, social) 9, 22–4, 27, 31, 35, 47–8, 59, 65, 98–9, 108, 139, 176, 183–4, 186, 189, 191, 207, 209–10
bilinguals, 2, 6, 20, 22–3, 80, 108, 113, 133–4, 165, 172–3, 176–7, 189, 191, 197, 207

Bogotá, 103, 128, 167, 219
Bolivia, 96, 100, 108, 130, 136, 163, 171, 184, 188
borders (*and* borderlands, borderlines), 23–24, 41, 45, 79–80, 110, 130–4, 161, 166–7, 181–2, 185–6, 192–3, 198
borrowing, 32, 35–6, 39, 46, 52–3, 59, 99, 118, 178, 208
brain (human), 11, 17, 23, 94, 207
Brazil, 41, 92, 104, 130–1, 184
Britain, 35, 51, 102, 127
Buenos Aires, 103, 108–9, 140, 146–7, 163, 184, 209
Burgos phase (of medieval Castilian koiné), 82–3

California, 88, 130–4, 185
Canary Islanders, 104, 146, 154
Caribbean, 41, 90–1, 94–5, 99, 105, 110, 127, 135, 145–6, 151, 167, 190
Cartagena, 19, 109, 115
Carthage, 63
castas (Spanish colonial racial category), 105, 109, 129
Castile, 23, 56–7, 72, 79–82, 84, 90
Catalonia, 146, 152, 154–5, 157
Catholic missions, 93, 95, 105
Caucasus, 61
Celtiberians, 63–4
Central America, 91, 93, 99, 103, 110, 130, 136, 166, 180
centrifugal triggers (*and* centripetal triggers), 182
Chicago, 47, 182, 184
Chicagoacán, 182
Chicanxs, 185, 191
Chihuahua, 144, 146
children, 2, 34, 47, 53–4, 66, 82, 95–7, 102, 141, 146–7, 149–50, 156–8, 168–9, 178, 182, 184, 192, 196, 205
Chile, 26, 49, 51, 91, 130, 136, 141–2, 167, 171, 179–80, 187, 198
Chinese (immigrants), 122, 144
Christian kingdoms (in medieval Iberia), 42, 72, 74, 80
cities *see* urban areas
ciudades dormitorio, 167, 177
clitic (object, omission, pronouns, redundant); *see also leísmo, loísmo*, 43, 85, 100, 121, 143, 159, 178, 194
coda (syllabic), 101, 121, 177
code-switching (intersentential,

intrasentential), 16, 38, 52, 86, 133, 191–2, 195–6, 200
cognition (individual speaker), 14, 16–17, 43–5, 49, 53–4, 203, 207
Colombia, 19, 52, 96, 109, 115, 166, 190
colonies (*and* colonialism), 12, 28, 90–6, 99, 101, 104–6, 108, 110, 119, 121, 124, 126–9, 145, 152, 195–6, 206
competence (individual), 13–14, 186, 209
competition (ecological process), 45, 155
complex adaptive systems (CASs), 14, 42–3, 203
complexity (morphological, sociolinguistic, systemic), 36, 84, 160, 180, 194
contact language (as a language category), 17, 37
contact typologies, 37
conventillos, 146–7, 155
convergence (dialectal grammatical, semantic, syntactic), 22, 24, 40, 53, 117, 134, 160, 172
conversational strategies, 52, 173, 191
copulas, 135, 160, 189, 196
Cordoba, 43
Costa Chica, 99
creole (languages), 19–20, 37, 96, 109, 121–3, 146
creolization, 36, 44, 52, 121
creoloids, 20, 37, 58
Cuba, 95, 105, 127, 129, 145, 148–51, 153–4, 179–80, 186, 196
cuña (model for medieval Castilian), 81–2
Cuzco, 89, 94, 103

Deaf (individuals), 204
de-colonization, 128, 166
dialect (change, contact, norms), 7, 9–10, 12, 15–17, 26–8, 31, 35, 37–41, 43–4, 49, 51, 61–2, 58, 82, 85, 102, 112, 125, 127, 132, 141–2, 186, 189–90, 204, 206
dialect continua, 10–11, 38, 43, 61, 165
differential object marking, 19, 23
differential replication, 16
diffusion (areal, geographical, inter-dialectal, social), 44, 49, 61–2, 64, 82, 111–12, 158
digital communication, 165–66, 198–9, 200–1
discourse markers, 124, 175, 197
discourses (monoglossic, of homogeneity, prescriptive) 7, 8–9, 28, 112, 128, 157, 174, 200

Dominican Republic, 132, 134, 179–80, 186
Dutch Antilles, 92, 149

early adopters, 50
Easter Island, 171
ecolinguistics, 16
ecology of language (*and* ecological factors), 16, 18, 45, 48, 93, 126, 141, 152, 166, 193, 201
education systems, 23, 161
Egypt, 70
e-languages, 12
El Salvador, 179–80, 188
emigrants, 154, 180
enregisterment, 48, 109, 140, 161, 171
entrenchment (*and* entrenched features), 23, 44, 48, 124, 140
Equatorial Guinea, 195
essences (languages as historical), 4–5, 44
Europeans, 86, 88–9, 91–6, 98, 105, 107, 143, 146, 188, 205
Euskaltzaindia, 155
Euzko Alderdi Jeltzalea, 155
evidence, metalinguistic, 126, 141, 158
evidentiality, 36, 173
evolution (of language), 28, 37, 39, 42, 71, 82, 94, 166
Extremadura, 155

factors in language change (internal vs external), 15, 27, 70, 72
feature pools, 16, 22, 42–3, 45, 48, 51, 71, 95–6, 108–9, 111, 114, 116, 122, 125, 137, 141, 143, 146–7, 150, 164, 167, 169, 172, 175–6, 178, 188, 190, 199, 210
feature selection (ecological process), 25, 49, 51, 81, 102, 122, 126, 207, 210
Filipinos, 121–2
Florida, 88, 183
founder effect, 68
fragmentation (linguistic), 6, 30, 49, 60–1, 86, 127
France, 63, 70, 102, 127, 132, 144, 181
frequency (of forms), 40, 44, 46–7, 70, 82, 112, 160, 187, 190, 198
function words, 124–5, 152
futurity, 190

Galicia, 80, 85, 146, 154–5
Gaul, 70

gender (grammatical), 19, 43–8, 58, 50, 83–4, 100, 135, 151, 160, 209
gender (identity) 43, 50, 163, 177–8, 200
generational partitions, 201
generativism, 33–4
Germanic tribes, 72
Gibraltar, 56, 72
Glosas Emilianenses, 3–4
grammar (historical), 7–8, 25, 27, 81
Granada, 43, 56, 79
Guam, 119, 124, 127
Guanajuato, 185
Guatemala, 103, 180, 186, 192, 198
Güegüense, 113–14
Gulf of Mexico, 91, 101, 130

Haiti, 102, 129–30, 132, 149, 186
heritage (attrition in, communities, language dominance, speakers), 46–8, 134, 144, 146, 189, 207
heteroglossic practices, 18, 163, 165, 186
Hispania, 58, 63, 66–7, 86
Hispaniola, 95, 129
historical linguistics, 7, 10, 17, 25–6, 42, 72
historical sociolinguistics; *see also* sociohistorical evidence, sociolinguistics, 24, 59
Honduras, 179–80, 186, 193
Houston, 46, 188
hybridization (*and* hybridism, hybridity in language contact), 10, 12, 18, 24, 48, 118, 135, 171–2, 193, 200

Iberian Peninsula, 3, 23, 26–7, 56, 63–4, 66, 68–9, 72–5, 78, 82, 91, 125, 152
Iceland, 60
identity (ethnic, ethnolinguistic, linguistic, national social), 13, 17–18, 23, 27–8, 45, 48–9, 51, 67, 78, 109, 112, 120, 138, 140, 149, 150, 161, 168, 170, 174, 179, 184, 188, 209
ideologies (language, monoglossic, power, social), 15, 23, 33, 43, 45, 158, 169, 192, 199, 212
idiolects, 16, 25, 42–5, 48, 50, 203, 207
i-languages, 12, 33
immigrants (*and* immigration), 24, 130, 136, 143–4, 146–7, 149, 152, 161–2, 164, 168, 180, 182, 184, 186–8, 200, 205, 207–8
imposition (contact process), 24, 35, 46, 53, 98, 111, 115

Inca, 89, 96–7
indentured workers, 46, 143, 145–8, 150
Indigenous languages, 67, 69, 98, 102, 111, 115–16, 138–9, 161, 163–4, 169, 171, 208
Indigenous populations, 88, 91–3, 95, 98, 105, 111, 113, 116–17, 119–21, 169, 179–80, 208
individual speakers (as sociolinguistic agents, monolingual, bilingual, semiliterate), 2–3, 11–17, 20, 25–7, 32–5, 38, 40, 44–50, 53, 59, 70, 82, 94, 116, 126, 132, 157, 168–9, 171, 198, 203, 207–10
innovations (cultural, diachronic, geographical, internal, linguistic, shared), 2, 22–3, 30–4, 36, 42, 48–51, 53, 61–3, 68, 84, 125, 140, 167, 198, 210, 212
innovators, 50
input, 33–4, 40, 47, 53, 70–1, 85, 96, 189
Institut d'Estudis Catalans, 155
intelligibility (mutual), 10–11, 20, 38–9
interference (contact process), 35, 70, 111, 116, 125
interlanguage, 98
intonation, 149
introgression *see* recombination
isoglosses, 39, 192
isolation (geographical, social), 74, 95–6, 98, 110, 131, 148–50
Italic Peninsula, 62
Italy, 62–4, 68, 72, 144

Jamaica, 92, 102
Japan, 88
Jewish (communities, populations; Sephardic Jews), 56, 80, 126, 163, 195

koinéization (and koiné), 36–8, 51, 58, 82, 98, 101–2, 110, 164
Koreans, 12, 144
Kurgan hypothesis; *see also* steppe hypothesis, 60–1

L1, 27, 96, 100, 115, 121, 143, 149, 160, 191, 195–6
L2, 19, 27, 53, 108, 120, 191
Lake Miwok, 117
language attitudes, 11, 16, 158, 163, 171, 183–4, 186–7, 198
language boundaries, 10, 20, 22–3, 37–8, 41, 134, 164, 199, 212

language change, 10, 13–14, 16–19, 24, 26, 29–37, 41–55, 73–4, 81, 205–7, 209–12
language death, 49
language evolution, 8, 17, 26, 28, 37, 39, 42, 48, 73–4, 94, 127, 191, 207
language funnel metaphor, 208
language histories (*and* historiography), 13, 18, 25–6, 42, 49, 54, 81, 126, 162, 205, 207–8
language learning (*and* learners, native, non-native, bilingual); *see also* acquisition, 19, 25, 33, 35–6, 40–1, 49, 53, 66, 69–70, 72, 85, 95, 97, 102, 111–12, 115, 120, 123, 134–5, 141, 149–51, 200
language shift (community-wide, generational, large-scale); *see also* verticalization, 22, 33, 35–6, 49, 63–4, 68, 98, 111, 138–9, 157, 164, 168–9, 171, 175–6, 184–6, 210
language speciation, 49
language variation (*and* varieties), 9–10, 12, 16, 18, 29, 31, 33, 35–6, 45, 48, 54, 143, 165, 207
languages as species (biological analogy, organic metaphor), 4, 16, 42–5
lateralization, 177, 187
Latin America, 5, 127–9, 138, 140, 144–6, 153, 155, 161, 170, 192
Lazio, 62
Lebanese immigrants, 144
leísmo, 178
lenguaje inclusivo; *see also* non-binary language, 212
lenition, 69–70
leveling (dialectal), 82, 84, 100, 164
lexicon, 24, 33, 35, 37, 42, 98–9, 124–5, 127, 176, 205
lexifiers, 19–20, 96, 195
LGBTQ+, 208
loanwords, 46, 70, 74, 99, 117, 123–4, 132, 135, 195, 198–9
loísmo, 178
Los Angeles, 51, 188–9
Louisiana, 104

Madrid, 127–8, 153, 155–8, 164, 167, 188, 205
Maghreb, 26, 195
Majorca, 157
Maluku Islands (*and* Moluccas), 118–19, 121

Manila, 90, 118–19, 121, 123–4
Mapudungun, 99, 117, 170
Mediterranean, 63–5
Mennonites, 144, 146
Mesoamerica, 93, 117
mestizos, 90, 92–3, 95, 102, 105–6, 108, 116, 119–22, 186, 194, 205
Mexica, 89, 94
Mexican Americans, 185, 188
Mexico, 2, 46–47, 89, 91–2, 99, 103, 105–6, 108, 110–11, 116–17, 129–31, 136, 138, 144, 167–9, 171–2, 175–7, 179–82, 184–7
Mexico City (*and* Mexico-Tenochtitlan), 89–90, 92, 94, 97, 103, 136–7, 143, 167–8, 171, 176–7, 186–7
MexiRicans, 184
Miami, 49, 183
Michoacán, 45, 169, 172, 182
Middle East, 60, 144
migrants (*and* migration, country-to-city, cross-border, cyclical, first-generation, internal, international, intranational, large-scale, temporary, transnational), 45, 61, 106, 129, 136, 153–5, 157, 161, 164–70, 176–80, 182, 184–5, 187
mixed languages, 37, 118, 170
mobility (socioeconomic, speaker), 130, 139, 147, 149, 156–9, 165–6, 170, 182, 198, 207
Montevideo, 105, 140, 149
Moroccans (*and* Morocco), 180–1, 195–7
morphology (*and* morphological categories, change), 4, 8, 26, 36, 49, 58, 68, 71, 74, 77–8, 84, 102, 112, 116–18, 125, 127, 141, 175, 190, 194, 200, 205, 209–10
multiple causation, 24, 49, 72, 115, 124, 149, 173
multiplex ties; *see also* social networks, 50
Muslim Iberia, 4, 56, 73, 79, 89, 121
myth (discrete language, monolingual), 9, 12, 201

national varieties, 27, 109, 140, 205
nations (*and* nation-states), 45, 54, 57, 96, 130, 133, 138, 154, 169, 176, 182
native speaker (*and* non-native speaker); *see also* learners, speakers, 20, 24, 27, 71, 95, 112, 122, 149, 209
Navarre, 78, 156–7
negation, double, 151–2
networks *see* social networks

New Castile, 155
new dialect formation, 44, 51, 110–11, 216
New Mexico, 91, 110–11, 130–1, 134
New Spain, 118–19, 123, 130
New York City (NYC), 40, 49, 51, 190
Nicaragua, 113–14, 181, 198
non-binary language; *see also* lenguaje inclusivo, 163, 212
non-native speaker *see* native speaker
norms (communal, competing, conservative, national, regional, rural, sociolinguistic, vernacular), 2, 8, 12–15, 16, 25, 44, 50–1, 72, 96–8, 101, 112, 140–2, 155, 165, 169, 171–2, 177, 184, 204–6
North America, 104, 117, 243
North Carolina, 51

Oaxaca, 99, 176
organisms; *see also* types, 5, 16, 19, 42–4, 127

Pacific Rim, 118–19
palenques, 19, 21, 95–6, 109, 115
Paraguay, 91, 95–6, 104, 111, 130, 144, 146, 173, 175–6
parasitic species (languages as), 16, 43, 203
parents, 150, 158–9
peak alignment (early, late), 150
Pennsylvania, 184
Peru, 91–2, 96, 103, 105, 129–30, 136, 139, 144–5, 179–80
Philippines, 26, 118–21, 123–5, 127
Phoenicians, 63
phonology (*and* phonological categories, change), 4, 8, 10, 13, 20, 26, 28, 53, 62, 69–71, 81, 102, 110–11, 117, 151, 157, 178, 185, 191, 196, 205, 206, 210
pidgin, 96, 121, 125, 152
Pizkundea, 155
Pontic-Caspian region, 60–1, 205
populations, 16, 29, 42–6, 48–51, 59–60, 62, 65, 75, 88, 91, 103–8, 111–12, 130–2, 136, 138–9, 147, 152–6, 161, 165–7, 176, 184–5, 204, 206–8, 210
Portugal, 23, 79, 104, 119, 186
post-colonial settings, 129, 152, 195
post-structuralism, 9, 12, 14–15, 17
pre-Columbian cultures, 2, 89, 93
prescription (*and* prescriptivism), 8, 138, 172, 197–8, 200

proficiency, 33, 40, 66, 112, 120, 169, 183, 210
pronouns (subject, object); *see also* address, clitic, 40–1, 43, 46, 49, 58, 70, 122–3, 150–1, 169, 191
proto-language, 37, 60
psycholinguistic processes, 20, 23–4, 35, 51
Puebla, 103, 110, 169
Puerto Rico, 95, 127, 129, 154, 177
punctuated equilibrium, 15
purism (linguistic), 23, 171, 175, 199
Pyrenees, 63, 72, 78, 80

Quito, 103, 170

ranchos (*and* rancheros), 107, 112, 130, 138, 182
Real Academia Española, 6, 75, 198, 209
Real Academia Galega, 155
reallocation, 51
reanalysis, 151
recombination (ecological process); *see also* restructuring, 29, 42–3, 48, 54, 68, 86, 115–16, 118, 120–1, 123, 149, 170, 172, 175, 189
Reconquista, 78–80, 86
refugees, 166, 180–1, 196, 200
registers (stylistic), 12, 25, 174
relexification, 35–6, 118, 125, 178
Renaixença, 155
repertoires (individual, communicative, hybrid, rural, urban), 2, 12, 16–18, 20, 24, 26, 38, 42–4, 46, 67, 74, 90, 93, 98, 115, 117, 120–3, 126, 130–1, 133–4, 138, 143, 147, 149, 161, 169, 174, 176–8, 182, 184, 186–7, 192–4, 204–05, 209–10
representativeness (of historical data), 55, 79, 99, 114, 126, 151, 204, 209, 211
resettlement, 83–4, 110–11, 121
restructuring (ecological process) *see* recombination
Rexurdimento, 155
Río de la Plata (*and* River Plate), 91–3, 105, 140–2, 144, 146, 149, 150, 155, 205
Roman Empire, 36, 63, 58, 65, 67–8, 70, 72
Romanians, 37, 180
Rome, 57, 63, 70, 72
rural areas, 66, 103, 106, 120, 136, 140, 144, 146, 156, 159, 169–72
Russia, 144

Saguntum, 65
Sahrawi Arab Democratic Republic (SADR) (*and* Sahrawis); *see also* Western Sahara, 196–7
salience (linguistic, sociolinguistic), 6, 40, 48–9, 108, 210
Samaná Peninsula, 132
San Basilio de Palenque 19, 21, 109
San Diego, 185
San Sebastián, 157
Santiago, 103, 140, 172
Santo Domingo, 90, 97
schools (*and* schooling; city, community, ecclesiastical, municipal, public, rural, universal); *see also* teachers, 120, 124, 131, 138–9, 146, 155–6, 158, 163, 168–70, 193, 210
Scotland, 15
scribes, 2, 80, 94, 101, 117
selection (ecological process), 17, 48–9, 58, 171
semantic calques, 112
semantic extensions, 117
semi-creoles, 20, 37
Senegal, 184
seseo, 101–2, 109, 121, 206
settlers, 43, 63–4, 73, 80, 85, 98, 111
Seville (*and* Seville phase of Castilian koiné), 43, 82–3, 85, 155
sibilants; *see also seseo*, 102, 121, 140, 206
simplification (grammatical), 36, 46, 71, 83, 85, 100–1
slaves (*and* slavery), 66, 88, 90, 92, 95–6, 105, 108, 114–15, 143, 145, 149, 161–2, 195, 208
social networks (age-based effects, dense, global, individual, local, open, rural, theory, tight-knit, weak) 12–14, 16, 33–4, 44, 50–1, 66, 68, 80, 84, 95, 105, 107, 112, 138, 141, 145–6, 148, 156, 167–9, 171–2, 177, 182, 184, 187, 198, 201, 205
social stratification, 93, 95, 155, 158
sociohistorical evidence, 69, 115, 125, 159–60
sociolinguistics, 9, 16, 32, 35, 37, 60, 75, 94, 111–12
socio-pragmatic (approach to language change), 11–14, 18, 29
Sonora, 130, 176
South America, 105, 117
Southeast Asia, 91, 118
Southern Cone, 110, 136, 144

Spain, 5–6, 41, 46, 56–91, 95–7, 101–29, 144–6, 152, 154–5, 160–1, 167, 179–81, 195–6
Spaniards, 91–97, 100, 105, 108, 116, 119–20, 144, 146, 153, 195–6, 206
speech community, 30, 33, 169
spelling, 63, 74, 77, 79, 111, 117, 159
spirantization, 176–7
Stammbaum (language tree), 30–1
standard languages, 7–8, 10, 25–6, 58, 155, 208
steppe hypothesis, 60–1
stratum, 37, 59, 69
stress shifts, 176, 196
structuralism (*and* structuralist approaches), 9–10, 31, 33, 44
subject-verb agreement, 19, 46, 151
substrates (*and* substratum); *see also* stratum, 31–2, 37, 59, 70–1, 172
super-diversity, 165
superstrates; *see also* stratum, 59, 75
symbolic values, 51, 139, 169, 171–2, 177, 184, 207
syntax; *see also* word order, 46, 71, 78, 133, 149, 160, 205

tabula rasa settings, 63
Taiwan, 119
Tartessians, 63
Taxco, 1–2, 26, 93–4
teachers, 138, 175, 189, 195, 202
tense-mood-aspect (TMA) particles, 21, 189
Texas, 130–1, 134, 144
Toledo (*and* Toledo phase of Castilian koiné), 43, 74, 79, 82–5
tourism, 181
transfer (grammatical, phonological), 39, 53, 62, 69, 71, 98, 110–11, 117, 149, 196
translingual approach (to language contact), 13, 18, 23, 192
transmission (language), 19, 30, 36, 42, 48, 54, 58, 61–2, 90, 105
transplantation, 27, 161, 206
tú, 8, 40, 109–10, 123, 135, 140–2, 143, 158
types (languages as), 44, 203

typologies (linguistic, social), 20, 32, 37, 50, 117
typology (linguistic), 39, 58

uniformitarian approach, 207
universities, 96, 107, 138
urban areas (*and* urbanization), 28, 65, 75, 103, 107, 111, 113, 130–1, 136–7, 138, 141, 143, 147, 157–8, 166–7, 171–2, 176, 184
Uruguay, 41, 131–3, 136, 138, 144, 146, 186, 193–4
usage-based accounts, 14, 18, 44
US Latinxs, 165, 183–5, 188, 191, 210
US Southwest, 117, 185, 190
usted, 113, 143, 158–9, 188

variation (sociolinguistic), 4, 7–8, 19, 25, 31, 33, 37, 45, 48, 51, 72, 78, 101, 121, 132, 140, 142, 165, 184, 186, 201, 206, 209
Venezuela (*and* Venezuelans), 92, 154, 166, 181
vernacular universals, 49, 112
verticalization (model of language shift), 139, 210
Visayans, 121
Visigoths, 72, 74–5, 77–8
vos (*and voseo*) 8, 109–10, 123, 138, 140–2, 146, 149, 172, 188
vosotras/os, 100–1, 122–3, 188

Welsh immigrants, 146
Western linguistics (scholarly tradition), 9, 30, 54, 60, 165
Western Sahara, 128, 196–7
West Indies, 132
word order, 25, 46, 71, 78, 159

yeísmo, 50, 110–11, 140, 157–8
Yucatan, 111, 117, 144
Yucatan Peninsula, 117
Yungas region, 96, 108

Zacatecas, 93, 110
Zamboanga, 121